# REVIEW FOR THE GRADUATE MANAGEMENT ADMISSIONS TEST (GMAT)

Complete review of skills

By
Andrew Bobby, Ed.D.
Deanna Corona, M.A.
Robert Neeman, M. S.
Jerome Hollander, M. S.
Michael Romeo, M.S.

This book is correlated to the video tapes produced by
COMEX Systems, Inc.
Review for The
Graduate Management Admissions Test (GMAT) ©1992
they may be obtained from

*comex systems, inc.*
**The Mill Cottage**
**Mendham, NJ 07945**

Excerpt on page 91 is from The Soviet Economy, by Marshall I Goldman. Copyright 1968. Used with permission of Prentice-Hall, Inc. Englewood Cliffs, NJ.

Excerpt on page 97 is from The Best Defense, by Alan Dershowitz. Copyright 1982. Used with the permission of Random House, Inc. New York, New York.

Excerpt on pages 99 is from A Treasury of the Theater, edited by John Gassner. Copyright 1963. Used with permission of Simon and Schuster, Inc. New York, New York.



**Published by**

***comex systems, inc.***
**The Mill Cottage**
**Mendham, NJ 07945**

**ISBN 1-56030-124-4**

# Contents

# INTRODUCTION

The **COMEX Systems, Inc. Graduate Management Admission Test Preparation** study guide is designed to help develop the test-taking abilities of the aspiring applicant for advanced study in business and management. Specifically, this program has been designed to help the applicant perform more effectively and efficiently on the **Graduate Management Admission Test** by (1) helping the student become thoroughly familiar with the format of the test; (2) providing the student with time-tested, test-taking strategies; and (3) helping the student become familiar with the specific types of questions. The **GMAT** is now administered as a computer adaptive test (**CAT**). The question types found in this guide are the same as those that appear in the computer adaptive version. However, the format and presentation of the questions are different. The computer adaptive version (**GMAT CAT**) differences are as follows:

Only one question at a time appears on the computer screen.

Each multiple-choice question **must** be answered before you can move onto the next one. You **cannot** skip a question or return to one after you have confirmed your answer and moved on to the next question.

The computer adaptive version is constantly trying to target your individual ability. This means that the question presented depends on your answers to previous questions. Each person's test will vary depending on his/her individual ability.

On the actual computer adaptive test, the multiple-choice quantitative and verbal questions appear in separate sections. Within these sections, questions of different types may appear in any order. In this guide, we review procedures for working with questions by question type and sample questions of that type are provided at the end of each review section.

The two Analytical Writing Sections are timed separately. You write your answers for these sections using a word processor that is provided as part of the computer based test.

## FORMAT

The **GMAT CAT** does not test specific knowledge of subject matter; therefore, cramming for a particular subject matter test will not help. The **GMAT CAT** does, however, evaluate a variety of skills and abilities that you will demonstrate as you respond to the various types of test questions. Your understanding of particular concepts and techniques will help you respond more effectively and efficiently to **GMAT CAT** questions.

As in the case of the Olympic athlete preparing for the decathlon event, the examinee must develop and master a number of skills and abilities to do well on the test as a whole. Because one major weakness can do much to lower your test score, it is necessary that you identify your weaknesses and then develop the techniques that will enable you to remedy the situation. Similar to the Olympic athlete, the examinee must study the terrain, identify the obstacles, and then practice diligently to develop the specific skill needed to overcome the identified weakness.

This study guide gives you descriptions and explanations of complex test questions and suggests techniques for responding to the test format effectively and efficiently. Each question type is presented with an explanation of its format, techniques for responding to the question, and sample questions for practice.

The descriptions of question types and discussions of test-taking techniques pertain to the most recent editions of the **GMAT CAT**. A general review of basic verbal and mathematical skills and concepts will prove helpful in responding to the respective sections of the test.

# FORMAT OF TEST AND QUESTION TYPES

There are 4 separately timed sections on the **GMAT CAT.** The first two sections each consist of a 30-minute writing task. The third section contains 37 multiple choice quantitative questions. You are given 75 minutes to work in the quantitative section. The fourth section is also 75 minutes in length and consists of 41 verbal questions.

Each of the multiple-choice sections contains trial questions that will be used in future tests. These are not identified, are not counted in the scoring of your test and appear at various times within the test. Because the **GMAT CAT** continually evaluates your ability level, only one question at a time appears on the computer screen. Each question must be answered and confirmed **before** you can be given another question. **Once an answer is confirmed, you may not go back to it.** Your past answers determine the level of your next question.

## Quantitative Section

There are two types of questions in the multi-choice quantitative section - Problem Solving and Data Sufficiency. These questions are designed to test:

(1) your skill with basic mathematics,

(2) your understanding of elementary mathematical concepts, and

(3) your ability to reason quantitatively while solving quantitative problems.

### Problem Solving

Most of the problems are expressed in practical living situations. The rest are presented in a purely mathematical setting. Specifically, problem solving questions place emphasis on testing your ability to understand verbal descriptions of situations which require basic knowledge in arithmetic, elementary algebra, and general principles of geometry.

### Data Sufficiency

The second type of question is the Data Sufficiency problem. These questions include initial (given) information and two statements. The examinee must determine if and in what combination the two statements provide sufficient information to determine a unique solution to the quantitative question. There are five possible combinations: either is sufficient, both are sufficient and necessary, the first is sufficient and the second is not, the second is sufficient and the first is not, or more information is necessary to uniquely solve the problem. This type of question measures your ability to analyze a problem, to discriminate between relevant and irrelevant information, and to recognize the point at which enough information has been given to solve the problem. You are not required to solve the problem or compute an answer.

Problem solving and data sufficiency questions are intermingled throughout the quantitative section.

## Verbal Section

The verbal section of the **GMAT CAT** measures your ability to read and comprehend written material, evaluate arguments and correct written material to conform to standard written English. There are three types of multiple choice questions in the verbal section:

Reading Comprehension

Sentence Correction

Critical Reasoning

The Reading Comprehension section presents reading passages of approximately three hundred and fifty words. These passages discuss general topics in the physical and biological sciences, the social sciences, the humanities and business related fields such as marketing. You need not be knowledgeable in the various subject areas. You will, however, be expected to interpret information, recall information, and draw inferences from the passage in order to answer the questions.

### Reading Comprehension Questions

Reading Comprehension questions measure your ability:

(1) to understand what you read,

(2) to interpret and analyze the information, and

(3) to apply your conclusions.

In depth knowledge of the material is not required because all questions are based on what is stated or implied in the passage.

Although vocabulary is not tested in this section, your ability to react to specialized terms in context is tested, as well as the connotation of words and phrases. Also measured is the ability to make value judgments in reference to the arguments and ideas in a passage. Inferences must be drawn from factual statements or information specifically stated in the passage. In addition, your interpretation of a passage may be given in numerical terms to test your ability to make simple arithmetical calculations.

### Sentence Correction Questions

Sentence Correction questions measure your ability to recognize and demonstrate your familiarity with stylistic conventions and grammatical rules of standard written English. You are asked to improve incorrect or ineffective expressions. The questions consist of five choices from which you are expected to choose the one that corrects or best improves the original statement.

Two general areas of language proficiency are addressed: correct expression and effective expression. Correct expression conforms to all the rules of standard written English including pronoun case and consistency, subject-verb agreement, and verb tense sequence. A correct sentence will be structurally sound and, therefore, will not have misplaced or dangling modifiers, unidiomatic or inconsistent expressions, nor will it have faults in parallel construction.

Effective expression in sentence form includes not only grammatically correct construction but also the clear and concise communication of ideas. This implies that there are no redundancies with respect to words or phrases. Clearly written expression includes the use of proper diction, which means using the appropriate word in a particular context. Remember also that word choices that are inaccurate or inappropriate cloud the intended meaning.

### Critical Reasoning Questions

The Critical Reasoning section of the **GMAT CAT** examination tests your ability to reason in a logical manner. As in the Reading Comprehension section of the test, the topics may be drawn from literature and the arts, the social sciences, the physical sciences, and business situations.

Each of the questions in this section requires that you examine the situations presented and analyze the data for the accuracy and reliability of the conclusions that have been drawn from that data. The arguments presented may or may not be logical and the conclusions drawn from those arguments may or may not be valid. You do not need to have specific knowledge about the topics presented. You are only required to determine whether the conclusions follow logically from the statements given. The correctness of the arguments presented depends on the form of the argument, including valid and invalid premises, hidden premises, and correct formation of the conclusions.

### Analytical Writing Assessment

This recently developed section of the **GMAT CAT** requires that you compose a response to each of two distinct writing tasks. You are given 30 minutes for each writing task. The first task, Analysis of an Issue, requires that you analyze a designated circumstance or opinion and then provide relevant reasons or illustrations to support your point of view on the subject.

For the second writing task, Analysis of an Argument, you will be asked to analyze the rational behind the argument that is presented. Basically you are challenged to develop a convincing coherent, fluid and organized essay that would critique that argument - what assumption underlies the thinking, what might weaken or strengthen the argument.

Both these writing responses, Analysis of an Issue and Analysis of an Argument, will be evaluated by college and university faculty members who will determine how well you write. They will consider not only the quality of your ideas about the issues, but also how well you develop a convincing, coherent, fluid and organized essay that demonstrates effective, appropriate and correct written expression.

## TEST-TAKING SUGGESTIONS AND TECHNIQUES

If you are familiar with various test-taking techniques and actually practice them, your score should be improved. The degree of improvement is related to many factors, but one fact is certain: practice will not hurt your score!

1. It is important that you lessen the tension that arises in a test-taking atmosphere. This can only be accomplished by becoming thoroughly familiar with the format of the test including the question, kinds of materials, and directions.

2. Pay particular attention to the directions. Develop the habit of reading all test directions carefully. Directions tell you exactly what you must do in order to answer a particular type of question. Past experience tells us that many examinees would have chosen the correct answer if they had followed the directions more carefully.

3. Do not spend too much time on one question. Remember you cannot move to the next question until you have confirmed the answer to the present one. If you find you have to guess at a question in the multiple-choice sections of the test - be sure it is an educated guess. Eliminate as many possible answers as you can and then take your guess. Do not worry if you have to guess. No one is expected to get a perfect score.

4. Read each question carefully. Be sure you know exactly what is being asked before you determine your answer.

5. For the analytical writing sections take a few minutes to think about the question and plan a response before you begin writing. Leave time to reread your response so that you can revise your writing if you think it would improve your response.

6. Arrive at the test site early.

7. An experienced jogger can pace himself in reference to speed and time. With practice, you, as a test-taker, should be able to do the same. Remember, do not spend too much time on any one question. Move along, answering all the items you can in the shortest time possible. Remember each question must be answered and confirmed before you are given another question.

8. Above all, go to the test knowing that you have done all you could do in preparation for the test. You would not expect to play a piano concert or win a tough tennis match without many hours of practice and preparation.

# OTHER IMPORTANT PREPARATION INFORMATION

It is possible to take an actual computer adaptive **GMAT** practice test in a test center setting. Call **1-800-GMAT NOW** to set up an appointment and find out the current cost of taking the practice test.

**http://www.gmat.org** will provide you with the latest **GMAT** information, sample test questions, sample essay topics, list of testing sites/phone numbers as well as information about 500 business schools and answers about financial aid, etc.

Now it is time to begin your review.

# WRITING ABILITY

The Writing Ability section of the **GMAT** tests your ability to apply the basic rules of English grammar, diction and syntax. A thorough and complete review of grammar and usage rules would no doubt prove helpful, but it is not necessary for you to become a grammarian with the ability to label parts of speech, define grammatical concepts, or explain the technicalities in the use of the English language. In general, the examinee taking the **GMAT** will be familiar with basic grammatical concepts; therefore, our review will be directed toward improving your ability to recognize and correct errors.

Before we begin our review, however, it would be beneficial for you to become familiar with the format of the Writing Ability question. Each sentence in this section will be completely or partially underlined. Your task is to decide which of five multiple choices is the best phrasing of the part of the sentence which is underlined. Keep in mind that choice A is always the same as the original and may be the best choice. For example:

1. Weeding in the garden, my neighbor's dog startled me.

   A. Weeding in the garden, my neighbor's dog
   B. While my neighbor's dog was weeding in the garden, he
   C. While I was weeding in the garden, my neighbor's dog
   D. My neighbor's dog, weeding in the garden
   E. While my neighbor was weeding in the garden, the dog

You must establish who was weeding the garden. Unless the dog was exceptionally well trained beyond an ability to fetch a tossed ball, we can rule out choices A, B, and D. The intended meaning of the sentence indicates that "I" was weeding the garden, thereby ruling out choice E. The only correct answer is choice C because it clearly tells who was weeding.

Now that you have been exposed to the format of the Sentence Correction question, you realize that the **GMAT** does not, as the title suggests, test your ability to write. So if you feel insecure about your ability to write flowingly and clearly, relax. What is evaluated is your ability to recognize and correct specific types of language expression errors. After a brief review of basic grammatical elements, we will focus your study on the specific types of errors often presented in the **GMAT** that you should be able to identify and correct.

## ENGLISH GRAMMAR TERMS

The following list of English grammar terms should help you as you review. You do not need to memorize the information, but you should be familiar with each of the terms. Use this list as a preview and again as a review.

**ADJECTIVE** - word used to describe a noun or pronoun; one of the eight parts of speech

**ADVERB** - a word used to describe a verb, adjective, or other adverb; one of the eight parts of speech

**AGREEMENT**

**PRONOUN, ANTECEDENT** - pronouns should agree with their noun-antecedents in number (singular or plural) and gender (male, female, neuter)

**AGREEMENT**

**SUBJECT, VERB** - verbs and their subjects must agree in number; singular verbs should match singular subjects and plural verbs should match plural subjects

**AMBIGUITY** - use of words that could have two meanings

**CAPITALS** - upper case letters; used for the first word of every sentence and for proper nouns

**COHERENCE** - logical connection of ideas

**COLON** - punctuation used to introduce a long list or a formal explanation

**COMMA** - punctuation used to indicate a pause

**CONJUNCTION** - a word used to connect words, phrases, or clauses; one of the eight parts of speech

**COORDINATING**

**CONJUNCTIONS** - words that connect clauses of equal importance.

**DANGLING MODIFIERS** - a clause or phrase that is not placed properly in the sentence.

**END PUNCTUATION** - marks used to signal the end of a sentence; this includes the period, question mark and exclamation point.

**GENDER** - male, female, or neutral

**IDIOM** - expression peculiar to a given language

**INTERJECTION** - a word used to express sudden or strong feeling; one of the eight parts of speech

**NOUN** - the name of a person, place, thing, or idea; one of the eight parts of speech

**PARAGRAPH** - a group of sentences expressing a central idea

**PARALLEL STRUCTURE** - the consistent use of the same type of phrase, clause, or sentence structure

**PLURAL** - more than one in number

**PREPOSITION** - a word used to state the relationship between a verb and a noun or a noun and a noun; one of the eight parts of speech

**PRONOUN** - a word used to take the place of a noun; one of the eight parts of speech

**PRONOUN REFERENCE** - the word to which the pronoun refers is the antecedent, should be clear

**RUN ON SENTENCE** - a series of complete thoughts strung together in one sentence

**SEMI-COLON** - punctuation used between main clauses of compound sentences when they are not joined by coordinating conjunctions

**SENTENCE** - a group of words containing a subject and a predicate that expresses a complete thought

**SENTENCE FRAGMENT** - a group of words, phrases, or clauses that does not express a complete thought

**SINGULAR** - one in number

**SLANG** - not used in formal English

**STANDARD ENGLISH** - the language of schools, business and government

**SUBORDINATING CONJUNCTIONS** - words that connect clauses of unequal importance

**SUBORDINATION** - the placing of less important details into clauses

**VERB** - states action or state of being; one of the eight parts of speech

Add to this list other words you find in the text that are unfamiliar to you on first reading.

# SECTION 1 - PARTS OF SPEECH

Each word in a sentence can be designated by its function or its relationship to other words within the sentence. There are eight possible functions that comprise the eight parts of speech:

1) NOUNS
2) PRONOUNS
3) ADJECTIVES
4) VERBS
5) ADVERBS
6) PREPOSITIONS
7) CONJUNCTIONS
8) INTERJECTIONS

Let us begin by briefly reviewing each part of speech.

## NOUNS

The first part of speech is called a <u>noun</u>. A <u>noun</u> is defined as a word used to name a person, place, thing, or idea.

Nouns may be classified in each of these three ways: a) proper or common, b) concrete or abstract, and c) collective.

a) A **proper noun** names a particular person, place, or thing and is always capitalized.

EXAMPLE: **J**ames, **V**ermont, **I**ndependence **H**all

A **common noun** does <u>not</u> name a particular person, place, or thing.

EXAMPLE: man, state, historic site

b) A **concrete noun** names an object that can be sensed.

EXAMPLE: person, land, building

An **abstract noun** names an idea or quality.

EXAMPLE: beauty, truth, justice

c) A **collective noun** names a group of persons, objects, etc.

EXAMPLE: flock, laundry, data

# PRONOUNS

The second part of speech is called a **pronoun**. A pronoun is a word used in place of a noun.

There are several kinds of pronouns.

a) PERSONAL

b) POSSESSIVE

c) REFLEXIVE-INTENSIVE

d) RELATIVE

e) INTERROGATIVE

f) DEMONSTRATIVE

g) INDEFINITE

a) **PERSONAL PRONOUNS** are listed below.

| SINGULAR | PLURAL |
|---|---|
| I | we |
| you | you |
| he, she, it | they |
| me | us |
| you | you |
| him, her, it | them |

b) **POSSESSIVE PRONOUNS** are listed below.

| SINGULAR | PLURAL |
|---|---|
| my, mine | our, ours |
| your, yours | your, yours |
| his, her, hers, its | their, theirs |

c) REFLEXIVE - INTENSIVE PRONOUNS are listed below.

| SINGULAR | PLURAL |
|---|---|
| myself | ourselves |
| yourself | yourselves |

| | |
|---|---|
| himself, herself, itself | themselves |

REFLEXIVE PRONOUNS point back to the antecedent.

EXAMPLE: He gave <u>himself</u> the book.

INTENSIVE PRONOUNS emphasize the antecedent.

EXAMPLE: He <u>himself</u> gave the book to her.

d) RELATIVE PRONOUNS are used to introduce subordinate clauses.

| | |
|---|---|
| who | whom |
| which | what |
| that | whose |

EXAMPLE: Mike married Debbie, who is Dave's sister.

e) INTERROGATIVE PRONOUNS ask a question.

who...? whom...? whose...? which...? what...?

f) DEMONSTRATIVE PRONOUNS point out specific persons, places, things, or ideas from many.

| **SINGULAR** | **PLURAL** |
|---|---|
| this | these |
| that | those |

g. INDEFINITE PRONOUNS do <u>not</u> refer to a particular person, place or thing.

| | | | |
|---|---|---|---|
| all | each | many | one |
| any | either | most | others |
| anybody | everybody | neither | several |
| anyone | everyone | nobody | some |
| both | few | none | somebody |
| | | no one | someone |

The word that replaces a pronoun in a sentence is called an ANTECEDENT of the pronoun.

EXAMPLE: Thomas fell and broke his leg.

He cracked it in two places.

The pronoun <u>he</u> takes the place of the proper noun, <u>Thomas</u>.

The pronoun <u>it</u> takes the place of the common noun, <u>leg</u>.

<u>Thomas</u> is the antecedent of <u>he</u>.

Leg is the antecedent of it.

# ADJECTIVE

The third part of speech is called an **adjective.** An adjective is a word used to modify a noun or a pronoun.

The words a, an, and the are called **articles** and are considered adjectives.

Now, let us discuss the following uses of adjectives.

a) PRONOUNS AS ADJECTIVES

b) PREDICATE ADJECTIVES

c) ADJECTIVE PLACEMENT

d) COMPARISON OF ADJECTIVES

## PRONOUNS AS ADJECTIVES

Some words may be used as either a pronoun or an adjective.

EXAMPLE: I love this. (pronoun)

I love this child. (adjective)

The following words may be used either as pronouns or adjectives.

| | | | |
|---|---|---|---|
| all | either | one | these |
| another | few | other | this |
| any | many | several | those |
| both | more | some | what |
| each | neither | that | which |

## PREDICATE ADJECTIVE

An adjective that follows a linking verb and completes the subject is called a **predicate adjective.**

There are two kinds of linking verbs:

a) forms of the verb to be (is, are, etc.), and

b) certain verbs that refer to the five senses.

EXAMPLE: The starlet is beautiful.

Beautiful modifies starlet.

Is is the linking verb.

EXAMPLE: The corn looks tall.

Tall modifies corn.

Looks is the linking verb.

Is could be substituted for the word looks. (The corn is tall.)

## Adjective Placement

Adjectives usually come before the nouns they modify.

EXAMPLE: The colorful float won the prize.

For variation, adjectives modifying nouns can come after the noun they modify.

EXAMPLE: The float, colorful and bright, won the prize.

**Comparison of Adjectives**

Adjectives can be stated in comparison. The three forms are the **POSITIVE**, the **COMPARATIVE**, and the **SUPERLATIVE**.

The **POSITIVE FORM** is the adjective itself.

EXAMPLE: She took a small portion.

The **COMPARATIVE FORM** is formed by use of -er or the words more or less.

EXAMPLE: She took a smaller portion than John.

The **SUPERLATIVE FORM** is formed by use of -est or the words most or least. Some adjective comparisons are irregular.

EXAMPLE: She took the smallest portion.

EXAMPLES: fast, faster, fastest (-er, -est)

beautiful, more beautiful, most beautiful (more, most)

good, better, best (irregular)

## VERBS

The fourth part of speech is called a **verb**. A verb is a word that shows action or states being.

a) PHYSICAL ACTION

b) MENTAL ACTION

c) STATE OF BEING

d) TRANSITIVE - INTRANSITIVE

e) TENSE

A **physical action verb** indicates any activity that can be seen.

EXAMPLE: John throws the ball.

A **mental activity verb** expresses an activity carried on in the mind.

EXAMPLE: John dreams about the game.

A **state of being** verb shows that something exists; it states that a thing or condition is.

EXAMPLE: John is the quarterback.

A **transitive verb** is an action verb that takes an object. An **object** is a noun or pronoun that completes the action by showing who or what is receiving the action of the verb.

EXAMPLE: The player tossed the ball.

An **intransitive verb** shows an action without taking an object.

EXAMPLE: The child cried.

Most verbs in English can be either transitive or intransitive depending on how they are used in the sentence.

In order to show the correct time relationship of the action or statement of being in a sentence, the verb or verbs of a sentence can change form. These forms are called **tense**.

Here are examples of the six tenses using the pronoun I and the verb talk.

| | |
|---|---|
| **PRESENT** | I talk today. |
| **PAST** | I talked yesterday. |
| **FUTURE** | I shall talk tomorrow. |
| **PRESENT PERFECT** | I have talked often. |
| **PAST PERFECT** | I had talked to her before I talked to you. |
| **FUTURE PERFECT** | I shall have talked to her by tomorrow afternoon. |

The **present tense** is used to express an action (or state of being) going on at the present time.

EXAMPLE: I talk today.

The **past tense** is used to express an action (or state of being) that took place in the past but did not continue into the present.

Adding ed to the present tense forms the past tense of most regular verbs.

EXAMPLE: I talked yesterday.

The **future tense** is used to express an action (or state of being) going on at some time in the future.

EXAMPLE: I shall talk tomorrow.

Form the future tense of regular verbs by adding the auxiliary verbs shall or will to the present tense of the verb.

The **present perfect tense** is used to express an action (or state of being) that was stated in the past and continues into the present.

EXAMPLE: I have talked often.

The **past perfect tense** is used to express an action (or state of being) which went on and was completed in the past before some other past action took place.

EXAMPLE: I had talked to her before I talked to you.

The **future perfect tense** is used to express an action (or state of being) which will take place and be completed at some time in the future before some other future event.

EXAMPLE: I shall have talked to her by tomorrow afternoon.

Many verb errors are caused by irregular verbs. These verbs, sometimes referred to as strong verbs, do not form the past, future and perfect tenses in the same manner as regular verbs. The following list may help you identify these irregular verbs and can be used as a handy reference tool.

## Principal Parts of Irregular Verbs

| Present | Past | Past Participle |
|---|---|---|
| bear | bore | borne |
| beat | beat | beaten |
| become | became | become |
| begin | began | begun |
| bite | bit | bitten |
| bleed | bled | bled |
| blow | blew | blown |
| break | broke | broken |
| bring | brought | brought |
| build | built | built |
| buy | bought | bought |
| catch | caught | caught |
| choose | chose | chosen |
| come | came | come |
| dig | dug | dug |
| dive | dove, dived | dived, dove |
| do | did | done |
| draw | drew | drawn |
| dream | dreamed, dreamt | dreamed, dreamt |
| drink | drank | drunk |
| drive | drove | driven |
| eat | ate | eaten |
| fall | fell | fallen |
| fight | fought | fought |
| find | found | found |
| fight | fought | fought |
| flee | fled | fled |
| fly | flew | flown |
| forbid | forbade | forbidden |
| forget | forgot | forgotten, forgot |
| freeze | froze | frozen |
| get | got | gotten |
| give | gave | given |
| go | went | gone |
| grow | grew | grown |
| hang (on a wall) | hung | hung |
| hang (execute) | hanged | hanged |
| have | had | had |
| hear | heard | heard |
| hide | hid | hidden |
| hurt | hurt | hurt |
| keep | kept | kept |
| know | knew | known |
| lay | laid | laid |
| lead | led | led |
| leave | left | left |
| lend | lent | lent |
| let | let | let |
| lie | lay | lain |
| light | lighted, lit | lighted, lit |
| lose | lost | lost |

| Present | Past | Past Participle |
|---|---|---|
| make | made | made |
| meet | met | met |
| pay | paid | paid |
| plead | pleaded, plead, pled | pleaded, plead, |
| prove | proved | proved, proven |
| put | put | put |
| ride | rode | ridden |
| ring | rang | rung |
| rise | rose | risen |
| run | ran | run |
| say | said | said |
| see | saw | seen |
| seek | sought | sought |
| sell | sold | sold |
| set | set | set |
| shake | shook | shaken |
| shine | shone, shined | shone, shined |
| show | showed | showed, shown |
| shrink | shrank, shrunk | shrunk |
| sing | sang | sung |
| sink | sank | sunk |
| sit | sat | sat |
| slay | slew | slain |
| slide | slid | slid |
| sow | sowed | sown |
| speak | spoke | spoken |
| spin | spun | spun |
| spit | spat | spat |
| spring | sprang | sprung |
| stand | stood | stood |
| steal | stole | stolen |
| sting | stung | stung |
| stink | stunk, stank | stunk |
| strike | struck | struck |
| swear | swore | sworn |
| swim | swam | swum |
| swing | swung | swung |
| take | took | taken |
| teach | taught | taught |
| tear | tore | torn |
| think | thought | thought |
| throw | threw | thrown |
| tread | trod | trodden |
| wake | waked, woke | waked, woken, woke |
| wear | wore | worn |
| weave | wove, weaved | woven, weaved |
| win | won | won |
| wind | wound | wound |
| wring | wrung | wrung |
| write | wrote | written |

# ADVERBS

The fifth part of speech is called an **adverb**. An adverb is a word used to modify a verb, an adjective or another adverb.

Let us discuss the following uses of adverbs.

a) ADVERBS USED TO ANSWER QUESTIONS

b) ADVERBS USED TO ASK QUESTIONS

c) PLACEMENT OF ADVERBS

d) COMPARISON OF ADVERBS

## Adverbs Answer Questions

Adverbs can answer the following questions:

| | |
|---|---|
| When? | EXAMPLE: Jim came early. |
| Where? | EXAMPLE: Jim came here. |
| How? | EXAMPLE: Jim came quickly. |
| To what extent? | EXAMPLE: Jim came very early. |

## Adverbs Ask Questions

The following words are used to ask questions and act as adverbs. You may find that it is helpful to rewrite a sentence of this type.

When...?, Where...?, How...?, Why...?

EXAMPLES:

When? When did the package arrive?
(The package did arrive when?)
The word when acts as an adverb.

Where? Where were the dishes placed?
(The dishes were placed where?)
The word where acts as an adverb.

How? How do you do this?
(You do this how?)
The word how acts as an adverb.

Why? Why are you going?
(You are going why?)
The word why acts as an adverb.

## Adverb Placement

Adverbs that modify verbs usually follow the word modified.

EXAMPLE: Alexis sat quietly.

Adverbs that modify adjectives usually come before the word modified.

EXAMPLE: Her dress is very pretty.

Certain adverbs are sometimes put in front of the verb modified in order to put emphasis on the action.

EXAMPLE: Alexis quietly sat down.

### Adverbs in Comparison

Adverbs can be stated in comparison. The three forms are the **POSITIVE**, the **COMPARATIVE**, and the **SUPERLATIVE**.

The **POSITIVE** form is the adverb itself.

EXAMPLE: Mary ran slowly.

The **COMPARATIVE** is formed by use of -er or the words more or less.

EXAMPLE: Mary ran slower than Rick.

The **SUPERLATIVE** is formed by use of -est or the words most or least.

EXAMPLE: Mary ran slowest of all the contestants.

## PREPOSITIONS

The sixth part of speech is the **preposition**. A preposition is a word that states a relationship between a noun and a noun or a verb and a noun.

### Between a Noun and Noun

EXAMPLE: The coat on the hanger is mine.

In this sentence the word on expresses the relationship between coat and hanger.

### Between a Verb and Noun

EXAMPLE: The boy ran into the street.

In this sentence, the word into expresses the relationship between ran and street.

**A List of Prepositions**

| | | | |
|---|---|---|---|
| aboard | about | above | according to |
| across | after | against | ahead of |
| along | amid | among | apart |
| around | as far as | as to | at |
| back | because | before | before |
| behind | below | beneath | betwixt |
| between | beyond | by | concerning |
| contrary | despite | down | due to |
| during | for | from | in |
| into | like | near | of |
| off | onto | out of | over |
| past | per | round | since |
| through | throughout | to | toward |
| under | until | unto | up |
| upon | with | within | |

# CONJUNCTION

The seventh part of speech is the **conjunction**. A conjunction is a word that connects words or groups of words. There are three types of conjunctions.

a) Coordinating Conjunctions

b) Subordination Conjunctions

c) Correlative Conjunctions

**Coordinating Conjunctions**

Coordinating conjunctions connect words, phrases and other word groups, and complete thoughts that are of equal importance. The coordinating conjunctions are and, or, but, nor, for.

**Subordinating Conjunctions**

Subordinating conjunctions connect complete thoughts that are of unequal importance.

The most common subordinating conjunctions are:

| | | | |
|---|---|---|---|
| after | before | provided | unless |
| although | how | since | until |
| as | if | than | when |
| as much as | in order that | that | where |
| because | in as much as | though | while |

**Correlative conjunctions**

Correlative conjunctions connect words, phrases and other word groups, and complete thoughts that are of equal importance. They differ from coordinating conjunctions in that correlative conjunctions are always used in pairs.

The most common correlative conjunctions are:

| | |
|---|---|
| either...or | not only...but also |
| neither...nor | whether...or |
| both...and | |

# INTERJECTION

The eighth part of speech is the **interjection**. An interjection is a word that shows emotion but has no grammatical relation to any other word in the sentence.

EXAMPLE: Quick! Hide behind the tree.

# PUNCTUATION

## THE COMMA

There are many uses for the comma. The primary use is to form logical groups of words within sentences. There are also special uses for the comma which are dictated by custom.

**RULE 1:** Commas separate items in a series.

EXAMPLES: The secretary was proficient on IBM, Wang, and Apple word processors.

The presents included a tie for father, a blouse for mother, and a doll for the baby.

It is acceptable to omit the comma before the <u>and</u> which joins the last two items of a series.

NOTE: Occasionally sentences may not be clear or the meaning of a sentence may be altered if the comma is omitted.

EXAMPLE: He ordered a huge breakfast of juice, pancakes, bacon and eggs, and coffee.

Custom dictates that *bacon and eggs* is <u>one</u> item. To represent it clearly as one item commas must come <u>before</u> and <u>after</u> this item.

EXAMPLES: The conductor insisted he loved all types of music: classical, pop, folk and rock.

(2 commas - 3 types)

In this sentence we use <u>2</u> commas and have <u>3</u> types of music. *Folk and rock* are grouped together.

There is an <u>exception</u> to this rule. When <u>all</u> the items in a series are separated by either <u>and</u> or <u>or</u>, no commas are used.

EXAMPLES: The murdered was either June or Mr. Reba or Michael.

I didn't know whether to laugh or cry or faint.

**<u>RULE 2</u>:** Commas are used to separate two or more adjectives preceding a noun.

EXAMPLES: He arrived on a cold, damp, blustery December day.

*<u>December day</u>* is one item. December is <u>not</u> modifying day. *<u>December day</u>* is taken as a single noun.

The second exception is similar. Do not use a comma between adjectives in a series if one of the adjectives modifies another adjective in the series.

EXAMPLE: Emma bought a shocking red car.

*<u>Shocking</u>* modifies *<u>red</u>*.

**<u>RULE 3:</u>** Use a comma before the conjunctions <u>and</u>, <u>but</u>, <u>or</u>, <u>nor</u>, <u>for</u>, and <u>yet</u> when they join two complete thoughts.

EXAMPLES: I understand why the critics' reactions were negative, but I can't accept personal attacks on the actors.

The school was closed because of the measles, and it will remain closed for a week.

When two complete thoughts are short, no comma is necessary.

EXAMPLE: You travel ahead and I'll catch you later.

**<u>RULE 4:</u>** Place a comma after certain introductory elements of sentences.

Place a comma after two or more introductory prepositional phrases.

EXAMPLES: <u>After three weeks on the job,</u> Tom decided to quit.

<u>At the end of the lane behind the barn,</u> we found the evidence.

**NOTE:** A comma need not but may be used after a single introductory prepositional phrase.

Place a comma after introductory participle phrases.

| | |
|---|---|
| EXAMPLE: | Forced to walk like a duck, the young actor soon tired of his role. |
| **NOTE:** | Use caution. Do not confuse participles with gerunds. |
| EXAMPLE: | Singing and dancing are my best subjects. |
| | (*Singing and dancing* are special nouns known as gerunds. In this sentence they are used as subjects.) |
| | *Singing and dancing* in the rain, I felt young again. (Introductory participial phrase - commas must be used.) |

Place a comma after an introductory adverbial clause.

| | |
|---|---|
| EXAMPLE: | While I iced the birthday cake, Dad cooked supper. |
| **NOTE**: | If the sentence elements were reversed, no commas would be necessary. |
| EXAMPLE: | Dad cooked the supper while I iced the birthday cake. |
| **RULE 5:** | Use a comma to separate items in a date. |
| EXAMPLE: | The first atomic bomb was dropped on August 6, 1945. |
| **NOTE:** | If only the month and date are used, no comma is necessary. |
| **RULE 6:** | Use a comma to separate items in an address. |
| EXAMPLE: | His address is 135 Lenox Drive, Phoenix, Arizona. |
| **NOTE:** | If prepositions are used between the elements of an address, no commas are necessary. |
| EXAMPLE: | He lived at 135 Lenox Drive in Phoenix, Arizona. |
| **RULE 7:** | Place a comma after a name followed by Jr., Sr., Ph.D., M.D., etc. |
| EXAMPLES: | His full name is Robert Clark Hoover, Jr. |
| | I guess we should call him Thomas Hume, Ph.D. |
| **RULE 8:** | Place a comma after the salutation of a friendly letter and after the closing of any letter. |
| EXAMPLES: | Dear Mary, |
| | Sincerely yours, |
| **RULE 9:** | Separate appositives from the sentence with commas. |

An **APPOSITIVE** is a word or phrase that follows a noun or pronoun and helps to further identify or explain the noun or pronoun. Appositives have modifiers.

EXAMPLES: The research by Jules Baer, a professor of psychology, will be published.

Some appositives are so closely related to the words they modify that no commas are necessary.

| | |
|---|---|
| EXAMPLES: | Alexander the Great died a premature death at the age of thirty-three. |
| | The novel Huckleberry Finn was written by Mark Twain. |
| | No commas are necessary between "Alexander" and "the Great" or between "novel" and "Huckleberry Finn." |
| **RULE 10:** | Use commas to set off words in direct address from the rest of the sentence. |

When you speak directly to a person using his name, this is known as direct address.

EXAMPLE: Dad, may I borrow the car tonight?

You are going, Richard, even if it is not convenient.

**RULE 11:** The following parenthetical expressions are set off by commas.

| | | |
|---|---|---|
| I believe | on the contrary | in fact |
| I think | on the other hand | indeed |
| I know | after all | naturally |
| I hope | by the way | of course |
| I am sure | incidentally | in my opinion |
| for example | nevertheless | to tell the truth |
| however | in as much | therefore |

EXAMPLES: He is, by the way, never on time.

I have decided, therefore, not to attend Harvard.

Tom is, I am sure, too old to attend the academy.

**RULE 12:** Use commas to separate nonessential information from the sentence.

Nonessential information is a complete thought or phrase that adds extra information to another complete thought.

EXAMPLE: William Rogers, who is an accountant, will receive an MBA from Rutgers this year.

The main idea of the sentence is that *William Rogers will receive an MBA from Rutgers this year*. The nonessential information is *who is an accountant.* The nonessential information does NOT change the meaning of the main idea if it is removed.

The opposite condition may occur. The added information may be essential to the main idea.

EXAMPLE: William Rogers is the only accountant who will receive an MBA from Rutgers this year.

In this sentence the underlined clause is essential; no commas are necessary. Without the clause the sentence would mean something else:

William Rogers is the only accountant.

## Key Points - The Comma

- Commas separate items in a series. (Rule 1)
- Commas separate two or more adjectives preceding a noun. (Rule 2)
- Commas separate two complete thoughts joined by certain coordinating conjunctions. (Rule 3)
- Commas set off certain introductory elements of sentences. (Rule 4)
- Commas separate items in a date. (Rule 5)
- Commas separate items in an address. (Rule 6)

- Commas separate the abbreviations Jr., Sr., Ph. D., etc. from the name preceding the abbreviation. (Rule 7)
- Place commas after the salutation of a friendly letter and after the complimentary close of any letter. (Rule 8)
- Separate appositives from the antecedent with commas. (Rule 9)
- Separate direct address from the sentence with commas. (Rule 10)
- Separate certain parenthetical expressions from the sentence with commas. (Rule 11)
- Separate nonessential clauses and phrases from the main idea with commas. (Rule 12)

## THE SEMICOLON

Although semicolons are not used as frequently as commas, they are very important punctuation marks. Semicolons are used in two instances. Rules 1 and 2 deal with the first use, while Rule 3 discusses the second.

**RULE 1:** Insert semicolons between complete thoughts (sentences) which are closely related but are not separated by a coordinating conjunction.

EXAMPLES: Include only pertinent information in your paragraphs; omit all nonessential items.

White provided a big lift to the team with some clutch pitching; Bently chipped in with some timely hitting.

**RULE 2:** Insert a semicolon between complete thoughts that are joined by expressions such as:

| | | |
|---|---|---|
| for instance | that is | besides |
| accordingly | moreover | nevertheless |
| furthermore | otherwise | therefore |
| however | consequently | instead |
| hence | for example | so |

EXAMPLES: The reservoir fell below 50% of capacity; therefore, the mayor has initiated special conservation measures.

The strike was not settled; nevertheless, many of the nurses returned to work.

**RULE 3:** For the sake of clarity, semicolons are sometimes used in place of commas.

EXAMPLE 1: Items in a series containing commas.

Four of state's players made the All-Star Team: Ted French, pitcher; Walt Finley, shortstop; Terry Laurino, centerfielder; and James Blueberry, who was selected for the third consecutive year, left fielder.

EXAMPLE 2: Between complete thoughts already containing commas.

My uncle Al, who never had children of his own, always brought toys, candies, games and good cheer to our Christmas celebration; we children, needless to say, were uncontrollable until he arrived.

A semicolon is necessary only when there are so many commas in the two sentences that not using a semicolon will cause confusion.

## THE COLON

A colon is a strong punctuation mark that can be translated as "note the following."

**RULE 1:** Use a colon to introduce a list.

EXAMPLE: He tied everything to the roof of the car: the bicycles, the cooler and the raft.

**EXCEPTION**: Do not use a colon after a verb or preposition that introduces a list.

EXAMPLE: The items he tied on the roof included a bicycle, a cooler and a raft. [Verb]

The professor was a specialist in history, economics and sociology. [Preposition]

**RULE 2:** Use a colon after the salutation in a business letter.

EXAMPLE: Dear Sir:

Dear Mrs. Wilson:

**NOTE:** Remember use a comma after the salutation in a friendly letter.

EXAMPLES: Dear Mom,

Dear Mary,

**RULE 3:** Use a colon between number divisions showing time.

EXAMPLES: The presentation will start at 10:30 A.M. sharp.

The winning time was 3:57.

### Key Points - Semicolons and Colons

- Use semicolons between complete thoughts not separated by a conjunction.
- Use a semicolon between complete thoughts that are joined by certain expressions such as therefore, however, for example, etc.
- To prevent confusion semicolons are sometimes used in place of commas.
- A colon is used to introduce a list.
- A colon is used after the salutation of a business letter.
- Use a colon to separate elements in expressions of time.

# AGREEMENT

## AGREEMENT BETWEEN SUBJECT AND VERB

Agreement of subject and verb is a key element in English grammar and composition. There are a number of special rules in the area of subject/verb agreement that you will review in this section.

## A Verb and Its Subject Must Agree in Number

Agreeing in number means that if the subject is singular, the verb must also be singular. So, too, if the subject is plural, the verb must be plural.

Remember that singular means one single thing and that plural means two or more things.

EXAMPLE #1: The dog walks down the street.

In this sentence the subject *dog* is singular and so is the verb *walks*. Most verbs ending in a single s are singular.

EXAMPLE #2: The dogs walk down the street.

In this sentence the subject *dogs* is plural and so is the verb *walk*.

## Phrases between Subjects and Verbs

Sometimes choosing the correct verb is complicated by the introduction of a prepositional phrase that is placed between the subject and verb. It is important to determine the correct subject before you choose the verb.

Most people will correctly say -

"The pipes are clogged."

but, some people might have problems with -

"The pipes in the bathroom is/are clogged."

In the second sentence the subject is *pipes* and the correct verb is *are*. But some people might mistakenly think that the noun *bathroom* is the subject and so select the verb is. The noun *bathroom* is the object of the preposition in, and this prepositional phrase is an adjective phrase modifying the subject *pipes*. If you have problems deciding which word is the subject, cross out the prepositional phrase.

EXAMPLE: The pipes ~~in the bathroom~~ is/are clogged.

## Indefinite Pronouns That Are Usually Singular

The pronouns that follow are usually singular and require a singular verb.

| | | | |
|---|---|---|---|
| each | one | no one | someone |
| either | everyone | nobody | somebody |
| neither | everybody | anyone | |

While these pronouns suggest groups of people, they actually point to individual members of the group.

EXAMPLE: See the children. Each wants a piece of candy.

In the above example, the pronoun *Each* refers to the children individually and requires the singular verb wants.

EXAMPLE: No one went to the store.

In this example, the pronoun *No one* means that not one person went to the store.

## Indefinite Pronouns that can be either Singular or Plural

The following pronouns can be either singular or plural depending upon how they are used in the sentence.

some all most

EXAMPLE #1: Some of the candy is missing.

In the above sentence the pronoun *some* is followed by the adjective phrase *of the candy*. *Candy* is singular and so the word *some* is used singularly. The verb is is singular.

EXAMPLE #2: Some of the candies are missing.

In the above sentence the pronoun *some* is followed by the adjective phrase *of the candies*. *Candies* is plural and so the word *some* is treated as plural. The verb are is plural.

## Indefinite Pronouns That Are Plural

The following indefinite pronouns are plural and require a plural verb.

several few both many

EXAMPLE: Several of the dancers wear ribbons in their hair.

In this sentence the pronoun *several* is the subject; the verb *wear* is the correct form.

## Compound Subjects Joined by And

Most compound subjects joined by and are plural and take a plural verb.

EXAMPLE #1: The spoon and dish are on the table.

In this sentence the nouns *spoon* and *dish* are joined by the word *and*. This compound subject is followed by the plural verb *are*.

EXAMPLE #2: The cat in the basket and the dog by the fireplace make a pretty picture.

In this sentence the nouns *cat* and *dog* are joined by the word *and*. *In the basket* and *by the fireplace* are prepositional phrases modifying the nouns *cat* and *dog*. *Cat* and *dog* make up the compound subject; the plural, make, is the correct verb form. Again, you might find it helpful to cross out the prepositional phrases when choosing the correct verb.

Some compound subjects are considered a single item.

EXAMPLE: Spaghetti and meatballs is my favorite dinner.

In this sentence the nouns *spaghetti* and *meatballs* make up the compound subject, but because they are often served together, we consider them a single dish. The singular verb form is used.

## Compound Subjects Joined by Or, Nor, Either... Or, Neither... Nor

If the subjects joined by or, nor, either...or, or neither...nor are singular, the verb is singular.

EXAMPLE: Either the doctor or the nurse visits the patient daily.

In this sentence the nouns *doctor* and *nurse* are the subjects joined by *either...or*. Both subjects are singular and so the verb *visits* is singular. Notice that the sentence states that only one person, either the doctor or the nurse, visits the patient daily.

If one of the subjects joined by _or_, _nor_, _either...or_, or _neither...nor_ is singular and the other subject is plural, the verb agrees with the subject that is closest to it.

EXAMPLE: Neither the coach nor the players are going to lunch.

In this sentence the nouns _coach_ and _players_ are the subjects joined by _Neither...nor_. The subject _coach_ is singular and the subject _players_ is plural. Because the subject _players_ is closer to the verb, the verb are going is plural.

EXAMPLE: Neither the players nor the coach is going to lunch.

In this sentence the noun _players_ and _coach_ are the subjects joined by _Neither...nor_. The subject players is plural and the subject _coach_ is singular. Because the subject _coach_ is closer to the verb, the verb _is going_ is singular.

## Collective Nouns

A **collective noun** refers to a group of persons or things. Use a singular verb if the noun is used to refer to the group as a _whole_. Use a plural verb if the members of the group are acting as _individuals_.

EXAMPLE: The team wins the game.

In this sentence the _team_ acts as a whole in order to win the game, and so the verb _wins_ is singular.

EXAMPLE: The team eat their sandwiches.

In this sentence the _team_ acts as individuals as they each eat their own sandwiches, and so the verb _eat_ is plural.

## Other Subject - Verb Agreement Problems

The words here, there, and where are never the subject of a sentence. Instead, the subject follows the verb, and so the subject must be found in order to use the correct verb form.

EXAMPLE 1: Where is the hat?

**NOTE**: It is sometimes helpful to restate the sentence.

**RESTATED**: The hat is where?

In this sentence the subject is _hat_. _Hat_ is singular and so is the verb _is_.

EXAMPLE 2: Here are the hats.

**RESTATED**: The hats are here

In this sentence the subject is _hats_. _Hats_ is plural and so is the verb _are_.

Words stating amount are usually singular.

EXAMPLE: Fifty dollars is the correct amount.

In this sentence the noun _dollars_ is the subject. It refers to _one_ payment and so the verb _is_ is singular.

Some nouns ending in s are considered singular.

EXAMPLE: Mathematics is my favorite class.

In this sentence the noun _mathematics_ ends in **s**. It is, however, one subject and so the verb _is_ is singular.

### Key Points - Subject and Verb Agreement

- A verb and its subject must agree in number.
- Agreeing in number means that if the subject is singular the verb must also be singular. So, too, if the subject is plural, the verb must be plural.
- The verb agrees with the <u>subject</u> and not other words that may be between the subject and the verb.
- The following pronouns are usually singular.

| | | | |
|---|---|---|---|
| each | one | no one | someone |
| either | everyone | nobody | somebody |
| neither | everybody | anyone | |

- The following pronouns can be either singular or plural depending upon how they are used in the sentence.

  some all most

- The following pronouns are plural.

  several few both many

- Most compound subjects joined by <u>and</u> are plural and take a plural verb.
- Some compound subjects are considered singular because they are considered a single item.
- If the subjects joined by <u>or</u>, <u>nor</u>, <u>either</u>...<u>or</u>, or <u>neither</u>...<u>nor</u> are singular, the verb is singular.
- If one of the subjects joined by <u>or</u>, <u>nor</u>, <u>either</u>...<u>or</u>, or <u>neither</u>...<u>nor</u> is singular and the other subject is plural, the verb agrees with the subject that is closest to it.
- A collective noun refers to a group of persons or things. Use a singular verb if the subject noun is used to refer to the group as a whole. Use a plural verb if the subject noun is used to refer to the individual members of the group.
- The words <u>here</u>, <u>there</u>, and <u>where</u> are <u>never</u> the subject of a sentence. Instead, the subject follows the verb, and so the subject must be found in order to use the correct verb form.
- Words stating amount are usually singular. Some nouns ending in <u>s</u> are considered singular.

## USING PRONOUNS CORRECTLY

Another skill measured by the **GMAT CAT** is your knowledge of pronoun usage. Selecting the correct pronoun is a matter of knowing the types of pronouns and their various forms and uses. This section will help you review proper pronoun usage.

### Using Pronouns Correctly as Subjects and Predicate Nominatives

The following personal pronouns are used as subjects and predicate nominatives.

| **SINGULAR** | **PLURAL** |
|---|---|
| I | we |

| | |
|---|---|
| you | you |
| he, she, it | they |

EXAMPLE 1: She is the captain of the cheerleaders.

In this sentence the pronoun *She* is the subject of the sentence.

EXAMPLE 2: Jill and she are the captains of the cheerleaders.

In this sentence the proper noun *Jill* and the pronoun *she* are the subjects of the sentence. Some people who might say, "Jill and her are the captains" would never say, "Her is the captain." If the subject is compound, use the pronoun by itself to be certain you have selected the correct pronoun.

EXAMPLE 3: I know it was he at the game.

In this sentence the predicate nominative *he* follows the linking verb *was*. Although it is becoming acceptable to say, "It's me," it is still better to use the correct pronoun for the predicate nominative.

EXAMPLE 4: We girls are going to lunch.

In this sentence the subject pronoun *We* is followed by the noun girls. Read the sentence without the noun in order to be certain you have chosen the correct pronoun. (*We* are going to lunch).

## Using Pronouns Correctly as Direct Objects, Indirect Objects, and Objects of the Preposition

The following personal pronouns are used as direct objects, indirect objects, and objects of the preposition.

| SINGULAR | PLURAL |
|---|---|
| me | us |
| you | you |
| him, her, it | them |

EXAMPLE 1: The coach praised him.

In this sentence the pronoun *him* is the direct object of the sentence.

EXAMPLE 2: The coach praised the quarterback and him.

In this sentence the noun *quarterback* and the pronoun *him* are the direct objects of the sentence. Some people who might say, "*The coach praised the quarterback and he*" would never say, "*The coach praised he.*" If the direct object is compound, use the pronoun by itself to be certain you have selected the correct pronoun.

EXAMPLE 3: The coach told the reporter and him the score.

In this sentence the noun *reporter* and the pronoun *him* are the indirect objects of the sentence. If the pronoun were the only indirect object in this sentence, it would read, "*The coach told him the score.*" This is correct.

EXAMPLE 4: The coach gave the play to the captain and him.

In this sentence the noun *captain* and the pronoun *him* are the objects of the preposition *to*. If the pronoun were the only object of the preposition in this sentence, it would read, *"The coach gave the play to him."* This is correct.

## Using Who and Whom Correctly

Who and whom can be either interrogative pronouns or relative pronouns.

When used as interrogative pronouns, use who for subjects and whom for direct objects and objects of the preposition.

EXAMPLE 1: Who is the trainer?

In this sentence the interrogative pronoun *Who* is the subject of the sentence.

EXAMPLE 2: Whom did the commissioner appoint?

In this sentence the pronoun *Whom* is the direct object of the verb *did appoint*. You may find it is helpful to re-write the sentence. The commissioner did appoint *whom*?

EXAMPLE 3: To whom did you address your letter?

In this sentence the interrogative pronoun *whom* is the object of the preposition *to*. Whom is the correct interrogative pronoun to use after prepositions.

When used as relative pronouns, who or whom should be used correctly within the subordinate clause it begins. Do not refer to words outside the clause when deciding which word to use.

EXAMPLE 1: The boy who is in my class is young.

In this sentence the relative pronoun *who* is the subject in the subordinate clause "*who is in my class.*"

EXAMPLE 2: The boy whom I met is young.

In this sentence the relative pronoun *whom* is the object in the subordinate clause "*whom I met*" *("I met whom").*

EXAMPLE 3: Do you know who the new boy is?

In this sentence the relative pronoun *who* is the predicate nominative in the subordinate clause *"who the new boy is" ("The new boy is who").*

## Other Problems When Using Pronouns

### Sentences with Comparisons

Sentences that make comparisons often use the words than and as. These sentences are frequently "incomplete" to avoid repetition. Use the pronoun you would use if the sentence were "complete".

EXAMPLE: Mark is stronger than he.

In this sentence the pronoun *he* is correct. If the sentence were "completed," it would read *"Mark is stronger than he is strong."*

You would not say - *"Mark is stronger than him is strong."* That would be grammatically incorrect.

Consider the following two sentences:

I like Jennie more than she.

I like Jennie more than her.

If the first sentence is "completed," it would read, *"I like Jennie more than she likes Jennie."* If the second sentence is "completed," it would read. *"I like Jennie more than I like her."*

**NOTE**: Some sentences can be completed either way while others can be completed only one way.

### Use Possessive Case before Gerunds

Use possessive personal pronouns before nouns formed by a **verb** plus **ing**.

EXAMPLE: Her ice-skating is at championship level.

In this sentence the possessive pronoun **her** modifies the noun **skating**. Note that **skating** is the name of an activity and is made up of the verb **skate** and an **ing** ending.

### Use Objective Case for the Subject of Infinitive Verbs

Use the personal pronouns me, him, her, you, it, us, them as subjects of verbs made up of to and the verb.

EXAMPLE: Mother warned her to be careful.

In this sentence *her* is the subject of the verb *to be*. This is the only time *her*, not *she*, would be the subject of the sentence.

## AGREEMENT OF PRONOUN AND ITS ANTECEDENT

### Pronouns Agree in Number and Gender

Pronouns agree with their antecedents in number (singular/plural) and gender (masculine/feminine/neuter).

EXAMPLE: The girl stated her opinion.

In this sentence the pronoun *her* refers to the noun *girl* which is *singular* and *feminine*.

The following indefinite pronouns are singular and are referred to by singular personal pronouns.

| | | | |
|---|---|---|---|
| each | one | no one | anyone |
| either | everyone | nobody | someone |
| neither | everybody | anybody | somebody |

EXAMPLE: Each of the girls stated her opinions.

In this sentence the pronoun *Each* is singular and the prepositional phrase *of the girls* indicates the feminine gender. *Her* is the correct possessive pronoun.

### Singular Nouns Joined by Or are Singular

Singular nouns or pronouns joined by or or nor are referred to by singular pronouns.

EXAMPLE: Frank or he will bring his wrench.

In this sentence the subjects *Frank* and *he* are joined by *or*. Both are masculine and so *his* is correct.

## Nouns Joined by And are Plural

Nouns or pronouns joined by and are referred to by plural pronouns.

EXAMPLE: The boss and the workers will eat their sandwiches.

In this sentence the subjects **boss** and **workers** are joined by **and**. **Their** is correct.

## Relative Pronouns Take Number of Antecedent

In sentences using the relative pronouns who, which, or that, the number of the antecedent determines the number of the verb that follows the relative pronoun.

EXAMPLE: The hat which is ripped no longer fits.

## KEY POINTS - USING PRONOUNS CORRECTLY

- Use the following personal pronouns as subjects and predicate nominatives.

| | |
|---|---|
| I | we |
| you | you |
| he, she, it | they |

- Use the following personal pronouns as direct objects, indirect objects, and objects of the preposition.

| | |
|---|---|
| me | us |
| you | you |
| him, her, it | them |

- Who and whom can be either interrogative pronouns or relative pronouns.
- When used as interrogative pronouns, use who for subjects and whom for direct objects and objects of the preposition.
- When used as a relative pronoun, who or whom should be used correctly within the subordinate clause it begins. Do not refer to words outside the clause when deciding which word to use.
- Sentences that make comparisons often use the words than and as. These sentences are frequently "incomplete" to avoid repetition. Use the pronoun you would use if the sentence were complete.
- Use possessive personal pronouns before nouns formed by verbs plus ing.
- Use the personal pronouns me, him, her as subjects of verbs made up of to and the verb.
- Pronouns agree with their antecedents in number (singular /plural) and gender (masculine/feminine/neuter).
- The indefinite pronouns that follow are singular and are referred to by singular personal pronouns.

| | | | |
|---|---|---|---|
| each | one | no one | anyone |
| either | everyone | nobody | someone |
| neither | everybody | anybody | somebody |

- Singular nouns or pronouns joined by or or nor are referred to by singular pronouns.
- Nouns or pronouns joined by and are referred to by plural pronouns.
- In sentences using the relative pronouns who, which, or that, the number of the antecedent determines the number of the verb that follows the relative pronoun.

# MODIFIERS

## MISPLACED MODIFIERS

Phrases and clauses that modify other words should be placed as close as possible to the words they modify.

EXAMPLE: The seawater rose and spilled over the wall up to the top of the stone.

In this sentence the adverb *up* and the prepositional phrases *to the top* and *of the stone* are misplaced. While it is possible that the water could spill over the wall to the top of some stone on the other side of the wall, it is more likely that the wall itself is made of stone. In any event the adverb *up* is clearly misplaced; water does not spill *up*!

**IMPROVED:** The seawater rose *up to the top of the stone* and spilled over the wall.

EXAMPLE: The fish was caught this morning from the dock that is being served for dinner.

In this sentence the clause *which is being served for dinner* is misplaced. The idea is ridiculous. This sentence makes it sound as if the dock is being served for dinner.

**IMPROVED:** The fish *that is being served for dinner* was caught this morning from the dock.

EXAMPLE: The boat glided from shore with its sails unfurled in the last of the early morning mist and its crew setting about their chores.

In this sentence the phrases *in the last* and *of the early morning mist* are misplaced. Since it would be awkward to place them close to the word they modify (glided), place them at the beginning of the sentence.

**IMPROVED:** In the last of the early morning mist, the boat glided from shore with its sails unfurled and its crew setting about their chores.

## DANGLING MODIFIERS

A dangling modifier is a phrase or clause that acts as a modifier but has no word in the sentence that it sensibly modifies. It is a modifier unattached to any word in the sentence.

EXAMPLE: Running to the bus, the passing car splattered me with mud.

In this sentence the phrase *Running to the bus* is a dangling modifier. Even though the sense of the sentence suggests that this phrase refers to the speaker of the sentence, *me*, grammatically the phrase modifies the word *car*. In other words, the sentence as it is now written is equal to saying, "The passing car running to the bus splattered me with mud." This of course makes no sense.

The sentence can be corrected by changing the phrase *Running to the bus* to a clause.

**IMPROVED:** The passing car splattered me with mud as I was running to the bus.

**OR:** As I was running to the bus, the passing car splattered me with mud.

**NOTE:** This sentence can also be improved by altering the main clause.

EXAMPLE: Running to the bus I was splattered with mud by *a passing car.*

Notice in this improvement that the speaker me is changed to I.

## MODIFIERS THAT CAN HAVE TWO MEANINGS

Sometimes a modifier is placed in a sentence where it can have two meanings because there are two words it could be modifying.

EXAMPLE: Jimmy decided after the game was completed to call Grandma.

With the clause *after the game was completed* in its present position, the exact meaning of the sentence is unclear.

**IMPROVED**: After the game was completed, Jimmy decided to call Grandma.

**OR**: Jimmy decided to call Grandma after the game was completed.

In the first improved version Jimmy did not make his decision to call until after the game was completed. In the second version Jimmy decided either before or during the game to make the call to Grandma sometime after the conclusion of the game. Either way is correct.

### KEY POINTS - MODIFIERS

- Phrases and clauses that modify other words should be placed as close as possible to the words they modify.
- A dangling modifier is a phrase or clause that acts as a modifier but has no word in the sentence that it can modify sensibly. It is a modifier unattached to any word in the sentence.

# COORDINATION AND SUBORDINATION

A sentence must contain one complete thought, but may contain more than one. When a sentence contains more than one idea, it is possible that these ideas may or may not be equal. The problem of coordination and subordination of these equal or unequal elements is addressed in this section.

## COORDINATION

Coordination means literally of equal rank or kind. When a sentence contains two ideas that are equal they must be properly coordinated.

EXAMPLES: I pitched the first game, and Tim pitched the second game.

Today I am president of the company, but twenty years ago I started in the mailroom.

In the preceding sentences the two ideas expressed in each sentence are equal; therefore each idea receives equal emphasis. These equal parts are called coordinate clauses.

There are four kinds of relationships between coordinate clauses: addition, contrast, choice, and result.

### Addition

The following words demonstrate that the second clause is supplemental information:

| | | |
|---|---|---|
| also | furthermore | then |
| and | likewise | |
| besides | moreover | |

EXAMPLES: I composed a song, and she wrote a poem.

I finished my assignment, then we went to dinner.

Father doesn't like to dance, besides his arthritis has been acting up.

### Contrast

The following words demonstrate that the second clause contrasts or conflicts with the first:

| | | |
|---|---|---|
| but | however | yet |
| nevertheless | still | |

EXAMPLES: Wendell kept his end of the bargain, but his sister did not.

The team broke a record, yet the coach was not happy because of the sloppy play.

The mosquitoes drive me crazy; however, I still like to hike.

### Choice

The following words or pairs of words indicate a choice is being made:

| | |
|---|---|
| either...or | neither...nor |
| otherwise | |

EXAMPLES: The contract must be signed; otherwise the deal will fall through.

Either sign the contract now or let the opportunity slip away forever.

### Result

The following words indicate a result or consequence of the preceding clause:

| | |
|---|---|
| accordingly | consequently |
| hence | therefore |

EXAMPLES: His lawyer posted his bail; consequently, he will be released from jail within the hour.

She finished the race; therefore, she will receive a certificate for her effort.

## SUBORDINATION

Subordination means of lower rank or not equal. When a sentence contains two ideas, with one subordinate to the other, appropriate conjunctions must be selected to express the sentence clearly.

There are four common types of subordinate relationships: time, cause or reason, purpose or result, and condition.

## Time

The following words are often subordinating conjunctions used to indicate time:

| | | | |
|---|---|---|---|
| after | as | before | since |
| until | when | whenever | while |

EXAMPLES: The players celebrated after the game was over.

Whenever it is not raining, you will find him on the links.

## Cause or Reason

The following words are often subordinating conjunctions used to indicate cause or reason:

| | |
|---|---|
| as | because |
| since | whereas |

EXAMPLES: The truck crashed because the brakes failed.

Since the victory was assured, the team started to celebrate.

## Purpose or Result

The following words are often subordinating conjunctions used to indicate purpose or result:

| | |
|---|---|
| that | in order that |
| so that | |

EXAMPLES: The workshop received a workbook so that they might gain actual experience.

In order that they might handle any emergency, police trainees are now trained as emergency technicians.

## Condition

The following words are often subordinating conjunctions used to indicate condition:

| | |
|---|---|
| although | even though |
| though | while |
| unless | provided |
| if | |

EXAMPLES: You will pass the course only if you receive an "A" on this examination.

I have no choice even though everyone says I do.

## KEY POINTS - COORDINATES AND SUBORDINATES

- When a sentence contains two ideas that are equal, the ideas must be properly coordinated.
- There are four kinds of relationships between coordinate clauses: addition, contrast, choice, and result.
- When a sentence contains two ideas, with one subordinate to the other, appropriate conjunctions must be selected to express the sentence clearly.

- There are four types of subordinate relationships: time, cause or effect, purpose or result, and condition.

## PARALLEL STRUCTURE

When you write, you will achieve parallel structure if you use the *same form of expression consistently* throughout the sentence.

If the ideas you are expressing are of equal importance, you will join them with the coordinate conjunctions and, or, but, or nor. Be sure to join nouns with nouns, infinitives with infinitives, phrases with phrases, and clauses with clauses.

EXAMPLE 1: I like to sing, to dance, and playing ice hockey.

In this sentence the infinitive form (to + verb) is used twice (to sing, to dance). These infinitives are followed by a noun (gerund) playing ice hockey (a GERUND is a noun made up of a verb + ing; it is the name of an activity.) The sentence can be corrected by either changing all items to the infinitive form or all to the gerund form.

**IMPROVED**: I like to sing, to dance, and to play ice hockey.

**OR**: I like singing, dancing, and playing ice hockey.

EXAMPLE 2: Profits, losses, and motivating salespeople in the Western region were the topics of Tuesday's meeting.

In this sentence the noun form is used twice (profits, losses). These nouns are followed by a phrase *motivating salespeople in the Western region*. Again, this sentence can be improved two ways.

**IMPROVED**: Profits, losses and motivation of the Western region's salespeople were the topics of Tuesday's meeting.

In this improved example the sentence was made consistent by changing all items to the noun form - profits, losses and motivation.

The sentence can also be improved by changing all items to the phrase form.

**IMPROVED**: Increasing profits, decreasing losses, and motivating salespeople in the Western region were the topics of Tuesday's meeting.

EXAMPLE 3: The shop steward demanded a work stoppage and that the fired employees be reinstated.

In this sentence the noun *stoppage* is paired with a clause *that the fired employees be reinstated*.

Again there are several ways to improve the sentence.

**IMPROVED**: The shop steward demanded a work stoppage and the reinstatement of the fired employees.

In this improved version the noun form, reinstatement, was used.

The sentence can also be improved by using the clause form.

**IMPROVED**: The shop steward demanded that the employees honor a work stoppage and that the fired employees be reinstated.

As you can determine from the examples given so far, parallel structure can be achieved in different ways. The important point to remember is to be consistent in using the same form of expression throughout the entire sentence.

## CONTRASTING AND PARALLEL IDEAS

The same rule applies when either contrasting or comparing parallel ideas, be sure to use whatever form you select consistently.

EXAMPLE 1: Sean complained that sitting with the girls was more embarrassing than to sit with the two-year olds.

In this sentence the gerund form *sitting with the girls* is paired with the infinitive form *to sit with the two-year olds*.

Look at two ways to improve this sentence. Either way correctly balances the two ideas.

**IMPROVED**: Sean complained that sitting with the girls was more embarrassing than sitting with the two-year-olds.

**OR**: Sean complained that to sit with the girls was more embarrassing than to sit with the two-year olds.

Both sentences now have parallel construction.

EXAMPLE 2: Honesty is as important a virtue as to not be selfish.

In this sentence the noun *honesty* is paired with the infinitive *to not be selfish*.

**IMPROVED**: Honesty is as important a virtue as selflessness.

Parallel construction was achieved by using the noun form, selflessness.

## CORRELATIVE IDEAS

Correlative ideas are always parallel. Nouns should be paired with nouns, phrases with phrases, infinitives with infinitives, and clauses with clauses.

Remember the correlative conjunctions are:

both....are

either....or

neither....nor

not only....but also

EXAMPLE: Not only was the train late but also needing cleaning.

In this sentence the clause *was the train late* is paired with the phrase *needing cleaning*.

Parallel construction is easily achieved by using it as the subject of the second clause.

**IMPROVED**: Not only was the train late but it also needed cleaning.

## COMPLETE THE PARALLEL STATEMENT CLEARLY AND CORRECTLY

When using parallel structure, be sure to repeat whatever words are necessary to make your meaning clear.

EXAMPLE 1: While shopping for groceries, Fran met her butcher and baker.

In this sentence it is not clear whether the butcher and baker are one person or two.

**IMPROVED**: While shopping for groceries, Fran met her butcher and her baker.

Be sure to place the correlative conjunctions immediately before each parallel statement.

EXAMPLE 2: The child both spoke to her mother and her father.

In this sentence the correlative conjunction both is misplaced.

**IMPROVED**: The child spoke to both her mother and her father.

When using parallel structure, be sure that you have included all the words necessary to make the construction complete.

EXAMPLE 3: The path at the far end of the park is more narrow than the main entrance.

In this sentence *path* is compared to *entrance*. This does not make sense. You would expect a path to be narrower than a main entrance. To correct this problem more words are added to the sentence.

**IMPROVED**: The path at the far end of the park is more narrow than the path near the main entrance.

## KEY POINTS - PARALLEL STRUCTURE

- When you write, you will achieve parallel structure if you use the same form of expression consistently throughout the sentence.
- If the ideas you are expressing are of equal importance, you will join them with the coordinate conjunction and, or, but, or nor. Be sure to join nouns with nouns, infinitives with infinitives, phrases with phrases, and clauses with clauses.
- When either contrasting or comparing parallel ideas, be sure to use whatever form you select consistently.
- Correlative ideas are always parallel and so nouns should be paired with nouns, phrases with phrases, infinitives with infinitives, and clauses with clauses.
- When using parallel structure, be sure to repeat whatever words necessary to make your meaning clear.
- Be sure to place the correlative conjunctions immediately before each parallel statement.
- When using parallel structure, be sure that you have included all the words necessary to make the construction complete.

# DICTION

There are many misused words and confusing pairs of words in the English language. Knowing which word to use in a specific situation is diction.

Some words are confused with one another because they look alike, or sound alike, or have similar spellings. Some pairs actually contain a word that is substandard and should not be used. Other pairs are often used incorrectly because the meanings of the words are confused.

This chapter will help you review some of the more commonly confused and/or misused words or pairs of words.

**ACCEPT/EXCEPT**

accept - to take what is offered

except - not including

except - to leave out

I accept your offer of employment.

Everyone except me went to the party.

The king stated, "All the lords are fools, present company excepted."

**AFFECT/EFFECT**

affect - to influence

effect - a result

effect - to bring about

His speech affected the audience.

The effect of his speech was incredible.

He effected a change in the way we think.

**ALL WAYS/ALWAYS**

all ways - in every possible way

always - at all times

The work you have done is good in all ways.

Your work is always good.

**ANYWHERES/ANYWHERE**

anywheres - unacceptable for anywhere

Go anywhere (NOT anywheres) you would like for vacation.

**BESIDE/BESIDES**

beside - close to

besides - in addition

The dog is lying beside the bed.

Bring the camera besides.

**BROKE/BURST/BUST**

burst - is correct for broke, exploded

bust - is unacceptable for broke

The balloon burst (not busted).

**CHOICE/CHOOSE/CHOSE**

choice - a selection

choose - to select (rhymes with snooze)

chose - selected (rhymes with rose)

You must make a choice.

Choose your favorite color.

I chose gray.

**CORE/CORPS/CORPSE**

core - the central part

corps - a military group

corpse - a dead body

The deer nibbled the apple core.

The young man joined the army corps.

The detective discovered the corpse.

**DIFFERENT FROM/DIFFERENT THAN**

different from - acceptable

different than - unacceptable

(Remember that different from has 3 fs and you'll know the correct usage.)

Yours is different from (NOT different than) mine.

**FARTHER/FURTHER**

farther - used to describe physical distance

further - used to describe thought and ideas

I walked farther than you.

Please explain your idea further.

**HANGED/HUNG**

hanged - to hang a person - past tense

hung - to hang a thing - past tense

The posse hanged the robber.

The painter hung his picture on the wall.

**REGARDLESS/IRREGARDLESS**

regardless - acceptable

irregardless - unacceptable

You may not go to the movies regardless (NOT irregardless) of what your friends are doing.

**LOTS/MANY**

lots - unacceptable when used as much, many, a great deal

There are many (NOT lots) to choose from.

**NOWHERE/NOWHERES**

nowhere - acceptable

nowheres - unacceptable

The child was nowhere (NOT nowheres) to be found.

**PLAIN/PLANE**

plain - simple; flat area of land; clear

plane - aircraft; tool; flat surface

The design of the furniture is plain.

The buffalo roamed the plains.

His statement is plain and simple.

See the plane in the air!

The carpenter used the plane.

The geometry teacher illustrated the plane.

**STATIONARY/STATIONERY**

stationary - standing still, unmovable

stationery - writing materials

The statue is stationary.

Please order my stationery in white or gray.

**TRY TO/TRY AND**

try to - acceptable

try and - unacceptable

Try to (NOT Try and) visit us when you return to this area.

**ACCESS/EXCESS**

access - means of getting

excess - too much; extra amount

The employees have access to the building on weekends.

Unfortunately, he drinks to excess.

She threw the excess away.

**AFFECTION/AFFECTATION**

affection - feeling for another

affectation - artificial behavior

Anna has great affection for dogs.

His affectations disturbed everyone.

**ALLOT/ALOT**

allot - apportion

alot - unacceptable when used as very much

The building manager will allot the parking spaces.

I like candy very much (NOT alot).

**AROUND/ABOUT/NEAR**

around - unacceptable when used as about or near

Meet me about (NOT around) five o'clock.

**BETTER/WELL**

better - recovering

well - completely recovered

Ricky's father is getting better.

Ricky's father now is well.

**CAN/MAY**

can - physically able to do

may - having permission to do

I can lift 50 pounds.

I may go to the movies.

**CLOTHS/CLOTHES**

cloths - pieces of fabric

clothes - fabric fashioned into wearable items

The cloths were cut from rags.

Mother hung the clothes in the closet.

**COULD OF/COULD HAVE**

could of - unacceptable for could have

I could have (NOT could of) been a contender.

**DUAL/DUEL**

dual - relating to two

duel - a fight between two people

This is a dual engine jet.

This gentleman challenged his rival to a duel.

**FEWER/LESS**

fewer - related to persons or things that can be counted

less - related to something considered a mass

Fewer than 500 people returned their ballot.

There is less fruit in the basket today.

**HEALTHY/HEALTHFUL**

healthy - having health

healthful - giving health

This baby is healthy!

Fruit juice is a healthful beverage.

**ITS/IT'S**

its - possessive of it

it's - contraction for it is

The cat chased its tail.

It's funny to watch.

**LEAD/LED**

lead - to direct (rhymes with need)

lead - a bluish-gray metal (rhymes with bed)

led - to lead - past tense (rhymes with bed)

I lead the parade every year.

The pipe is made of lead.

The teacher led the children to the playground.

**OFF OF/OFF**

off of - unacceptable; delete of

Get off (NOT off of) the chair.

**PRINCIPAL/PRINCIPLE**

principal - main

principal - leader

principle - a basic belief or truth

He is the principal player.

Mr. Smith is the principal of our school.

It is against my principles to lie.

**REASON IS BECAUSE/REASON IS THAT**

reason is because - unacceptable for reason is that

The reason for water restrictions is that (NOT is because) we have not had sufficient rain.

**STOP/STAY**

stop - cease

stay - remain

Stop running.

Stay where you are.

**TO/TOO/TWO**

to - used as a preposition; used to introduce an infinitive

too - also

two - one plus one

Let's go to the party.

I want to go, too.

The two of us will go.

**YOUR/YOU'RE**

your - possessive of you

you're - you are

Your mittens are here.

You're welcome here.

**ADAPT/ADEPT/ADOPT**

adapt - to adjust

adept - skillful

adopt - to take as one's own

I will have to adapt to this warm climate.

Jack is adept at building model ships.

The couple plans to adopt a child.

**AISLE/ISLE**

aisle - passageway

isle - island

The bride walked down the aisle.

My, what a beautiful isle.

**ALTAR/ALTER**

altar - a sacred table used in a place of worship

alter - to change

The bride and groom joined hands at the altar.

The tailor altered the suit.

**AS/LIKE**

as - this word is a conjunction

like - this word is a preposition

As the curtain fell, the audience applauded.

The boy wanted a boat like that one.

Behave as (NOT like) you should.

**BREATH/BREATHE/BREADTH**

breath - air taken into the lungs

breathe - to take air in and let it out

breadth - width

She took a deep breath.

Breathe deeply.

The man measured the breadth of the object.

**CAN'T HARDLY**

can't hardly - unacceptable; it is a double negative.

I can't (NOT can't hardly) hear you.

**COARSE/COURSE**

coarse - rough, unfinished

course - path; part of a meal; a class

This blanket is too coarse for the baby.

Dad is on the golf course.

Broiled fish is the main course.

Geometry is my hardest course this year.

**DECENT/DESCENT/DISSENT**

decent - suitable

descent - downward motion

dissent - to disagree; disagreement

Jim did a decent job cleaning the room.

The airplane began its descent.

When the chairman took the vote, no one dissented.

The crowd's dissent is obvious.

**EMIGRATE/IMMIGRATE**

emigrate - to leave one's own country for another

immigrate - to enter a country other than one's own.

Many people emigrated from Ireland in both the nineteenth and twentieth centuries.

Scott decided to immigrate to Australia.

**FORMALLY/FORMERLY**

formally - properly

formerly - in the past

She formally addressed the group.

She was formerly of Washington, D.C.

**HOLY/HOLEY/WHOLLY**

holy - sacred

holey - with holes

wholly - completely

He is holy man.

His socks are holey.

He is wholly innocent.

**KIND OF/SORT OF/RATHER**

kind of/sort of - unacceptable for rather

This program is rather (NOT kind of) boring.

**LOOSE/LOSE**

loose - not tight (rhymes with caboose)

lose - to suffer a loss (rhymes with snooze)

The rope became loose and the boat drifted from the dock.

Try not to lose all your money at once.

**PASSED/PAST**

passed - to go by (past tense); to make the grade

past - before the present

He passed the market on the way to school.

He passed the test.

In the past he was a great star.

**PROPHECY/PROPHESY**

prophecy - prediction (rhymes with bee)

prophesy - to make a prediction (rhymes with by)

The prophecy became true.

The old man prophesied the war.

**RESPECTABLY/RESPECTFULLY/RESPECTIVELY**

respectably - deserving respect

respectfully - with respect

respectively - in the order given

The quarterback played respectably.

I respectfully ask your opinion.

Here are the players respectively, Tom, Dick and Harry.

**SUSPICIONED/SUSPECTED**

suspicioned - unacceptable for suspected

I suspected (NOT suspicioned) him all along.

**WAIST/WASTE**

waist - area of the body just above the hips

waste - discarded material; to misuse

The seamstress measured the woman's waist.

The contractor removed the waste.

Don't waste paper.

**ADDITION/EDITION**

addition - process of adding

edition - a book; an issue of a publication

The bookkeeper completed the addition.

This is a rare edition.

Look at this old edition of the school newspaper.

**ALL READY/ALREADY/ALL RIGHT/ALRIGHT**

all ready - everyone is ready

already - done previously

all right - all correct

alright - unacceptable form of all right.

The children are all ready for the picnic.

The basket has already been packed.

Everything is all right (NOT alright).

**AMONG/BETWEEN**

among - in the company of three or more

between - in the company of two

Keep this information among yourselves.

Keep this information between you and me.

**AT**

at - unacceptable if not necessary to complete the meaning of the sentence.

Tell me where you are (NOT are at).

**BRING/TAKE**

bring - to carry to

take - to carry from

Bring this package to Suzy.

Take this bag from me when you go.

**CAPITAL/CAPITOL**

capital - punishable by death

capital - seat of government

capital - money

capitol - building where the legislature meets

The governor signed the capital punishment bill.

Trenton is the capital of New Jersey.

We need capital to start our business.

The senators met at the Capitol Building.

**COMPLEMENT/COMPLIMENT**

complement - something that completes

compliment - praise

These gloves complement your outfit.

Thank you for the compliment.

**DESERT/DESSERT**

desert - a dry region (DES ert)

desert - to abandon (de SERT)

dessert - a meal's last course

Cacti grow in the desert.

The mother cat would not desert her kittens.

We're having ice cream for dessert.

**EVERY ONE/EVERYONE**

every one - all individually

everyone - all together

The coach gave a certificate to every one of his players.

Everyone liked the show.

**FORMER/LATTER/LATER**

former - first mentioned of two

latter - second mentioned of two

later - more late

Debbie and Mike are coming; the former is a ballerina and the latter is a halfback.

They will arrive later.

**IF/WHETHER**

if - begins a statement of condition

whether - begins a statement of choice

I'll buy you a sweater if I go to Ireland.

I don't know whether I will go.

**MANY/MUCH**

many - counted in numbers

much - measured in bulk

There are many apples in the basket.

There is much fruit in the basket.

**PIECE/PEACE**

piece - part of a whole

peace - opposite of war

May I please have a piece of pie?

(Note that the word piece has pie in it.)

Let there be peace on earth.

**QUIET/QUIT/QUITE**

quiet - silent

quit - to leave

quite - wholly; to a great extent

The hospital was quiet.

Kevin quit his job.

I think this ice cream is quite delicious.

**ROB/STEAL**

rob - a person is robbed

steal - a thing is stolen

The thug robbed the old man.

The thug stole the old man's wallet.

**THAN/THEN**

than - a conjunction

then - an adverb, at that time

Diane is more graceful than Margaret (is).

He then turned the corner and sped down the street.

**WHO'S/WHOSE**

who's - contraction for who is

whose - possessive for who

Who's in charge here?

Whose hat is this?

**ADVICE/ADVISE**

advice - suggestion (rhymes with ice)

advise - to give advice (rhymes with eyes)

I need your advice.

Please advise me.

**ALL TOGETHER/ALTOGETHER**

all together - everyone/everything together

altogether - completely

The team went to the party all together.

This game is altogether silly.

**ANY/AT ALL**

any - unacceptable when used to mean at all

I don't like it at all (NOT any).

**AWFUL/VERY/UGLY**

awful - unacceptable when used to mean very or ugly

This television show is very (NOT awful) boring.

**BUNCH/GROUP**

bunch - used for things

group - used for persons or things

What a delicious bunch of grapes!

The group (NOT bunch) arrived at the stadium gate.

**CERTAINLY/SURE**

certainly - an adverb

sure - an adjective

Your speech was certainly effective.

I am sure you will like the coat.

**CONSUL/COUNCIL/COUNSEL**

consul - a government representative

council - an assembly

counsel - advice; to advise

The consul entered the chamber.

The town council passed the motion.

Please counsel my son.

The child sought his older brother's counsel.

**DEVICE/DEVISE**

device - a thing made to carry out some activity (rhymes with ice)

devise - to work out (rhymes with eyes)

This can opener is a handy device.

The engineer devised a special mixer.

**EVERYWHERE/EVERYWHERES**

everywheres - unacceptable for everywhere

The butterflies are everywhere (NOT everywheres).

**FORTH/FOURTH**

forth - forward

fourth - comes between third and fifth

The commander ordered his men to go forth.

I am fourth in line at the bank.

**IMPLY/INFER**

imply - to suggest

infer - to conclude

The lawyer implied that I am guilty.

I infer that he thinks I'm the thief.

**MINER/MINOR**

miner - one who mines

minor - under legal age; not as important

My great grandfather was a coal miner.

It is illegal to sell alcohol to minors.

That fact is a minor detail.

**MORAL/MORALE**

moral – ethical

morale – spirit

Many consider his decision a moral one.

The victory lifted the team's morale.

The moral of the story is to be fair.

**PERSONAL/PERSONNEL**

personal - individual

personnel - the people employed by a company

Life insurance is a personal decision.

Mr. Rogers represents our personnel at company meetings.

**RAIN/REIGN/REIN**

rain - water falling from the sky in droplets

reign - a period of rule; to rule

rein - a leather strap used to guide a horse

The rain fell for hours.

The king began his reign with a celebration.

The king reigned wisely.

The rider pulled on the horse's rein.

**SOMETIME/SOMETIMES**

sometime - at an unspecified time in the future

sometimes - on occasion

We should meet sometime for lunch.

I sometimes walk to work.

**THAT THERE/THAT**

**THIS HERE/THIS**

that there - unacceptable for that

this here - unacceptable for this

That (NOT That there) is a nice dog.

This (NOT This here) is a good piece of work.

**THEIR/THERE/THEY'RE**

their - possessive of they

there - at that place

they're - contraction for they are

Their bus is over here.

There is the bus.

They're walking toward the bus.

**WOULD HAVE/HAD**

would have - unacceptable for had

I wish you had (NOT would have) told me.

# SAMPLE TEST QUESTIONS FOR SENTENCE CORRECTION

These sample test questions represent roughly a third of the 41 questions to be presented to you by the **GMAT CAT**. The other two-thirds are categorized as **Reading Comprehension** and **Critical Reasoning** type questions. These question types are significantly different and each individual will respond at different rates for each. Remember that the GMAT CAT does not allow you to return to or to skip over any question. When you get stuck, you will need a strategy for taking your best guess so as to move on to questions that you will be able to answer.

You will be given 75 minutes time to answer 41 questions. This is roughly 110 seconds, under 2 minutes, per question. As you practice using the following questions, time yourself noting the rate at which you dispatch each. As you note that some questions take you too long, you will develop a sensitivity to timing. During the test this sense will help you to transition from looking for the "right" answer to picking what you think is the "most likely" answer.

Remember, that as you first read the answers for any question, some answers may be eliminated initially. You should practice this in this section by remaining aware of the fact that you are making value judgements as you read each answer. In fact you may develop a method of noting these judgements on scratch paper to aid you in more quickly identifying the educated guess. No matter how you may organize this aspect of taking the **GMAT CAT**, by practicing it here in these sample questions it will be easier for you to enter your stride during the actual test.

**Directions:** These sample test questions consist of a number of sentences, in which some part or the whole is underlined. Each sentence is followed by five alternative versions of the underlined portion. Select the alternative you consider both most correct and most effective according to the requirements of standard written English. Answer A is the same as the original version; if you think the original version is best, select answer A.

In considering the answer choices, be attentive to matters of grammar, diction, and syntax, as well as clarity, precision, and fluency. Do not select an answer which alters the meaning of the original sentence.

1. Who but him would have reported that the traitor was he.

   (A) him would have reported that the traitor was he
   (B) he would have reported that the thief was him
   (C) he would have reported the thief was him
   (D) him would have reported that the thief was him
   (E) he would have reported that the thief was he

2. Fritz Jackson, together with his four assistants, are looking for workers who will choose to rise early.

   (A) are looking for workers who will choose to rise early
   (B) are looking for workers whom will choose to rise early
   (C) are looking for workers who choose to rise early
   (D) is looking for workers who will choose to rise early
   (E) is looking for workers whom will choose to rise early

3. A few friends and I had gone to the beach earlier then the crowd but by evening all had left but I.

(A) then the crowd but by evening all had left but I
(B) than the crowd but by evening all had left but I
(C) then the crowd but by evening all had left but me
(D) than the crowd but by evening all had left but me
(E) than the crowd but by evening all left but me

4. Arriving at the scene, debris was scattered everywhere and reported by the investigators.

(A) debris was scattered everywhere and reported by the investigators
(B) debris, scattered everywhere, was reported by the investigators
(C) scattered everywhere was debris which was reported by the investigators
(D) debris were scattered everywhere and reported by the investigators
(E) investigators reported that debris was scattered everywhere

5. Mr. Semple, who is president, asked for an accounting of all members whom, he said, were late with their reports.

(A) whom, he said, were late with their reports
(B) who, he said, was late with their reports
(C) who, he said, were late with their reports
(D) who, he said, was late with their reports
(E) whom, he said, were late with there reports

6. If the stock would have risen in price, than I could have sold it and made a profit within a week's time.

(A) If the stock would have risen in price, than
(B) If the stock had risen in price, than
(C) If the stock had risen in price then,
(D) If the stock rose in price, than
(E) If the stock rose in price then,

7. I felt badly when I saw her lying on the hospital bed.

(A) I felt badly when I saw her lying
(B) I felt bad when I saw her lying
(C) I felt bad when I saw her lieing
(D) I felt badly when I saw her laying
(E) I felt badly when I seen her lying

8. Newark is larger than any city in New Jersey and boast one of the finest airports in the nation.

(A) Newark is larger than any city in New Jersey and boast
(B) Newark is larger than any city in New Jersey and boasts
(C) Newark is larger then any city in New Jersey and boasts
(D) Newark is larger then any city in New Jersey and boast
(E) Newark is larger than any other city in New Jersey and boasts

9. Because he was frightened of heights, he descended down the ladder as quickly as he could.

(A) Because he was frightened of heights, he descended down the ladder as quickly as he could
(B) Because he was frightened by heights, he descended the ladder as quickly as he could
(C) Because he was frightened of heights, he descended the ladder as quickly as he could
(D) Because he was frightened by heights, he descended down the ladder as quick as he could
(E) Because he was frightened by heights, he descended the ladder as quick as possible

10. The end of the novel is not resolved; therefore, we cannot draw any precise conclusion.

(A) resolved; therefore, we cannot draw any precise conclusion
(B) resolved: therefore we cannot draw any precise conclusion
(C) resolved therefore, we cannot draw any precise conclusion
(D) resolved, therefore, we cannot draw any precise conclusion
(E) resolved therefore we cannot draw any precise conclusion

11. Gary drove the ball into the center-field bleachers and the game was finished before seven o'clock that evening.

(A) Gary drove the ball into the center-field bleachers and the game was finished
(B) Gary drove the ball into the center-field bleachers, and the game was finished
(C) Gary drove the ball in the center-field bleachers, and the game was finished
(D) Gary drove the ball into the center-field bleachers and ended the game
(E) Gary drove the ball into the center field bleachers, and the game was over

12. The hero was tall, strong, and had much vigor as he acted out an extremely difficult role.

(A) and had much vigor as he acted out an extremely difficult role
(B) and had much vigor as he acted out an extreme difficult role
(C) and vigorously acted out an extremely difficult role
(D) and with vigor acted out an extremely difficult role
(E) and vigorous as he acted out an extremely difficlut role

13. Jim's collection of cars, which included the earliest Oaklands, was presented and sold to its original owner.

(A) which included the earliest Oaklands, was presented and sold to its original owner
(B) which included the earliest Oakland's, were presented and sold to its original owner
(C) that included the earliest Oaklands, were presented and sold to its original owner
(D) which included the earliest Oaklands, was presented and sold to it's original owner
(E) which included the earliest Oaklands, were presented and sold to its original owner

14. We have two choices; we can go to meet them, or we can wait until they call.

(A) two choices; we can go to meet them, or we
(B) two choices, we can go to meet them, or we
(C) two choices:  we can go to meet them, or we
(D) two choices:  we can go to meet them or we
(E) two choices; we can go to meet them or we

15. Since the recent increase of foreign small cars, the American car industry had taken steps to improve its process and product.

(A) the American car industry had taken steps to improve its process and product
(B) the American car industry took steps to improve its process and product
(C) the American car industry will have taken steps to improve its process and product
(D) the American car industry has taken steps to improve its process and product
(E) the American car industry has taken steps to improve their process and product

16. The number of large car sales which was decreasing has grown recently, but it may not continue.

(A) has grown recently, but it may not continue
(B) had grown recently, but it may not continue
(C) has grown recently, but the growth may not continue
(D) has grown recently, but the growth of cars may not continue
(E) has grown recently but it may not continue

17. The Yankees demonstrated that their pitching staff was weak but could never win a close game.

(A) their pitching staff was weak but could never
(B) their pitching staff was weak and could never
(C) their pitching staff was weak and, therefore, could never
(D) their pitching staff were weak and, therefore could never
(E) there pitching staff was weak but could never

18. Everyone in the classroom did their homework and handed it to the teacher in time.

(A) did their homework and handed it to the teacher
(B) did his homework and handed it to the teacher
(C) done their homework and handed it to the teacher
(D) did their homework, and handed it to the teacher
(E) did his homework, and handed it to the teacher

19. Her mother did not approve of the girls' playing their records so loudly.

(A) did not approve of the girls' playing their records so loudly
(B) did not approve of the girls playing their records so loudly
(C) did not approve of the girls' playing their records so loud
(D) did not approve of the girl's playing her records so loudly
(E) did not approve of the girl playing  there records so loudly

20. Neither the teachers nor the administrator are ready to report who the recipient is.

(A) are ready to report who the recipient is
(B) is ready to report who the recipient is
(C) are ready to report whom the recipient is
(D) are ready too report who the recipient is
(E) is ready to report whom the recipient is

21. One reason for the rise of prices for farm goods is because of last years locust attack on farm crops.

(A) is because of last years locust attack on farm crops
(B) is due to last years locust attack on farm crops
(C) is because of last year's locust attack on farm crops
(D) are due to last years locust attack on farm crops
(E) is that the locust attacked farm crops last year

22. Realizing that the end of the flight was near, the successful trip was celebrated by its crew.

(A) the successful trip was celebrated by its crew
(B) the successful trip had been celebrated by its crew
(C) the crew began to celebrate the successful trip
(D) the successful trip was to be celebrated by its crew
(E) the celebration was planned by its crew for a successful trip

23. He might have made a different decision if he was the president of the bank.

(A) decision if he was the president of the bank
(B) decision if he had been the president of the bank
(C) decision, if he was to be the president of the bank
(D) decision, if he were the president of the bank
(E) decision. If he were the president of the bank.

24. Municipal bonds rather than industrial stocks are most attractive to older, conservative investors who must consider income.

(A) Municipal bonds rather than industrial stocks are most attractive to
(B) Municipal bonds rather then industrial stocks are most attractive to
(C) Municipal bonds rather than industrial stocks are more attractive to
(D) Municipal bonds rather then industrial stocks are more attractive too
(E) Municipal bonds rather than industrial stocks are more attracted to

25. If we agree on who we should appoint as chairman, let us get on with the agenda.

(A) who we should appoint as chairman
(B) whom we should appoint as chairman
(C) who is to be appointed as chairman
(D) whom should be appointed as chairman
(E) who we ought to appoint as chairman

## Answers to Sample Test Questions for Writing Ability

1. A — The preposition "but" (meaning "except") is always followed by an objective case pronoun except when that pronoun is the subject of a verb. The linking verb "was" is always followed by the nominative case "he."

2. D — The subject, Fritz Jackson, is singular and requires the singular verb "is looking." The phrase, "together with his four brothers," is parenthetical and is not included as part of the subject.

3. D — Use "than" after the comparative adverb earlier. Use the objective case pronoun "me" after the preposition "but."

4. E — "Investigators" is the word being modified by the introductory phrase and must follow it directly.

5. C — The subject of the verb "were" must be in the nominative case "who."

6. C — The sequence of action calls for the first action to occur before the second action and should read, "... stock had risen..." The comma after "then" expresses the intended meaning.

7. B — A verb of the senses such as feel, smell, taste, etc. requires the adjective form "bad." "Lying " is the correct verb form for "lie" meaning "to rest."

8. E — The comparison must read "any other city" because one thing cannot be compared to itself.

9. B — "Descended down" is redundant. "Frightened of" is not idiomatic.

10. A — A semi-colon before and a comma following the conjunctive adverb "therefore" are used when the conjunctive adverb joins two independent clauses.

11. D — The verb shift between the first and second independent clauses goes from active to passive voice unnecessarily. The choice in letter D keeps them both active.

12. E — The lack of parallelism must be corrected by replacing the phrase "had much vigor" with the adjective "vigorous."

13. A — The subject "collection" is singular and requires the singular verb "was presented."

14. C — A colon is used before an explanation or to introduce a list.

15. D — The present perfect "has taken" is necessary to show action taken in the past and continuing into the present.

16. C — The pronoun "it" has no logical referent and so must be replaced by the noun it refers to, "growth."

17. C — The conjunction "but" expresses a reversal in thought which is not logical in this context. Choice C most logically continues the thought expressed in the first part of the sentence.

18. B — "Everyone" is singular; therefore, the pronoun which refers to it must also be singular.

19. A — The plural possessive "girls'" is necessary before the gerund "playing." Letter D is correct grammatically but it changes the intended meaning in the original sentence.

20. B Neither – nor constructions require that the verb agree with the noun or pronoun which immediately precedes it.

21. E "One reason... because" is redundant and requires a relative clause which is linked to the noun "reason."

22. C The introductory dangling modifier must have something logical to modify.

23. B This statement expresses a past conditional and requires the past perfect in the conditional clause.

24. C When only two things are being compared (municipal bonds and industrial stocks) "more" rather than "most" is used.

25. B The object of the verb "should appoint" is "whom."

# Vocabulary Development

The **GMAT** examination does not have a specific section on vocabulary study or the meaning of words; however, a wide and diversified vocabulary can help you to understand the ideas presented in the passage in a more meaningful way. Understanding the relationship between words, the subtle shades of meaning and the emotional potential or connotation of words can enhance your comprehension of the entire passage, paragraph by paragraph. Some questions are based on one word answers which are not contained in the passage. Other questions may ask specifically for the definition of a word used in a different, unusual or particularly meaningful way. The following list may be a helpful starting point in reviewing frequently used words. Concentrate on the words you <u>almost</u> know first; master those words and move on to words you have seen before, but have never committed to memory. Do not try to master a long list of unfamiliar words out of context.

## WORD LIST

### A

abase—to degrade
abash—to embarrass
abdicate—to renounce
aberration—deviation
abhor—to hate
abiogenesis—spontaneous generation
abjure—to renounce
abominate—to loathe
aboriginal—native to an area
abrade—to scrape
abrogate—to cancel
abstemious—sparing in eating and drinking
abstruse—hard to understand
abyss—bottomless pit
a cappella—without musical accompaniment
acclivity—upward slope
accolade—honor
accord—agreement
accredit—to accept as believable
accretion—increase
acetic—vinegary
acidulous—sharp, caustic
acme—high point
acolyte—helper
acquiesce—to comply
acrimonious—bitter
acrophobia—fear of heights
acumen—mentally sharp
adage—saying
adduce—to offer as proof
adieu—good-bye
adipose—fatty
adjacent—near or next to
adjure—to make an oath
admonish—to warn
adobe—sun-dried brick of mud
adroit—clever
adulterate—to corrupt
adumbrate—to overshadow
adventitious—accidental
aegis—shield
affinity—likeness
agape—open-mouthed
aggrandize—to increase in power
agnostic—one who doubts the existence of God
agoraphobia—fear of open spaces
alchemy—chemistry of the medieval period
alimentary—relating to food
allay—to calm
allegory—fable
altercation—quarrel
altruism—selfless devotion
aloft—above the ground
ambiguous—vague
ameliorate—to better
amenities—courtesies
amorphous—shapeless

anachronism—a thing out of time or place
anathema—curse
ancillary—auxiliary
anhydrous—without water
antediluvian—ancient
anterior—front
antimacassar—a cover to protect furniture
antipathy—strong dislike
antithesis—the opposite of
aperture—opening
apex—highest point
apiary—place where bees are kept
aplomb—poise
apocryphal—false
apoplexy—loss of consciousness; stroke
apothegm—short saying
apprise—to inform
appurtenances—additional possessions
aptitude—talent
archipelago—chain of islands
arduous—difficult
argot—slang
arrant—complete
artifice—trickery
artisan—skilled worker
ascetic—one who denies himself pleasure
asinine—stupid
asperity—bitterness
aspersion—false statement about another
assiduity—care
assuage—to ease
astringent—austere
atheist—one who denies the existence of God
atrophy—to waste away
audacity—bold behavior
augur—to predict
austere—severe; strict
autocrat—monarch with absolute power
avant-garde—experimenters in art
avarice—greed
aversion—strong dislike
aviary—place where birds are kept
avuncular—like an uncle
axiom—a truth that is self-evident
azure—sky-blue

## B

bacchanalian—drunken and wild
badinage—teasing talk
bagatelle—trifle
balustrade—railing
banal—commonplace
bateau—long light boat
bathos—loss of meaning at the conclusion
bawdy—obscene
bedizen—dressed gaudily
bedlam—confusion
behest—command
bellicose—warlike
belligerent—waging war
bicameral—two chambered
biennial—every two years
bilious—ill-tempered
billet-doux—love letter
biopsy—examination of body tissue
bivouac—camp
blasé—bored
blasphemy—irreverence
blazon—coat of arms
blithe—happy
bombast—pompous speech
bovine—relating to cattle
breach—breaking of a contract
brine—salty water
broach—to touch upon
browbeat—to intimidate
bucolic—rustic; pertaining to the country
buoyant—cheerful
burnish—to polish
butte—hill
buxom—plump

## C

cabal—secret group; intrigue
cacophony—discordant sound
cajole—to persuade
callous—hard
callow—inexperienced
calumniate—to slander
campanile—bell tower

canard—rumor
canto—a division of a long poem
cantilever—brace
capitulate—to give in
capricious—marked by whim; changeable
captious—blaming, fault-finding
caricature—exaggerated drawing
carmine—deep red
carnal—of the flesh
carrion—decaying flesh
castigate—to punish
cataclysm—violent upheaval
catalyst—change agent
cathartic—purifying, relieving
cavil—to quibble
celibate—unmarried
cerebral—of the intellect
charlatan—faker
chary—watchful
cherubic—angelic
chicanery—trickery
chimerical—of the imagination
choleric—inclined to anger
clandestine—secret
clarion—shrill
clemency—mercy
cloy—to glut
coalesce—to join forces
codger—miser
cogitate—to meditate
cognizant—aware
cohort—band of warriors
collate—to arrange in order
collation—light meal
collier—coal miner
colloquy—conference
colombiad—heavy cannon
comestible—eatable
comity—courtesy
comminatory—threatening
commodious—convenient
compendium—abridgment
comport—to behave
concatenate—to link together
concupiscence—overwhelming desire
conflagration—fire
congruous—in agreement
connubial—related to marriage
consanguinity—blood ties
conscript—to force into service
construe—to interpret
consummate—(adj.) perfect; (verb) to complete or perfect
contemn—to view with scorn
contentious—argumentative
contiguous—touching
controvert—to dispute
contumely—rude behavior
conundrum—puzzle
copious—plentiful
coquette—flirt
corollary—deduction
corporeal—related to the body
corroborate—to confirm
cortege—escort
coterie—social group
covenant—agreement
cozen—to trick
craven—cowardly
culpable—deserving blame
cupidity—greed
cynic—skeptic
cynosure—center of attraction

## D

dearth—scarcity
debacle—collapse
debauch—to corrupt
decadence—gradual decay
decant—to pour
décolleté—low-necked
decorous—dignified
decorum—propriety
deleterious—harmful
demagogue—false leader
denigrate—to belittle
denizen—inhabitant
depilate—to remove hair
deprecate—to disapprove of with regret; protest strongly
depreciate—to lessen in value
desiccate—to dry up
desuetude—disuse
desultory—unmethodical

detritus—refuse, waste
devolve—to hand down
diabolic—fiendish
diametric—opposite
diaphanous—sheer
diatribe—insulting speech
didactic—instructive
dilatory—delaying
dilettante—one who dabbles in the arts
disingenuous—sophisticated
disparage—to belittle
dissolute—morally weak
distrait—absent-minded
divers—many
doggerel—poor verse
dolt—stupid person
dotage—senility
dregs—sediment
droll—laughable
dross—refuse
drover—cattle man
dubitable—open to doubt
duenna—older female chaperon
dyspepsia—indigestion
dysphasia—difficulty in speech

## E

ebullient—showing enthusiasm
éclat—glory
eclectic—derived from many sources
educe—to draw forth
effete—worn-out
effluvium—noxious smell
effrontery—boldness
effusive—very emotional
egregious—flagrant; outstanding
elation—great happiness
elegy—funeral song
emaciated—painfully thin; haggard
emanate—to issue forth
emblazon—to outfit in bright colors
embrasure—opening in a fort for a cannon
emend—to correct
emetic—substance causing vomiting
émigré—refugee
emissary—person sent on a mission
encomium—speech of praise
endemic—peculiar to a location
enervate—to sap the energy of
enfranchise—to give the right to vote
ennui—boredom
ephemeral—short-lived
epigram—witty saying
epitaph—inscription
epithet—descriptive word or phrase
equanimity—calmness
equine—related to a horse
equivocal—doubtful
ersatz—artificial
esoteric—select
ethnology—study of the races
exculpate—to free from blame
exhort—to urge
exigency—situation of urgency
exiguous—small
expatiate—to talk at length
expiate—to made amends
expurgate—to cleanse of offensive passages
extirpate—to annihilate
extraneous—irrelevant
extrude—to force out
exude—to give forth

## F

facade—front of a building
facetious—joking
facile—easy
factitious—false
fait accompli—thing accomplished and presumed irrevocable
fallacy—erroneous idea
fallible—liable to error
fallow—uncultivated
farce—ludicrous drama
fastidious—hard to please
fathom—to get to the bottom of
fatuous—foolish, silly
faux pas—error in manners
fealty—loyalty
fecund—productive
felicitate—to wish one joy
fell—cruel
fervid—ardent
fete—to honor with a party

fetid—bad-smelling
fettle—condition
fiat—decree
fiduciary—held in trust
filch—to pilfer
filial—like a son or daughter
filigree—ornamental work
flaccid—soft and limp
flagitious—evil
flippant—pert
florescence—flowering
flotsam—floating wreckage of a ship
foment—to stir up
forensic—relating to court or debate
fractious—unruly, irritable
fratricide—the killing of one's own brother
fraught—filled
frenetic—frenzied
freshet—sudden flood
froward—disobedient
fulminate—to explode
fulsome—disgusting
funereal—sad
fustian—pompous

### G

galleon—Spanish ship
gambol—to frolic
garish—showy
garrulous—talkative
gelatinous—containing jelly
gelid—frozen
genocide—extermination of an ethnic group
genus—group with similar characteristics
germane—relevant
gibbet—gallows
gloaming—twilight
glutinous—sticky
gluttonous—greedy for food
gossamer—filmy substance
gormand, gourmand—person excessively fond of food
gratuitous—given freely
gregarious—sociable
grenadier—foot soldier
grommet—metal ring
gusset—piece of cloth
gustatory—affecting the sense of taste
gyre—circular motion

### H

hackneyed—trite, common-place
halcyon—calm
harangue—long speech
harbinger—forerunner
harlot—lewd woman
hauteur—disdainful pride
hedonist—lover of pleasure
hegemony—dominance of authority
hegira—a flight
heinous—evil
hermaphrodite—of both sexes
heterodox—rejection of accepted doctrines
hexagon—six-sided figure
hippodrome—circus
hircine—goat like
hirsute—hairy
hoary—white with age
holocaust—complete destruction
homogeneous—uniform
homologous—corresponding in structure
horology—science of measuring time
hostler—groom
hovel—hut
hussar—a horse soldier
hyperbole—exaggeration for effect
hypothesis—assumption

### I

ibex—mountain goat
iconoclast—a destroyer of idols
idiosyncrasy—whim
idyl, idyll—pastoral poem
igneous—produced by fire
ignominy—shame
imbroglio—difficult situation
immolate—to offer a sacrifice
impalpable—vague
impecunious—poor
imprecate—to curse
impromptu—without previous preparation
incarcerate—to imprison

incognito—disguised state
incorrigible—beyond correction
indigenous—native
indigent—poor
indigo—a blue dye
indite—to write
indolence—laziness
indurate—hardened
ineffable—indescribable
inept—incompetent
inexorable—relentless
inference—logical conclusion
infrastructure—basic framework
ingenious—clever
ingenuous—naive
inimical—unfriendly
iniquitous—unjust
innate—inborn
innocuous—harmless
insensate—without feeling
insipid—dull, flat
insular—like an island; narrow-minded
intaglio—etching
interlocutor—one who questions
interpolate—to change with new material
inundate—to flood
inured—accustomed
inveigle—to lead astray
inveterate—firmly established
irascible—easily angered
itinerant—wandering

## J

Jacobin—revolutionist
jaded—tired
japan—to varnish
jejune—barren
jetsam—items thrown overboard to lighten a sinking ship
jocose—humorous
junket—feast or picnic
junta—council
jurisprudence—study of law
juxtaposed—placed side by side

## K

ken—range of knowledge
kimbo—bent
kinetic—producing motion
kiosk—summer house
kismet—fate
kith—friends

## L

labyrinth—maze
labyrinthine—perplexing
lachrymose—producing tears
laconic—brief, concise
landau—covered carriage
languid—listless
largess—generous gift
lascivious—indecent
lassitude—weariness
laudatory—expressing praise
lethargic—tired
levity—lightness
libertine—debauched person
libido—emotional desires
licentious—unrestrained
limpid—clear
lionize—to show attention
lissom, lissome—agile
loquacious—talkative
lucent—shining
lugubrious—mournful, sad
lunular—crescent-shaped
lupine—wolf-like
luxuriate—to flourish
lyceum—literary association

## M

macabre—gruesome
machinations—schemes
mackintosh—waterproof coat
madrigal—pastoral song
maelstrom—whirlpool
magnanimous—benevolent
maladroit—clumsy
malediction—curse
malevolent—desiring evil ways; spiteful
mandate—order
martinet—strict disciplinarian
matricide—act of killing one's own mother
maudlin—overly sentimental
mélange—mixture
mellifluous—smooth-flowing

mendacious—false
mendicant—beggar
mercurial—changing
meretricious—falsely alluring
mesa—steep, flat-topped hill
mettle—spirit
miasma—foul atmosphere
mien—air, manner
milieu—environment
misanthrope—hater of mankind
miscreant—villain
misogynist—hater of women
misoneism—hatred of anything new
mitigate—moderate
mnemonics—memory device
moiety—part
moratorium—legal delay of payment
mordant—sarcastic
moribund—dying
mulct—to defraud; a penalty
multifarious—diverse
myrmidon—obedient follower

## N

nadir—lowest point
naiveté—lack of sophistication
narcissism—love of self
nascent—beginning to grow
nebulous—unclear
necromancy—black magic
nefarious—evil, wicked
nemesis—enemy
neophyte—beginner
noisome—foul-smelling
nonage—legal minority
nonpareil—unequaled
notary—officer
notoriety—publicity
nuance—hint of difference
numismatics—study of coins
nymph—nature goddess

## O

obdurate—stubborn
obeisance—bow
obfuscate—to obscure
objurgatory—reproving
obloquy—a speech made against a person or thing
obsequious—extremely attentive; fawning
obtrude—to push forward
obtuse—stupid
obviate—to make unnecessary
occidental—of the west
odious—hateful
officious—meddlesome
oleaginous—like oil
oligarchy—rule by a few
omnipotent—all-powerful
omniscient—all-knowing
onus—burden
opacous—dark
opalescent—iridescent
opprobrious—reproachful
opulence—wealth
opus—composition
ordinance—statue
ordnance—artillery
ornithology—study of birds
orthodox—generally accepted
oscillate—waver
osier—willow
osseous—bony
ostensible—professed
ostentatious—showing off
ostracize—to ban
oust—to expel
ovine—like a sheep

## P

paean—song of praise
palatable—agreeable
palaver—misleading speech
palladium—safeguard
palliate—to ease pain
pallid—pale
palpable—tangible
palpitate—to throb
panacea—remedy for all ills
panegyric—formal praise
parable—story which teaches a lesson
paradigm—model
paradox—contradictory statement which may be true
paragon—model of perfection
pariah—outcast

parlance—language
parody—humorous imitation
paroxysm—violent emotion
parsimony—stinginess
pastoral—rural
pathos—something that arouses pity
patricide—the killing of one's own father
paucity—lack
peccadillo—minor offense
peculate—to rob
pedagogue—dull teacher
pedant—teacher who emphasizes trivia
pejorative—making worse
pelf—wealth
penurious—stingy
penury—poverty
perdition—damnation
perfidy—violation of trust; treachery
perfunctory—superficial; spiritless
peripatetic—itinerant
peristyle—rows of columns around a court
perjury—false statement given under oath
permeable—porous
permeate—to spread
pernicious—highly destructive
perquisite—bonus
perspicacious—having keen judgment
perspicuous—easily understood
pertinacious—persistent
perversion—corruption
pervious—penetrable
pestiferous—evil
petulant—impatient
philander—flirt
philanthropist—lover of mankind
philistine—one interested only in material gain
philogyny—love of women
philology—study of language
phlegmatic—calm; sluggish
pinion—to restrain
piquant—pleasantly stimulating
piscine—like a fish
pithy—concise
placate—to calm
plagiarism—stealing another's ideas
plaintive—sad
platitude—trite statement
plausible—reasonable
plebeian—common
plenary—full
plethora—excess, super-abundance
polemic—disputable
politic—prudent
poltroon—coward
polyglot—speaking several languages
porcine—of a pig
portend—foretell
portentous—serious
posit —to set down as fact
potentate—ruler
poultice—mixture applied to a wound
practicable—feasible
practical—useful
prate—to chatter
precipitous—steep
precis—brief summary
preclude—to eliminate
precursor—forerunner
predilection—inclination
prefatory—introductory
preponderate—to outweigh
preposterous—ridiculous
presage—to foretell
prevaricate—to lie
primordial—existing at the start
pristine—unspoiled
probity—honesty
procrastinate—to put off
prodigal—wasteful
prodigious—enormous
profligate—wasteful
progeny—offspring
prolific—highly productive or inventive
prolix—verbose
propinquity—nearness
propitious—favorable
prosaic—commonplace
provender—dry food
provincial—narrow in interests
proxy—agent authorized by another
puerile—childish
pugnacious—belligerent

puissant—powerful
pulchritude—beauty
punctilious—very exact
purloin—to steal
purview—scope
pusillanimous—cowardly
pyrrhic—gained at too great a cost

## Q

quaff—to drink
quagmire—bog
qualms—misgivings
quandary—dilemma
quay—dock
querulous—fretful, constantly complaining
query—inquiry
quiddity—essential quality
quiescent—at rest
quintessence—perfect form
quip—taunt
quixotic—absurd
quorum—enough members to conduct business

## R

raconteur—storyteller
raillery—pleasantry
raison d'être—reason for being
rancid—unpleasant odor
rancor—hatred
rapacious—grasping
rapprochement—reconciliation
ratiocination—reasoning
raucous—harsh
ravening—seeking prey
ravenous—hungry
ravine—gorge
recalcitrant—disobedient
recant—to renounce
recondite—profound
recreant—coward
rectitude—integrity
recumbent—lying down
redolent—fragrant
redoubt—temporary retreat
redundant—wordy
refectory—dining hall
refractory—hard to manage
regale—to entertain
regicide—killing of a king
regime—government
relegate—to banish
remiss—negligent
remonstrate—to protest; reason earnestly
remunerate—to pay
renegade—deserter
renege—to go back on a promise
repartee—clever response
repast—meal
replete—filled
reprobate—scoundrel
requiem—mass for the dead
requisite—requirement
requite—to repay
respite—rest
retinue—followers
retribution—compensation
retrograde—degenerating
revelry—merrymaking
reverie—daydream
revile—to slander
rhetoric—art of communication
ribald—vulgar
rife—abundant
rime—frost
riposte—quick retort
risible—exciting laughter
rococo—ornate
rote—repetition
rubicund—ruddy
rudiment—basic principle
ruminate—to ponder
ruse—trick
rusticate—to live in the country

## S

saccharine—overly sweet
sacrilegious—irreverent
sacrosanct—most sacred
saffron—orange-colored
sagacious—wise
salacious—lustful, highly indecent
salient—prominent
sallow—yellowish
salubrious—healthful

salutary—wholesome
salutatory—welcoming address
sang-froid—composure
sanguinary—bloody, gory
sanguine—cheerful
sapid—savory
sapient—wise
sardonic—bitterly sarcastic
sartorial—related to tailoring
saturnine—gloomy
savant—scholar
schism—division
scintilla—tiny bit
scion—descendant
scurrilous—obscene
sebaceous—secreting fat
secular—of the world
sedition—rebellion
sedulous—diligent
seine—net for catching fish
senescent—becoming old
sententious—terse, meaningful
serpentine—snakelike
shallop—small, open boat
shamble—to walk awkwardly
shoal—shallow place
simian—like a monkey
sinecure—easy, well-paid job
siren—enticing woman
skittish—lively
skulk—to move secretly
slake—to quench
slattern—untidy woman
sluice—man-made water channel
sobriquet—nickname
solecism—improper grammar
solicitous—concerned
soliloquy—talking to oneself
Solon—legislator
somatic—of the body
somniferous—inducing sleep
somnolent—half asleep
sophistry—clever but deceptive reasoning
soporific—causing sleep
sororicide—killing of one's own sister
specious—seemingly reasonable, but not really so
spectral—ghostly
spurious—false
squalid—dirty
staid—sedate
stentorian—loud
stoic—person indifferent to pain
stolid—dull
stratagem—deceptive plan
stricture—adverse criticism
stringent—strict
stultify—to make foolish
stupor—daze
suave—polite
subaltern—subordinate
subjoin—to add on
subjugate—to conquer
subservient—submissive
subterfuge—pretense, deceitful evasion
succinct—brief
succor—aid
succulent—juicy
suffuse—to spread over
sully—to soil
sunder—to separate
sundry—many
superannuated—retired
supercilious—haughty, arrogantly proud
supernal—exalted
supersede—to replace
supine—lying on one's back
surcease—ending
surfeit—to overfeed
surreptitious—secret
svelte—slender
swathe—to bandage
sycophant—flatterer
syllogism—conclusion based on two premises
sylvan—rustic
synod—church council
synopsis—summary
synthesis—combining parts to create a whole
synthetic—artificial

## T

tacit—unspoken

taciturn—usually quiet
tact—sensitivity to appropriate behavior
tactile—able to be touched
talisman—charm
tangent—touching
tantamount—equivalent
taurine—of a bull
tautology—repetition of an idea using different words
tawdry—cheap
taxonomy—classification
tedium—boredom
temerity—boldness
tenable—capable of being defended
tenacious—holding fast, unyielding
tenancy—period of occupancy
tenet—doctrine
tenuous—thin
tepid—lukewarm
termagant—scolding woman
terpsichorean—related to dancing
terrestrial—earthly
terse—concise
tertiary—third
theocracy—rule by church leaders
theology—study of religion
thespian—related to drama
thrall—slave
timorous—shy, fearful
tirade—long scolding
titanic—gigantic
tithe—tax of one-tenth
titular—in name only
toady—to flatter for favors
tome—large volume
toothsome—pleasing to the taste
torpid—dormant
torrid—burning
torsion—act of twisting
tort—a wrong
tractable—controllable, docile
traduce—to expose to shame
transgress—to violate
translucent—partially transparent
travail—hard work
travesty—parody
treatise—thoroughly written study
trenchant—sharp
tribulation—suffering
tribunal—court of justice
trilogy—group of three works
truckle—to submit to a superior
truculent—aggressive
truism—self-evident truth
trumpery—objects without value
truncated—shortened
tryst—meeting
turbid—muddy
turgid—swollen
turpitude—baseness
tutelage—training
twit—to tease
tyro—novice

## U

ubiquitous—present everywhere
ulterior—unstated
ultimatum—last demand
umbrage—offense
unassuaged—not soothed
unbridled—uncontrolled
uncanny—mysterious
unconscionable—unscrupulous
unction—anointing with oil
undulate—to move in waves
unequivocal—plain
unfeigned—genuine
unguent—ointment
unipod—one-legged stand
unmitigated—harsh
unseemly—unbecoming
untoward—unfavorable
unwonted—unaccustomed
upbraid—scold
urbane—refined
ursine—like a bear
usurp—to take over
usury—lending money at an illegal interest rate
utopian—visionary ideal
uxorious—foolishly fond of one's wife

## V

vacillate—to waver
vacuous—empty
vagabond—one who wanders

vagary—whim
vanguard—front line of an army
vapid—insipid
vaunt—to boast
vellum—parchment
venal—mercenary
vendetta—feud
venial—forgivable
veracious—truthful
verbiage—profusion of words
verbose—wordy
verdant—green
verisimilitude—truth
vermilion—bright red
vernacular—native speech of an area
vertex—high point
vestige—remains
viaduct—bridge
viand—food
vicarious—as a substitute; sharing another's experience
vicissitude—change
vignette—literary sketch
vilify—to slander
vindicate—to clear of accusations
vindictive—revengeful
virago—domineering woman
virulent—poisonous
visage—face
viscid—sticky
viscous—sticky
vitiate—to spoil
vitreous—of glass
vitriolic—sarcastic
vituperative—scolding
vixen—female fox
vociferous—clamorous
voluble—fluent
voracious—ravenous
votary—devoted follower
vulpine—like a fox

## W

waft—to carry through the air
waggish—sportive
wan—pale
wane—to grow smaller
wanton—unchaste
warp—lengthwise threads of fabric
welter—turmoil
winsome—agreeable
wizened—withered
wont—custom
woof—threads running across fabric
wraith—ghost
wrath—anger
wrest—to pull away

## Y

yeoman—small landowner

## Z

zealot—fanatic
zenith—highest point; peak
zephyr—west wind

Two other essential approaches used to expand word power are **Structural Analysis - Word Formation** and **Context Clues**. These two techniques are equally important skills for you to develop as you approach the Reading Comprehension/Recall Section of the examination.

# STRUCTURAL ANALYSIS - WORD FORMATION

The first technique, Structural Analysis - Word Formation, unlocks the meaning of thousands of unfamiliar words. The three parts of words - prefix, root, and suffix - can be used to help you determine the meaning of an unknown word. Reviewing the following list of often utilized prefix, root and suffix definitions will enable you to work more efficiently with an unfamiliar term.

## PREFIXES

A word part added before the root is a **prefix**. Note that the spelling of some of the prefixes varies according to the root.

| PREFIX | MEANING | EXAMPLE |
|---|---|---|
| **a, an** | not, without | atheism |
| **ab, abs** | from, away | absent |
| **ad, ac, af, ag, an, ap, ar, as, at** | to, towards | apparition, attest |
| **ambi** | both | ambidextrous |
| **ante** | before | antebellum |
| **anti** | against | antiseptic |
| **arch** | chief | archbishop |
| **auto** | self | automobile |
| **bi** | two | bicycle |
| **cata** | down | cataract |
| **circum** | around | circumnavigate |
| **com, co, col, con, cor** | together, with | communicate, consent |
| **contra** | against | contrary |
| **de** | away, from | decline |
| **dia** | across | diameter |
| **dis, dif** | away, opposing, not | diffuse, dislike |
| **duo, dup** | two | duodecimal |
| **dys** | bad, ill | dysentery |
| **ecto** | outside | ectoderm |
| **endo** | within | endoskeleton |
| **equi** | equal | equidistant |
| **eu** | well | euphoria |
| **ex, exo, e** | out, former | eject, expatriate |
| **extra** | beyond | extraterrestrial |
| **hetero** | different | heterogeneous |
| **homo** | same | homogenized |
| **hyper** | excessive | hyperactive |
| **hypo** | under | hypodermic |
| **in, il, im, ir** | in, within, into, not | insert, illogical |
| **inter** | between | interject |
| **intro, intra** | within, inward | introduce, intramural |
| **macro** | large | macrocosm |
| **mal** | bad | malodorous |

| PREFIX | MEANING | EXAMPLE |
| --- | --- | --- |
| **micro** | small | microscopic |
| **mis** | not, incorrect | mistake, misnomer |
| **mono** | one | monologue |
| **neo** | new | neoclassical |
| **non** | not | nonprofit |
| **para** | by the side of | paraphrase |
| **per** | through | persist |
| **peri** | around, about | periscope |
| **poly** | many | polysyllabic |
| **post** | after | posthumous |
| **pre** | before | preheat |
| **pro** | for | profess |
| **pseudo** | false | pseudonym |
| **quad** | four | quadrangle |
| **re** | again, back | reset, rebate |
| **retro** | backward | retroactive |
| **semi, hemi, demi** | half | semicircle, hemisphere |
| **sub** | under | subterranean |
| **super** | above, over | supersonic |
| **syn, sym, syl** | same | synonym, syllogism |
| **tri** | three | tripod |
| **trans** | across | transcontinental |
| **ultra** | beyond, excessively | ultramodern |
| **un** | not, opposite | unserved, untie |
| **uni** | one | unicycle |

## ROOT

The word part that acts as the core of the word is the **root**. Prefixes and/or suffixes are added to the root to form specific words.

| ROOT | MEANING | EXAMPLE |
| --- | --- | --- |
| **ac, acr** | sharp | acrid |
| **aev** | era | medieval |
| **ag, act** | do | agent, action |
| **agog** | leader | pedagogue |
| **agri, agari, agro** | field | agrology |
| **ali** | another | alien |
| **am, amic** | friend | amiable, amicable |
| **ambulat** | walk | ambulatory |
| **anim** | soul | animate |
| **ann, enn** | year | centennial |
| **anthrop** | man | misanthropic |
| **aqu** | water | aqueduct |
| **arch** | first | matriarch |
| **aster, astr** | star | astrology |
| **aud, audit** | hear | auditory |
| **auto** | self | automation |
| **belli** | war | bellicose |
| **ben, bon** | good | benevolent |
| **bibli** | book | bibliography |

| ROOT | MEANING | EXAMPLE |
|---|---|---|
| **bio** | life | biology |
| **brev, breve** | short | abbreviate |
| **cad, cas** | fall | cadence, cascade |
| **cand** | light, source | candescent, candidate |
| **cap, capt, cep, cip** | take | captivate, anticipate |
| **cap** | head | decapitate |
| **ced** | go | secede |
| **cent** | hundred | centurion |
| **chrom** | color | monochromatic |
| **chrono** | time | anachronism |
| **cid, ci** | cut, kill | decision |
| **cit, citat** | arouse | cite, excitation |
| **civi** | citizen | civilize |
| **clam, clamat** | cry out | clamor, exclamation |
| **claud, claus, clos, clud** | close | clause, include |
| **clin** | bend | incline |
| **cognos, cogni** | learn | recognition |
| **comp** | fill | complement |
| **cord** | heart | record |
| **corpor** | body | corpulent |
| **cosm** | universe | cosmopolitan |
| **cred** | believe | credence |
| **cryp** | hidden | crypt |
| **culp** | blame | culprit |
| **cur** | care | curator |
| **curr, curs** | run | discursive |
| **cycl** | circle | cyclical |
| **da, dat** | give | mandate |
| **deb, debit** | owe | debit |
| **demo** | people | demotic |
| **derm** | skin | hypodermic |
| **di, diurn** | day | diary |
| **dic, dict** | say | Dictaphone |
| **doc, doct** | teach | doctrinaire |
| **dom, domin** | rule | domain |
| **dorm** | sleep | dormancy |
| **duc, duct** | lead | aqueduct |
| **dynam** | power | dynamometer |
| **ego** | I | egotistic |
| **rg, urg** | work | urgency |
| **err** | stray | erratic |
| **fac, fec, fect, fic** | make | manufacture, infect, fiction |
| **fall, fals** | deceive | fallacy |
| **fer** | bear | vociferous |
| **fid, fin** | belief | fiduciary |
| **flect, flex** | bend | reflection |
| **fract, frag** | break | infraction |
| **frater, fratri** | brother | fraternity |
| **fus** | pour | infuse |

| ROOT | MEANING | EXAMPLE |
| --- | --- | --- |
| **gam** | marriage | bigamy |
| **gen, gener** | class | generic |
| **geo** | earth | geophysics |
| **grad, gress** | step | gradient |
| **graph** | write | polygraph |
| **grat** | thank | ingratiate |
| **greg** | flock | congregation |
| **heli, helio** | sun | heliocentric |
| **hydr** | water | dehydrated |
| **itiner** | journey | itinerary |
| **jec, ject** | throw | project |
| **jud** | judge | judicial |
| **jug** | yoke | jugular |
| **junct** | join | conjunction |
| **jur, jurat** | swear | jury |
| **labor, laborat** | work | elaborate |
| **leg, lect, lig** | choose | elect, eligible |
| **leg** | law | legitimize |
| **lib, libr, liber** | book | library |
| **loc** | place | local |
| **log, logy** | study | biology |
| **loqu, locut** | talk | elocution |
| **luc** | light | lucent |
| **magn** | great | magnify |
| **man, manu** | hand | manual |
| **mand, mandat** | order | countermand |
| **mar** | sea | aquamarine |
| **mater, matri** | mother | maternal |
| **miss, mitt** | send | missive |
| **mon, monit** | warn | admonish |
| **mori, mort** | death | postmortem |
| **morph** | shape | ectomorphic |
| **nav** | sail | circumnavigate |
| **nym** | name | synonymous |
| **mni** | all | omnifarious |
| **oper** | work | operant |
| **orth** | straight | orthodontist |
| **pac** | peace | pacifier |
| **pan** | all | pandemic |
| **para** | ward off | parasol |
| **pater, parti** | father | patriarch |
| **path** | feeling | apathy |
| **ped, pod** | foot | bipedal |
| **pel, puls** | drive | propulsion |
| **pend, pens** | hang | pendulum, pensive |
| **pet, petit** | seek | compete, petition |
| **phil** | love | philosophy |
| **phobia** | fear | claustrophobia |
| **phon** | sound | phonetic |
| **pon, posit** | place | postpone, deposit |
| **port, portat** | carry | portable |

| ROOT | MEANING | EXAMPLE |
|---|---|---|
| **preda** | prey | predator |
| **prehend, prehens** | seize | comprehend |
| **prim** | first | primogeniture |
| **proto** | first | protocol |
| **psych** | soul, mind | psychology |
| **punct** | point | punctilious |
| **put, putat** | cut off, calculate | deputy, amputate |
| **ques, quis** | ask | question, inquiry |
| **reg, rig, rect** | rule | regal, direct |
| **rid, ris** | laugh | deride |
| **rog, rogat** | ask | interrogation |
| **rupt** | break | eruption |
| **sci** | know | scientific |
| **scrib, script** | write | scribble, scripture |
| **sed, sess, sid** | sit | sediment, session |
| **sens, sent** | feel, think | sensation, present |
| **sequ, secut** | follow | sequence, consecutive |
| **solv, solut** | loosen | solvent, solution |
| **son** | sound | sonar |
| **soph** | wise | sophistry |
| **spec, spect** | see | specify, spectacle |
| **spir** | breath | aspirate |
| **string, strict** | bind | astringent, restrict |
| **tang, tact** | touch | tangible, tactile |
| **tele** | far | television |
| **tempor** | time | contemporary |
| **ten, tent** | hold | tenure, tentative |
| **terr** | earth | terrain |
| **theo** | god | theologian |
| **tors, tort** | twist | torsion, distort |
| **tract** | pull | contract |
| **urb** | city | urbane |
| **vent** | come | advent |
| **verb** | word | verbose |
| **vers, vert** | turn | versatile, revert |
| **veri** | truth | veracity |
| **via** | way | viaduct |
| **vid, vis** | see | video, vista |
| **vinc, vict** | conquer | invincible, victor |
| **vict** | life | vital |
| **viv** | live | vivisection |
| **voc, vocat** | call | vocal, vocation |
| **vor** | eat | voracious |
| **volv, voult** | roll | revolve, convoluted |
| **zo** | animal | zoology |

# SUFFIXES

A word part added after the root is a **suffix**. Knowledge of suffixes can often help one determine the word's part of speech.

| SUFFIX | MEANING | EXAMPLE |
|---|---|---|
| **-able, -ible** | able to be | drinkable |
| **-age** | act, condition, result of | marriage |
| **-al, -ile, -eal, -ial** | pertaining to | local, genial |
| **-an, -ian, -n** | of that place | American, Floridian |
| **-ance, -ence** | act of, quality of | dominance, essence |
| **-ant** | person or thing that... | pendant |
| **-cle, -cule** | small | follicle, miniscule |
| **-cracy** | rule | theocracy |
| **-cy** | state of being condition | lunacy |
| **-ee** | one who is ... | retiree |
| **-eer** | one who has to do with ... | mountaineer |
| **-en** | to make | wooden |
| **-ence, -ency** | state of being | regency |
| **-er, -or** | one who ... | teacher, sailor |
| **-esque** | in the style of | picturesque |
| **-et, -ette** | little, female | statuette, majorette |
| **-fic** | make | terrific |
| **-ful** | having, full of | wonderful |
| **-fy, -ify** | to make ... | beautify |
| **-hood** | condition | priesthood |
| **-ic** | pertaining to | volcanic |
| **-ice** | condition | justice |
| **-il, -ile** | capable of | civil, servile |
| **-ion, -sion, -tion, -ation** | act of | diction, recitation |
| **-ious** | full of | rebellious |
| **-ish** | like, characteristic of | childish |
| **-ism** | act of, result of | terrorism |
| **-ist** | one who does | linguist |
| **-ity, -ive** | state of | paucity |
| **-ive** | of, relating to | creative |
| **-ize, -ise** | to cause to be | hypnotize |
| **-less** | without | senseless |
| **-like** | similar to | warlike |
| **-ling** | small, one who is of | duckling, earthling |
| **-ly** | in the manner of | happily |
| **-ness** | state of being | contentment |
| **-ous** | full of | hazardous |
| **-some** | like, tending to | lonesome |
| **-tude** | having the quality of | certitude |
| **-wise** | in a manner | clockwise |
| **-y** | having or possessing | healthy |

# CONTEXT CLUES

The second technique used to enlarge vocabulary is the most common word attack skill of adults - **context clues**. Context clues are key words that come before or after unfamiliar terminology which help us ascertain the right meaning of words and assist us in word attack experiences. For example, let us say that you do not know the meaning of the word *obnoxious* in the following sentence.

> The insulting and ***obnoxious*** remarks of the players truly annoyed and irritated the coach.

First examine the words around the unknown word. The adjective *insulting* and the verbs *annoyed and irritated* present a perspective and clue in regard to the meaning of the word *obnoxious*. These synonymous and more familiar terms help you determine the definition; consequently we have, *obnoxious*: offensive, abusive.

A second way to determine the definition of an unfamiliar word by utilizing context clues is to note the meaning indicated in the sentence. For example, if you did not know the meaning of the word *aerobic* in the following sentence:

> Most organisms are ***aerobic***, that is, they require oxygen to release energy for life functions.

You can determine the meaning of the word *aerobic* by examining the phrase, "*...that is, they require oxygen to release energy for life functions.*" In this sentence there is actually a supplied definition.

The third way to use context clues in determining the meaning of unfamiliar terms is to make **inferences** about the probable meaning from the words around it. For example:

> In his works the author ***eschewed*** the obvious in favor of the obscure.

You can *infer* from the words around it that the meaning of the word *eschewed* is *to pass over.*

The fourth way context clues may be used to determine a word's definition is through **contrast**. Certain words signal that what will follow is the opposite of the first part of the sentence; these words include; *but, however, although, and in contrast to.* For example:

> The term ***sea*** usually implies the waters are ***saline***, but the Sea of Galilee is not salty.

In this example, the conjuction "*but*" is a signal the definition which follows is the opposite of the meaning of saline. By examining the phrase, "*... but the Sea of Galilee is not salty,*" and by realizing that the meaning of the word saline is the opposite of this phrase, you can determine the definition of *saline* to be *salty.*

Appropriate preparation and practice at finding context clues will enhance your vocabulary development. Wide and diverse reading, keeping a record of unfamiliar vocabulary you encounter, and whenever possible doing accomplished crossword puzzles such as those found in the New York Times will strengthen your skill in this area.

# READING COMPREHENSION

The verbal portion of the GMAT examination is comprised of three parts: Reading Comprehension, Critical Reasoning, and Sentence Correction. The skills required for the Reading Comprehension portion of the test are similar to those required for the Critical Reasoning test; however, the format of the two tests varies markedly. The Reading Comprehension section of the test is comprised of three passages, each approximately 350 words, dealing with business related topics, social science topics, the humanities, and the sciences. The business passages may be based on topics such as management, economics, marketing and human resources. The science passage may deal with the biological sciences, the physical sciences or other science-related fields. The social science passage may deal with topics in anthropology, history and sociology. The humanities passage may deal with topics dealing with the arts or literature or criticism of the arts or literature.

Timing is a very important consideration when dealing with the Reading Comprehension section of the examination. Some topics may be easier for you than others because you are familiar with the material. Even if you are familiar with the topic, *be sure to base your answers only on the material in the passage* and move at a pace which allows you to work efficiently through the **GMAT CAT**.

Although it may at first appear that each reading comprehension passage is followed by completely different questions, the basic skills being tested in each passage are the same. Mastering the skills in this text will provide the background needed for ALL reading comprehension tests.

## THE MAIN IDEA QUESTIONS

The first and most important skill you will need is the ability to determine the *main idea* of the passage. Although each passage may be followed by questions from several of the skills areas included in this list, this particular skill is tested in almost every reading comprehension passage.

The main idea is the central thought that unifies the passage. In most well-written essays, the first sentence is usually the topic sentence, the statement of the purpose of the author. The main idea of the passage is developed by each succeeding sentence in the paragraph and by each paragraph in the essay. When you are trying to determine the main idea of the passage, remember that the idea must be general enough to include every sentence in every paragraph in the passage. It must not, however, be so general that any additional ideas could be included under the same heading.

Let us look at a very simple sample paragraph.

> Scientists have recently discovered that honeybees are able to communicate with each other by using a series of dance-like movements. Through careful observation and with the assistance of knowledgeable beekeepers, insect physiologists have determined that concrete ideas, such as distance, and abstract ideas, such as quality of the nectar, can be expressed through these movements. Slight variations in their movements indicate the type of flower and the distance of that flower from the hive. Scientists have observed that after receiving such a message, a honeybee will fly to the exact location danced by the foraging worker-bee.

BROAD IDEAS

If this were a passage on the GMAT examination there are several ways you might be asked to find the main idea. Such a question might be phrased in any of these forms.

- What is the author's primary purpose in writing this passage?
- Which of the following would be the most appropriate title for this passage?
- Which of the following best expresses the author's main point?
- Which of the following is the principal topic of the passage?

The topic sentence in this paragraph is obviously the first sentence. The answer to any form of the main idea question would be a paraphrase of that sentence. It would contain words that cover the key points of scientist, discovery, honeybees, and communicate with movements. Anything less specific would not cover the topic and anything more specific would leave out some of the ideas in the paragraph.

When dealing with a multi-paragraph essay, you must be certain to include all the paragraphs in your consideration of the answer. Be sure to note keywords such as *however, in addition, moreover, on the other hand* and other transition words. They signal that contrasting or additional information is coming. Be certain that if a passage is constructed as an argument, you consider both sides of the argument in your answer choice. If the passage is based on a comparison of two points of view, both viewpoints should be included in the title of the passage.

In addition to finding the topic sentence in the introductory paragraph, you must also consider the first sentence of each paragraph as a topic sentence. Finally, the last paragraph will act as a summary and either restate the topic in a comprehensive manner, or unify the details from all the preceding paragraphs.

## SUPPORTING DETAILS QUESTIONS

Questions about the supporting details in a passage ask you to differentiate between the main idea or general theme and those ideas which substantiate or support the main idea. You must also be able to differentiate between those ideas which are stated explicitly in the passage and those ideas which are merely implied by the author. When dealing with the main idea of a passage, the entire passage must be considered. When dealing with supporting details, each sentence must be regarded as an individual statement of fact. Answers to supporting detail questions will be in the form of a paraphrase of a specific sentence or two.

Questions about supporting details can be phrased in the following manner:

- According to the passage ______________
- In line XX the author specifically states that...
- All of the following are mentioned by the author *except*...
- The passage provides information that would answer which of the following questions?
- Which of the following statements is true according to the author?

The most commonly used form of the supporting detail question is the first form on the list. The blank line will contain specific information from the passage which you must then complete by choosing one of the five answers given. For example, using the paragraph about the honeybees, a supporting detail question might be phrased in this way:

According to the passage, honeybees are able to communicate both

A) ______________
B) ______________

C) ____________

D) ____________

E) ____________

A possible answer would contain the information given in the sixth line of the paragraph in a paraphrase form. This statement supports the main idea that scientists have discovered that honeybees are able to communicate with each other. It gives specific information telling exactly what honeybees are able to communicate. This information is given and you are not expected to draw a conclusion or make an inference. You are expected to read the information and give it back in another form to show your understanding of the specific details.

One difficulty in answering a supporting detail question is choosing the answer that *"best fits the question"*. Each of the five possible answers may be a paraphrase of a sentence or two in the passage; however, only one answer choice specifically answers the question. The other four answers are correct according to the passage, but they **do not** answer the question. For example, once again using the honeybee paragraph, five possible answer choices might be:

According to the passage, honeybees are able to communicate both

A) with insect physiologists and beekeepers

B) with foraging worker bees and honeybees

C) concrete and abstract ideas

D) with dance-like movements and careful observations

E) slight variations and observations of messages

The correct answer is C). Although all the other words can be found in the paragraph, only *concrete and abstract ideas* answers the question.

## SPECIFIC FACTS QUESTIONS

Specific fact questions are actually the easiest ones to answer. At times you may be asked to perform some simple mathematical calculations; other times you may be asked a question in a negative fashion, but usually you will only need to read carefully and respond appropriately. When you read the questions through briefly before beginning a careful reading of the selection, make a mental note of the specific details that the questions require you to observe. During your careful reading of the selection, mark those places which contain the answers to the fact questions. You may even wish to stop reading the passage and answer the fact questions immediately. This can be of special advantage to those examinees who read slowly and find they are unable to complete all the questions in the given time. You will at least have answered those questions that are most direct and which you can probably answer most easily.

When dealing with *mathematical questions*, be sure to read carefully and examine **all** possible answers. Let us look at an example based on the following sentence:

In 6000 BC during one of the invasions of the Nile valley, several valuable examples of early Egyptian art were entombed in a pile of rubble and discovered only in this century.

The early examples of Egyptian art discovered in this century are

A) 2,000 years old

B) 4,000 years old

C) 6,000 years old

D) 8,000 years old

E) 10,000 years old

A less than careful reading may result in choosing the most obvious answer, letter C. This, of course, is incorrect. If the simple arithmetic problem is done incorrectly, an examinee might choose letter B, subtracting 2000 years to bring the time up to this century instead of adding them. The correct answer is, of course, D, 8000 years old. You must add 2000 years for the time from 1 AD to the present, which is almost 2000 AD, to 6000, the time from 6000 BC to 1 AD

Let us use the passage about honey bees to demonstrate an example of a question asked in a negative form.

> Scientists have recently discovered that honeybees are able to communicate with each other by using a series of dance-like movements. Through careful observation and with the assistance of knowledgeable beekeepers, insect physiologists have determined that concrete ideas, such as distance, and abstract ideas, such as quality of the nectar, can be expressed through these movements. Slight variations in their movements indicate the type of flower and the distance of that flower from the hive. Scientists have observed that after receiving such a message, a honeybee will fly to the exact location danced by the foraging worker-bee.
>
> According to the passage, honeybees are able to communicate all of the following except
>
> A) location and quality of the nectar.
> B) distance from the hive of desired nectar.
> C) messages to other bees.
> D) variations of flowers.
> E) careful observations with insect physiologists.

It is important to select only the one answer which is incorrect. Sometimes this can be more difficult than choosing the correct answer from a group of wrong answers. In this example the obvious answer is letter E. All the other choices are mentioned specifically in the passage. Although the words *careful observations* and *insect physiologists* are included in the passage, the observations are not communicated by the bees, but performed by the insect physiologists. Letter E does not answer the question.

## TONE OR ATTITUDE QUESTIONS

The author's attitude towards his subject and his audience sets the *tone or mood* of the passage. An author can reveal that he thinks highly of himself and his subject, but little of his audience. This would produce a tone that is *sarcastic or condescending.* He can feel that his topic is really unimportant, but still treat that topic in an important manner. This would produce a tone that is *whimsical or light-hearted.* He can be cynical, serious, optimistic, pessimistic, sympathetic, or hostile, or any of a long list of words which describe an author's tone or mood.

This type of question is not objective, as is the specific detail question. You cannot find the answer in any specific place in the passage. You must determine the answer by using context clues, looking for descriptive words, and determining the connotation (emotional meaning) of words. Whether the author uses mostly positive words to describe his subject or mostly negative words is an important part in determining the mood of a passage or the author's tone.

Perhaps the most difficult aspect of this type of question is the vocabulary used in the answer choices.

Here is an example of a tone question based on the following sentences:

> Johnny's bedtime causes a battle of heroic proportions. He is a three year old military genius who can out-maneuver any senior ranking officer, otherwise known as a parent.
>
> Which of the following best describes the attitude of the author of the above statement?
>
> A) Disdainful
> B) Sardonic
> C) Facetious
> D) Laconic
> E) Antagonistic

In this case, it is merely a question of knowing the meaning of the five answer choices. The correct answer is obviously letter C, facetious, which means lightly joking. The other answers are all inappropriate. Disdainful means full of scorn or aloof contempt; sardonic means bitterly ironic or sarcastic; laconic means expressing much in a few words, and antagonistic means combative.

Let us look at an another example using the same five answer choices.

> My father told me, "Work for the masses, you'll live with the classes; work for the classes, you'll live with the masses." However, if I must soil my hands with work at all, I would prefer, at least, to deal with people who have class and breeding.
>
> Which of the following words best describes the attitude of the author of the above statement?
>
> A) Disdainful
> B) Sardonic
> C) Facetious
> D) Laconic
> E) Antagonistic

Here the first answer is obviously the correct choice. The author is disdainful; his attitude is one of scorn or aloof contempt for the masses and for work itself. This question is more difficult to answer because three of the five choices are negative, and because the passage indicates that a negative tone is present, it is harder to make easy eliminations simply based on positive or negative connotations.

Choice B, sardonic, is incorrect because the author is not saying one thing but meaning another which would produce irony or sarcasm. The answer is not letter C, facetious, since the author is serious in his attitude and does not mean to amuse the reader. Although one might think that the pithy quote from the author's father might be laconic, saying much in a few words, that is not the *author's attitude* towards his subject or his reader. The final choice, antagonistic, might be the best wrong answer. It almost seems as if the author is trying to pick a fight with someone; yet, his attitude is so demeaning, superior and supercilious, that choice A is a much better answer.

## APPLICATION QUESTIONS

All **GMAT** Reading Comprehension questions are based on information that is provided in the passage, but certain questions also ask you to use your general knowledge and make comparisons between situations in the reading passage and situations not discussed in the passage, but about which you should have some knowledge. This type of question is called an *application* question because you are being asked to apply what you have read in the passage to another situation. The answer *cannot* be found in a specific place in the passage. You must make a judgment based on your general knowledge.

The sample question following the passage below is a simplified example of an application question.

> Of the many causes for the French Revolution, probably the most obvious would have to be the extravagances of King Louis XVI and his queen, Marie Antoinette. Not only did they spend in excess of the tax revenues, but they spent the money on themselves.
>
> Which ruling couple could be considered analogous to Queen Marie Antoinette and Louis XVI?
>
> A) Ronald and Nancy Reagan of the U.S.A.
> B) Imelda and Ferdinand Marcos of the Philippines
> C) Raisa and Mikhail Gorbachev of the USSR
> D) Barbara and George Bush of the U.S.A.
> E) King Ferdinand and Queen Isabella of Spain

It is important to recognize this type of question in order to avoid spending unnecessary time searching the passage for the answer.

You would be expected to have some common knowledge about the various rulers. The obvious answer is letter B, Imelda and Ferdinand Marcos of the Philippines.

Although Nancy and Ronald Reagan did seem more extravagant than some presidential couples, they did not spend tax money on themselves. That would be impossible with present day media reporters acting as the watchdogs of our society.

Raisa and Mikhail Gorbachev would also find it difficult, if not impossible, to divert revenues from the government for their own purposes.

Although Barbara and George Bush are from traditionally wealthy backgrounds, they are not known for their lavish spending habits.

There is no common knowledge of lavish spending by Ferdinand and Isabella of Spain, either; this choice was probably included to confuse you with similar names.

You are probably aware of the overthrow of the Marcos regime in the Philippines just a few years ago. At this time the lavish life style of the rulers was exposed. This common knowledge provides the basis for your answer.

## INFERENCE QUESTIONS

One of the most important skills necessary for success on the GMAT is the ability to read between the lines or to make judgments about the passage from the information you have read. The answers to inference questions are not directly or explicitly stated as they are in questions dealing with specific facts. They may be suggested or implied by the author and must, therefore, be assumed by the reader. This type of question is more challenging and sometimes more difficult than questions about specific facts.

As we have seen in the section on Tone or Attitude, answers are not specifically given but must be determined by the reader based on such things as the connotations (emotional meanings) of the words used by the author. From these subtle hints, you can determine the author's attitude toward his subject and toward the reader. This is one type of inference question.

Another type of inference question tests your ability to determine facts or premises that are not stated specifically, but can be *assumed*, based on the information given. Here is an example:

> In 1976 the United States suffered the worst weather conditions possible for the production of soy beans. The normal production of almost 50 million metric tons was decreased by almost 10%. Yet, in that same year, the United States commodities market was still able to sell almost 50 million tons of soybeans, the same amount it had sold in previous years.
>
> Which of the following statements must be true based on the information in the passage?
>
> A) The soybean farmers suffered serious financial loses in 1976.
> B) The normal production of soybeans usually exceeds 50 million metric tons.
> C) In 1976 the United States produced the fewest metric tons of soybeans in its history.
> D) In 1976 the commodities market sold surplus tons of soybeans from previous years.
> E) The commodities market is indifferent to the plight of the farmers.

Now let us examine each of the answers. It is clear that this is an inference question because the answer is NOT stated specifically in the passage. Information is given and a conclusion must be drawn based on that information. You cannot go back to the passage and find the answer either in exact words or in a paraphrase.

Letter A is not the correct answer because you cannot *assume* that the farmers suffered serious financial losses since there is no discussion of the amount of money paid each year for each ton of soybeans. Although fewer tons of soybeans were produced, the price might vary enough from year to year or supply and demand might alter the price so that farmers would not incur *serious* financial loses. Even if you felt that the passage *implies* that the farmers suffered financial loses, there is no way to assess whether or not these loses were serious. This one word in the answer choice makes it unacceptable.

Letter B is incorrect because it is factually wrong. The passage specifically states that soybean production is normally *almost* 50 million metric tons, not *more* than 50 million tons.

Letter C is incorrect because it is impossible to determine what the production levels in other years might have been. We know that production in 1976 was down 10% due to the worst possible weather conditions, but we have no way of knowing whether other years might have been lower due to other problems, such as insect infestation, etc. This answer is wrong because it leaves no room for error. The word *worst* requires that you are certain of all previous years' production rates.

Letter E is incorrect because we have no information on which to base this supposition. If we were told that others profited from the soybean plight while the farmers suffered, we might be able to assume that this was caused by the traders on the commodities market, but the passage gives no indication that the farmers suffered in any way.

This leaves us with Letter D as the only possible choice. In order to sell the same amount of soybeans in 1976 as it had sold in previous years, the missing five million tons of soybeans had to come from surplus stocks. You cannot sell what you do not have. Letter D is correct.

Let us look at another example of an inference question which asks you to supply a conclusion based on the facts.

During the middle ages in western Europe, the office of reeve of the shire, or sheriff, as it came to be called, was commonly a hereditary position. One of the main roles of the sheriff was the collection of tax monies owed to the Lord of the manor. Often this role was not pursued with the zeal the Lords would have liked. Mills were operated illegally without permits and the Lords lost the tax money that was supposed to be generated by operating the only available mill.

According to the passage, which of the following is probably true?

A) The tax collectors skimmed money from their collections that belonged to the Lord of the manor.
B) Because their jobs were secure, tax collectors became lax in their endeavors on their Lords' behalf.
C) Illegal mills were being operated by the tax collectors.
D) Lack of sufficient mills available caused a loss in tax money for the Lords of the manors.
E) The Lords lost money by operating the only available mill.

The question makes it obvious that the answer cannot be found in a specific place in the passage. The word *probably* is the clue. There is no *definite* answer. You must make an assumption based on the information given.

Letter A is incorrect because there is no reason to jump to this conclusion. The passage states that the role of tax collector was not pursued the way the Lord would like, but it does not give us any reason to believe that the sheriffs were anything more than lazy. Dishonesty is mentioned, but it is not clear who was committing the illegal acts.

Letter B is correct. The passage specifically states that the job of the tax collector was hereditary, that is, handed down from father to son. This makes the job a rather secure one. It is logical to conclude that this job security was responsible for the laxity or lack of enthusiasm in collecting the tax monies. The passage says that endeavors of the tax collectors were not all that the Lords would have liked.

Letter C is incorrect because although illegal mills were being operated, there is no evidence in the passage that these mills were being operated by the tax collectors themselves.

Letter D is incorrect because there is no mention of the number of mills being insufficient for the needs of the people. The illegal mills made the number of available mills even greater. There is no indication that these mills were established for any reason other than to avoid taxes.

Letter E is incorrect because the Lords were losing money because their mills were NOT the only mills available. They would have received tax money from the use of these mills, but illegal mills were siphoning off their income.

**HINT:** You will find that the largest number of questions on the GMAT appear to be inference questions. This is usually the case for most examinations because the inference question tests your ability to read beyond the simplistic and obvious meaning of the words. You must absorb all of the information and make good judgments in order to answer inference questions. Also, the inference question lends itself to a greater variety of topics than any other skill being tested. However, you must not feel that every question calls for a judgment on your part. Even some questions that include the word *infer* or *inference* in the question format might actually have specific answers in the passage.

# TECHNIQUES AND STRUCTURE QUESTIONS

Each passage is written for a specific purpose and each author utilizes certain techniques to accomplish that purpose. For example, if a passage is written to give knowledge, you can expect to find a good deal of factual information and specific details to educate the reader. In addition, the author would organize that information in a logical manner so that the information could be absorbed in an efficient fashion. That would be the structure of the passage. You will be expected to determine the purpose of the passage, the techniques used to accomplish that purpose, and the structure of the passage as it relates to the content.

A passage can also be written to convince the reader of a particular point of view; to show one side of an argument; to present two sides of an argument; to give a cause and show its effects; to show results and let the reader determine what actually caused the results; to create a mood; to analyze a problem. Some of the techniques an author might use include examples, comparisons, explanations, descriptions, facts, opinions, and arguments. You should be able to tell the difference between a fact and an opinion; tell whether an argument is weak or well developed; evaluate the correctness of a comparison and the effectiveness of its use.

A passage can be organized as a list of facts; one side of an argument followed by the other side; a list of opinions; a fact in favor of a viewpoint followed by a fact refuting the viewpoint; a series of problems with a solution; a series of problems with no solution; one problem with many solutions.

Let us look at a very simple example of a question about the technique and structure of a passage.

> In recent times America has come to question its role as policeman of the world. Saddam Hussein and the Persian Gulf War brought many of these concerns to the surface. Is it really the responsibility of our nation to determine the moral code for the entire world? Yet can we stand back and let another Hitler decide the fate of defenseless people?

**1. What is the purpose of the last question in the passage?**

A) to give a third point of view
B) to give a specific fact about a subject
C) to draw an analogy between the two people mentioned
D) to question the reader's knowledge of the subject
E) to give a possible solution to the dilemma presented

**2. How is the passage organized?**

A) a series of facts
B) one side of an argument
C) two sides of an argument
D) a problem is presented and a solution is given
E) a hypothesis is presented to be followed by observations

The answer to question #1 is letter C. The purpose of the question is to draw our attention to the possible similarity between Saddam Hussein and Hitler. This was done many times by the media to convince the American people of the correctness of their position in this conflict.

Letter A is incorrect because the last question in the passage does not give a third point of view; two points of view are being argued.

Letter B is incorrect because the last question is not a fact, but an opinion. The examinee is expected to be able to distinguish between the two.

Letter D is incorrect because the question was not meant to be answered by the reader. It is a rhetorical question posed to arouse interest.

Letter E is incorrect because although a dilemma (two negative possibilities) is presented, the last question in the passage is not a solution, but simply an opinion for one side of an argument.

The answer to question #2 is letter C. The author is presenting two sides of an argument. First he states the negative side in the role America must play; then he states the negative side of failing to play that role. Letter A is clearly wrong. There are no facts presented. Letter B is incorrect because although it appears that the author is going to take a particular side in this argument, he does present TWO viewpoints, not one. Letter D is incorrect because although a problem is presented, no solution is given. Letter E is incorrect because there is no hypothesis followed by observations; this structure is usually used in scientific passages.

## WORDS IN CONTEXT QUESTIONS

Another type of question used on the GMAT asks the examinee to show that he understands the meaning of words in context. Sometimes one word is substituted for a large idea encompassing several sentences; other times a word is used in an unusual manner; other times a word is unique to a particular topic and its meaning is probably unknown to most examinees but can be ascertained by using context clues.

Let us look at a simple passage and sample questions examining each of these possibilities.

> Elena Mendosa's travel agency experienced five economically strong years which encouraged her to expand her base of operations. She re-mortgaged her office building to purchase another building in another town. She used her reserve capital to furnish the new office and she used her operating capital to purchase necessary supplies and pay her staff until the new business could become self-sustaining. This left her in a precarious financial position.
>
> Which of the following statements could be substituted for the word **<u>this</u>** in line 6 without changing the meaning of the passage?
>
> A) The expansion of Elena Mendosa's business
> B) The use of her operating capital to pay for supplies and staff salaries
> C) The inability of the new business to sustain itself
> D) All the means used by Elena Mendosa to finance the expansion of her business
> E) The difficulties experienced by Elena Mendosa in obtaining financing for her new business

Let us examine each answer. Letter A is incorrect. Although it appears that the expansion is responsible for her precarious or dangerous position, it is not the expansion itself, but the way Ms. Mendosa financed the expansion that is dangerous.

Letter B is only partially correct. Using her operating capital to pay for current expenses on her second business is only one of three financing measures Ms. Mendosa used. It is the combination of these measures, not one act only, that placed her in jeopardy.

Letter C is incorrect because this situation is only temporary and one which Ms. Mendosa took into account as a calculated risk. This is only one risk; the accumulated practices, not one situation alone, constitute the danger.

Letter D is correct. The word *this* refers to all three methods mentioned in the passage for financing this operation. It is the cumulative effect of these measures which puts Ms. Mendosa's business at risk.

Letter E is incorrect because we have no information about *difficulty* in financing the expansion. It appears that Ms. Mendosa has completed the task of financing the expansion, but there is no indication that there was a problem in doing so.

**HINT:** This question is more than just a word in context question. You must understand the meaning of the passage as a whole in order to make the correct selection. Often a single word refers to more than the simple or obvious answer and you must look beyond the line in which the word can be found. When a word comes after a series of thoughts, you must look at all the information that precedes it. Do not concentrate ***only*** on the line in which the word can be found.

Let us look at another type of word in context question, one which requires determining the meaning of an unknown word by the context clues around it.

> In the late 17th century in France, the Controller General of Finance, Jean Baptiste Colbert, developed a sound economic system based on the theory of mercantilism. But even this policy of economic self-sufficiency based on a favorable balance of trade could not sustain the expensive wars inspired by Louis XIV's desire for glory.
>
> What is the meaning of the word **mercantilism** as it is used in line 3 of this passage?
>
> A) An economic system of trade based on exchanges during wartime.
> B) A self-sufficient economic system based on a policy of expensive foreign wars.
> C) A self-sufficient system of economic control.
> D) An expensive social system inspired by Louis XIV.
> E) A self-sufficient economy based on wealth generated by a trade surplus.

Letter A is incorrect. Although all of the words used in this and subsequent answers can be found in the passage, they are used incorrectly. The trade in the system of mercantilism is not based on exchanges during wartime.

Letter B is incorrect because mercantilism is not based on expensive foreign wars.

Letter C is incorrect because control is not part of the meaning of mercantilism as it is used in this passage.

Letter D is incorrect because Louis XIV did not create this system; according to the passage, it was Colbert. Also, there is no mention of mercantilism being a social system, just an economic one.

Letter E is correct. It is a paraphrase of the definition of mercantilism given in the passage.

# TIPS FOR ALL READING COMPREHENSION QUESTIONS

The length of each reading comprehension passage makes it difficult to read the passage and remember all the important information necessary to answer the questions which follow each selection. It is important, therefore, to read the passage with a specific focus in mind. In order to know exactly what to look for, the following steps may be helpful.

**Skim the passage**; read just enough to know which category the selection fits into. Use skimming techniques such as locating key words, underlined words and words which make it clear that the selection deals with a specific topic. Pay special attention to the topic sentence of the passage and the topic sentence of each paragraph. Look for transition words such as: ***therefore, however, moreover, on the other hand, in contrast, although, despite, nevertheless, and yet.*** These words indicate that more than one opinion or idea is being presented. During the skimming process, which should take about 45-60 seconds, you should be able to determine the topic of the passage, the main idea, and important secondary ideas.

**Read the question stem.** Do not bother to read all the possible answers because at this time you are unprepared to make choices and the possibilities will confuse you and slow down your reading. You should be able to determine if the question is general or specific. If the question refers to a specific line in the text, immediately identify that line by noting it on a piece of scratch paper.

**Read the passage.** Now that you have read the question, you have a focus for a careful reading of the selection. If you are able to answer the question before you finish reading the passage, do so ***immediately.*** Keep in mind that you must work quickly and try to answer each question as quickly as possible.

**Always check all five answers** in case there is a catch to the question. The most obvious answer may not always be the correct one.

# HELPFUL HINTS FOR THE READING COMPREHENSION TEST

Improving your reading speed will aid you in the reading comprehension section of the **GMAT**. Word by word reading is slow and inefficient; instead try to read phrases or clusters of words. A key to speed reading is to widen your eye span and to build your concentration. Keep reading forward; do not regress; read the material a second time rather than stopping in the middle of a paragraph. Shift the rate of reading according to the type of material; adjust reading rate to the *purposes* for reading.

Now it is time to try all these skills together. The sample passage which follows includes most of the types of questions we have just covered. Time yourself and allow two minutes to read the passage and slightly less than one minute for each answer, or around twelve minutes in all.

## READING COMPREHENSION SAMPLE TEST PASSAGE

As the pragmatist once said, it is hard to argue with success. Because the Russians have carried themselves from the rear ranks of the Russian laggards to the front ranks of the world leaders, they have managed to forestall many arguments. But even if it is conceded that the Russians might have grown at a significantly lower rate of growth if they had adopted some other form of economic organization, it might nonetheless be possible to show that equally rapid rates of growth could also have been achieved in some other way. If we could find that there was no other alternative that could have assured the same success, then indeed it is necessary to acknowledge that some of the political excesses of the Stalinist period might have been needed to produce rapid economic growth. By the same token, however, if it can be demonstrated that equally rapid growth or almost as rapid growth could have been obtained by some other less draconic methods, then it seems fair to conclude that Soviet economic growth may not have been worth the cost of a Stalinist regime.

Under the best of circumstances, such questions require some very heroic assumptions, but they must be made if thoughtful guidance is to be provided other countries which confront the same situation. With the passage of time, there is less and less tendency to ask such questions because history tends to favor the dramatic. Historians concentrate on the greater glory that was Egypt under the Pharaohs, Rome under Caesar and France under Napoleon. The suffering inflicted on the enemy or the out-of-favor is neglected in the rush to admire the monuments that survive. The same thing is beginning to happen within the Soviet Union. There are some who are trying to forget Stalin's excesses. Therefore, to ensure balance in judging history, it is necessary periodically to ask if collectivization, forced draft industrialization, and Stalin were necessary.

The first point to remember is that, prior to Russia's entrance into World War I, it was experiencing a very rapid rate of growth. Although there were bad as well as good years, we noticed earlier that Alexander Gorschenkron has estimated that the average annual rate of growth in the 1890s was as high as 8 per cent and about 6 percent between 1905 and 1914. Conceivably, somewhat similar rates could have been maintained after the war without much more strain than had been required earlier. Nonetheless, fifteen years later under Stalin it became fashionable to argue that such high rates of growth require large and, it was thought, unavailable capital resources. In contrast, not many in the pre-revolutionary period seemed to feel that future rapid growth would require a radical uprooting of the economy and the society. Perhaps it was not a sudden problem then because it was assumed there would always be substantial inflows of foreign capital. Yet some authorities like Gerschenkron argue that economic growth in Russia was in fact becoming self-sustaining without the need for large quantities of outside aid. In any case, a small amount of foreign investment, whatever its disadvantages, might have been better than the chaos and suffering which eventually ensued during the collectivization of agriculture in the late 1920s and early 1930s. Perhaps it was just for this reason that Lenin and much later Khrushchev did seek outside credits and investments. Stalin refused to do this. The result was death and destruction.

## Questions for Reading Comprehension Test Sample Passage

**1. This passage is probably an excerpt from**

(A) a political history of Europe.
(B) an economic history of Europe.
(C) an economic history of the Soviet Union.
(D) anti-Soviet propaganda.
(E) an information pamphlet on agriculture.

**2. The author's purpose in writing this passage is to**

(A) explain the development of the Soviet economy.
(B) instruct developing countries in economic matters.
(C) explain and justify the reasons for collectivization.
(D) debunk the myth that Stalin's measures were necessary for rapid economic growth.
(E) enumerate the various methods used by Stalin to produce rapid economic growth.

**3. To what do the *draconic methods* in line 13 refer?**

(A) rapid growth rates
(B) political excesses
(C) slower growth rates
(D) alternative successes
(E) political growth

**4. The author's attitude towards Stalin is one of**

(A) benign indulgence.
(B) sardonic hostility.
(C) intellectual detachment.
(D) sympathetic cynicism.
(E) righteous indignation.

**5. The author would agree with all of the following except**

(A) The Russians advanced from economic inferiority to economic leadership.
(B) If there were no other way to achieve economic growth, some of Stalin's excesses might have been necessary.
(C) History tends to see only the results of dramatic actions and ignores some of the drawbacks.
(D) It is possible that Russia could have achieved rapid economic growth without foreign investment and without austere measures.
(E) Before World War I, Russia's dependence on foreign aid produced its rapid rate of economic growth but was also responsible for much of the painful chaos in Russian society.

**6. The author alludes to Egypt, Rome and France in lines 20 and 21 in order to**

(A) draw an analogy between the suffering inflicted on the helpless by historical dictators and the results of Stalin's methods.
(B) remind the reader that it is sometimes necessary to use harsh measures to achieve desirable ends.
(C) prove that collectivization and forced draft industrialization were necessary.
(D) show that Stalin's dramatic achievements were as glorious as those of Caesar and Napoleon
(E) draw an analogy between monuments left by historical leaders and those left by Stalin to serve as an example to countries in a similar situation.

**7. Which of the following premises are part of the basis for the author's arguments?**

**I. The radical uprooting of the economy and social structure of Russia was caused by a need to bring about rapid economic growth.**

**II. Stalin's methods were a response to the economic needs of the nation, although his ideas were flawed.**

**III. All political actions are merely a response to the economic needs of all nations.**

(A) I only
(B) I and II only
(C) I and III only
(D) II and III only
(E) I, II, and III

**8. The annual rate of growth for the first decade of the twentieth century was**

(A) 2% higher than the previous decade.
(B) 4% higher than the previous decade.
(C) 6% higher than the previous decade.
(D) 2% lower than the previous decade.
(E) 4% lower than the previous decade.

**9. Which of the following can be inferred from the passage?**

(A) Khrushchev and Lenin both designed their economic policies around a plan to circumvent the deficiencies of dependency on foreign aid.
(B) Khrushchev was aware of the drawbacks of Stalin's methods and relied on a small amount of foreign aid instead.
(C) Stalin was unaware of the drawbacks of foreign investment.
(D) Stalin could not avoid the destruction that resulted from his economic reforms.
(E) The Russian economy was self-sustaining and did not require foreign investment for growth.

## Answers and Explanations for Reading Comprehension Test Sample Passage

1. (C) This excerpt is probably from an economic history of the Soviet Union. This is not a political history; Europe is too broad of a topic; answers D and E are too general.

2. (D) This is a general question. The answer must contain the main idea and all aspects of that idea. First the general idea is stated; then the rest of the passage refutes the necessity of Stalin's measures. (A) is too general; (B) is too specific; (C) is incorrect; the author's purpose was not to explain collectivization, but to show that it was unnecessary. (E) is incorrect because the author never lists the methods used by Stalin.

3. (B) In lines 8-11 the author states that some of the political excesses might have been necessary if no other way could be found. In line 13 he refers to these excesses as "draconic methods." Remember that you must look at lines before and sometimes after the line indicated to find the answer. All the other words were used in the passage, but they were not the draconic methods to which the author referred.

4. (E) The author is not in favor of Stalin so we know the answer cannot be positive. This immediately eliminates answers A and D. Answer B, sardonic hostility, is much too strong. The author is not sneering or ranting about Stalin but treating him in an intellectually proper manner. The two remaining choices, C and E are both good possibilities. If you look carefully at the last four sentences, it is evident that the author is angry with Stalin by the use of words such as suffering and chaos. He is sympathetic towards the victims of Stalin's programs. This would eliminate intellectual detachment as an answer. The author is not detached, but emotionally involved. He is affronted or indignant by Stalin's refusal to behave in a moderate manner; he is righteously indignant.

5. (E) All the other answers are specifically stated in the passage. Only part of answer E is correct; the second half of the answer is exactly the opposite of what occurred according to the author.

6. (A) The author wants the reader to see that there is a similarity between the suffering in previous eras and the suffering caused by Stalin. He does not want Stalin's successes to wash away his excesses as has happened to dictators in the past.

7. (B) In the first paragraph, the author states that the rapid economic growth of Russia was responsible for the upheaval of the people. In the second and third paragraph Stalin's excesses are directly related to the rapid economic growth he achieved. I and II are therefore, correct. III, is much too limited in its scope. The word all leaves no room for any possibilities outside this answer to exist, and there is no way of making such broad claims.

8. (D) This is a simple specific detail question asked in a mathematical format. Growth in the 1890s was 8% and growth in 1905 was 6%; therefore, the rate of growth was 2% less than the previous decade.

9. (B) Lines 45 and 47 of the text state that perhaps it was possible that Khrushchev was trying to avoid the chaos and the suffering of Stalin's methods; from this sentence we know Khrushchev was aware of Stalin's methods and we know that he did seek a small amount of foreign investment. It is safe to assume that his knowledge influenced his

decision to allow outside credits. Letter A is incorrect because lines 46 and 47 state that Lenin and Khrushchev did allow outside credits and a small amount of foreign aid. Letter C is incorrect because the next to the last line in the text states that Stalin refused to allow outside credits. From this we can assume that he weighed the choices and made a decision. Letter D is incorrect because the author believes that Lenin and Khrushchev were faced with the same problems as Stalin, but made better choices. Letter E is incorrect because lines 41 and 42 state that Russia was becoming self-sustaining. It had not achieved this result at the time of the passage.

# SAMPLE TEST QUESTIONS FOR READING COMPREHENSION

These sample test questions represent roughly a third of the 41 questions to be presented to you by the **GMAT CAT**. The other two-thirds are categorized as **Sentence Correction** and **Critical Reasoning** type questions. These question types are significantly different and each individual will respond at different rates for each. Remember that the **GMAT CAT** does not allow you to return to or to skip over any question. When you get stuck, you will need a strategy for taking your best guess so as to move on to questions that you will be able to answer.

You will be given 75 minutes time to answer 41 questions. This is roughly 110 seconds, under 2 minutes, per question. As you practice using the following questions, time yourself noting the rate at which you dispatch each. As you note that some questions take you too long, you will develop a sensitivity to timing. During the test this sense will help you to transition from looking for the "right" answer to picking what you think is the "most likely" answer.

Remember, that as you first read the answers for any question, some answers may be eliminated initially. You should practice this in this section by remaining aware of the fact that you are making value judgements as you read each answer. In fact you may develop a method of noting these judgements on scratch paper to aid you in more quickly identifying the educated guess. No matter how you may organize this aspect of taking the **GMAT CAT**, by practicing it here in these sample questions it will be easier for you to enter your stride during the actual test.

**DIRECTIONS:** Each passage in this group is followed by questions based on its content. After reading a passage, choose the best answer to each question and blacken the corresponding space on the answer sheet. Answer all questions following a passage on the basis of what is <u>stated</u> or <u>implied</u> in that passage.

**Passage 1:**

One of the truest tests of a free country is how it treats those whose job it is to defend the guilty and the despised. In most repressive countries there is no independent defense bar. Indeed, a sure sign that repression is on the way is when the government goes after the defense attorneys. Shakespeare said, "The first thing we do, let's kill all the lawyers." Hitler, Stalin, the Greek Colonels, and the Chinese Cultural Revolutionaries may not have killed all the lawyers first, but they surely placed defense attorneys - especially vigorous and independent ones - high on their hit lists.

One of the surest ways of undercutting the independence of defense attorneys is to question the propriety of their representing the guilty. Those who argue that defense attorneys should limit their representation to the innocent, or indeed to any specific group or category, open the door to a system where the government decides who is, and who is not, entitled to a defense. Granting that power to the government, to the bar, or to any establishment, marks the beginning of the end of an independent defense bar - and the beginning of the end of liberty.

The role of the defense attorney who defends guilty clients is the hardest role in the criminal justice system to explain to the public. In 1980 I traveled to China to advise the People's Republic on its criminal justice system. Most Chinese lawyers seemed to understand the need for free and independent judges and prosecutors. But hardly anyone - even those lawyers who had suffered most under the Cultural Revolution - seemed willing to justify the actions of a defense attorney representing a client whom he knew to be guilty and "counterrevolutionary." (Every society has its own favorite epithets for those it most despises.) "Why should our government pay someone to stand in the way of socialist justice?" was the question I was most often asked. I tried to explain that justice - whether socialist, capitalist, or anything else - is a process, not only an end; and that for the process to operate fairly, all persons charged with a crime must have a right to a defense. Since not all defendants are created equally in their ability to speak effectively, think logically, and argue forcefully, the role of a defense attorney - trained in these and other skills - is to perform those functions for the defendant. The process of determining whether a defendant should be deemed guilty and punished requires that the government be put to its proof and that the accused have a fair opportunity to defend.

To me the most persuasive argument for defending the guilty and the despised is to consider the alternative. Those governments that forbid or discourage such representation have little to teach us about justice. Their systems are far more corrupt, less fair, and generally even less efficient than ours. What Winston Churchill once said about democracy can probably also be said about the adversary system of criminal justice: It may well be the worst system of justice, "except [for] all the other [systems] that have been tried from time to time."

1. The primary purpose of this passage is to

   (A) explain the need for defense attorneys
   (B) explain the democratic system of justice
   (C) argue the need to defend the innocent
   (D) argue the need to defend the guilty
   (E) defend the defense attorneys from excessive criticism

2. The purpose of the allusions to historical figures in lines 5 and 6 is to

   (A) show the author's familiarity with Shakespeare's works
   (B) remind the reader of the place in history occupied by these men
   (C) remind the reader of historical situations that were highly undesirable
   (D) argue against the philosophies of these men
   (E) show the author's familiarity with history

3. The author's tone is

(A) pessimistic
(B) highly indignant
(C) persuasive
(D) insulting
(E) indifferent

4. The author discusses his experiences in China in order to

(A) give an example of the difficulty of explaining the purpose of an independent defense bar
(B) show the extent of repression under Communist rule
(C) show his widespread travels and vast experience
(D) give another point of view about his topic to show that he is capable of understanding opposing viewpoints
(E) show the superiority of western thought and culture over eastern practices

5. According to the author the word "counterrevolutionary" in line 21 actually means

(A) a Chinese counter cultural revolutionary group
(B) those who caused the greatest suffering during the cultural revolution
(C) a person who is guilty of a crime
(D) an innocent person wrongly accused of a crime
(E) a person who is currently out of favor with Chinese society and is hated for being different

6. The author would agree with all of the following statements except

(A) defense lawyers must be free to defend the guilty as well as the innocent
(B) it is surprising that those who suffered the must from a lack of justice fail to realize the importance of defending the guilty
(C) the absence of defense attorneys will result in the government deciding who is guilty or innocent
(D) paying someone to defend the guilty stands in the way of socialist justice
(E) justice is not an end in itself

7. It can be inferred from the passage that defense lawyers are necessary because

(A) it is difficult to determine who is guilty or innocent on the basis of what an accused person might say on his own behalf
(B) defense lawyers find it difficult to defend the guilty but they do it to preserve the system
(C) governments should be made to pay lawyers for their defense of the guilty
(D) those who suffered under the Cultural Revolution are probably afraid to speak out in defense of others
(E) it is sometimes necessary to use the system of justice unfairly in order to bring about a desired end.

8. According to the passage, it is the purpose of government to

(A) teach other nations about the system of justice
(B) prove a person's guilt
(C) represent all the accused in an effective, logical and forceful manner
(D) provide alternatives for the guilty and the despised
(E) determine who is and who is not entitled to a defense

9. The quote from Winston Churchill is a fitting conclusion for this passage because

(A) it shows that there is little else that can be said about justice
(B) it acknowledges that our system has flaws which makes the author seem less rigid in his views
(C) it leaves it up to the reader to decide which system of justce is really the worst
(D) it invites the reader to study the topic in greater depth
(E) it leaves no doubt in the reader's mind about which system of justice the author feels is superior to all others

1870

**Passage 2:**

Until the advent of realistic styles and techniques, the nineteenth-century stage was a flimsy anachronism, made tolerable by some brilliant virtuoso acting. Up to the eighteen-seventies, most of the plays clung to the conventions of a decadent romanticism, even when they dealt with contemporary characters and problems. Alert and earnest men of the theater could not fail to realize that a wide rift had occurred between these conventions and the realities of the nineteenth century. It was time to end the cleavage, as John Mason Brown has said, "between the grotesque and the commonplace, the picturesque and the factual, the Gothic revival and the scientific spirit, the cloak and swords of yesteryear and the slums of today." The novelists were already facing the modern world, as anyone could see in the work of such masters as Balzac, Flaubert, and Tolstoy. The dramatists could not trail behind them any longer.

Adapting the drama to reality was more difficult than attuning the novel to modern times, because a playwright is dependent upon the stage for which he is writing. And the stage held on to antiquated styles of production. Its stock scenery represented the vested interests of playhouse proprietors, and the acting profession would not willingly, and could not easily, unlearn lifetime habits of theatrical declamation and ostentatious performance. Dramaturgy, moreover, presents more intricate problems than narrative art. No matter how strongly the playwright tries to make his play conform to life, he has to provide effective entrances and exits, convincing time-covering scenes, and act endings that will bring the audience back into the theater after the intermissions. He must also telescope events that the novelist would present in separate chapters, and intermingle characters whom a novelist would keep separate. Kitty and Anna, for example, can live apart for long periods in Tolstoy's Anna Karenina and still belong to the same book, whereas a stage version in which their lives merely ran parallel to each other would disintegrate and fail to sustain interest. In truth, the dramatist had, and still has, a hard time of it whenever he tries to realize standards of absolute realism. Nevertheless, playwrights began to infuse their work with the breath of life and to give their art a greater degree of verisimilitude than earlier dramatists had attained or considered necessary.

From their effort to approximate reality, moreover, the drama acquired more or less special attributes, and these are of signal importance in differentiating the modern realistic play from the dramatic work of previous ages. Not even the casual reader or playgoer can overlook the emphatic contrasts between plays written for the realistic stage and those written for the romantic theater of Schiller and Goethe, for the Renaissance theater of Shakespeare and Lope de Vega, or for the classic theater of Sophicles and Euripides.

10. Which of the following would be the most appropriate title for this passage?

(A) Problems of the Art of Drama
(B) Birth of a New Art Form
(C) The Theater - A Difficult Art Form
(D) The Transition of Drama from the Romantic to the Realstic
(E) Plays and Realism

11. According to the passage, one of the only things that saved the nineteenth century theater was

(A) the introduction of contemporary characters and problems
(B) alert and earnest men of the theater
(C) flimsy anachronisms
(D) experienced players
(E) dedicated members of the audience

12. The author of this passage is probably a

(A) theater critic
(B) playwriter
(C) actor
(D) member of the audience
(E) novelist

13. The author's attitude towards the nineteenth century stage can best be described as

(A) sympathetic
(B) disinterested
(C) deferential
(D) disappointed
(E) disdainful

14. All of the following were problems in adapting drama to the age of realism except

(A) props that belonged to the owners of the theaters
(B) providing entrances and exits
(C) actors who refused to change their techniques
(D) shortening the time intervals between events
(E) adapting novelists characters, like Anna Karenina, to the stage

15. Balzac, Flaubert and Tolstoy were all of the following except

(A) realistic writers
(B) predecessors of the realistic dramatists
(C) acknowledged craftsmen in their field
(D) writers of the gothic revival and the slums of today
(E) aware of the modern world

16. According to the passage, it is much more difficult to achieve realism in drama than to achieve realism in novels because

(A) novels were able to concentrate on problems of the modern age that would bore playgoers
(B) characters that can lead parallel story lives in a novel would have to appear on the stage simultaneously to sustain audience interest
(C) standards of absolute realism are higher for drama
(D) audiences often do not return to a play after intermission
(E) realism was not considered necessary by dramatists

17. The word "versimilitude" in line 28 means

(A) realism in drama
(B) a "breath of life" for drama
(C) parallelism in drama
(D) time covering scenes in drama
(E) absolute standards in drama

18. The author takes for granted that his audience

(A) will agree with him
(B) will be able to appreciate the differences between the periods of drama
(C) is familiar with the writers Schiller and Goethe
(D) enjoys the works he is discussing
(E) are sophisticated theater goers

**Passage 3:**

A new concept is emerging in the realm of foreign policy: "managed trade." At one time this philosophical perspective was strictly reserved for hard-liners. However, many moderate business people are monitoring and adjusting their views in the interest of a more balanced trade arrangement for America.

Basically, "managed trade" sets a specific amount of imports a nation targets as appropriate. "Free" or "open" trade allows competitive elements to dictate amounts. Recently, the Japanese system has truly overwhelmed the U.S. market. This "controlled" action plan would necessitate concessions from this Far Eastern magnate.

This managed approach would ultimately discourage discrimination against foreign goods by Japan. Presently, the Japanese system is fundamentally different from the American; it relies on negotiated results, rather than market forces to improve the trade balance. Since the deficit of the United States has severely increased in relation to it's imports vs. exports, a more feasible solution to offset this disparity is imperative.

This procedure would entail a process approach to foreign trade equality. Initially, any country that discriminates against foreign goods would be forced to buy a specific amount of imports. The total would rise each year until a target is met. If a country failed to meet this standard, the United States would retaliate by limiting the offender's exports to America.

The second phase would focus on specific industries or market items. The United States would specify Japan purchase particular goods. This practice would not only benefit the overall situation, but also especially enhance the selling of commodities targeted for this purpose. A fairer rate of trade and distribution of products would result.

A third stage calls for "strict reciprocity." If a country delays in the purchasing or the issuing of contracts for items, the United States responds with the same procedures of rebuke. Without a give-and-take arrangement, the trade industry would prohibit further imports until equitable distribution across the board was achieved.

Opponents of this "managed trade" plan (proponents of free, or open trade) quickly cite the disadvantages of this process. They immediately warn these controlled practices could cause overall world trade to shrink. Furthermore, dissenters convey the feeling that prices in "managed" industries and commodities would rise. Another disadvantage in this negative mode is governments would tend to dictate what people can buy and sell. Trade wars may result in complete chaos and price instability. Cohorts of "free trade" also feel the United States should upgrade its productive elements to attain quality appraisal in world trade.

As this controversy intensifies, members of each group are seeking aspects of compromise. The Advisory Committee for Trade Policy and Negotiations has proposed a "results oriented trade strategy." The United States under this concept would identify and ultimately select, situations and sectors where competitive actions are possible. Then, United States' representatives would negotiate goals for a reasonable percentage of goods that Japan would be expected to import.

As the chasm between cohorts of "managed" and "open" trade widens, it is obvious some practical and necessary concessions must be made by each group. While these tactics of "management" could create a bureaucratic nightmare, some reform must occur with some realistic format. "Free traders" must realize "open" arrangements are not working now, and the future looks even bleaker for the United States. Additionally, Japan already responds positively to European pressures of this type. The Japanese trade industry constantly yields to demands of this type to settle disputes. Precedents from the Common Market, South Korea and other business adjustments have been established. Whatever, this "managed" approach deserves a long, hard look before dismissal as a pragmatic solution.

19. The primary purpose of the passage is to:

(A) explain Japan's dominance over the world's trade markets
(B) compare and contrast "managed trade" and "free trade"
(C) persuade the reader to change his/her mind about "managed trade"
(D) describe the process, advantages and disadvantages of "managed trade"
(E) provide guidelines and criteria for "negotiated trade"

20. The tone of the passage could best be described as:

(A) ambivalent
(B) pedagogical
(C) argumentative
(D) chauvinistic
(E) satirical

21. According to the passage, the second phase of "managed trade" would be:

(A) to force the nation to buy a specific amount of American goods
(B) to identify specific industries
(C) to call for "strict reciprocity"
(D) to prohibit further imports
(E) to achieve equitable distribution

22. The author mentions that the reason behind this directive, "managed trade", would be to:

(A) adjust business leaders' views
(B) change the hard-liners minds and actions
(C) achieve a more balanced trade situation for the United States
(D) force business people to utilize a process approach to trade negotiations
(E) overcome Japan as the world's greatest exporter

23. The term "negotiated results" (line 11) can best be interpreted as meaning that:

(A) parameters are rigidly set in relation to the amount of imports
(B) this practice would encompass a process approach
(C) elements of retaliation would be arranged for designated infractions of trading
(D) the Advisory Committee for Trade Policy and Negotiations would dictate and control contract items
(E) trade discussions would be openly arranged and settled in relation to need and quality of contract items

24. It can be inferred the major difference between "managed" and "open" trade is:

(A) a consortium overrules price guidelines in open practices
(B) each country must arrange for amounts exchanged
(C) specified limits are established to enhance productive concerns
(D) Japan would predominate perspectives of discussion and procedure
(E) meaningful strategies are utilized in "controlled" vs. "free" trade

25. It can be inferred from the passage's context, unless concessions are made by each side:

(A) Japan's trade advantage would diminish
(B) experts will take over the adjustments of world trade
(C) the deficit of imports for the United States would intensify and worsen
(D) the Advisory Committee for Trade Policy will override the actions and process of world trade
(E) the Common Market will overtake Japan as the leader in the trade

## Answers for Sample Test Questions for Reading Comprehension

1. D The opening paragraph and the concluding paragraph both deal with the need to defend the guilty. This idea is fully developed in the body of the passage as well. All other ideas are only mentioned in one place in the passage.

2. C The author wants the reader to see what the alternatives to defending the guilty can be. Using an allusion to historical situations that most people find highly undesirable helps him make his point.

3. C The author is trying to persuade the reader that his ideas are the only sensible ones. He is not pessimistic because he believes his system is a good one; he is not indignant, which would mean that he is annoyed and insulted by the audience; he is not insulting his audience since this would defeat his purpose; he is passionate about his topic and cannot be called indifferent.

4. A The author is trying to convince the reader of the benefit of an independent defense bar. He knows that even readers in western cultures have difficulty accepting the idea of defending the guilty, so he used an example from another culture to make his point.

5. E The words in the parenthesis following the word "counterrevolutionary" explain what the author means by that term.

6. D Each of the other answers are specifically mentioned in the passage. This is a negative specific fact question.

7. A Lines 26-29 explain this answer quite clearly. The use of the word "infer" in the question does not preclude the possibility that the answer may be stated somewhere in the passage specifically.

8. B This is a specific fact question and the answer can be found in line 30.

9. E Although answers A, B, and D are partially correct, answer E encompasses the author's philosophy completely and the quote is a perfect summary of that philosophy.

10. D The opening sentence of the passage states specifically that the passage is about the transition from romanticism to realism in the theater. The rest of the passage deals with the difficulties of the transition.

11. D This is a specific fact question and the answer can be found in line 2. Virtuoso acting is the same as experienced players.

12. A The author makes it clear that he is knowledgeable about the theater both in the past and in the present. The purpose of this passage is to inform the reader about the changes in drama from the viewpoint of one who is able to view all aspects of the theater. This is the job of a critic rather than a novelist, playwright, or actor. A member of the audience may be that well informed, but a critic is a better choice.

13. E The author uses words such as flimsy anachronism and decadent romanticism; he makes statements such as, "dramatists could not trail behind them [novelists] any longer." He is quite scornful of the nineteenth century stage. He becomes sympathetic later in the passage when discussing the difficulties involved in making the changes necessary to bring the stage up to date, but his sympathy is only with

the dramatists who dare to change, not with those who maintained the conventions of the past.

14. E — Anna Karenina is mentioned, but not as a problem in adapting her role to the stage.

15. D — This is a specific fact question. The author placed <u>gothic revivals</u> and <u>slums of today</u> in the same sentence to show the contrast between the two. The novelists were ahead of the playwrights and, therefore, were beyond the gothic revivals.

16. B — In lines 20-22 this specific fact question is answered quite clearly.

17. A — In lines 25 and 26 the author explains the difficulty in attaining realism. In lines 27-29 he states that despite the difficulties, strides were make toward achieving versimilitude, which must, therefore, be a synonym for realism. This is a supplied definition.

18. C — In lines 32-33 the author states that "Not even the casual reader or playgoer can overlook the emphatic contrasts between... of Schiller and Goethe..." as if even those less informed would be aware of these writers.

19. D — The major rationale of the writer is to depict the phases of this perspective. This is the central <u>focus</u> of the article. Benefits and detractions are covered.

20. C — The author basically is presenting many viewpoints in this area.

21. B — This is a supporting detail presented explicitly in the passage (line 19).

22. C — The author specifically conveys this element. The rationale is depicted quite clearly. We can effectively scan the passage for this choice.

23. E — This meaning can be discerned through the use of context clues. We must identify key terms to clarify definition and purpose.

24. B — Through the author's suggestions, hints and implications in the context of the passage, we can select this choice. Please refer to paragraphs five and six.

25. C — Through the overall comprehension of literal and inferential aspects, this is the best choice. Please refer especially, to the final, summary paragraph.

# CRITICAL REASONING

The critical reasoning section of the **GMAT** examination tests your ability to reason in a logical manner. This section of the test was added to the **GMAT** examination in 1988 and replaces what had been called Analysis of Situations - Practical Business Judgment. This newer version covers a more general approach to reasoning in a logical manner than the previous test. As in the Reading Comprehension section of the test, the topics may be drawn from literature and the arts, the social sciences, the physical sciences, and business situations, although most questions are based on the final category.

This section of the test contains twenty questions, which must be answered in thirty minutes. You have slightly more than one minute per question. Some examinees feel that the questions increase in difficulty from first to last; therefore, you may wish to pace yourself accordingly, reserving more time for the difficult questions at the end.

Each question is comprised of a short passage of from three sentences to two paragraphs followed by a question with five possible answer choices.

Each of the questions in this section requires that you examine the situations presented and analyze the data for the accuracy and reliability of the conclusions that have been drawn from that data. The arguments presented may or may not be logical and the conclusions drawn from those arguments may or may not be valid. You do not need to have specific knowledge about the topics presented. You are only required to determine whether the conclusions follow logically from the statements given. The correctness of the arguments presented depends on the form of the argument, including valid and invalid premises, hidden premises, and correct formation of the conclusions.

## TYPES OF ARGUMENTS - DEDUCTIVE REASONING

Although it is not necessary to be trained in formal logic, some understanding of the basis of argument construction is helpful.

For example, it is **VALID** to make the following argument:

All men are mortal.

John is a man.

John is mortal.

It is not necessary for you to determine the accuracy of the statement that all men are mortal. This is a **PREMISE** that is given and you may accept it as true. You may also accept as true that John is a man. This is another **PREMISE**. It is your job to determine whether or not the **CONCLUSION** drawn from the statements is **VALID**. This argument is an example of deductive reasoning. The conclusion is a necessary consequence of the premises. If the premises are true, it is impossible for the conclusion to be false.

The preceding example is the most common type of argument form in deductive logic - the **syllogism**. A syllogism consists of two premises and a conclusion that can take the following forms: all A is B, some A is B, some A is not B, and no A is B. Aristotle developed six rules which govern syllogisms and his format has remained unchanged. These six rules are:

1) A syllogism must have exactly three terms. If any of these terms are ambiguous or open to other interpretations, then the syllogism is not valid. For example:

All fruits require earth and water to grow. Good deeds bear fruit. The fruits of good deeds require earth and water to grow.

The word fruit is ambiguous; therefore, this syllogism is invalid.

2) Two negative premises yield no conclusion. For example:

Blondes do not have more fun. Mary is not a blonde.

No conclusion can be drawn from these two premises.

3) Two positive premises always yield a positive conclusion. For example:

Blondes have more fun. Mary is a blonde. Mary has more fun.

This is a valid argument.

4) A positive and a negative premise can only yield a negative conclusion. For example:

All Martians have red hair. John does not have red hair. John is not a Martian.

This is a valid argument.

5) The words all or none must modify one of the terms that occurs in both premises. For example:

All Acme products are guaranteed unconditionally for one year. Mary's toaster is an Acme product. Mary's toaster is guaranteed for one year.

This is a valid argument because Acme product appears in both premises and is modified by the word all.

6) A term that appears in the conclusion modified by the word all or none must be modified by the word all or none in the premises. For example:

Students John, Martin, Alex, Mary, and Jane wrote letters to the president. All letters to the president are answered personally. All of the letters sent by the five students were answered personally.

This is a valid argument because the word all appears in both the premise and the conclusion.

Applying these rules to the arguments you encounter on the **GMAT** test will enable you to make immediate eliminations of incorrect answers to questions based on deductive reasoning. In addition, you may be able to discern faulty reasoning and invalid premises in other types of logic questions as well. Three additional rules will help you to recognize other valid deductive reasoning arguments. They are:

1) If the first premise implies the second premise and the second premise implies the third premise, then the first premise will also imply the third premise. For example:

If "The ice has melted" implies "The rivers are open" and if "The rivers are open" implies "Navigation can resume," then "The ice has melted" implies "Navigation can resume."

2) If the first premise implies the second premise and we can prove that the first premise is true, then the second premise is automatically true. For example:

The statement that 10 is an even number implies that 10 can be divided by 2. If we KNOW that 10 is an even number, then we can assert that 10 is divisible by 2.

3) If the first statement implies the second statement, and we can show that the second statement is false, then we know that the first statement is false also. For example:

> "This is the year 2001" implies that last year was 2000. If we can prove that last year was not 2000, then we know that this year is not 2001.

## PREMISE VS. CONCLUSION

Deductive reasoning is, perhaps, the simplest form of logical reasoning. The statements must follow a pattern and the pattern, if followed correctly, must yield the correct conclusion. It is important, however, to be able to differentiate between the premises of an argument and the conclusion of that argument. There are certain cue words that delineate which statements are the premises and which statements form the conclusions. The conclusion of an argument need not come after the premises. For example, the first example of a valid argument we used was:

> All men are mortals. John is a man. John is mortal.

This argument could have been written in the following ways:

> All men are mortals and John is a man; therefore, John is mortal.
>
> or
>
> John is mortal because all men are mortals and John is a man.
>
> or
>
> All men are mortals and John is mortal because John is a man.

In each of these examples the conclusion, "John is mortal," appears in a different place. The conclusion did not change, only its position in the argument. In each case different words signaled which statements were premises and which statements were conclusions. The following lists may be helpful in identifying which statements are which.

| Words used to signal a conclusion: | Words used to signal the premises: |
|---|---|
| therefore | since |
| it appears that | because |
| it can be inferred | in so far as |
| it seems that | as much as |
| it follows that | for |
| which means that | |
| which shows that | |
| which suggests that | |
| which proves that | |
| consequently | |
| so | |
| hence | |
| thus | |
| therefore | |
| resulting in | |

## PRACTICE PROBLEMS - PREMISE VS. CONCLUSION

The following sentences contain premises and conclusions. See if you can identify which parts of each are the premises and which part is the conclusion.

1. Only seniors are allowed on the class trip. I saw Ann on the class trip; therefore, Ann must be a senior.

2. Jeremy is a fine doctor because really good doctors have the ability to diagnose a patient using more than just laboratory tests. Jeremy is able to diagnose his patients even when the laboratory tests are inconclusive.

3. Every time it rains my shoulder aches from my old war wound. Rain is predicted for tomorrow so I guess I'm in for some shoulder pain.

4. Mary will be elected president of the garden club at the next election because the president of the garden club must have been a member of the club for at least five years and only Mary has been a member for five years.

5. I received a traffic ticket for making an improper right turn on a red light at 6:04 p.m. This ticket should not have been issued since right turns are allowed after 6:00 p.m.

6. This year the million dollar sales club of the Jones Marketing firm will hold its meeting in Bermuda as an incentive to inspire the sales representatives to earn membership in this club. It appears that Mary will be going to Bermuda this year because she finally sold enough products to join the club.

7. The Japanese have very rigid price protection tariffs on food imports and other products which America produces and exports to other countries. Our balance of trade with the Japanese is a serious drain on the American economy because America allows many more products to be imported than those we export.

8. Many of our children are seriously overweight and out of shape because local school boards do not always mandate proper diet and exercise programs for our school children.

9. Overwashing hair can cause it to become dry and difficult to manage. I have been overwashing my hair and thus it is dry and difficult.

10. Our team has lost so many football games and the school budget has been cut drastically; consequently, this results in the cutting of the football team.

## ANSWERS - PREMISE VS. CONCLUSION

The premises are contained in the brackets, [], and the conclusion is contained between the parenthesis, ().

1. [Only seniors are allowed on the class trip.] [I saw Ann on the class trip;] therefore, (Ann must be a senior.)

2. (Jeremy is a fine doctor) because [really good doctors have the ability to diagnose a patient using more than just laboratory tests.] [Jeremy is able to diagnose his patients even when the laboratory tests are inconclusive.]

3. [Every time it rains my shoulder aches from my old war wound.] [Rain is predicted for tomorrow] so (I guess I'm in for some shoulder pain.)

4. (Mary will be elected president of the garden club at the next election) because [the president of the garden club must have been a member of the club for at least five years] and [only Mary has been a member for five years.]

5. [I received a traffic ticket for making an improper right turn on a red light at 6:04 p.m.] (This ticket should not have been issued) since [right turns are allowed after 6:00 p.m.]

6. [This year the million dollar sales club of the Jones Marketing firm will hold its meeting in Bermuda] as an incentive to inspire the sales representatives to earn

membership in this club. It appears that (Mary will be going to Bermuda this year) because [she finally sold enough products to join the club.]

7. [The Japanese have very rigid price protection tariffs on food imports and other products which America produces and exports to other countries.] (Our balance of trade with the Japanese is a serious drain on the American economy) because [America allows many more products to be imported than those we export.]

8. (Many of our children are seriously overweight and out of shape) because [local school boards do not always mandate proper diet and exercise programs for our school children.]

9. [Overwashing hair can cause it to become dry and difficult to manage.] [I have been overwashing my hair] and thus (it is dry and difficult.)

10. [Our team has lost so many football games] and [the school budget has been cut drastically]; consequently, (this results in the cutting of the football team.)

## THE HIDDEN PREMISE

In the ten examples above, it is easy to determine the premises and then to determine if the conclusion follows logically from the premises. However, in many circumstances, there are hidden premises, or ***implied*** premises that must be filled in to make the conclusion valid. For example:

> Mary is able to reach both high and low notes with great ease. Her range is amazing. Mary is the best singer in the class.

When this argument is examined, it is evident that a part of the argument is missing. There is an implicit or implied premise on which the conclusion is based.

**Premise** (explicit or stated) - Mary is able to reach both high and low notes with ease. Her range is amazing.

**Premise** (implied or implicit) - Range determines the value of a singer's voice.

**Conclusion** - Mary is the best singer in the class.

As is evident from this example, when the hidden premise is examined, there are difficulties with the argument. Another argument can be made using a different set of premises, both stated (explicit) and implied (implicit). For example:

> I beg to differ with you. Jane is the best singer in the class. Her voice has strength and clarity at the same time.

Here the breakdown of the argument would look like this:

**Premise** (Stated or explicit) - Jane's voice has strength and clarity at the same time.

**Premise** (implicit or implied) Strength and clarity determine the value of a singer's voice.

**Conclusion** - Jane is the best singer in the class.

Because the two arguments are using different sets of premises and one of the hidden premises excludes the possibility of the other, there is no possibility of arriving at a conclusion that is valid according to both sets of premises.

Although in this example the hidden premise made the argument invalid, this is not necessarily the case in all situations. Many times the hidden premise is valid and the argument produces a valid conclusion. The important thing to remember when dealing with hidden premises is that they exist and they must be considered as part of the argument.

It is important to be able to determine the hidden premise because, on the **GMAT** examination, some questions specifically ask what assumptions the argument makes. This is the same as asking what the hidden premise might be. At this point it may be helpful to practice the following exercises.

## PRACTICE PROBLEMS - HIDDEN PREMISE

Find the hidden premise in the following arguments.

1. Ted O'Brien cheated on his exams at Harvard. Ted O'Brien is an immoral man.
2. John Smith is a fabulous soccer player. John will have no trouble getting into a good college.
3. April 15th is the present deadline for filing one's income tax. If the deadline were extended to April 30th, most people would file their taxes on midnight of April 30th.
4. The present speed limit on most New Jersey roads is 55 m.p.h. If the speed limit were changed to 65 m.p.h., more cars would travel at 70 and 75 m.p.h.
5. There are many drugs that are not available to the public. If the FDA would release these drugs, it would be possible to save many lives.
6. John finished his **GMAT** preparation class the day before the test took place. If John had completed an earlier course or taken a later exam, he would have received a higher score on the test.
7. Mary Smith has tremendous sex appeal. She will rise very quickly in this company.
8. Mary Elizabeth woke up late; therefore, she had a headache all morning at work because she was hungry.
9. Many driving accidents occur when there is a full moon. It will be unsafe to drive two days from now.
10. When a salesperson breaks a company record, he is rewarded with a new car. John is presently shopping around to determine which car he wants as his prize.

## ANSWERS - HIDDEN PREMISE PROBLEMS

1. Cheating on exams is immoral.
2. Good soccer players have no trouble getting into good colleges.
3. Most people wait until midnight of April 15th to file their income taxes.
4. Most people travel five or ten miles over the speed limit.
5. The drugs that are still unavailable to the public have the ability to save lives.
6. If John had more time, he would have studied or absorbed the information he just received in a more advantageous manner.
7. Sex appeal is an important quality in rising up quickly in this company.
8. Waking up late prevented Mary Elizabeth from eating before going to work.
9. In two days from now the moon will be full.
10. John has either broken a company sales record or believes he is about to break a company sales record.

The ability to determine the hidden premise is important in those questions which ask you to strengthen or weaken the argument. These are sometimes difficult questions because the hidden premise may be difficult to locate or it may not be obvious that there is an assumption based on a hidden premise in the argument. Premises may not be intentionally hidden merely as a trick question, but because some truths are generally accepted and the writer may not feel that it is necessary to state each step of his argument. For example, in the first example, it may be taken for granted in a certain audience that all persons would acknowledge that cheating is immoral and it would not be necessary for the writer or speaker to make this a formal part of his argument.

## INDUCTIVE REASONING

Inductive reasoning differs from deductive reasoning in that the process of deduction proves with certainty that a conclusion is valid if the given premises are true. Inductive reasoning questions the truth of the premises, the authority of the premises or the grounds for the beliefs. Inductive reasoning yields **probable** conclusions, as opposed to **certain** conclusions.

Grounds for belief may be based on generalizations, analogies, or causal connections.

A person may observe that the sun rises and sets at a certain difference in time each day and may, therefore, **infer** that the sun will rise and set with this same certainty and time difference for the next few days, weeks, months, or years. This is a **generalization**. A generalization is a principle that makes an inference or assertion about a whole class of objects or continuance of events based on specific observations.

A person may observe that Jane and Mary are both good swimmers. Jane is also a good tennis player. It is possible to argue that Mary is probably a good tennis player, too, since both girls share similar athletic characteristics. This would be an **analogy** - the comparison of two or more subjects that share similar characteristics.

This same tennis player, Jane, may notice that when she serves a ball with overhand topspin, she gets a pain in her shoulder. It is logical, then, for Jane to assume, or draw the conclusion, that putting topspin on her serves causes her pain in her shoulder. This is arguing from **cause and effect**.

Many questions on the **GMAT** examination deal with **inductive** reasoning because this allows the examinee to display more sophisticated critical reasoning skills than deductive logic alone. These skills require the use of many of the reading comprehension techniques discussed in the first section of this review.

Both deductive and inductive reasoning are important techniques in determining the accuracy of a conclusion and neither is more or less important than the other. Both methods are used to compliment each other and sometimes serve different purposes.

To summarize, there are three areas of inductive reasoning that we will be dealing with as we discuss possible questions on the **GMAT** examination:

1. Generalization
2. Analogy
3. Cause and Effect

## GENERALIZATION

As mentioned previously, inductive reasoning makes use of different criteria for determining the validity of the premises used in forming a logical argument than does deductive reasoning. In fact, it is not the function of deductive reasoning to examine the validity of a premise at all. The premises are given and if the argument is developed properly, a conclusion must follow. The purpose of inductive reasoning is to gather the data necessary to form the premises in the first place.

One method of forming a premise deals with collecting specific examples and then applying a general rule to the collection of examples. For example, in a supermarket a food tester may ask 50 people to taste a particular type of cereal and give their opinions on that brand. When the data is collected and analyzed, generalizations can be made. A premise then can be formed stating:

> Most people prefer the taste of Yummy cereal over other brands tested.

This may not necessarily be an untruth, but such statements can be manipulated to suit the purposes of the speaker. Whether most means 26 people as opposed to 24, or, if several different cereals were used, 11 people as opposed to 10, 10, 10, and 9, the listener has no way to judge.

Even generalizations using specific figures can be misleading. For example:

> Nine out of ten dentists recommend sugarless gum for their patients who chew gum.

It is not apparent how many dentists were surveyed, or if those dentists who were surveyed are against chewing gum under any circumstances, but find sugarless gum to be less harmful than regular gum.

Questions on the **GMAT** examination that might be concerned with generalizations are those which ask you to strengthen or weaken the argument. If a premise is less than convincing, additional facts would be needed to strengthen the argument. If you wish to weaken the argument, you must find the flaw in the premise.

Try the following example:

> A recent survey of families in district five of the town of Plainville showed that almost all families consider liberal spending by one of the parties a cause of spiraling inflation. Although certain social programs were deemed necessary, it was felt that spending in general should be curbed. This is a message that should be heeded by the party.

Which of the following statements would strengthen the above argument?

(A) The town of Plainville is suffering disproportionately greater from the recession that has swept the nation than other towns of similar size.

(B) Many of the people in the town of Plainville are receiving assistance from those social programs established by the offending party.

(C) District five is a cross-section of people representing most of the socio-economic groups who live in Plainville.

(D) District five is the largest voting district in the town of Plainville.

(E) The offending party is known for over-spending and must make adjustments if it wants to remain in power.

The correct answer is (C). There is an assumption or hidden premise in this statement that what the people of district five say has great validity. This is a generalization, generalizing from one district to all of the districts. In order to strengthen that hidden assumption and give clout to the generalization that as district five goes, so goes the town, district five must represent all the people of the town.

Although (A) sounds as if the people of Plainville need some inflationary relief, it is unclear whether this relief should be bought by cutting government spending or increasing it. (B) would actually weaken any argument to cut government spending since most of the people of the town are dependent on it. Although (D) states that there are more people in district five than in any other district, it is possible that district five could be an anomaly in Plainville, a district socially and economically different from the other districts in the town. In this case, the other districts combined could out-vote district five.

In addition to strengthening the argument, you should be able to pick out the flaw in a generalization that would weaken the argument.

Try the following example:

> Last season the television sitcom "One Life, One Wife" received over 52% of the ratings in the Thursday, 8:30 p.m. slot using the Ralston rating system. It is hoped that ratings will improve significantly this year since the biggest ratings rival, "Family Frolics," with 36% of the audience, will be moving to the Wednesday, 8:00 p.m. time slot. Since both programs are considered family viewing, there is a good chance that "One Life, One Wife" will pick up a good portion of the audience that had watched "Family Frolics." The marketing company, The Valerie Mac Agency, that solicits advertising for "One Life, One Wife", is highlighting this fact in all of its negotiations with prospective advertisers.

Which factor would most seriously weaken the position of The Valerie Mac Agency?

(A) One of the secondary actors in the sitcom, "One Life, One Wife" is not returning to the show next season.

(B) The Valerie Mac Agency has been asked to represent "Family Frolics" this season.

(C) 52% of the ratings is already quite high. It is unlikely that advertisers would care about a larger audience.

(D) A sports commentary will be taking the place of "Family Frolics" opposite "One Life, One Wife."

(E) The Ralston rating system surveyed a small suburban sample and the ratings listed above are for November 21st, which happened to be Thanksgiving night.

Although (A) might hurt the show, it is unlikely that changing a secondary actor would have enough of an impact on a popular show to seriously reduce its audience ratings, thereby affecting its advertisers. Although (B) might be a conflict of interest for the Valerie Mac Agency, since the two shows are going to be on different nights, this conflict should not make too much of a difference in the Agency's representation of "One Life, One Wife." It seems unlikely that (C) would be much of a worry for the Agency. The Agency would still be negotiating from a position of strength. It is also unlikely that (D) would be much of a problem since the two programs are aimed at different audiences; this might actually strengthen the agency's position since the 36% audience rating for "Family Frolics" is a family sitcom oriented audience.

The correct answer is (E) because if the sample taken by the Ralston Rating system is **NOT** representative, the Valerie Mac Agency's entire premise falls apart. The most important aspect of the agency's argument is that a large number of people are watching the show; therefore, advertising time reaches a large audience. The agency's argument is weakened if the area surveyed, a suburb, is not representative of urban and rural populations. Also, since Thanksgiving is a family holiday, more family viewers might be inclined to watch t.v. together than would normally be the case on a regular weeknight. This would also affect the results of the survey. A <u>generalization</u> must be significantly representational to be valid.

## ANALOGY

When an argument is based on an analogy, it is important to be certain that the analogy is valid and that the items being compared do have validity. In some instances the analogy structure itself is the faulty premise in an argument. For example, Jane and Mary, our two athletes several pages ago, do share many common characteristics. Using inductive reasoning, one can *ASSUME* a *PROBABLE CONCLUSION.* This is a *VALID* argument construction. We get into trouble when we use an analogy or a comparison as a *DEFINATE* premise for drawing a conclusion. Jane and Mary are both good swimmers and Jane is also a good tennis player. It is acceptable to assume Mary is *PROBABLY* a good tennis player also, but we cannot make this a definite assertion. Using this analogy as a premise will cause a faulty argument and make a conclusion invalid. For example:

> Both Jane and Mary are good swimmers and Jane is a good tennis player as well. Mary is probably a good tennis player, too, so let's buy her a new tennis racquet cover for her birthday.

This is, of course, an extreme example. We are not even sure if Mary plays tennis or owns a racquet. We have carried the analogy too far and have based a conclusion on a very shaky premise.

However, analogies can be valid forms of arguing in the right circumstances and should not always be dismissed as invalid. For example:

> Mr. Smith was the school superintendent of two small school districts that regionalized with each other under his direction. Both schools had suburban, homogeneous populations of upper-middle income students whose parents were intensely involved in the merger. Mr. Smith managed to engineer this merger with great diplomacy and the merger was successfully completed despite the fact that the parents held very strong, and sometimes contradictory, views. Our districts are similar to the ones with which Mr. Smith was involved. Mr. Smith would be a good choice for superintendent for our districts if we wish to merge as successfully as the two districts he directed last year.

In this case the conclusion is valid because the analogy is valid. Evidently, the speaker is looking for a superintendent to direct the merger of two school districts. It is *LOGICAL* to look for someone who has experience that is similar or analogous to the job description that must be filled.

The following practice question is based on an analogous relationship.

> Last year, in an effort to increase holiday sales, the J.P. Smith Company used a variety of items as "lost leaders" to bring people into the store. Many of these items were sold at cost which caused a small loss for the store; however, it was felt that overall sales increased because of these items. This year, the buyers are suggesting that a similar program be used to increase this year's sales and they have already selected a number of items to be used as this year's leaders.

Which of the following statements, if true, would not weaken the position of the store's buyers on using "lost leaders" this year?

(A) Last year the items chosen as inducements were the "hot" items of the season; this year the buyers have selected more traditional items that are always available in the store.

(B) Last year the country was in a serious recession; this year the economy is recovering and consumer spending is up.

(C) Many of the buyers who promoted the program last year have left the store or are working in other jobs.

(D) The items chosen by the buyers will also be on sale in other stores at similar prices.

(E) Although the inducement items are very attractively priced this year, other prices have gone up considerably on non-sale merchandise in the store.

The correct answer is (C). The fact that different buyers are using the strategy that worked last year should make no difference in the success of the promotion. The similarity between the situations is still very convincing. Sell certain items cheaply and people will come into the store. Who selects the items or who is working in the store is not part of this argument. The buyers may have moved on because they were successful.

Answer (A) would weaken the buyers position because the inducement items are what attracted the buyers. Change the nature of the items and you change the similarity between the situations. (B) would also weaken the buyers' need to induce customers to come into the store.

If consumer spending is up, it may be too costly to take a loss on certain items; customers may spend more without inducements. The change in the economy changes the relationship between the two situations. (D) would seriously weaken the position of the buyers because there would be no reason for customers to shop in one store when another has the same merchandise equally inexpensively priced. (E) would also seriously weaken the buyers' position because customers may be smart enough to purchase the inducement items and leave the store if the higher prices turn them away.

This question is tricky because the question was phrased in a negative manner. All answers had to be rejected as negatively affecting the buyers' position before the correct answer could be chosen.

# CAUSE AND EFFECT

Arguments based on cause and effect argue that one factor brings about a result. For example: Ragweed makes Jim sneeze; Jim is sneezing. There must be ragweed in this area. The result, Jim's sneezing, may be attributable to ragweed in the area. This is a possible conclusion that may be drawn from the usual cause, ragweed. Or another example might be: Hamlet's Department Store gave a $50.00 discount certificate to every customer who spent $200.00 in one day. Sales were up 120% the day the certificates were given. The promotion evidently caused the increase in sales.

It is important NOT to consider as a *cause and effect* relationship things that happen sequentially. For example, company A changed managers in 1990 and profits have been up since that time. The change in managers may not have caused the increase in profits. These items may only be linked sequentially; first came the manager, then came the profits. The profits may be due to any number of factors exclusive of the competence or prowess of the new manager.

Try the following example of a faulty cause and effect type question.

> In an effort to bring more customers into the store during the holiday season when spending is the greatest, ShopBest supermarket offered a free holiday turkey to customers whose total bill exceeded $250.00 on any one shopping day in the seven days preceding Thanksgiving. The store manager felt that this program was a success because bills in excess of $250.00 were up over 37% during this promotion.

Which of the following statements, if true, would most seriously weaken the above argument?

(A) The cost of the turkeys cut into the profits gained by the promotion.

(B) After the holiday promotion, customers returned to their former supermarkets to shop.

(C) Some people who came into the store for the turkey promotion were dissatisfied with the size of the turkey they received.

(D) Many of the people who came just for the turkey promotion bought extra items that they would not normally have bought just to attain the $250.00 total.

(E) Many of the customers whose bills exceeded $250.00 during the turkey promotion were regular customers who would have spent that much anyway, but over a period of days instead of at one time. They simply saved all their shopping for one big trip.

The correct answer is (E). The premise is the store manager's desire to have more people spend large amounts of money just before the holiday. If the same people are simply redistributing their shopping dollars to get the free turkeys, no additional money would be realized.

(A) is incorrect because the cost of the turkeys must already have been considered and covered by the profit on $250.00 worth of groceries. (B) is incorrect because the purpose of the promotion as stated in the premise was simply to lure customers in during the peak spending period before the holiday. This was not a promotion aimed at long-term customer retention. (C) is extraneous information that neither strengthens or weakens the premise, although the store manager might not end up as popular as he had hoped! (D) is the desired goal of the store manager. This is exactly what he hoped to achieve and this would strengthen his position.

# CRITICAL REASONING PRACTICE PROBLEMS

1. There are six people at a breakfast table. The person with scrambled eggs and bacon is next to the person with scrambled eggs and ham. The person with cereal is next to the person with fruit and the person with fried eggs. The person with steak is across from the person with fried eggs and the person with fried eggs is next to the person with ham.

   Who sits beside the person with steak?

   (A) fruit and ham
   (B) fruit and cereal
   (C) bacon and fruit
   (D) fried egg and bacon
   (E) cereal and fried egg

2. The theory of evolution states that man and apes both arose from a common ancestor. Anyone who believes otherwise is obviously wrong.

   What is the major flaw in this author's argument?

   (A) There are many people who believe that men are not related to apes.
   (B) He is arguing a theory as a fact.
   (C) It goes against religious beliefs.
   (D) Man and apes do not even look alike.
   (E) Frogs and snakes also would have a common ancestor.

3. Genetic engineering is going to kill us all. If one of the experimental viruses or bacteria escape we will all die due to lack of immunity.

   Which of the following, if true, is the strongest argument against the author's statement?

   (A) New strains of viruses and bacteria occur all the time in nature.
   (B) The chances of an escape are small.
   (C) A vaccine would probably already have been made for the virus.
   (D) Most viruses and bacteria could not live outside the laboratory.
   (E) The potential benefits greatly outweigh the dangers.

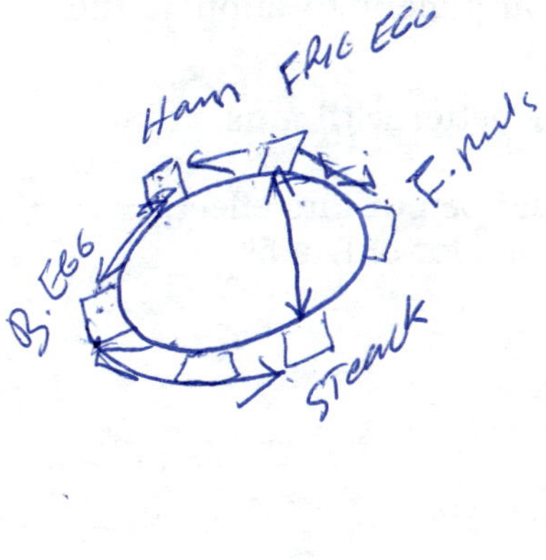

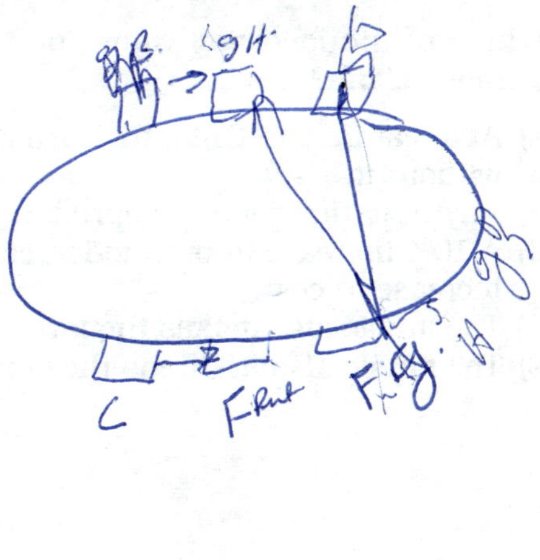

4. Putting lasers up in space could either be a dangerous escalation in the arms race or they could be a great defensive gain. What the cross bow did to the knight in shining armor, lasers could do to nuclear missiles. The threat of nuclear weapons could be eliminated.

The author would be most likely to agree with which of the following statements?

**I. Laser technology should be a major area of research.**

**II. Defensive weapons are better than offensive ones.**

**III. Nuclear weapons are here to stay.**

(A) I only
(B) II only
(C) I and II
(D) II and III
(E) I, II and III

5. Nuclear power is unsafe and should be eliminated. Even though a plant can operate for many years without causing any casualties, a minor accident can kill many people. How could anyone with a conscience sleep at night if even one person were harmed from nuclear power?

The above argument assumes which of the following?

**I. That people care if someone dies from nuclear power.**

**II. That alternative forms of power do not harm anyone.**

**III. That it will cost less to use nuclear power.**

(A) I only
(B) I and II only
(C) III only
(D) II and III
(E) I, II and III

6. Plants do not grow as well when they are yelled at. They also grow much better when classical music is played around them. Therefore, music should be played in cornfields around the country.

Which of the following would be the best argument to support the author's claim?

(A) At a test field in Ohio, the corn grew 10% better with music than without it.
(B) Anything that increases production should be put into effect.
(C) A 10% increase in production can be gained for only a 5% increase in cost.
(D) The music also makes the farmers work better.
(E) The music also frightens the crows.

7. I hate to fly on airlines because once you are in the air you are not in control of your own destiny. If the pilot makes a mistake or the plane fails, you are dead.

Which of the following would the author be least likely to do?

(A) ski
(B) jog
(C) drive a race car
(D) ride a bobsled
(E) sail a racing yacht

8. So little thought is given to plants in today's world and yet they do so much for us. They clean our air and make our buildings more pleasant to look at. I think the world would be a much better place if everyday we all stopped to thank a plant.

With which of the following would the author most likely agree?

**I. Stricter air pollution should be put on factories.**

**II. A little love and understanding would solve a lot of the world's problems.**

**III. Tests on laboratory animals should be stopped.**

(A) I only
(B) II only
(C) I and II
(D) I and III
(E) I, II and III

9. Mary Fine is delighted with all the new ('light') beers on the market. She has increased her input of this beverage daily. She truly feels her weight reduction program is going very successfully.

Which of the following distinctions would be the most useful in analyzing a <u>major flaw</u> in Mary Fine's reasoning?

(A) diet vs. regular beverages
(B) exercise vs. weight training
(C) one element vs. over all diet
(D) name vs. generic brands
(E) doctors vs. health counselors

10. If college students enroll in American Literature courses, they study selected masterpieces of recognized authors. The criteria for analysis are presented in detail. All genres are represented.

Which of the following inferences can the reader draw from the above passage?

(A) More students major in American Literature than General Business programs of study.
(B) Students who take American Literature coursework on the college level receive a balanced preparation of authors, works, and critiques.
(C) American Literature coursework prepares prospective educators more comprehensively.
(D) College courses in literature should have definitive course objectives and student proficiencies.
(E) Guidance counselors in high school should advise high school graduates to take balanced American Literature courses.

11. In 1950 the percentage of single parent households was 10. By 1970 it was 22. Today, this percentage is 40. It appears that this trend is continuing.

Each of the following if true could relate to this trend <u>except</u>?

(A) The divorce rate has increased.
(B) Civil Rights legislation has been passed.
(C) The enrollment of children in day-care centers has increased.
(D) The number of couples "living together" has increased.
(E) The number of women in the workforce has increased.

12. From a letter to the editor of a newspaper:

"In the June 22 issue, you addressed the issue of automobile insurance in the state. From my perspective your report missed the important point. While reform is necessary, you have convoluted the major issue - price reduction. You clearly stated that, because of industry's needs, the present rates were imperative; in fact, you saw a need for increases. You have clearly excluded the consumer in favor of the insurance companies."

The writer of the letter makes which of the following assumptions?

(A) All areas of the issue were covered in detail.
(B) The editor has stock in companies that foster car insurance.
(C) Only one side of this issue was delineated.
(D) Significant resources from industry were utilized to assess this area.
(E) There is a definite need to reduce rates on auto insurance.

13. During Governor Macon's term in office, the sales tax has increased by 20%. If Macon is re-elected, more increases will certainly occur. Do not vote for or support Macon!

The argument above is analogous to which of the following arguments?

(A) Ever since the State house was moved to Greenville, public services have decreased. Save our state. Move the State house back to Newton.
(B) The law to make 55 mph the maximum speed on our nation's highways has resulted in fewer accidents. We should keep this regulation in force.
(C) Since smoking has been prohibited in our public schools, 50% of our staff has quit this habit. Let's keep this statute.
(D) Our test scores have risen 25% this year. The law of averages shows that next year's results will be lower.
(E) 'Earth Day' was instituted last year in our city. Since that situation, people have become more conscious of recycling efforts. Let's keep this occasion!

14. Drug abuse has reached disastrous proportions. Much blame must be given to the lack of effective and appropriate prevention programs. Definite steps must be taken immediately to address this serious problem. Without relevant and successful strategies and procedures to combat this malady, these negative practices will be out of control.

If the statements above are true, it follows that

**I. Drugs will be eliminated when all the pushers are taken out of business.**

**II. Laws are too lenient relative to drug sales.**

**III. Studies should be undertaken to research successful programs in relation to drug abuse prevention.**

(A) I only
(B) II only
(C) III only
(D) I and II only
(E) II and III only

15. Last year, foreign car sales rose by 6%. Increases such as this have occurred consistently during the last ten years. This statistic proves that the American auto industry is in serious trouble. The United States must immediately upgrade its auto products.

Which of the following statements objects to the premises of the above argument?

**I. More quality control procedures must be instituted at American automobile plants.**

**II. American workers in this industry must be evaluated on a more stringent basis.**

**III. American auto representatives should review foreign car elements of production and sales.**

(A) I only
(B) II and III only
(C) I and III only
(D) All of the above
(E) None of the above

16. In 1985, students entering the ninth grade in New Jersey had to pass the New Jersey High School Proficiency Test (HSPT) to gain a high school diploma. Although this regulation is still in effect, educators are reviewing the efficacy of this program.

Which of the following statements can be inferred from the above passage?

(A) The HSPT first appeared in the 1980's.
(B) Some students in New Jersey had to take the HSPT before 1985.
(C) All students entering New Jersey high schools after 1985 had to pass the HSPT.
(D) The HSPT had three sections - Reading, Writing and Mathematics.
(E) Educators have reviewed this policy and have found it to be efficacious.

17. In order to develop appropriate and effective skills in the teaching profession, educators must keep abreast of the latest research in teaching and learning. Instructional strategies and procedures definitely affect learning styles.

The argument above assumes that

(A) influences outside the field of education strongly affect the teaching/learning process.
(B) comprehension of material is enhanced by successful instructional practices.
(C) all teachers should attend workshops to enhance their skills.
(D) educators should maintain a library of the latest journals in their profession.
(E) liberal arts' graduates do much better in teaching than subject-matter specialists.

18. Joe Acomb has concluded he would be better off if he raised his prices for mechanical repairs. Parts and labor are expensive elements for Joe. People will pay for effective service. Joe figured he should check the competition, but that would take too long.

Which of the following distinctions would be the most useful in analyzing a <u>major flaw</u> in Joe Acomb's reasoning?

(A) individual vs. group rates
(B) mechanics vs. technology
(C) law of supply and demand
(D) market research vs. consumer appeal
(E) Joe vs. himself

**For Questions 19 and 20**

In one town there are five chemical companies. Company I produces A. Company II uses A to make B and C. Company III uses C to make D and it also makes B. Company IV uses B to make C. Company V uses B to make C and D. III will only sell to IV.

19. If employees of I go on strike, what plants will have to close?

(A) I and II only
(B) I, II, and III
(C) II and V
(D) II and III
(E) I, II, and V

20. If D is the only product sold out of town, which companies would probably be better off if they merged to form one company?

(A) I and III
(B) I and II
(C) II and V
(D) II and III
(E) III and V

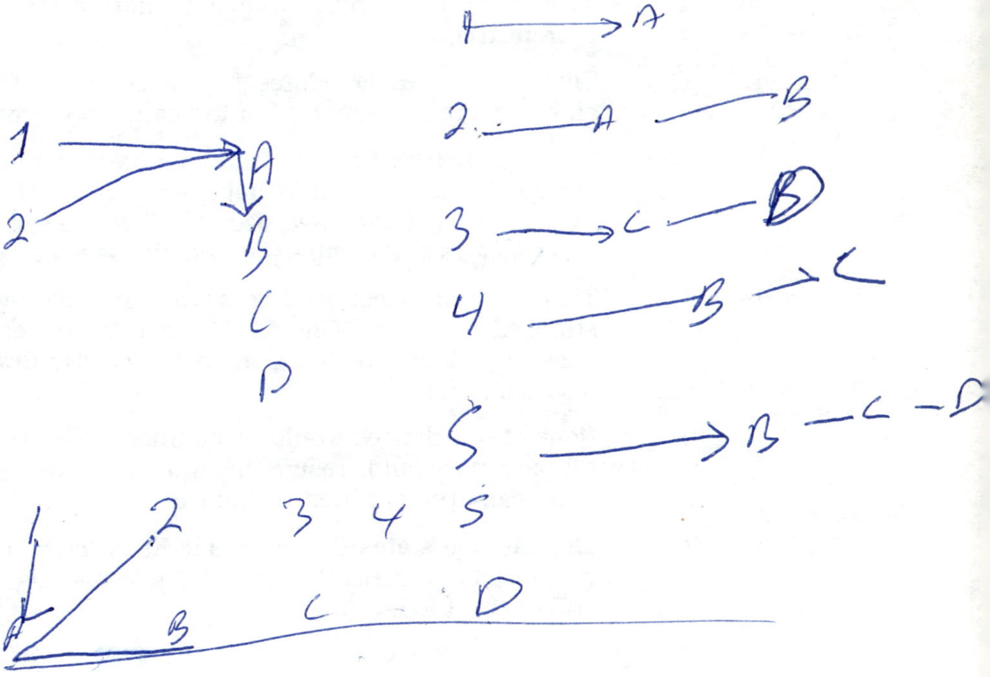

# CRITICAL REASONING PRACTICE PROBLEMS ANSWERS AND EXPLANATIONS

1. C — The person with steak sits across from fried egg which immediately eliminates answers D and E. Ham is next to fried egg, so he is two away from steak, eliminating answer A. Cereal is next to fruit and fried eggs which leaves only bacon and fruit as the correct answer.

2. B — This is the best answer because it does not necessarily mean you are against the author's point of view; you are merely pointing out his/her flaw and dealing only with factual information.

3. A — The author is afraid of new viruses, but he/she encounters hundreds of new viruses every day that occur naturally.

4. C — The author believes that lasers might be able to make nuclear weapons obsolete. Choices I and II agree with that point, but III does not.

5. B — Both I and II are assumed. The third point is an economic issue which is not brought up in the statement.

6. A — This choice directly substantiates the author's claim. It provides specific verification of his/her thesis.

7. D — In the sport of bobsledding, more than one person is required to control the sled. The other activities or choices entail individual performance.

8. E — The author would most likely agree with all three statements. The reader could make this inference in relation to the passage's content and magnanimous tone.

9. C — The primary error in judgment would be to assess only one aspect of an overall weight reduction - diet program.

10. B — The passage specifically states the three items listed in answer B. All other answers require information not available in the passage.

11. B — This is the only choice that does not correlate with the aspects of the current trend.

12. C — This choice clearly relates to the essence of the test item. All other choices were not apparent or indicated in the passage.

13. A — The logical flaw in this argument is a simple one - the speaker has assumed a situation that happened during Governor Macon's term (rise in sales tax) must have occurred because of Governor Macon. Many other factors and complex, economic issues affect this aspect.

14. C — This type of question forces you to make inferences relative to the supplied material. Choices I and II were not stated or implied in the passage. Choice III is a conclusion clearly drawn from the focus of the test item.

15. E — None of the choices would be counter to the substance of the paragraph. All actions could result in practices to upgrade and improve the American auto production and sales.

16. C — The passage states that all students entering the ninth grade after 1985 had to pass the HSPT test. The passage also states that this policy is still in effect today.

| | | |
|---|---|---|
| 17. | D | The passage states that it is important to keep up with the latest trends in education. Only answer D provides a means to follow that directive. |
| 18. | C | Joe must take into consideration the prices charged by the competition. His service may be good, but that is not the only criteria to use when evaluating a price increase. |
| 19. | E | I, II, and V would all have to close. II because it gets its material from I; V because it gets its material from B. |
| 20. | B | I and II would probably be the best merger because I sells all its products to II and II gets all its products from I. |

# SAMPLE TEST QUESTIONS FOR CRITICAL REASONING

These sample test questions represent roughly a third of the 41 questions to be presented to you by the **GMAT CAT**. The other two-thirds are categorized as **Sentence Correction** and **Critical Reasoning** type questions. These question types are significantly different and each individual will respond at different rates for each. Remember that the GMAT CAT does not allow you to return to or to skip over any question. When you get stuck, you will need a strategy for taking your best guess so as to move on to questions that you will be able to answer.

You will be given 75 minutes time to answer 41 questions. This is roughly 110 seconds, under 2 minutes, per question. As you practice using the following questions, time yourself noting the rate at which you dispatch each. As you note that some questions take you too long, you will develop a sensitivity to timing. During the test this sense will help you to transition from looking for the "right" answer to picking what you think is the "most likely" answer.

Remember, that as you first read the answers for any question, some answers may be eliminated initially. You should practice this in this section by remaining aware of the fact that you are making value judgements as you read each answer. In fact you may develop a method of noting these judgements on scratch paper to aid you in more quickly identifying the educated guess. No matter how you may organize this aspect of taking the **GMAT CAT**, by practicing it here in these sample questions it will be easier for you to enter your stride during the actual test.

**DIRECTIONS:** For each question in this section, select the best answer from the choices given.

1. Four salesmen traveled to four cities and each made a sale of his respective merchandise. One salesmen sold a computer software package and another traveled to Chicago. The salesman who sold a mutual fund package did not go to Denver. Neither Max nor the person who sold medical insurance went to New York. The man who sold a food service program (which was not sold by Howard) did not go to Denver. Tom did not go to Seattle. Neither Alex nor the mutual fund salesman went to New York.

   Which of the following statements are true according to the information given?

   **I. Howard sold a computer software package in New York.**
   **II. Tom sold a food service program in Chicago.**
   **III. Alex sold medical insurance in Seattle.**

   (A) I only
   (B) II only
   (C) III only
   (D) I and II only
   (E) I, II and III

2. At a time when technology has become more important than the products it produces, our nation has become increasingly an exporter of services rather than of hard commodities. Although this is good for business in some aspects, this causes great problems for our economy in other aspects. Fewer people are needed to sell services than to produce hard goods.

What is the underlying assumption of the above passage?

(A) Goods created by our nation's technology are not being made in this country.
(B) There is greater profit in selling hard goods than in selling technology.
(C) Unemployment is growing as a result of technologic imports.
(D) Our economy is undergoing a period of great difficulty.
(E) Technology and hard goods are the basis for our economy.

3. In one New Jersey town only two out of eight Town Committeemen showed concern about a new development planned for an environmentally sensitive swamp area. In previous decades when an airport site was needed, many of the town legislators fought hard to prevent this airport from being located in this same environmentally sensitive swampland. It seems somewhat unusual that, at this time when many more townspeople are involved in local environmental issues than ever before, elected officials are failing to lead.

Which of the following conclusions can be drawn from the passage?

(A) More committeemen are needed to support environmental legislation.
(B) In order to represent the townspeople's views more fairly, the Town Committeemen must take a protective stand about the environmentally sensitive swampland.
(C) State officials must enforce legislation about environmentally sensitive areas when towns fail to do so.
(D) The six committeemen who failed to protect the Great Swamp should be removed from office.
(E) Only the two committeemen who showed concern for the environment should be re-elected.

4-5. In order to compete in the business of baseball, it is necessary to have a certain number of fans in attendance. For the past three years our attendance has dropped below that level and our team has dropped in the standings. It has become evident, therefore, that we must move the team.

4. The conclusion is based on which of the following assumptions?

(A) Moving the team will increase the number of spectators.
(B) One of the causes for the team's losses is the poor attendance of the fans.
(C) The team is no longer competitive.
(D) The fans are in some way responsible for the success or failure of a team.
(E) The business of baseball is pleasing the crowds.

5. Which of the following statements would weaken the speaker's argument?

(A) A winning team is what attracts the fans to the stadium.
(B) The stadium is old and needs remodeling.
(C) Many players were injured in the last season.
(D) The fans cannot watch the games on TV because of the blackout on local stations.
(E) The costs of moving are less than what might be expected for a corporate move in a similar situation.

6. The postal system should be removed from federal control because it becomes a political football when it tries to raise the prices of stamps or instigate cost-saving cutbacks in service or layoffs of employees. Private companies would be more efficient because a profit motive would control behavior instead of political expediency.

What conclusion can be drawn from the above statements?

(A) All government run agencies should be replaced by private companies.
(B) Cost-saving cutbacks are more popular with the voters if instigated by private companies rather than by government agencies.
(C) Private industry can derive a profit from the same industries that government operates at a loss.
(D) Private industry would cut back services making the postal service less responsive to the needs of the people.
(E) Private companies could run the postal service more efficiently because they would not have to be responsive to political pressure.

7-8. In a recent drug survey taken in our local public high school, the sophomore class had the highest number of students who had used drugs or alcohol in the past twelve months. This surprised many parents who had assumed that the senior class would certainly have the highest number simply because those students were older. However, the numbers for the sophomore class remained constant in all categories (for example, drinking before school in the morning, using substances within the drug-free safety zone, etc.) while the numbers fluctuated for all categories in the other classes, sometimes falling below those of the sophomore class, and sometimes rising above those of the sophomore class. Many parents called for greater drug awareness programs in the school and stronger supervision of students during school hours, especially for the sophomore class.

7. Which of the following statements, if true, would weaken the argument of the parents?

(A) Drug awareness programs might make the students more interested in trying the substances.
(B) The survey showed that statistically no students were taking drugs or using alcohol in the school during school hours.
(C) The senior class was providing the sophomores with the substances.
(D) Most students were not interested in the results of the survey.
(E) The survey showed that students were very aware of the hazards of drinking and driving and the survey showed that not even one student checked yes to drinking and driving.

8. Which of the following, if true, should lesson the fears of the parents about the sophomores?

(A) there are more sophomores in the school than in any other grade so it was logical for their numbers to be higher
(B) no students were drinking and driving and that is what parents fear most
(C) the teachers would now be watching that class especially closely making it harder for them misbehave
(D) the sophomore numbers were constant and showed that the same students were responsible for most of the drug use in the grade, while other classes had fluctuating numbers and showed that different students were involved in each of the categories making their overall numbers greater
(E) the statistical percentage of error is greater when dealing with fewer numbers than with larger numbers; since the school is so small compared to other schools participating in the survey, the margin of error is likely to be much greater for our school than for the others.

9. During Mary's tenure in office as president of the local Chamber of Commerce, six new stores were added to the town square area increasing the tax revenues for the town. Also, a tree lighting project for the holiday season was begun, a gazebo was built with funds donated by customers in the local shops and the local theater group was able to rebuild its theater. Is it any wonder Mary is receiving the "Outstanding Citizen of the Year" award?

Which of the following statements most seriously weakens the conclusion drawn in this passage?

(A) Previous recipients of the award had accomplished much more than Mary.
(B) Mary was a recent resident of the town and had only been a member of the Chamber of Commerce for two years before becoming president.
(C) The gazebo project was initiated by one of the local architects in town and the holiday lighting project was begun by a local minister. The theater group had started rebuilding the theater before Mary became president.
(D) Despite Mary's many accomplishments in town, there are people who feel she really has not pulled the town together on some serious issues that had been a problem before her tenure as president and which she said she would try to address during her term.
(E) The Citizen of the Year award has lost its luster over the years and has gone from an award for outstanding heroism or unusual service to an award that recognizes those people whose accomplishments are readily visible.

For Questions 10-12.

There are seven people standing in a line that goes around the corner of a wall. The fourth person, who is at the corner, can see everyone. All the other people can only see the people in a straight line. There are four people wearing hats. Three are wearing blue shirts, 2 green, one white and one red. The sixth person in line knows that only one of the two people wearing a green shirt has a hat. The green shirt with the hat knows that there are at least two people with blue shirts and hats and that only one person with a green shirt has a hat.

10. If the white shirt is on the end, what color shirts must he be able to see?

(A) 2 blue, 1 white, 1 green
(B) 2 green, 1 white, 1 blue
(C) 2 green, 1 red, 1 white
(D) 1 white, 3 blue
(E) 1 green, 1 red, 1 white, 1 blue

11. If there are not four hats in a row, which of the following could be possible combinations?

**I.** **blue, green, blue, blue, green, red, white**
**II.** **blue, blue, green, green, blue, red, white**
**III.** **blue, blue, green, green, red, blue, white**

(A) I only
(B) II only
(C) I and II only
(D) II and III only
(E) I, II, and III

12. If white is not next to a hat, green is not surrounded by blue shirts, and all blue shirts are wearing hats, what is the order of the shirts?

(A) blue, blue, green, green, blue, red, white
(B) blue, blue, green, green, red, blue, white
(C) blue, green, blue, green, red, white, blue
(D) blue, green, blue, green, white, red, blue
(E) blue, blue, green, white, green, red, blue

13. During the 1989 holiday season and again in the 1990 season, the police found that an unusual number of crimes were committed that could be classified as mischief. Because of the nature of these crimes it is assumed that they are the work of juveniles rather than adults. Already this season several Christmas trees have been stolen from the local non-profit tree stall sometime during the middle of the night. For this reason the police are mandating a 10 p.m. curfew for all people under the age of twenty-one.

What is the major flaw in the police policy of a 10 p.m. curfew for under twenty-one year olds?

(A) Most people consider juveniles to be under eighteen, not twenty-one.
(B) The crimes are not really serious enough to warrant such drastic measures.
(C) Young people have an uncanny way of avoiding detection when they so desire; a curfew will only keep the "good" kids off the streets.
(D) The police have not determined who has committed these "crimes" and should not punish an entire group of people without proof. Even if some teenagers are responsible, all teenagers should not be punished.
(E) Although the mischief may be annoying and sometimes costly, the holidays are a time for merry-making and some latitude must be allowed to all citizens, teenagers and adults alike.

14. Linda Salinger, an economist, has noticed that people who live in areas where housing prices are higher tend to buy more expensive cars than the national average, while people who live in areas where housing prices are lower, tend to buy less expensive cars. She contends that people spend a constant percentage of their home value for cars.

Bob Smith, however, contends that car price is more closely related to the amount of expendable income an individual has rather than to the cost of housing.

Which of the following, if true, would most seriously weaken Linda Salinger's argument?

(A) People who bought their homes in 1960 when housing costs were very low, all drive expensive cars.
(B) There are many more car dealers in expensive housing areas than in other parts of the country.
(C) When the stock market goes down, people still buy expensive cars.
(D) People who live in good homes in depressed areas often buy expensive cars rather than putting the money into housing.
(E) It is impossible to determine the true extent of people's expendable income because of tax dodges that favor only certain people.

15. Double trailer trucks on our nation's highways are dangerous. Studies have shown that they are 80% more likely to have an accident than a single truck. Double trailer trucks should be banned.

Which of the following, if true, is the best argument against the author's point of view.

(A) More jobs are created by having only single trailer trucks.
(B) Most truck accidents occur in cities.
(C) Most double trailer accidents are not serious.
(D) Double trailer trucks are more economical.
(E) Double trailer trucks have 80% more accidents, but since they move twice the cargo they are safer than two single trucks.

16. President Bush has addressed the issue of teenage unemployment by suggesting that government enforced minimum wage laws be suspended for teenage workers.

Which of the following assumptions is the president making by suggesting this policy?

**I. Teenage workers do not need as much money as older workers.**
**II. Cheap teenage labor would encourage more employers to hire extra help.**
**III. Cheap teenage labor would deprive older workers of their jobs.**

(A) I only
(B) II only
(C) III only
(D) I and II
(E) I, II and III

17. Many video rental stores are complaining that cable viewers who illegally pirate movies from cable channels are seriously hurting their business. This is probably untrue because

(A) by the time the movies come to cable television, they are old anyway
(B) the number of movies copied from cable television is low compared to the number of video movies that are rented
(C) the overall volume of rental videos is great enough not to be hurt by pirated copies of television movies
(D) those who copy television movies already have access to these movies on their cable channels and would not be renting them from video stores anyway
(E) the quality of movies copied from cable television is not as good as the quality of movies available for rental

18. Commercial Fisherman are now using modern technology such as radar which has increased their catches significantly. Sports anglers feel that the seas are being overfished because they are finding fewer fish and bringing home smaller catches. Some sport fisherman have already quit the sport and others are discouraged enough to do so.

Which of the following, if true, would encourage legislators to put restrictions on commercial fishing?

(A) Commercial fishing is a billion dollar industry
(B) Commercial catches are being reduced
(C) Many people die on commercial boats
(D) Many people die on sports boats
(E) Sports fishing is a multi-billion dollar industry

19. Has the advent of the personal computer really made the business world more efficient? First of all, since filling out forms is so much easier, more forms are now filled out. Second, with the advent of desk-top publishing, instead of just typing a report, it now has to be "designed" as well. The time saved in planning and writing is now lost in design.

The author of the above article would probably agree with which of the following statements?

(A) Computers have made business less efficient
(B) Computers have made business more efficient
(C) The time saved by computers in writing reports is shifted to other areas
(D) Computers cause many errors that are difficult to solve
(E) Workers must now be more and more skilled in order to be able to use computers

20. Environmental Activist:

The spotted owl is an endangered species and must be protected at all costs. Spotted owls can only live in old growth forest. All cutting of trees in old growth forest must stop so that the owls can be saved.

Company Official:

What we are talking about here is lives. Owls lives vs. people's lives. If it is necessary to stop the lumbering here, not only will our industry suffer, but all of the people who provide food, clothing and shelter to the large number of people who work for us will suffer. The lumbering of the forests must continue.

Which of the following, if true, would weaken the argument of the environmental activists?

(A) 15,000 people would lose their jobs if the lumbering ceases
(B) the price of lumbering would increase 20% if lumbering ceases
(C) the spotted owl has been found living in other forest areas that had previously been cut
(D) the spotted owl carries a bacterium in its intestines used in making a new drug
(E) the state economy has an unemployment rate above 10% now, while lumbering is still continuing

## Answers for Sample Test Questions for Critical Reasoning

1. E The easiest way to solve this problem is to write a list of what cannot be done and then check the choices against it. Choice 1, mutual fund and Alex did not go there. Also Max and medical insurance did not go there. Yes, Howard could sell computer software in New York. Tom and food service are both allowed in Chicago, so 2 is allowed. Alex and medical insurance are both allowed in Seattle, so 3 is allowed.

2. A The problem with selling technology is that these services allow other countries to produce hard goods. The passage states that we are becoming a nation which exports technology, NOT commodities themselves.

3. B Since more people are concerned about the environment, the legislators must represent these views. A is incorrect because more committee members are not needed. There are already eight members; those members must be representatives of their constituents. The arguments in answers C, D and E are not brought up in the passage.

4. A The conclusion of the passage is that the team should be moved. Answer A is the only answer that discusses the moving of the team.

5. A The speaker has put the cart before the horse in thinking that another city would produce more spectators.

6. E Answer E rephrases the last line of the passage which is the conclusion.

7. B The parents' request for greater supervision in school is unnecessary if no drug problem exists during school hours.

8. D Although there are a greater number of positive responses to drug use in the sophomore class, the fact that the same number of students make the same positive responses indicates that the same students are responding to each question. In other classes where there are different numbers of students responding to each question, and some numbers are actually greater in some categories than those of the sophomore class, a more diverse group of students are giving positive responses to drug use and those numbers, overall, are higher than the sophomore class.

9. C This is a cause and effect question which displays faulty reasoning. The effects attributed to Mary's tenure in office are merely sequentially related to Mary. She did not cause those effects to occur.

10. E The person with a green shirt with a hat must be able to see all four hats or he must be able to see the green shirt without a hat. Since the sixth person can also figure out that only one person has a hat, he must be able to see either all four hats, both green shirts, or a green shirt without a hat and only one hat. The only way for both of these to work together is for the sixth person to see the green shirt without a hat and for him to see only one hat. This means that the green hat is not at the corner, so the white shirt has to see one of each color.

11. E All three combinations are possible.

12. A All the other combinations have white next to a hat or green surrounded by blue.

13. D The police are basing their actions on a conclusion that has not been proven.

14. D In areas where housing prices are depressed, the housing prices are lower. If people in those areas with nice houses are buying expensive cars then Linda Salanger's assumption is wrong.

15. E This is the best answer because it is arguing safety and states that, in essence, double trailer trucks are actually safer overall. This answer is the best argument against the author's perspective. Choice A really supports the author's argument.

16. D In order to suggest paying one group of people less than another, there must be some valid reasons. If a group has fewer responsibilities in life, this would be a reason for reduced wages. Also, if the purpose of suspending the minimum wage is to help reduce teenage unemployment, it must be assumed that this will increase the number of jobs for teenagers for whatever reasons.

17. D This assumption is faulty because the video rental stores are complaining about lost business. The viewers who watch cable TV are not part of their business income anyway.

18. E You are being asked to determine what priorities govern legislative action. The conclusion is that industry income which produces tax revenue is the determining factor.

19. E Because computers can do more, workers are expected to be able to use all of a computer's capabilities.

20. C The environmentalists argument is based on the fact that the owls cannot survive without an old growth forest. That the owls can survive in new growth forests negates the only argument put forth by the activists. All the other arguments are in support of the company official, but do not weaken the argument of the environmentalist.

# ANALYTICAL WRITING ASSESSMENT

This recently developed section of the **GMAT CAT** requires you to compose a thirty minute response to each of two distinct writing tasks. The first experience "Analysis of an Issue" requires you review a designated circumstance or opinion and then provide relevant reasons and/or illustrations from your frame of reference. The second writing prompt entails an "Analysis of an Argument." Upon completion of your reading an argumentative essay, you must conceptualize the rationale behind the argument. Then, you must design an evaluation of this persuasive piece. Basically, you are challenged to develop a convincing, coherent, fluid and organized essay that demonstrates effective, appropriate and correct written expression. These writing samples provide further insight of a candidate's literacy, ability and educational background/training.

## SCORING

Both of these papers - "Analysis of an Issue" and "Analysis of an Argument" of the Analytical Writing Assessment section are evaluated with a scoring rubric/scale from 6, the highest score to 1, the lowest rating. Candidates receive a 0 for illegible, off-topic, or inappropriate response, and NR for no response. Specific elements to delineate and embellish these ratings involve:

| | |
|---|---|
| 6 = **Superior** | demonstration of the highest level of written expression; very well organized, unified, cohesive and outstanding portrayal and control of language; cogent, logical and smooth transitions. |
| 5 = **Strong** | command of the written skills; clear control of language (diction and sentence variety/structure); well developed critique. |
| 4 = **Satisfactory** | mastery of the aspects of effective/correct writing; competent organization; adequate and substantial content; some flaws in language but no pattern of grammatical errors. |
| 3 = **Minimal** | representation of the components of composition; poor organization; partial substance; definite pattern of grammatical errors (punctuation, capitalization, spelling). |
| 2 = **Unsatisfactory** | portrayal of the language arts; major problems in grammar, syntax, and mechanics; loose organization; no substance. |
| 1 = **Poor** | depiction in the area of composing papers; severe deficiencies of basic skills of grammar, usage and mechanics; incoherent presentation of confused ideas; no structure. |

0 = **Illegible, Off-Topic, Unrelated, Inappropriate**

NR = **No Response**

## STRATEGIES FOR WORKING WITH ESSAY QUESTIONS

**Step One** = Read and review the elements of the writing prompt. Consider all parts of the question carefully.

**Step Two** = Employ the successful and time-tested perspectives of prewriting. Brainstorm all aspects of the response. Take a few moments to outline your major topic and supporting details. Organize the essential components of the issue/argument.

**Step Three** = Compose a three to five paragraph response to the issue/argument. State your position/critique clearly. Support your main ideas with specific details, examples and factors. Be convincing, explicit and literate. Demonstrate complete mastery of grammar, usage, syntax and mechanics.

**Step Four** = Proofread and edit diligently. Consider the following criteria: organization/content, sentence construction, usage, mechanics, and spelling.

## COMPOSING THE ESSAY

The essay that you are challenged to write measures whether you can write unified, coherent paragraphs, can organize ideas, can develop a logical, fluid argument, can provide specific, relevant examples, can use complete, diversified sentence structure, can spell, can interest or relate to the reader, can maintain a consistent tone, and can express thoughts precisely. The ability to write an effective essay is essential for all GMAT candidates. Here are some pertinent points to remember as you address the questions in the analytical writing assessment portion:

**(1) First Paragraph - Introduction**

State the main idea, topic and/or your position of the paper. Convey and clarify the main ideas; provide some background on the subject and/or articulately reveal your thesis.

**(2) Second - Fourth Paragraphs – Body**

Develop the supporting and corroborating elements of the essay. Relate appropriate substantiation for your main idea or thesis. Utilize opinions, examples, facts, details and transitional devices. Embellish the explanatory/persuasive descriptive/expository perspectives of your primary purpose.

**(3) Final Paragraph - Conclusion**

Present a summary of your main ideas. Reinforce the aspects of your position. Correlate main ideas, topic, position and thesis statement. Culminate your writing assessment with a clincher (final statement) to leave a lasting impression. Review major points. Emphasize your thesis/main objective. Give a viable solution.

# EXAMPLE ESSAYS

Following are examples of both types of writing tasks and sample responses that have been critiqued.

## ANALYSIS OF AN ISSUE

**Directions:** In this section, you will need to analyze the issue presented and explain your views on it. There is no "correct" answer. Instead, you should consider various perspectives as you develop your own position on the issue.

### Sample Question - "Analysis of an Issue"

There are two distinct points of view relative to the training and background of management personnel in business. One group feels very strongly that leaders should possess specialized skills and course work that promote technological perspectives. The other segment of the business community says quite conclusively that generalists with a diverse program of study will be more humane and receptive of their employees'/associates' needs and concerns.

Which line of reasoning do you perceive as more successful? Present, explain and support your position. Use pertinent aspects of rationale and illustrations/factors drawn from your own frame of reference/prior knowledge.

### Sample Papers - Sample 1

I am definitely in favor of specialized and technical training, education and hands-on experiences for future managers and business leaders. A jack-of-all trades/master-of-none coordinator is an unnecessary element in today's highly sophisticated world of commerce. The kindest and gentlest leader does not realize the depth and breadth in contemporary issues of private enterprise.

Manufacturing plants and computerized accounting procedures require the ultimate in expertise and meaningful implementation of relevant strategies. Competent leaders facilitate the highest level of performance and excellence from their staff. Various aspects of management by objectives necessitate leaders with specialized backgrounds in the specific realm of production and record keeping. "Lean and mean" companies are led by managers with degrees in particular courses of study (e.g. business administration, finance, market analysis, computer technology, industrial management, etc.). Today, graduate work with the largest and up-to-date perspectives and techniques must be designed, developed and promulgated at financial/industrial sites.

Therefore, I reiterate and reinforce my primary position and point-of-view in this presentation. Managers must bring very precise and accurate academic training and pragmatic involvement to their leadership professions. They are required to focus on the most successful means to an end. Worthwhile leaders need to understand, analyze, synthesize and evaluate comprehensive attention to detail. None of this is possible without specialized skills and technological attainment.

### Explanation Of Score 5/6

Strong/Superior demonstration/command of the highest level of written expression; clear and masterful control of language/written skills (e.g. grammar, usage, syntax, mechanics); very well-organized; more than substantial content; beautifully developed position paper; a thorough balanced presentation with an introduction, body and conclusion.

## Sample Papers - Sample 2

Business leaders whom have many skills in the technical field sometime make better managers in the field. Irregardless they have no care for there workers? neither of these persons were prepared alright. All people with these training' should go back to school and learn to manage Nobody cares for workers anyways.

## Explanation Of Score – 1/2

Unsatisfactory/Minimal representation/portrayal of the art of composition; definite pattern of grammatical errors, usage, syntax and mechanics; loose organization of ideas; little, or no substance. Obviously, this is NOT a Satisfactory/Adequate mastery of the aspects of effective/appropriate/correct expression in standard written English. There is a definite and prevailing pattern of language errors. Certainly, elements of coherence and logic are remiss. Substantial information is lacking.

# ANALYSIS OF AN ARGUMENT

**Directions:** In this section you will be asked to write a critique of the argument presented below. You are NOT being asked to present your own views on the subject.

## Sample Question - "ANALYSIS OF AN ARGUMENT"

Some members of the business community in the United States fervently support restrictions and tariffs on commodities from other countries. These people feel specified elements of managed trade and penalties on imports would compensate for labor practices overseas.

Discuss, in detail, how practical and convincing this solution is for the problem of equalized/balanced trade agreements for America. Relate an effective, coherent and organized essay that realistically assesses this situation.

## Sample Papers – Sample 1

I truly perceive that this argument, supporting restrictions and tariffs on commodities from other countries, is a feasible and convincing alternative to America's demise as a world leader in the business arena and world market. The United States is being decimated by less expensive/lower quality goods and materials from foreign concerns. Strong sanctions, restrictions and tariffs must be imposed immediately on imports to balance this commercial endeavor and to preclude this destructive, disturbing and negative trend.

My initial example to illustrate this concept is the automobile industry. Throughout my entire driving career over the past thirty years, I have personally witnessed the inundation of import models. Given union wages and benefits, the American companies simply cannot replicate the same machine at the reduced price structures and options offered by the foreign market. A second example would be the complete domination of electronic appliances by foreign companies. Relative to the earnings of international workers, these goods are brought into our wholesale/retail markets severely below American quality control standards/prices. Finally, the computer hardware/software elements further corroborate this aspect. Without equalization of America's import/export figures, foreign technological components will continue to destroy American efforts in this realm.

In summary, this is certainly a thorough and efficient manner to solve and rectify a disastrous situation/problem. Foreign business concerns must meet the convictions and resolve of American perspectives. Tariffs, sanctions and restrictions to balance our trade actions must be implemented and fostered before it is too late. Proactive aspects and measures must be initiated; these proposals would correspond to our present/future needs.

## Explanation Of Score 5/6

Strong/Superior/Outstanding. This paper clearly identifies and evaluates significant aspects of the argument. There is definitive control of language arts skills.

## Sample Papers – Sample 2

Without a doubt their must be some restrictions on stuff coming to our country many people loose jobs because of foreign goods, without laws to stop and prohibit these cheap labor and trade practices nothing will get finished. Equal and balanced arrangements and prices is important? Between you and I, we'd better pass some measures in our government. Being necessary at this time.

## Evaluation – 1/2

This evaluation of the argument truly depicts severe deficiencies in the area of grammar, usage, syntax and mechanics. These weaknesses pervade the composition. Additionally, very poor organizational elements and no development of thoughts further correlate with this negative rating.

# SAMPLE ANALYTICAL WRITING ASSIGNMENTS

Following are ten sample analytical writing assignments. Five are analysis of an issue and the latter five are analysis of an argument. During the **GMAT CAT** you will be assigned one of each and allowed 30 minutes for each assignment. You will be allowed an optional break between the two writing assignments.

# FIVE SAMPLE ANALYSIS OF AN ISSUE ASSIGNMENTS

**Directions:** In this section, you will need to analyze the issue presented and explain your views on it. There is no "correct" view. Instead, you should consider various perspectives as you develop your own position on the issue.

**Writing your response:** Take a few minutes to think about the issue and plan a response before writing. Be sure to organize and fully develop your ideas. Finally, leave time to reread and make any revisions.

Remember that your response will be evaluated for how well you

- organize, develop, and express your ideas on the issue,
- provide relevant supporting reasons and examples, and
- control the elements of standard written English.

### Analysis of an Issue Sample Number 1

1. In many cultures throughout the world, government regulations dictate an individual's vocational future. Stringent examinations categorize students into specific positions through strong, established criteria of selection. In your point of view, should these cultural elements and governmental restrictions indicate an individual's potential and choice. Explain fully your position on this topic with meaningful reasons, factors, examples and details to support your position.

### Analysis of an Issue Sample Number 2

2. There is an ongoing debate/controversy between public and private parochial education. For many years, sides have been drawn with very strong, emotional and cognitive perspectives and rationale. Recently, the aspects of vouchers and charter schools have evolved.

   Choose what you believe to be the most successful way to educate our youth from grades kindergarten through twelve (elementary, middle and high schools). Justify your selection with relevant and meaningful reasons, details and factors from your own experience, observations and/or reading.

### Analysis of an Issue Sample Number 3

3. Job satisfaction should be the most important element in choosing a profession. Discuss to what degree you agree or disagree with the point of view expressed above. Support your views with reasons, details and/or illustrations from your experience, observations and/or reading.

## Analysis of an Issue Sample Number 4

4. There is an ongoing controversy among universities and business: generalist versus specialist. Major universities/colleges advocate a well-rounded graduate educationally. Advisors in higher education develop programs of studies that incorporate the humanities and technical perspectives. Corporate human resource professionals recruit and hire graduates with specific, highly sophisticated expertise. Discuss to what degree you agree with either the university or business elements. Support your position/view with reasons, details and/or illustrations from you experience, observations and/or readings.

## Analysis of an Issue Sample Number 5

5. Two major forms of management exist today. The first system entails a strong, almost dictatorial leader. This manager makes all significant decisions. His/her policies/regulations/rules are clearly delineated with specified parameters. There is a distinction between administrator and staff. In complete contrast, there is the democratic/benevolent/collegial manager. He/she involves all employees in all important issues. Consensus must be reached with extensive aspects of overall and active participation at all levels. This manager develops a completely cooperative channel of performance. Choose a type of management system. Support your views with reasons, details and/or examples from your experience, observations and/or readings.

# FIVE SAMPLE ANALYSIS OF AN ARGUMENT ASSIGNMENTS

**Directions:** In this section you will be asked to write a critique of the argument presented below. You are NOT being asked to present your own views on the subject.

> Discuss how reasoned you find this argument. In your discussion, be sure to analyze and specify the line of reasoning and the use of evidence and level of validity.

- Organize, develop and completely express your perceptions about the argument presented.
- Provide meaningful supporting elements, reasons and examples.
- Utilize the highest level of standard written English. Be very cognizant of usage, mechanics, sentence construction and overall effective, grammatical principles.

### Analysis of an Argument Sample Number 1

The following appeared in a magazine advertisement for health foods:

> For the past ten years, studies have shown that people who use Herb-A-Life have better medical results than those individuals that do not use this product.

Discuss how well-reasoned you find this argument. In your discussion, analyze and incorporate the line of reasoning and the use of evidence in the argument. Organize, develop and express your critique with substantial illustrations and pertinent factors. Demonstrate the highest level of standard written English.

### Analysis of an Argument Sample Number 2

The following appeared in an editorial section of a newspaper:

> As the officials of business have become more conscientious in their efforts to address drug and alcohol abuse, costs of these programs have become prohibitive. This is a disturbing trend, and if it continues will be disastrous. Management should terminate all of these expensive programs. Employees should have more self-control.

Discuss how well-reasoned you find this argument. In your discussion, analyze and incorporate the line of reasoning and the use of evidence in the argument. Organize, develop and express your critique with substantial illustrations and pertinent factors. Demonstrate the highest level of standard written English.

### Analysis of an Argument Sample Number 3

The following appeared in a company memorandum from top-level management:

> Xerba Corporation should promote early retirements and buy-outs for middle management personnel. Furthermore, our company should reduce our workforce by laying-off twenty percent of our laborers; this action would motivate remaining workers and raise their level of concern for increasing productivity.

Discuss how well-reasoned you find this argument. In your discussion, analyze and incorporate the line of reasoning and the use of evidence in the argument. Organize, develop and express your critique with substantial illustrations and pertinent factors. Demonstrate the highest level of standard written English.

## Analysis of an Argument Sample Number 4

The following editorial appeared in the magazine Business World:

> Corporations have a major responsibility for establishing day care facilities with trained personnel on-site. Statistics have shown that more and more women must return to the workforce. These trained individuals have much to contribute. Additionally, this relevant action would reduce the roles of public assistance.

Discuss how well-reasoned you find this argument. In your discussion, analyze and incorporate the line of reasoning and the use of evidence in the argument. Organize, develop and express your critique with substantial illustrations and pertinent factors. Demonstrate the highest level of standard written English.

## Analysis of an Argument Sample Number 5

School districts should require at least a year of community service as a graduation pre-requisite. This procedure should relate to a two-year obligation to our Federal perspectives. This should be a very diversified opportunity: military, environmental agencies, hospitals, etc. These altruistic experiences would promote a more mature background and outlook for future elements of life. As an added incentive, colleges/technical institutes, etc. should award credits for this time and effort.

Discuss how well-reasoned you find this argument. In your discussion, analyze and incorporate the line of reasoning and the use of evidence in the argument. Organize, develop and express your critique with substantial illustrations and pertinent factors. Demonstrate the highest level of standard written English.

# THE GMAT MATHEMATICS SECTION

The mathematics portion of the **GMAT CAT** consists of two types of questions: problem solving and data sufficiency. Both types are multiple choice, with five possible selections for each question. Problems for the most part are oriented toward real situations. In problem solving you are asked to analyze a question and determine its solution. Select the best possible answer, confirm it and move on to the next question.

The **GMAT** utilizes basic arithmetic, first year-level algebra and geometry and includes the following topic areas:

**ARITHMETIC:** Fractions, decimals, percents, mean and median, powers and roots, ratios and proportions

**ALGEBRA:** Simplifying expressions, factoring quadratics, solving equations, absolute values and inequalities

**GEOMETRY:** Lines, angles, polygons, circles, solids and coordinate geometry

Data sufficiency measures your ability to analyze a problem by means of providing you with information which may (or may not) be relevant to its solution.

For both cases, problem solving and data sufficiency, the main objective of the test is to measure your ability to reason. Regardless of the type of problem or its complexity, the same basic math concepts are used over and over again.

### A GMAT CAT Test Taking Tip

You should attempt to solve each problem as quickly as possible. Since you cannot skip and return to questions on the **GMAT CAT**, simply pick/guess the best answer for each problem for which a solution eludes you. Each minute you spend after you have stopped making progress towards a solution is lost. Unless you have been averaging better than one problem a minute, it is to your advantage to guess on difficult problems and to proceed to problems you are more likely to solve.

## HOW IS THE MATHEMATICS PORTION OF THIS BOOK DESIGNED?

This book contains a review section for:

**ARITHMETIC**

**ALGEBRA**

**GEOMETRY**

The section on geometry includes a review of Coordinate Geometry. Each section contains sample problems with solutions which will assist you in the review of the concepts.

The descriptive section of data sufficiency problems contains sample questions and provides several examples.

The final sections cover interpretation of graphical data, useful formulas and mathematical terms with which you should be familiar.

# Arithmetic Review

Arithmetic necessary for success on the GMAT examination is reviewed here for completeness. Depending on your individual needs, you may wish to read this whole section or skim the section titles to only read that which is needed. Many will find that such topics as prime numbers, factors, exponents and square roots need to be reviewed since fewer disciplines use these topics and that which is not used tends to be lost.

## IMPORTANT NUMBER SYSTEMS (SETS)

There are many types of numbers or number systems. For the purpose of the GMAT examination the number systems described here are Integers, Rational Numbers (Fractions), and Real Numbers. The set of rational numbers is composed of all numbers that can be described as the division of two integers, thus a fraction. The set of real numbers is a richer set of numbers that includes such famous numbers as pi, $\pi$, and the square root of two, $\sqrt{2}$. Such numbers have been proven to not be fractions. In fact, it is told that when the Greeks discovered a proof that the root of two could not be described precisely by a fraction they offered a thousand bulls in sacrifice to the gods for their vast wisdom in making such a creation. For us this means that not all of the results of meaningful calculations can be represented as a fraction, and therefore other means must be employed.

## INTEGERS

Integers are the counting numbers, positive, negative, and zero (0). The set of integers is {... -3, -2, -1, 0, 1, 2, 3 ...}.

## IMPORTANT CONCEPTS AND PROPERTIES

Some important properties of integers and number concepts are highlighted here.

### Properties of Odd and Even for Addition and Subtraction

**even ± even ⇒ even**

EXAMPLES: 6 + 4 = 10 and 8 - 2 = 6.

**odd ± odd ⇒ even**

EXAMPLES: 3 + 5 = 8 and 11 - 1 = 10.

**even ± odd ⇒ odd**

EXAMPLES: 3 + 4 = 7 and 5 – 2 = 3.

In general the above statements can be summarized as:

**same ⇒ even**

**different ⇒ odd**

## Properties of Odd and Even for Multiplication

**(even)(even) ⇒ even**

EXAMPLE: (4)(6) = 24

**(even)(odd) ⇒ even**

EXAMPLE: (4)(3) = 12

**(odd)(odd) ⇒ odd**

EXAMPLE: (3)(5) = 15

In general if one of the multiplicands, or factors, is even the result is even. Otherwise, if all of the factors are odd the product is odd.

EXAMPLE: (even)(odd)(odd)(odd) = even (2)(3)(1)(5) = (2)(15) = 30, which is even.

## Factors

Given that X, Y, and Z are integers, X is a ***factor*** of Y **if** X divides into Y evenly (i.e. with no remainder). $\frac{Y}{X} = Z$ or $Y = X \cdot Z$

EXAMPLE: 6 is a factor of 24: $\frac{24}{6} = 4$ or $24 = (6)(4)$

EXAMPLE: 7 is not a factor 25: $\frac{25}{7} = 3\frac{4}{25}$ (with a remainder of 4).

The concept that an integer may have factors has implications. These implications come up in the concept of prime numbers later.

### Special Properties of Factors

Some factors can be determined by special properties exhibited by integers containing the factor. One such property is that all even numbers are divisible by 2. Following are properties for numbers divisible by 3, 5, 6, and 9.

3 is a factor of a number if the sum of the number's digits is divisible by 3 (i.e., 3 is a factor of the sum). For example the number 1011 is divisible by three because the sum of its digits is three: 1011 ⇒ 1 + 0 + 1 + 1 = 3. (Three is, of course, divisible by three.)

EXAMPLE: Is 2304 divisible by 3?

SOLUTION: 2304 ⇒ 2 + 3 + 0 + 4 = 9

Since 9 is divisible by 3, 2304 is divisible by 3.

EXERCISE: Apply this principle to the following list of numbers as you read the list: 12, 21, 30, 15, 24, 33, 42, 51, and 60. In each case the number sums to 3 or 6 and in each case the number is divisible by 3.

6 is a factor of a number if 2 and 3 are each factors of the number. Look at the numbers in the exercise above. You should be able to quickly identify that 12, 30, 24, 42, and 60 are divisible by 2 and 3 and are thus divisible by 6.

5 is a factor of a number if the number ends in 5 or 0. Some examples are 25, 50, 55, 75, 90, 125, 995.

9 is a factor of a number if the sum of the number's digits is divisible by 9 (i.e., 9 is a factor of the sum). Notice that 2304, as shown on the previous page, is divisible by 9 since its digits add to 9.

EXAMPLE: $774 \Rightarrow 7 + 7 + 4 = 18$. Since 18 is divisible by 9, 774 is divisible by 9.

## Multiple

The concept of a number being a multiple is the opposite of it being a factor.
Given that X, Y, and Z are integers, X is a ***multiple*** of Y **if** Y is a factor of X, i.e.,

$$\frac{X}{Y} = Z \text{ implies } YZ = X.$$

EXAMPLE: 24 is a multiple of 6: (6)(4) = 24.

## Closure Property

Closure means that the result of an operation is still a member of the set. Closure comes up on the GMAT test in questions where number properties are assigned to variables. You are expected to identify combinations of variables that will always result in a certain number type, such as integer.

Integers are closed under

1. addition EXAMPLE: $2 + 3 = 5$
2. subtraction EXAMPLE: $4 - 1 = 3$
3. multiplication EXAMPLE: $(3)(2) = 6$

The set of integers is <u>not closed</u> under division. Notice that it only takes <u>*one*</u> example to show that an operation is not closed.

EXAMPLE: $\frac{2}{3}, \frac{5}{2}$ are not integers.

To reiterate an operation, such as addition, is ***closed*** over a set, such as the set of integers, when every possible result of the operation is in the set. So we can say that addition is closed over the set of integers because the sum of any two integers always results in an integer. Some phrases that have precisely the same meaning are:

- Addition is closed over the set of integers.
- Integers are closed under addition.
- Integers are closed with respect to addition.
- Addition is closed on integers.

Let's use combinations of factors and multiples to test closure.

Given that X, Y, and Z are integers, X is a factor of Y, and Z is a multiple of X, each of the following examples can be shown to be integers (i.e. closure).

From the given we have $\frac{Y}{X} = A$ or Y=XA, where A is an integer, and Z = XB, where B is also an integer.

EXAMPLE: $\frac{Y+Z}{X} = \frac{XA+XB}{X} = \frac{X(A+B)}{X} = A + B$ Demonstration of closure under addition.

EXAMPLE: $\frac{X-Y}{X}=\frac{X-XA}{X}=\frac{X(1-A)}{X}=1-A$ Demonstration of closure under subtraction.

EXAMPLE: $\frac{YZ}{X}=\frac{(XA)(XB)}{X}=\frac{X^2AB}{X}=XAB$ Demonstration of closure under multiplication.

## Absolute Value

The absolute value of a number is always non-negative (i.e., positive or zero).

EXAMPLE: $|5| = 5$ and $|-5| = 5$.

### Common Traps

$|A| = A$ is not true if $A < 0$ (i.e. A is negative).

EXAMPLE: Let $A = -5$. Then, if $|A| = A$ were true it would follow that $|-5| = -5$, but this is certainly not the case. $|-5| \neq -5$ but $|-5| = 5$. The resolution is that $|A| = A$ if $A \geq 0$ and $|A| = -A$ if $A < 0$.

Absolute value is used to measure distance. Distance is the difference between 2 points and difference implies subtraction. Since distance is considered a positive value, absolute value is used.

EXAMPLE: The difference (distance) between -4 and 6 can be expressed as follows: $|-4 - 6| = |-10| = 10$ or $|6 - (-4)| = |10| = 10$.

### Use of Absolute Value for Addition and Subtraction

If the signs of the numbers are the same, add the absolute values of the numbers and insert the common sign.

EXAMPLE: $-4 - 5 = -(|-4| + |-5|) = -(4 + 5) = -9$

common sign absolute values

If the signs are different, subtract the absolute values of the numbers and insert the sign of the number with the greater absolute value.

EXAMPLE: $-4 + 7 = +(|7| - |-4|) = +(7 - 4) = 3$

greater value sign absolute values

EXAMPLE: $7 - 4 = +(|7| - |-4|) = +(7 - 4) = 3$

greater value sign absolute values

EXAMPLE: $-7 + 4 = -(|-7| - |4|) = -(7 - 4) = -3$

greater value sign absolute values

EXAMPLE: $4 - 7 = -(|-7| - |4|) = -(7 - 4) = -3$

greater value sign absolute values

It can be seen that $-4 + 7 = 7 - 4 = 3$ and $-7 + 4 = 4 - 7 = -3$.

If parentheses ( ) are involved some simple methods can be applied. If the two signs are the same the result is positive (i.e. +(+) ⇒ (+) and -(-) ⇒ (+)).

EXAMPLE: +(+4) = 4 (+) EXAMPLE: -(-4) = 4 (+)

If 2 signs are different the result is negative (i.e. +(-) ⇒ (-) and -(+) ⇒ (-)).

EXAMPLE: +(-3) = -3 (-) EXAMPLE: -(+3) = -3 (-)

When multiple numbers are combined, a good method is to proceed in logical stages

EXAMPLE: -3 + 5 - (+4) - (-6)

= -3 + 5 - 4 + 6 eliminate dual signs

= -7 + 11 combine like signs

= 4

## Consecutive Integers

Consecutive integers are in sequence, one after another, without skipping any numbers (i. e. no gaps).

EXAMPLE: 3, 4, 5, 6, are consecutive.

Consecutive integers can be expressed in a generic form as X, X + 1, X + 2, X + 3, ... where X is the first in the sequence.

EXAMPLE: if X = 3 then X, X + 1, X + 2, X + 3 would be 3, (3 + 1), (3 + 2), (3 + 3) or 3, 4, 5, 6.

You can also have consecutive even integers. Of course each odd number is skipped.

EXAMPLE: 2, 4, 6, 8 are consecutive even integers.

And as you would expect there are consecutive odd integers.

EXAMPLE: 3, 5, 7, 9.

Both odd and even consecutive integers can be expressed in the generic form X, X + 2, X + 4, X + 6...

EXAMPLE: If X = 4 then X, X + 2, X + 4, X + 6 would be 4, (4 + 2), (4 + 4), (4 + 6) or 4, 6, 8, 10.

EXAMPLE: If X = 3 then X, X + 2, X + 4, X + 6 would be 3, (3 + 2), (3 + 4), (3 + 6) or 3, 5, 7, 9.

### Counting Consecutive Integers

The number of integers between two specific integers, A and B, is $|A - B| - 1$. Note that this computation assumes that A and B are not included in the count, and that $A \neq B$.

EXAMPLE: What is the number of integers between 11 and 25?

SOLUTION: The hard way is to list the numbers and count:

12, 13, 14, 15, 16, 17, 18, 19, 20, 21, 22, 23, and 24.

Or $|25 - 11| - 1 = 14 - 1 = 13$, is an easier way.

EXAMPLE: How many numbers are in the sequence 5, 6, 7, ..., 22?

SOLUTION: This problem could be rewritten as, "How many integers are between 4 and 23?" Notice that the rewritten version fits our formula so the answer is simply $|23 - 4| - 1 = 19 - 1 = 18$.

Obviously these sort of questions are too simple for the GMAT exam, however, this method of counting consecutive numbers, or anything that can be numbered, is useful. Of special importance is counting correctly. If instead of using $|25 - 11| - 1$, you use $25 - 11$, not only is the result wrong, but more than likely that error has been anticipated in the available answers to trap you.

## Special Integers

Zero (0) is the addition and subtraction identity (i.e. $X + 0 = X$ and $X - 0 = X$).

Multiplication by zero yields zero (i.e. $0 \cdot X = 0$).

Zero divided by any non-zero number yields zero (i.e. $\frac{0}{X} = 0$).

Division by zero cannot be done (i.e. $\frac{X}{0}$ = undefined).

For integers X and Y if $X \neq Y$ and $XY = 0$ then either $X = 0$ or $Y = 0$.

One (1) is the multiplication (divisional) identity (i.e. $X \cdot 1 = X$ and $X \div 1 = X$).

## Primes

The set of primes is the subset of integers for which each number is only divisible by one (1) and itself.

EXAMPLE: 2, 3, 5, 7, 11, 13 are consecutive primes.

Note: one (1) is not considered prime and two (2) is the only even prime.

### Prime Closure

Since all primes, except the first prime, two (2), are odd and odd ± odd ⇒ even, it follows that primes are not closed under addition and subtraction.

Primes are not closed under multiplication since (A)(B) = C makes A and B factors of C.

Every integer can be expressed as a product of its primes.

EXAMPLE:

```
      8            15            24
     / \           / \          /   \
    2   4         3   5        4     6
       / \                    / \   / \
      2   2                  2   2 2   3
  8 = (2)(2)(2)   15 = (3)(5)   24 = (2)(2)(2)(3)
```

# FRACTIONS

A fraction, a rational number, is one integer divided by another (i.e. $\frac{A}{B}$).

## SOME FRACTION CONCEPTS

Some fundamental fraction concepts are equivalent fractions, reciprocals, and reduced fractions.

### Equivalent Fractions

Fractions are equivalent if they can be reduced to the same lowest terms.

EXAMPLE: $\frac{2}{3} = \frac{4}{6} = \frac{6}{9}$ are equivalent fractions.

### Reciprocal

The ***reciprocal*** of X is $\frac{1}{X}$. A number times its reciprocal equals 1 (i.e. $X \cdot \frac{1}{X} = \frac{X}{X} = 1$).

It can be shown that the reciprocal of any fraction is the fraction inverted (i.e. flipped).

EXAMPLE: The reciprocal of $\frac{X}{Y}$ is $\frac{Y}{X}$: $\frac{1}{\frac{X}{Y}} = 1 \cdot \frac{Y}{X} = \frac{Y}{X}$.

### Reducing Fractions

The process of reducing a fraction to its lowest terms involves dividing the numerator and denominator by their greatest common divisor (GCD). The GCD of two integers is the greatest number that is a factor of both.

EXAMPLE: To reduce $\frac{4}{6}$ compute GCD(4,6)=2, then divide: $\frac{4 \div 2}{6 \div 2} = \frac{2}{3}$.

And to reduce $\frac{6}{9}$ compute GCD(6,9)=3, so that $\frac{6 \div 3}{9 \div 3} = \frac{2}{3}$.

Though using a GCD is the most efficient means for reducing a fraction, it is not a requirement as seen in the example below.

EXAMPLE: $\frac{375 \div 25}{1000 \div 25} = \frac{15 \div 5}{40 \div 5} = \frac{3}{8}$ (i.e., keep dividing until you cannot divide again).

## MIXED NUMBERS

The combination of an integer followed by a fraction is called a ***mixed number***. In a mixed number addition is implied (i.e. $3\frac{3}{4} = 3 + \frac{3}{4}$). Mixed numbers can be converted into improper fractions (i.e. where the numerator is greater than the denominator).

EXAMPLE: From mixed form $2\frac{3}{4} = 2 \cdot \frac{4}{4} + \frac{3}{4} = \frac{8}{4} + \frac{3}{4} = \frac{11}{4}$ to improper fraction form.

A short cut to obtaining the numerator for a converted mixed number is to multiply the integer times the denominator and then add the numerator (remainder) (i.e. (integer)(denominator) + (numerator)). This new numerator goes over the original denominator.

EXAMPLE: $2\frac{3}{4} \Rightarrow (2)(4)+3 \Rightarrow \frac{11}{4}$

## ADDITION AND SUBTRACTION OF FRACTIONS

The preferred method for the addition of fractions requires finding the lowest common denominator (LCD) (i.e. lowest common multiple of the denominators).

EXAMPLE: $\frac{3}{4}+\frac{5}{6}$ LCD = 12 $\Rightarrow \frac{9}{12}+\frac{10}{12}=\frac{19}{12}=1\frac{7}{12}$

(Note: 12 is the lowest common multiple of 4 and 6.)

An alternate method to find a common denominator is to multiply the two denominators and then reduce.

EXAMPLE: $\frac{3}{4}+\frac{5}{6}$ Multiply denominators, (4)(6) = 24. $\frac{18}{24}+\frac{20}{24}=\frac{38}{24}=\frac{19}{12}=1\frac{7}{12}$

## MULTIPLICATION OF FRACTIONS

Multiplication is accomplished by multiplying numerator times numerator and denominator times denominator: $\frac{N_1}{D_1}\times\frac{N_2}{D_2}=\frac{N_1 \cdot N_2}{D_1 \cdot D_2}$.

EXAMPLE: $\left(\frac{3}{4}\right)\left(\frac{2}{5}\right)=\frac{3\cdot 2}{4\cdot 5}=\frac{6}{20}=\frac{3}{10}$

The method of cancellation can be applied to simplify the operation. By canceling factors common to the numerator and denominator of a fraction multiplication, you reduce the size of the numbers to be multiplied.

EXAMPLE: $\frac{3}{\overset{}{\cancel{4}}_{2}}\times\frac{\overset{1}{\cancel{2}}}{5}=\frac{3}{10}$ By first eliminating the common factor of 2 in 2 and 4, the step of reducing the answer is eliminated.

## DIVISION (COMPLEX FRACTIONS)

Complex fractions occur when a number is divided by a fraction. $\frac{3}{\frac{3}{4}}$ (3 divided by $\frac{3}{4}$) is an example of a complex fraction. This can be evaluated by multiplying the numerator by the reciprocal of the denominator:

$$\frac{3}{\frac{3}{4}}=\overset{1}{\cancel{3}}\cdot\frac{4}{\underset{1}{\cancel{3}}}=4$$

Note that this is valid since multiplying by the reciprocal is equivalent to division.

EXAMPLE: $\dfrac{\frac{3}{4}}{\frac{6}{8}} = \dfrac{\overset{1}{\cancel{3}}}{\underset{1}{\cancel{4}}} \cdot \dfrac{\overset{2}{\cancel{8}}}{\underset{2}{\cancel{6}}} = \dfrac{2}{2} = 1$

Note that $\frac{3}{4} = \frac{6}{8}$ are equivalent fractions. When you divide equivalent fractions you get one (i.e., anything divided by itself equals one.

## RATIO AND PROPORTION

A ***ratio*** is the comparison of one number to another: A to B ⇒ A : B ⇒ $\frac{A}{B}$. Note: The number being compared to is on the bottom of the fraction (i.e., denominator).

EXAMPLE: 3 to 5 = 3 : 5 = $\frac{3}{5}$

A ***proportion*** is comparison of two ratios: $A:B = C:D \Rightarrow \frac{A}{B} = \frac{C}{D}$. The easiest way to evaluate proportions is by cross multiplication:

$$\frac{A}{B} \times \frac{C}{D} \Rightarrow A \cdot D = B \cdot C$$

EXAMPLE: $\frac{3}{5} = \frac{N}{15} \Rightarrow 5N = 45$ or $N = 9$.

### Additional Properties of Proportion

Consider the following proportion: $\frac{2}{10} = \frac{8}{40}$. Each denominator is the same multiple of its corresponding numerator (i.e. 5). 10 is 5 times 2 just as 40 is 5 times 8. Further the numerators and denominators have the same multiplier (i.e. 4). 8 is 4 times 2 and 40 is 4 times 10. These two types of symmetry allow two different solution methods.

$$5\left(\frac{2}{10} \overset{4}{=} \frac{8}{40}\right)5 \quad (4 \text{ above and below})$$

EXAMPLE: $\frac{5}{15} = \frac{N}{60}$ can be solved in two ways. The ratio of 5 to 15 is 1:3, so 60 is 3 times N: 3N=60, which yields N=20. The ratio of 15 to 60 is 1:4, so N is 4 times 5, or 20.

$$3\left(\frac{5}{15} \overset{4}{=} \frac{N}{60}\right)3 \quad (4 \text{ above and below})$$

The concept of proportion can be used to compare fractions (i.e. which is larger or equal).

EXAMPLE: $\frac{2}{9} \overset{?}{=} \frac{6}{27}$ If this proportion is equal then the cross multiplication will be equal. $(2)(27) \overset{?}{=} (9)(6)$ which after multiplication is 54 = 54. Therefore they are equal. Alternately since the multiples of the numerators and denominators are the same, namely 3, the two fractions are equivalent.

EXAMPLE: Which is larger $\frac{2}{9} \overset{?}{=} \frac{5}{21}$?

SOLUTION: Using cross multiplication we see:

$$\frac{2}{9} \overset{?}{\times} \frac{5}{21}$$

$2 \cdot 21 \overset{?}{=} 9 \cdot 5$ or $42 < 45$. Since the right side is larger, the correct relationship is $\frac{2}{9} < \frac{5}{21}$. This can be verified by converting both to a common denominator.

## Application of Proportion

EXAMPLE: A flagpole and a man standing nearby both cast shadows. The flagpole's shadow is 8 feet long, whereas the man's shadow is only 2 feet long. Given that the man's height is 6 feet, what is the pole's height?

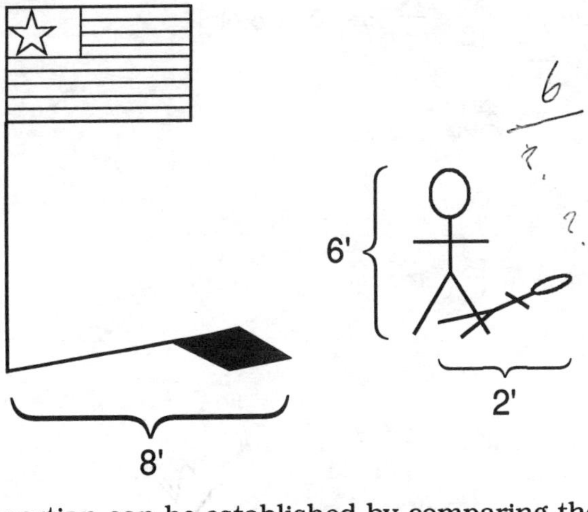


SOLUTION: The proportion can be established by comparing the height of the man to his shadow: $\frac{6}{2} = \frac{H}{8}$, where H is the height of the pole in feet.

There are 3 ways to evaluate this:

1. Cross multiplication: $\frac{H}{8} \times \frac{6}{2} \Rightarrow 2H = (8)(6) = 48 \Rightarrow H = 24$

2. Ratio of each side is 3: $3\left(\frac{H}{8} = \frac{6}{2}\right)3 \Rightarrow (3)(8) = H \Rightarrow H = 24$

3. Ratio of numerators and denominators is 4: $\frac{H}{8} = \frac{6}{2} \Rightarrow H = (6)(4) = 24$ (with 4 marked above and below the fractions)

The proportion could also have been established by comparing shadow to shadow and height to height: $\frac{2}{8} = \frac{6}{H} \Rightarrow 2H = (6)(8) \Rightarrow 2H = 48 \Rightarrow H = 24$. The result is the same.

## Inverse Proportion

An ***inverse proportion*** reverses the proportional relationship. A standard proportion problem occurs when the components increase together (as in the flagpole problem, where as the pole size increases the pole's shadow also increases). An inverse proportion problem occurs when one quantity increases while the other decreases (as seen in work problems, where as the number of workers on a project increases the time to completion decreases). This can best be explained by example.

EXAMPLE: A certain job takes 6 men 4 hours. How long would it take 12 men to do the job? The equation setup is as follows: $\frac{6 \text{ men}}{12 \text{ men}} = \frac{X \text{ hours}}{4 \text{ hours}}$. Note: The 2nd ratio is the reciprocal or inverse of a standard proportion. By cross multiplication 12X = 24 which simplifies to X = 2.

Alternately $\frac{6}{12} = \frac{X}{4} \Rightarrow 3X = 6$ or X = 2. (with 3 marked above and below the fractions)

# DECIMALS

Decimals are a form of a fraction where the denominator is understood to be a power of 10. Each decimal place is 10 times the previous one.

| Thousands | Hundreds | Tens | Ones | | Tenths | Hundredths | Thousandths |
|---|---|---|---|---|---|---|---|
| 9 | 3 | 5 | 4 | . | 2 | 7 | 1 |

Consider the following number: 9 3 5 4 . 2 7 1

## EQUIVALENT FRACTIONS

EXAMPLE: $.2 = \frac{2}{10}$

EXAMPLE: $.23 = \frac{2}{10} + \frac{3}{100} = \frac{20}{100} + \frac{3}{100} = \frac{23}{100}$

EXAMPLE: $.237 = \frac{2}{10} + \frac{3}{100} + \frac{7}{1000} = \frac{200}{1000} + \frac{30}{1000} + \frac{7}{1000} = \frac{237}{1000}$

EXAMPLE: $.4 = \frac{4}{10} = \frac{2}{5}$

## ROUNDING

To round a decimal number to a particular place, follow this procedure:

1. Mark place to be rounded.
2. If the previous place (the place to the right) is greater than or equal to 5, then increment the marked place by 1. If not, then the marked place remains the same.
3. All decimals following the marked place are dropped.

EXAMPLE: Round 278.468 to the nearest hundredth.

SOLUTION:

| | |
|---|---|
| $278.4\underline{6}8$ | mark place |
| $278.4\underline{6}\mathbf{8}$ | next significant $8 \geq 5$ therefore increment 6 |
| $278.4\underline{7}$ | drop the previous digits |

EXAMPLE: Round 35.247 to the nearest tenth.

| | |
|---|---|
| $35.\underline{2}47$ | mark place |
| $35.\underline{2}\mathbf{4}7$ | $4 \leq 5$ therefore 2 remains the same |
| $35.\underline{2}$ | drop the previous digits |

## ADDITION AND SUBTRACTION

To add or subtract decimals place the numbers vertical and line up the decimals.

EXAMPLE: $3.5 + 28 + .02$ $\qquad$ $21.4 - 17.26$

$$\begin{array}{r} 3.50 \\ 28.00 \\ +.02 \\ \hline 31.52 \end{array} \qquad \begin{array}{r} 21.40 \\ -17.26 \\ \hline 4.14 \end{array}$$

Don't forget to borrow.

Notice zeros are placed to locate the decimal, they do not change the value of the number.

## MULTIPLICATION

Multiply decimals as if they were all integers, then count the total number of decimal places in both numbers. This is the number of decimals in the final answer.

EXAMPLE:

$$\begin{array}{r} 6.25 \\ \times 3.2 \\ \hline 1250 \\ 1875\phantom{0} \\ \hline 20.000 \end{array}$$

There are 3 decimal places total, .25 and .2. So three of the zeros in 20000 are decimal digits to the right of the decimal place.

EXAMPLE:

$$\begin{array}{r} 0.325 \\ \times 1.8 \\ \hline 2600 \\ 325\phantom{0} \\ \hline .5850 \end{array}$$

There are 4 decimal places total, .325 and .8. So four of the zeros in 5850 are decimal digits to the right of the decimal place.

## DIVISION

To divide decimals follow these stages:

1. Convert divisor to an integer by moving the decimal point as many places to the right as necessary.
2. Move the decimal point of the dividend the same number of places.
3. Bring the point straight up from the dividend to the quotient.

EXAMPLE: 180 divided by 4.5: $4.5\overline{)180}$ ? (quotient: ?)

SOLUTION: $45\overline{)1800.}$ (quotient: ?.) Move both decimal places over by 1 place. Now 4.5 is 45.

$$\begin{array}{r} 40.0 \\ 45\overline{)1800} \\ \underline{180}\phantom{0} \\ 0\phantom{0} \end{array}$$

Place your decimal and then divide.

## CONVERTING FRACTIONS TO DECIMALS

Consider $\frac{5}{8}$. The bar in a fraction implies division, so to convert to decimal do the division.

$$
\begin{array}{r}
0.625 \\
8\overline{)5.000} \\
\underline{4.8} \\
20 \\
\underline{16} \\
40 \\
\underline{40}
\end{array}
$$

Note: Zeros were added after the decimal point to complete the division.

**Time saver**

Convert to an equivalent fraction with the denominator as a power of 10.

EXAMPLE: Convert $\frac{3}{5}$ to its decimal equivalent.

SOLUTION: $\left(\frac{3}{5}\right)\left(\frac{2}{2}\right) = \frac{6}{10} = 0.6$ When the denominator is a power of 5 just multiply the top and bottom by the same power of two.

EXAMPLE: Convert $\frac{7}{20}$ to its decimal equivalent.

SOLUTION: $\left(\frac{7}{20}\right)\left(\frac{5}{5}\right) = \frac{35}{100} = 0.35$ When the denominator has only 2s and 5s in its prime factorization ($20 = 2 \cdot 2 \cdot 5$), then multiply the top and bottom by the missing factors of 5 or 2 to make the denominator a power of ten.

A table of fractions with their decimal and percent equivalents is on page 163.

## PERCENT

***Percent*** means parts per hundred (100). There are 100 years in a <u>cent</u>ury, and 100 <u>cent</u>s in a dollar. A percent is a fraction in units of hundredths (i.e. denominator = 100). For instance $25\% = \frac{25}{100}$. **Note:** $\frac{100}{100} = 1 \Rightarrow$ one whole represents 100%.

To convert a percent to a decimal, move the decimal point 2 places to the left: 75% = .75. To convert a decimal to a percent, move the decimal point 2 places to the right: .40 = 40%.

## EQUIVALENT FORMS

EXAMPLE: $25\% = \frac{25}{100} = .25 = \frac{1}{4}$

EXAMPLE: $150\% = \frac{150}{100} = 1.5 = 1\frac{1}{2}$

## THREE BASIC FORMS OF PERCENT PROBLEMS

There are three places in a percent problem for an unknown. The three parts are the percent, the whole and the part of the whole. To evaluate the problems below remember, "OF" always means multiply and "IS" always means equals. Change each of the word problems to an algebraic equation.

EXAMPLE: 25% of 300 is ?

Convert the percent to a decimal, 25% ⇒ .25, of to ×, and ? to a variable (i.e. N):

$$.25 \times 300 = N$$

The solution is 75 = N.

An alternate method avoids decimal multiplication. Converting the percent to a fraction changes the problem from decimal multiplication to integer division, 300 divided by 4:

$$\frac{1}{4} \times 300 = 300 \div 4 = 75$$

EXAMPLE: 25% of ? is 45

$.25 \times N = 45$

$N = \frac{45}{.25} = 180$

Alternate solution

$\frac{1}{4} \times N = 45$

$N = \frac{45}{\frac{1}{4}} = 45 \times \frac{4}{1} = 180$

EXAMPLE: ? % of 360 is 90

$P \times 360 = 90$

$P = \frac{90}{360} = \frac{1}{4} = 25\%$

# FRACTION AND PERCENT CONVERSION TABLE

The following conversion table may be helpful in identifying patterns with conversions between fractions, decimals, and percents.

| Number | % | Decimal |
|---|---|---|
| $\frac{1}{2}$ | 50 | .5 |
| $\frac{1}{3}$ | $33\frac{1}{3}$ | .33... |
| $\frac{2}{3}$ | $66\frac{2}{3}$ | .66... |
| $\frac{1}{4}$ | 25 | .25 |
| $\frac{3}{4}$ | 75 | .75 |
| $\frac{1}{5}$ | 20 | .2 |
| $\frac{2}{5}$ | 40 | .4 |
| $\frac{3}{5}$ | 60 | .6 |
| $\frac{4}{5}$ | 80 | .8 |
| $\frac{1}{8}$ | $12\frac{1}{2}$ | .125 |
| $\frac{3}{8}$ | $37\frac{1}{2}$ | .375 |
| $\frac{5}{8}$ | $62\frac{1}{2}$ | .625 |
| $\frac{7}{8}$ | $87\frac{1}{2}$ | .875 |
| $1\frac{1}{2}$ | 150 | 1.5 |
| 2 | 200 | 2.0 |

## PERCENT CHANGE

Different terms can be used in stating a problem of percent change.

- Increase / Decrease
- Profit / Loss
- Markup / Markdown

All can be evaluated by the same method: $\% \text{ change} = \frac{\text{change (difference)}}{\text{original amount}}$.

EXAMPLE: What is the % increase from 30 to 40.

$$\frac{\text{change}}{\text{original}} = \frac{10}{30} = \frac{1}{3} = \frac{100\%}{3} = 33\frac{1}{3}\%$$

EXAMPLE: What is the % decrease from 50 to 30.

$$\frac{\text{change}}{\text{original}} = \frac{20}{50} = \frac{2}{5} = \frac{200\%}{5} = 40\%$$

## COMPOUND PROBLEMS

EXAMPLE: 30% of 500 is 10% of ?

SOLUTION: First convert to an expression: (.3)(500) = (.1) N. (Notice that each "of" is converted to multiplication and the "is" becomes "=" and the "?" becomes a variable.)

$$150 = .1(N)$$

$$\frac{150}{.1} = N$$

$$1500 = N$$

Alternate method with fractions:

$$\left(\frac{30}{100}\right)(500) = \frac{1}{10}N$$

$$(30)(5) = \frac{N}{10}$$

$$150 = \frac{N}{10}$$

$$1500 = N$$

EXAMPLE: 250% of 30 is ? % of 225

SOLUTION: First convert to an expression: (2.5)(30) = P (225).

$$75 = 225P$$

$$\frac{75}{225} = P$$

$$\frac{1}{3} = P$$

$$\frac{100\%}{3} = 33\frac{1}{3}\% = P$$

Alternate method with fractions:

$\left(\frac{250}{100}\right)(30) = P(225)$

$\left(\frac{25}{10}\right)(30) = P(225)$

$75 = P(225)$

$\frac{1}{3} = P$

$33\frac{1}{3}\% = P$

## Performing Percent Mentally

Doing percent problems mentally can save a lot of time. Some basic concepts are in order.

- 10% of a number ⇒ shift decimal place left one digit

EXAMPLE: 10% of 400 ⇒ 40.0 = 40

- 1% of a number ⇒ shift decimal place left two digits

EXAMPLE: 1% of 300 ⇒ 3.00 = 3

Consider the number 1600:

- If 10% of 1600 = 160 then

  5% of 1600 = 80 (5% is half of 10%, so 80 is half of 160).

- Similarly if 1% of 1600 = 16 then

  $\frac{1}{2}\%$ of 1600 = 8 ($\frac{1}{2}\%$ is half of 1%, so 8 is half of 16).

EXAMPLE: What is $2\frac{1}{2}\%$ of 360?

SOLUTION: 10% of 360 = 36

5% of 360 = 18 one-half of 36

$2\frac{1}{2}\%$ of 360 = 9 one-half of 18

EXAMPLE: What is 15% of 520?

SOLUTION:

| | | |
|---|---|---|
| 10% of 520 | = | 52 |
| + 5% of 520 | = | 26 |
| 15% | = | 78 |

Mental math involves taking more difficult tasks, such as multiplying by .15, and breaking each down into simpler tasks, such as taking 10% (shifting the decimal place by one place) taking half of whatever is 10% to get 5% and then adding the two to get the result. These "tricks" are applied throughout the rest of this review. As you start to apply mental math you will find that it eases many computations, improves your speed and increases accuracy.

# PERCENT OF PERCENTS

EXAMPLE: What is 20% of 10% of 3000?

SOLUTION: **Method 1, "Stages":**

$20\% \text{ of } \underbrace{10\% \text{ of } 3000}_{300}$

$\underbrace{20\% \text{ of } 300}$

20% of 300 = 60

**Method 2:**

"of" always means multiply:

$.2 \times .1 \times 3000 = .02 \times 3000 = 60$

**Method 3, "Mentally":**

$20\% = \frac{1}{5}$

$\frac{1}{5}$ of 10% = 2%

1% of 3000 = 30

2% of 3000 = 60

# REAL NUMBERS

Real numbers are composed of the set of integers and everything in between (i.e. fractions, decimals, roots, and many others). Real numbers can be viewed as any number that resides on the number line. It is true that many roots cannot be equated with a fraction. These roots, and other non-fractions, can be found on the number line, between many fractions.

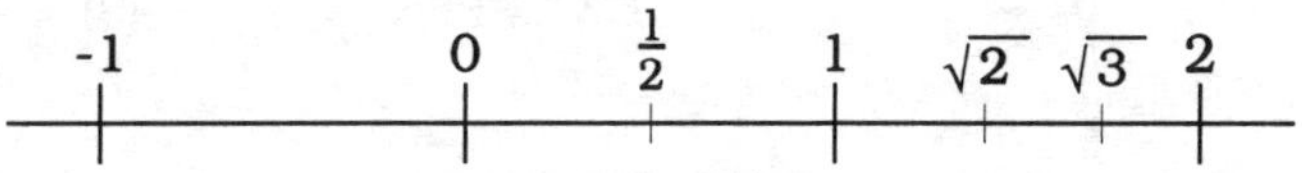


One must use ingenuity to successfully compare real numbers when they are not fractions.

# PROPERTIES OF SIGNS

## Multiplication

For multiplication there is a property of signs. This property is critical in algebra.

(+)(+) = (+) EXAMPLE: (3)(4) = 12

(+)(-) = (-) EXAMPLE: (3)(-4) = -12

(-)(-) = (+) EXAMPLE: (-3)(-4) = 12

In general, for two non-zero multiplicands, if the signs are the same the product is positive and if the signs are different the product is negative. In cases with more than two factors (all non-zero), an even number of negative signs makes the product positive, and an odd number of negative signs makes the product negative. If any factor is zero, the product is zero.

EXAMPLE: (+)(+)(-):

(+)(+) (-) =

(+) (-) ⇒ (-) i.e., (3)(5)(-2) = (15)(-2) = -30

EXAMPLE: (+)(-)(+)(-):

(+)(-) (+)(-) =

(-) (-) ⇒ (+) i.e., (3)(-1)(5)(-2) = (-3)(-10) = 30

## Division

For division there is a property of signs: $\frac{(+)}{(+)} = (+)$; $\frac{(+)}{(-)} = (-)$; $\frac{(-)}{(+)} = (-)$; $\frac{(-)}{(-)} = (+)$

In general if the signs are the same the quotient is positive and if the signs are different the quotient is negative, just as with multiplication.

Since the fraction itself may have a negative sign, it follows:

$$-\frac{(-)}{(-)} = -(+) = (-) \qquad -\frac{(+)}{(-)} = -(-) = (+)$$

Note: A negative sign preceding parentheses, ( ), is equivalent to multiplying by (-1).

EXAMPLE: -(-3) = (-1)(-3) = 3

Consider the following examples:

EXAMPLE: $\frac{2}{-3} = -\frac{2}{3}$

EXAMPLE: $\frac{-6}{-2} = 3$

EXAMPLE: $-\frac{-2}{3} = -\left(-\frac{2}{3}\right) = \frac{2}{3}$

EXAMPLE: $-\frac{-6}{-2} = -(3) = -3$

## CLOSURE

Real numbers are closed under addition, subtraction, and multiplication. Division is also closed when dividing by other than zero (0). This property is not easily shown here, but suffice it to say that the sum, difference, product, or ratio of any two non-zero real numbers is also a real number.

## POWERS

$X^n$ means X times itself n times (i.e. $X^3 = (X)(X)(X)$).

EXAMPLE: $5^3 = (5)(5)(5) = 125$

It is important to note that powers only apply to what they directly touch.

EXAMPLE: $3^2 = (3)(3) = 9$

EXAMPLE: $-3^2 = -(3)(3) = -9$. The power 2 only touches the 3 not the negative sign.

EXAMPLE: $(-3)^2 = (-3)(-3) = 9$. The power 2 touches the ( ).

### Properties of Powers

Consider $X^n$ where n is an integer. If X>1, then $X^n > X$ (i.e. $X^n$ gets larger when X>1).

EXAMPLE: $2^3 = 8 \Rightarrow 8 > 2$

However, if $0 < X < 1$ then $X^n < X$ (i.e. $X^n$ gets smaller).

EXAMPLE: $\left(\frac{1}{2}\right)^3 = \frac{1}{8} \Rightarrow \frac{1}{8} < \frac{1}{2}$

EXAMPLE: $(.2)^2 = .04 \Rightarrow .04 < .2$

If X is positive then $X^n$ is positive (i.e. if $X > 0 \Rightarrow X^n > 0$). If X is negative $X^n$ is positive if n is even and $X^n$ is negative if n is odd.

EXAMPLE: $(-3)^4 = (-3)(-3)(-3)(-3) = 81$ and $(-3)^3 = (-3)(-3)(-3) = -27$.

## Properties of Exponents with a Base of 10

Consider the following chart:

$$10^3 = 1000$$
$$10^2 = 100$$
$$10^1 = 10$$
$$10^0 = 1$$
$$10^{-1} = \frac{1}{10^1} = .1$$
$$10^{-2} = \frac{1}{10^2} = \frac{1}{100} = .01$$
$$10^{-3} = \frac{1}{10^3} = \frac{1}{1000} = .001$$

Note the shift of the decimal point one place to the right as the exponent increases (going up the chart) and one place to the left as the exponent decreases.

EXAMPLE: $10^4 = ?$

Since $10 = 10^1$, $10^4$ is an increase of 3 (three additional zeros or three place movements of the decimal). It follows:

$10^4 = 10\,0\,0\,0 = 10{,}000$ (shift 3 right)

EXAMPLE: $10^{-3} = ?$

Since $10 = 10^1$ to $10^{-3}$ is a decrease of 4, we have:

$10^{-3} = 0\,0\,1\,0 = .001$ (shift 4 left)

Alternately $10^{-3} = \frac{1}{10^3} = \frac{1}{1000} = .001$.

EXAMPLE: $10^2$ is how many times $(0.01)^2$?

SOLUTION: Alternately $(0.01)^2 = (0.01)(0.01) = 0.0001$:

0.0001 must shift right 6 places
(0.0 0 0 1 0 0) to equal 100

which is the equivalent of multiplying by $10^6$.

$$(0.01)^2 = \left(\frac{1}{100}\right)^2 = \left(\frac{1}{10^2}\right)^2 = \frac{1}{10^4} = 10^{-4}$$
$$10^2 = (10^x)(10^{-4})$$
$$10^2 = 10^{x-4}$$ (see Algebra, Rules of Exponents)
$$2 = x - 4$$
$$6 = x$$

## Roots

Roots are the inverse (opposite) of powers (i.e. $3^2 = 9 \Rightarrow \sqrt{9} = \sqrt{3^2} = \sqrt{3 \cdot 3} = 3$). Note: for $\sqrt{9}$ (square root) the 2 is implied (i.e. $\sqrt{9} = \sqrt[2]{9}$). For other roots, the number always appears (i.e. cube root $\sqrt[3]{\ }$ and fourth root $\sqrt[4]{\ }$). For instance the cube root of 27 is shown as $\sqrt[3]{27} = \sqrt[3]{3 \cdot 3 \cdot 3} = 3$ (i.e., what number multiplied by itself three times equals 27?).

EXAMPLE: $\sqrt{64} = \sqrt{8 \cdot 8} = 8$

$\sqrt[3]{64} = \sqrt[3]{4 \cdot 4 \cdot 4} = 4$

### Sign Properties of Roots

Roots have interesting sign properties. It is important to recognize that (-3)(-3) also equals 9, but $\sqrt{9}$ implies only the positive root 3, not -3. Therefore $\sqrt{X^2} = |X|$; the two are identical. Cube roots on the other hand preserve the sign: $\sqrt[3]{27} = 3$ and $\sqrt[3]{-27} = -3$.

EXAMPLE: $\sqrt[3]{125} = \sqrt[3]{5 \cdot 5 \cdot 5} = 5$

$\sqrt[3]{-125} = \sqrt[3]{(-5)(-5)(-5)} = -5$

$\sqrt{-1}$ does not exist (as a real number). There is no real number X such that $X \cdot X = -1$. (In fact no real number multiplied with itself can be negative.) But we have seen that cube roots of negative numbers exist (i.e. $\sqrt[3]{-27} = -3$). This suggests that $\sqrt[3]{X^3} = X$ versus $\sqrt{X^2} = |X|$. In general even roots of negative numbers do not exist and odd roots of negative numbers do exist .

### Simplifying Roots

A useful property is used to simplify roots: $\sqrt{xy} = \sqrt{x}\sqrt{y}$.

To simplify the $\sqrt{X}$, identify factors of X that are perfect squares. Each square factor removed from X can be moved out from under the root.

EXAMPLE: $\sqrt{75} = \sqrt{25 \cdot 3} = \sqrt{25}\sqrt{3} = 5\sqrt{3}$

Note: 75 can also be factored as 15 · 5, but neither is a square.

EXAMPLE: $\sqrt{108} = \sqrt{9 \cdot 4 \cdot 3} = \sqrt{9}\sqrt{4}\sqrt{3} = 3 \cdot 2\sqrt{3} = 6\sqrt{3}$

Note: 108 can also be factored as 36 · 3. The order in which factors are removed will not change the final answer. There is no one way to simplify roots, but there is only one simplified answer.

Consider $\sqrt{96}$:

$\sqrt{96} = \sqrt{3 \cdot 32}$ poor choice of factors (no perfect squares)

This next example is an okay choice but needs a second factoring:

$\sqrt{96} = \sqrt{4 \cdot 24}$

$\sqrt{96} = \sqrt{4 \cdot 4 \cdot 6}$

$\sqrt{96} = 2 \cdot 2 \cdot \sqrt{6}$

$\sqrt{96} = 4\sqrt{6}$

This last example is the best choice:

$\sqrt{96} = \sqrt{16 \cdot 6}$

$\sqrt{96} = 4\sqrt{6}$

**Comparison of Roots**

The method for comparing square roots involves removing the roots by squaring both sides.

EXAMPLE: Which is larger, $\sqrt{17}$ or $3\sqrt{2}$?

$\sqrt{17} \stackrel{?}{=} 3\sqrt{2}$

$\sqrt{17}^2 \stackrel{?}{=} (3\sqrt{2})^2$

$17 \stackrel{?}{=} 9 \cdot 2$

$17 < 18$

Therefore $3\sqrt{2}$ is larger than $\sqrt{17}$.

**Simplifying Higher Roots**

If the operation is cube root (i.e. $\sqrt[3]{\ }$), look for a perfect cube as a factor, and a similar process for higher roots.

EXAMPLE: $\sqrt[3]{54} = \sqrt[3]{27 \cdot 2} = 3\sqrt[3]{2}$

**Addition and Subtraction of Roots**

To add or subtract roots, the terms must be of the same type. For instance, $\sqrt{x} + \sqrt{x}$ can be combined ($2\sqrt{x}$), but $\sqrt{x} + \sqrt{y}$ cannot be combined without knowing more about x and y.

EXAMPLE: $3\sqrt{2} + 2\sqrt{2} = 5\sqrt{2}$

$3\sqrt{2} + \sqrt{3}$, not like terms

EXAMPLE: $\sqrt{12}+\sqrt{75}$

As is, these are not of the same type but by using simplification:

$= \sqrt{(3)(4)} + \sqrt{(3)(25)}$

$= 2\sqrt{3} + 5\sqrt{3}$

$= 7\sqrt{3}$

**Multiplication and Division of Roots**

If the roots are the same then the numbers can be multiplied (i.e. $\sqrt{3}\sqrt{5} = \sqrt{15}$ and $\sqrt[4]{9}\sqrt[4]{16} = \sqrt[4]{144}$). Similarly for division: $\sqrt{35} \div \sqrt{5} = \sqrt{7}$ and $\sqrt[3]{36} \div \sqrt[3]{12} = \sqrt[3]{3}$. But $\sqrt{5} \cdot \sqrt[3]{9}$ cannot be so easily combined.

EXAMPLE: $\sqrt{2}\sqrt{8} = \sqrt{(2)(8)} = \sqrt{16} = 4$

The next example uses a property similar to multiplication of roots, the division of roots property, to simplify: $\sqrt{\frac{x}{y}} = \frac{\sqrt{x}}{\sqrt{y}}$.

EXAMPLE: $\frac{\sqrt{8}}{\sqrt{2}} = \sqrt{\frac{8}{2}} = \sqrt{4} = 2$

# ORDER OF OPERATIONS

Numeric expressions are evaluated according to a set order of operations:

- Parentheses P
- Powers (exponents) E
- Multiplication / Division M D
- Addition / Subtraction A S

The word PEMDAS is often used to remember this order. It is the first letter of each operation.

EXAMPLE: Evaluate $-(-3+2-1)^2$.

| | |
|---|---|
| $= -(-2)^2$ | Do parentheses first. |
| = -(4) | Secondly, do exponents (powers). |
| = -4 | Finally, multiply by (-1). |

For nested parentheses, work from the inside out.

EXAMPLE: Evaluate (-3 - (4 - 3) + 1).

| | |
|---|---|
| = (-3 - (1) + 1) | Compute inside ( ) first. |
| = (-3 - 1 + 1) | Multiply by (-1). |
| = -3 | Then do addition and subtraction. |

# MEAN, MEDIAN, AND MODE

## Mean (Average)

The ***mean*** of a list of numbers is calculated by dividing the sum of the elements of the list by the number of elements in the list.

EXAMPLE: The average of X, Y, Z is $\frac{X+Y+Z}{3}$.

### Application of Mean

EXAMPLE: A student has 3 grades of 60, 70, 95 for the first 3 tests. What must he score on the final test to obtain an average of 80?

SOLUTION: $\frac{60+70+95+X}{4}=80$ There are four tests and one is unknown.

$(4)\frac{225+X}{4}=80(4)$ Multiply both sides by 4. (The fours on the left cancel.)

$225 + X = 320$ Subtract 225 from both sides.

$X = 95$

Therefore a 95 is required on the last test to have a final average of 80.

There is an alternate method which sometimes simplifies the solution of this type of problem. The first score, 60, is 20 less than 80. The second score, 70, is 10 less than 80. And 95 is 15 more than 80. To balance the amount less than 80 with the amount more than 80, 15 more is needed. Therefore the last test score needs to be 80 + 15 or 95.

## Median (Middle)

The ***median*** is the middle of a set of numbers arranged in ascending order.

EXAMPLE: Given 3, 5, $\underline{6}$, 8, 11: 6 is the median.

### Rules of median

For N numbers, if N is odd, then the median is the middle number.

EXAMPLE: 3, 6, 8, $\underline{9}$, 14, 17, 21: N = 7, median is 9.

If N is even, the median is the average of the two middle numbers.

EXAMPLE: 3, 5, $\underline{6, 7}$, 8, 11: N = 6, median $= \frac{6+7}{2} = 6.5$.

## Mode (Most Often)

The number that appears most often in a set is the mode.

EXAMPLE: 3, 4, $\underline{5, 5, 5}$, 6, 7: mode = 5.

EXAMPLE: 3, 4, 6, 8, 11: no mode.

EXAMPLE: $\underline{3, 3}$, 4, 5, $\underline{7, 7}$, 8: 2 modes, 3 and 7.

## Practice – Arithmetic

1. If the cost of a monthly car payment is $300, what is the monthly expense for food?

   A. $220
   B. $225
   C. $240
   D. $250
   E. $275

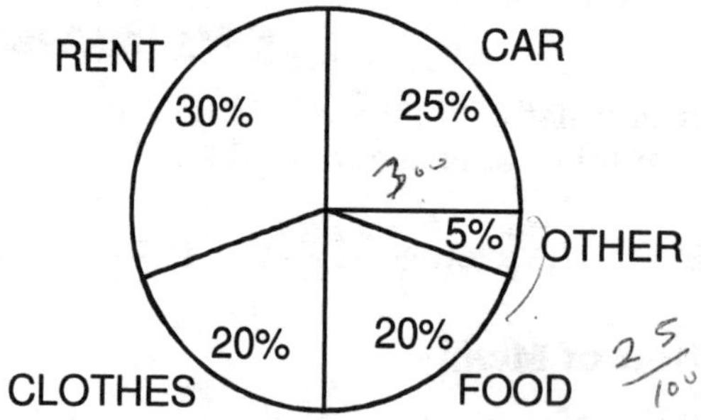


2. A professional bowler has bowled scores of 190, 185 and 205 for 3 games. He needs a 200 average for 4 games to qualify for the next round of the tournament. What is the least he can score on his 4$^{th}$ game to qualify?

   A. 200 B. 205 C. 210 D. 220 E. 225

3. An item which originally listed for $200 has a sign on it which says "take an additional 10% off the discounted price". If the item was discounted by 20% already, what is the total discount?

   A. $30 B. $50 C. $54 D. $56 E. $60

4. What is the total percent discount, in problem 3 above?

   A. 22½% B. 23% C. 25% D. 28 % E. 30%

5. $$\frac{\frac{1}{2}\left(\frac{\frac{2}{3}}{\frac{4}{3}}\right)}{\frac{1}{4}} =$$

   A. $\frac{1}{9}$ B. $\frac{1}{6}$ C. $\frac{2}{3}$ D. 1 E. 2

6. 5.07 – 3.614=

   A. 1.366 B. 1.464 C. 1.654 D. 1.456 E. 2.456

7. If $0.70 is equivalent to 1 peso, what is the value of $140 dollars in pesos?

   A. 42 B. 50 C. 98 D. 200 E. 210

8. If a sequence of 7 consecutive odd integers has 5 as the 5th term, what is the sum of the sequence?

   A. 21 B. 23 C. 25 D. 28 E. 29

9. 1 – [2 – (3 – 5) – 5] =

   A. -14 B. -8 C. -1 D. 0 E. 2

10. Which of the following is equal to ½ percent of 2200?

A. 4400 B. 3300 C. 1100 D. 110 E. 11

11. How many degrees are necessary to rotate the square counterclockwise around its center, so that D is where A is?

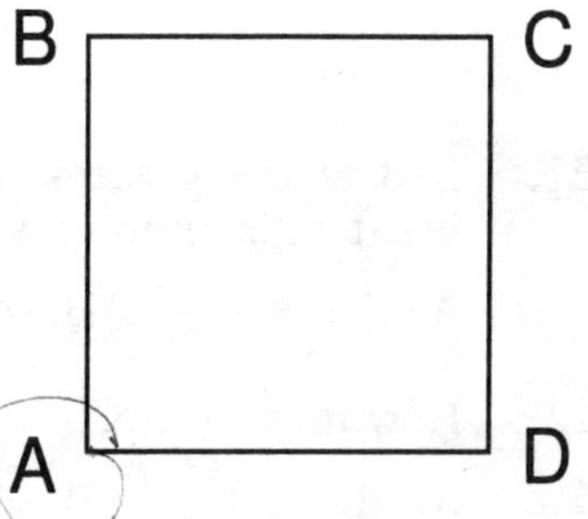


A. 90°
B. 180°
C. 225°
D. 270°
E. 315°

12. $\sqrt[4]{576}$ is between what pair of integers?

A. 3 and 4 B. 4 and 5 C. 5 and 6 D. 6 and 7 E. 7 and 8

13. Which of the following has at least one factor which is a perfect square other than 1?

A. 30 B. 35 C. 42 D. 50 E. 105

14. What is the average of 17, 18, 19, 19, 20 and 21?

A. 18 B. 18.5 C. 19 D. 19.5 E. 20

15. Which of the following is approximately equal to $\frac{(0.5)(5.95)}{9.97}$?

A. $\frac{3}{10}$ B. $\frac{1}{3}$ C. $\frac{1}{2}$ D. $\frac{3}{5}$ E. $\frac{2}{3}$

16. $-(-3)^2 - (-1)^2 =$

A. -10 B. -8 C. 4 D. 8 E. 10

17. A pharmacy charges $0.50 per fluid dram for a particular medicine. Seniors receive a 10% discount. What is the price for a senior customer for 4 fluid ounces of medicine if 1 ounce = 8 fluid drams?

A. $13.60 B. $14.40 C. $14.60 D. $15.40 E. $28.80

18. If x is an odd integer, which of the following is <u>not</u> even?

A. $3x + 1$ B. $6x + 2$ C. $4x + 5$ D. $x^2 + x$ E. $x^3 + x$

19. $\frac{5}{4}\left(39 \div \frac{3}{16}\right) =$

A. 0.171 B. 9.14 C. 130 D. 166.4 E. 260

20. If $\frac{2}{3} \times \frac{3}{5} \times \frac{5}{7} \times \frac{7}{P} = \frac{2}{5}$, then P =

A. $\frac{1}{10}$ B. $\frac{1}{5}$ C. 5 D. 10 E. 20

21. If 3 is the greatest common divisor of positive integers S and T, what is the greatest common divisor of 2S and 2T?

A. 3 B. 4 C. 6 D. 9 E. 12

22. How many prime numbers are between 10 and 30?

A. 4 B. 5 C. 6 D. 7 E. 8

23. How far is it from A to B?

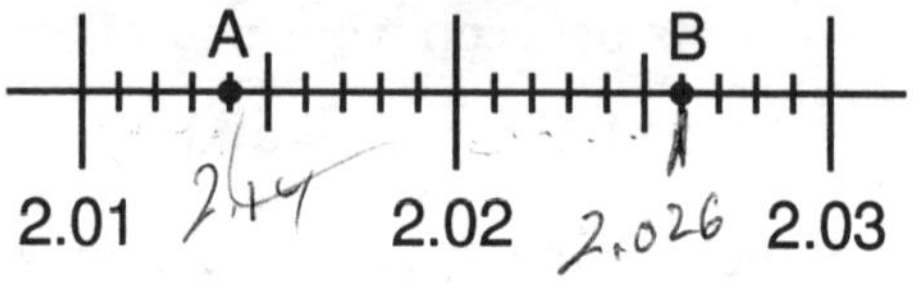


A. 12 B. 1.2 C. 0.13 D. 0.12 E. 0.012

24. Which of the following has a value greater than 1?

A. $3\left(\frac{7}{21}\right)$ B. $\left(\frac{7}{8}\right)^2$ C. $\frac{\sqrt{3}}{2}$ D. $\left(\frac{1}{2}\right)^3$ E. $\frac{3}{\sqrt{8}}$

25. Which of the following is equal to $\frac{39}{81}$?

A. $\frac{4}{9}$ B. $\frac{5}{9}$ C. $\frac{11}{27}$ D. $\frac{13}{27}$ E. $\frac{2}{3}$

26. Which has the largest prime factor?

A. 12 B. 15 C. 24 D. 27 E. 36

27. In a class of 56 students, the ratio of men to women is 3:4. The number of women in the class is:

A. 21 B. 24 C. 32 D. 36 E. 42

28. An even number is divided by another even number. The quotient is then squared. The result could be:

I. Odd
II. Even
III. Negative

A. I only B. II only C. I or II D. II or III E. I, II or III

29. The sale price of a jacket is $90 after being marked down 25%. The original price was:

A. $112.50 B. $115 C. $120 D. $125 E. $135

30. From 1996 to 1997 the population of a town decreased from 2700 to 2500. The next year it decreased by twice as much as the previous year. The percent decrease for the 2-year period is approximately:

A. 19% B. 22% C. 28% D. 30% E. 33%

31. Five machines produce 300 jars in one hour. How many jars can 10 machines produce in 20 minutes?

A. 200 B. 225 C. 240 D. 400 E. 600

32. Three men divide their winnings of a lottery ticket into ratios of 3:4:5. If the least amount was $5,000, what was the value of the ticket?

A. $12,000 B. $15,000 C. $16,000 D. $20,000 E. $25,000

33. C is the midpoint of AB. D is the midpoint of AC. What is the coordinate of D?

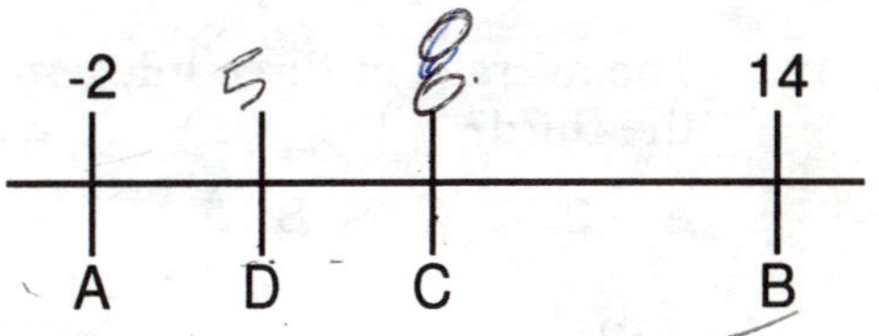


A. -1 B. 0 C. 1 D. 2 E. 4

34. If N is an integer, for what value of N is $0.0100100 \times 10^{N}$ greater than 100 but less than 1000?

A. -5 B. -4 C. 3 D. 4 E. 5

35. $\left(-\frac{1}{2}\right)^3 - \left(\frac{1}{2}\right)\left(\frac{1}{3}\right) =$

A. $-\frac{1}{2}$ B. $-\frac{7}{24}$ C. $-\frac{1}{24}$ D. $\frac{1}{24}$ E. $\frac{1}{2}$

36. Which of the following are reciprocals?

I. 4 and ¼
II. ½ and -½
III. $\sqrt{2}$ and $\frac{\sqrt{2}}{2}$

A. I only B. II only C. I and II D. I and III E. II and III

37. 35% of $\frac{3}{4}$ of 160 is:

A. 25 B. 35 C. 42 D. 50 E. 60

38. If x and y are prime, which of the following can not be the product of x and y?

A. 6 B. 8 C. 9 D. 15 E. 35

39. $\dfrac{6.06}{5.05} =$

A. 1.01 B. 1.02 C. 1.2 D. 1.25 E. 1.66

40. What is the decimal equivalent of $\left(\dfrac{1}{5}\right)^2$?

A. 0.04 B. 0.1 C. 0.16 D. 0.25 E. 0.4

41. $\dfrac{(-20)(2.5)-(10)(-5)}{5} =$

A. -20 B. -15 C. -5 D. 0 E. 20

42. The average of three integers is 2. If two of the integers are –3 and –1, what is the third?

A. -2 B. 2 C. 6 D. 9 E. 10

43. $\dfrac{125}{10{,}000}$ is equivalent to what percent?

A. 0.125% B. 0.8% C. 1.25% D. 8% E. 12.5%

44. How many unique prime factors are in 84?

A. 2 B. 3 C. 4 D. 5 E. 6

45. How many multiples of 6 are there between 18 and 96?

A. 12 B. 13 C. 14 D. 15 E. 16

46. Which of the following is greater than $\dfrac{2}{5}$?

A. $\dfrac{4}{11}$ B. $\dfrac{3}{8}$ C. $\dfrac{1}{3}$ D. $\dfrac{3}{7}$ E. $\dfrac{9}{23}$

47. A room is to be designed with each row to have the same number of seats. If there are 150 total seats, which of the following could <u>not</u> be the number of rows?

A. 6 B. 10 C. 12 D. 15 E. 25

48. $\sqrt{0.0036} =$

A. 0.0006 B. 0.006 C. 0.06 D. 0.36 E. 0.6

49. If $\dfrac{x}{\frac{y}{z}} = 6$ and x = 2, what is the value of $\dfrac{y}{z}$?

A. $\dfrac{1}{6}$ B. $\dfrac{1}{3}$ C. $\dfrac{2}{3}$ D. $\dfrac{3}{6}$ E. $\dfrac{5}{6}$

50. What percent of 15 is 40?

A. 37.5% B. 62.5% C. $166\frac{2}{3}\%$ D. 225% E. $266\frac{2}{3}\%$

51. Tom biked 20 miles in 1 hour and 20 minutes. What was his speed in miles per hour?

A. 12 B. 15 C. 16 D. 18 E. 20

52. What is the greatest integer less than $-1 - 1.1$?

A. -3 B. -2 C. -1 D. 0 E. 1

53. A laser printer can print 200 characters per second, which is four times faster than a bubble jet printer, which in turn is five times faster than a dot matrix printer. How many characters per minute can a dot matrix printer print?

A. 10 B. 50 C. 250 D. 300 E. 600

54. Three cars travel distances that are in ratios of 2:3:4. If the ratios of the traveling times are 4:3:2 respectively, what are the ratios of their respective average speeds?

A. 1:1:1 B. 2:3:4 C. 4:3:2 D. 1:2:4 E. 1:2:8

55. $5! - 4! =$

A. 1 B. 5 C. 24 D. 96 E. 120

56. $$\frac{0.005\times\frac{20}{3}\times 24}{2\times 0.0012\times\frac{5}{6}}$$

A. 0.4 B. 2 C. 200 D. 400 E. 800

57. What is the greatest possible product of 3 different integers, each of which is between $-10$ and 5 inclusive?

A. 50 B. 60 C. 200 D. 450 E. 720

58. Which is the ascending order of A, B, and C, if

$A = 3\sqrt{2}$

$B = 2 + 2\sqrt{2}$

$C = 3 + \sqrt{2}$

A. ABC B. ACB C. BCA D. CAB E. CBA

59. The average of 3 different positive integers is 200. If 250 is the largest, what is the least possible value of the smallest of the 3 integers?

A. 1 B. 11 C. 101 D. 110 E. 111

60. If w, x, y and z are single digit integers and $10w + 40{,}000x + 200y + 3000z = N$, what is the units digit of N?

A. 0 B. 1 C. 2 D. 3 E. 4

61. The average of 10 numbers is 53. After one of the numbers was removed, the new average was 52. What number was removed?

A. 1 B. 52 C. 53 D. 62 E. 72

62. For Sarah's Jellies and Jams, 30% of the jars are grape and the rest strawberry. Half are large and half are small. If 40 out of 200 are grape and small, how many are strawberry and large?

A. 60 B. 80 C. 100 D. 120 E. 140

63. A bus company charges $150 for an 800 mile trip. At that rate, how much would it cost for a trip T miles long?

A. $\frac{3}{16T}$ B. $\frac{3T}{16}$ C. $\frac{16T}{3}$ D. $\frac{16}{3T}$ E. $\frac{5T}{8}$

64. A clock gains 5 seconds every 15 minutes. If it is set accurately at 12 noon, what time will it display when it is 12 midnight?

A. 11:56 B. 11:59 C. 12:01 D. 12:04 E. 12:15

The following graphs are for problems 65 and 66, which follow.

Monthly Family Budget

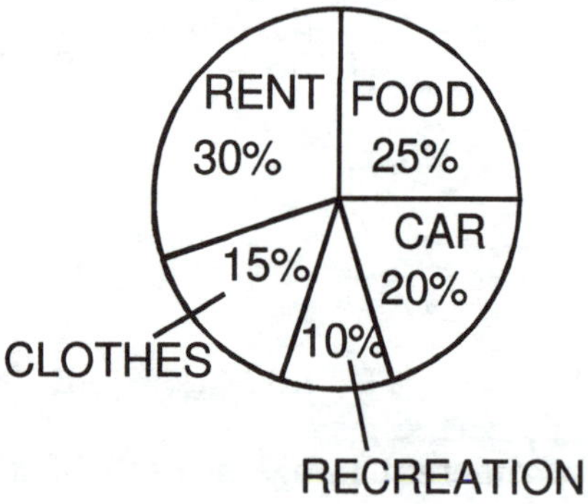


Monthly Food Budget

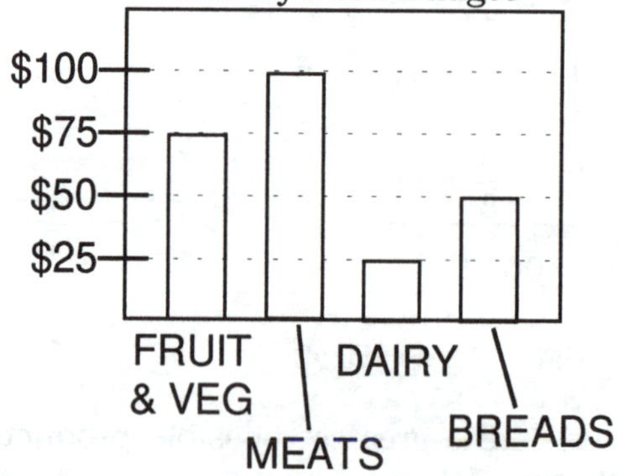


65. What percent of the total budget is Breads?

A. 4% B. 5% C. 10% D. 15% E. 25%

66. How much does the family spend for recreation each month?

A. $60 B. $80 C. $90 D. $100 E. $200

67. If the sum of the <u>odd</u> numbers from 1 to 100 is 2500, what is the sum of the even numbers from 1 to 100?

A. 2400 B. 2450 C. 2500 D. 2550 E. 2600

68. If b books cost d dollars, then at this rate, how much will 10 books cost?

A. 10bd B. $\frac{10d}{b}$ C. $\frac{10b}{d}$ D. $\frac{b}{10d}$ E. $\frac{d}{10b}$

69. If x and y are both positive even integers, which of the following must be even?

I. $x^{(y+1)}$
II. $x^{(y-2)}$
III. $(x+1)^y$

A. None B. I only C. I and II D. I and III E. I, II and III

70. On the number line, 1.6 is halfway between which of the following?

A. -1.6 and 2.6
B. 0.2 and 3.4
C. -0.3 and 3.5
D. 0.8 and 2.2
E. -0.8 and 2.2

71. A 5-gallon container has 3 gallons of a solution which is 30% alcohol and 70% water. If it is then filled to capacity with water, what % of the solution is alcohol?

A. 15% B. 16% C. 18% D. 20% E. 24%

72. A clothier bought a group of ties, $\frac{1}{3}$ of which were blue. He sold $\frac{2}{3}$ of the ties, including $\frac{3}{4}$ of the blue ties. What fraction of the unsold ties was blue?

A. $\frac{1}{6}$ B. $\frac{1}{4}$ C. $\frac{1}{3}$ D. $\frac{5}{12}$ E. $\frac{1}{2}$

73. A set of golf irons sells for $209. The matching metal woods sell for $89. If bought as a package, the total price is $249. What is the approximate percent savings by buying the package versus the irons and woods separately?

A. 14% B. 16% C. 20% D. 24% E. 33%

74. An 8-gallon container is filled with a solution of 30% salt and 70% water. If 2 gallons of water evaporate and are then replaced by more solution, what percent of the new solution is salt?

A. 30% B. $33\frac{1}{3}\%$ C. $37\frac{1}{2}\%$ D. 40% E. 50%

75. 40% of the employees of a company live outside the city limits. Of the employees outside the city, 40% take the train to work. If 30% of the company's employees take the train, what percent of the employees who live inside the city take the train?

A. 12% B. 14% C. 16% D. 20% E. 25%

76. A scalper bought a ticket to the World Series for $35 and sold it for $140. What was his percent profit?

A. 75% B. 105% C. 200% D. 300% E. 400%

77. After 4 games, a football team averaged 24 points. How many points must be scored in the 5th game to increase their average by K points?

A. K B. 5K C. 24K D. 24 + K E. 24 + 5K

78. Prior to an election, a poll showed 70% of the people surveyed said they would vote for candidate X. In the actual election, only 80% of those people voted for X. Of the people who said they would not vote for X, 10% actually did. What percent of the people voted for candidate X?

A. 53% B. 56% C. 59% D. 60% E. 62%

79. If B is the midpoint of line segment AD and C is the midpoint of BD, what is the ratio of AC to AB?

A. $\frac{2}{3}$ B. $\frac{3}{2}$ C. $\frac{4}{3}$ D. $\frac{2}{1}$ E. $\frac{3}{1}$

80. What is the greatest positive integer x such that $3^x$ is a factor of $18^{10}$?

A. 10 B. 12 C. 18 D. 20 E. 60

81. If x, y and z are consecutive positive integers in that order, which of the following must be an odd integer?

A. xyz
B. x + y + z
C. xy + z
D. (x + y)z
E. (x + y)(y + z)

82. $\sqrt{(29-4)(19+6)} =$

A. 5 B. 15 C. 25 D. 125 E. 625

83. $\frac{2^{20}-2^{19}}{2} =$

A. 1 B. 2 C. 4 D. $2^{18}$ E. $2^{19}$

84. What is the least value of x such that $\frac{1}{3^x} < 0.001$, where x is an integer?

A. 7 B. 11 C. 30 D. 31 E. Does not exist

85. 0.40%=

A. $\frac{1}{400}$ B. $\frac{1}{250}$ C. $\frac{1}{200}$ D. $\frac{1}{40}$ E $\frac{2}{5}$

86. A buyer of a car must choose 2 of 4 options from category A, and 4 of 5 options from category B. If the choices are independent (one does not necessitate another), how many different combinations of options can the buyer choose?

A. 8 B. 15 C. 20 D. 30 E. 40

87. $\frac{2}{\frac{2}{3}}+\frac{4}{\frac{4}{5}}+\frac{5}{\frac{5}{6}}=$

A. $\frac{1}{3}$ B. $\frac{11}{30}$ C. $\frac{4}{3}$ D. 11 E. 14

88. $(\sqrt{3}+\sqrt{2})(\sqrt{3}-\sqrt{2})=$

A. 1 B. $1-2\sqrt{6}$ C. 5 D. $5-2\sqrt{6}$ E. 10

89. An engine spins at 4800 revolutions per minute (RPM). How many revolutions will it make in T seconds?

A. 4800T B. $\frac{4800}{T}$ C. 80T D. $\frac{80}{T}$ E. $\frac{288{,}000}{T}$

90. If the sum of 2 integers is 3, which of the following could not be their product?

A. -10 B. -6 C. -4 D. 0 E. 2

91. If x is a non-zero integer, which of the following must be negative?

I. $-(3x^2 + 4)$
II. $-(-x)$
III. $(-x)^3$

A. None B. I only C. I and II D. I and III E. I, II and III

92. If N is an integer and $5^N < 30{,}000$, what is the greatest possible value of N?

A. 5 B. 6 C. 7 D. 8 E. 9

93. If $x=1+\frac{1}{2}+\frac{1}{4}+\frac{1}{8}$ and $y=\frac{1}{2}\left(1+\frac{1}{2}+\frac{1}{4}+\frac{1}{8}\right)$ then x exceeds y by:

A. $\frac{1}{16}$ B. $\frac{1}{8}$ C. $\frac{3}{4}$ D. $\frac{15}{16}$ E. $1\frac{1}{16}$

94. If x and y are integers and x – y = 4, then x + y can not be:

A. 0 B. <4 C. >6 D. even E. odd

95. $\frac{(13)(28)-(28)(6)}{13-6}=$

A. 0 B. 1 C. 4 D. 28 E. 196

96. What is the distance between two points on the number line if the coordinates of the points are $6+\sqrt{3}$ and $3-\sqrt{3}$?

A. 9 B. 3 C. $3+\sqrt{3}$ D. $3+2\sqrt{3}$ E. $3-2\sqrt{3}$

97. What is the greatest prime factor of $(2^4)^2 - 1$?

A. 2 B. 5 C. 11 D. 17 E. 29

98. If the average of 7, 11, A and B is 13, what is the average of (A + 2) and (B – 10)?

A. 13 B. 14 C. 17 D. 19 E. 21

99. $\left(1-\frac{1}{4}\right)^2\left(1-\frac{1}{3}\right)^2 =$

A. $\frac{1}{3}$ B. $\frac{1}{4}$ C. $\frac{5}{12}$ D. $\frac{7}{12}$ E. $\frac{3}{5}$

100. If x is an integer divisible by 6 but not by 4, then which of the following can not be an integer?

A. $\frac{x}{2}$ B. $\frac{x}{3}$ C. $\frac{x}{10}$ D. $\frac{x}{12}$ E. $\frac{x}{18}$

## Solutions – Arithmetic

1. (C) Circle graph solutions are almost always solved using proportion. $\frac{car\$}{car\%}=\frac{food\$}{food\%} \Rightarrow 12\left(\frac{300}{25}=\frac{F}{20}\right)12$

$\Rightarrow$ 12(20)=\$240. The answer is C.

2. (D) There will be 4 games, so by the definition of average:

$$\frac{190+185+205+L}{4}=200$$

$$\not{4}\,\frac{580+L}{\not{4}}=200\cdot 4$$

$$580+L=800$$

$$L=220$$

The answer is D

Alternate method:

| | | |
|---|---|---|
| 205 is | +5 | over the desired average of 200, |
| 190 is | –10 | under, |
| 185 is | –15 | under, |
| | –20 | under, all together, |

therefore the last game score must make up the 20 (i.e., 220).

3. (D) The discount percent must be applied separately and not combined as a flat rate of 30%.

20% of 200 = 40

200 – 40 = 160

10% of 160 = 16

40 + 16 = 56

The answer is D.

4. (D) This is a proportion:

$$2\left(\frac{100\%}{\$200}=\frac{P\%}{\$56}\right)2$$

$$2P=56$$

$$P=28$$

The answer is D.

5. (D) $$\frac{\frac{1}{2}\left(\frac{\frac{2}{3}}{\frac{4}{3}}\right)}{\frac{1}{4}}$$ Order of operations is not important since everything is multiplication and division.

One solution is: $$\frac{\frac{1}{2}\left(\frac{2}{3}\cdot\frac{3}{4}\right)}{\frac{1}{4}}=\frac{\frac{1}{2}\left(\frac{1}{2}\right)}{\frac{1}{4}}=\frac{\frac{1}{4}}{\frac{1}{4}}=1.$$

6. (D) 5.07 – 3.614 = ? To insure accuracy, solve vertically and line up the decimals:

```
  5.070
- 3.614     Note the addition of a zero to 5.07.
  1.456
```

The answer is D.

7. (D) This is a comparison which is solved by proportion:

$$\frac{.70}{1}=\frac{140}{D} \quad \text{or} \quad 200\left(\frac{.70}{140}=\frac{1}{D}\right)200$$

(200 above and below)

D = 200

The answer is D.

8. (A)

| Term# | 1 | 2 | 3 | 4 | 5 | 6 | 7 |
|---|---|---|---|---|---|---|---|
| | | | | | 5 | | |

The above is the given. We now fill in left and right with consecutive odd integers:

| Term# | 1 | 2 | 3 | 4 | 5 | 6 | 7 |
|---|---|---|---|---|---|---|---|
| | ~~-3~~ | ~~-1~~ | ~~1~~ | ~~3~~ | 5 | 7 | 9 |

What is crossed out cancels. 5 + 7 + 9 = 21. The answer is A.

9. (E) 1 – [2 – (3 – 5) – 5] = ? With "nested" parentheses or brackets, you work from the inside to the outside.

1 – [2 – (-2) – 5]
1 – [2 + 2 – 5]
1 – [ –1 ]
2
The answer is E.

10. (E) This is a trap question. Don't make the mistake of just taking half of 2200, which is 1100. You need ½% of 2200. The most efficient way is to first find 1% of 2200 by moving the decimal two places to the left, which gives you 22. Now since ½% is half of 1%, the answer is 11 or E.

11. (D) Since there are 4 sides, each turn required to change a letter is ¼ of a circle or 90°.

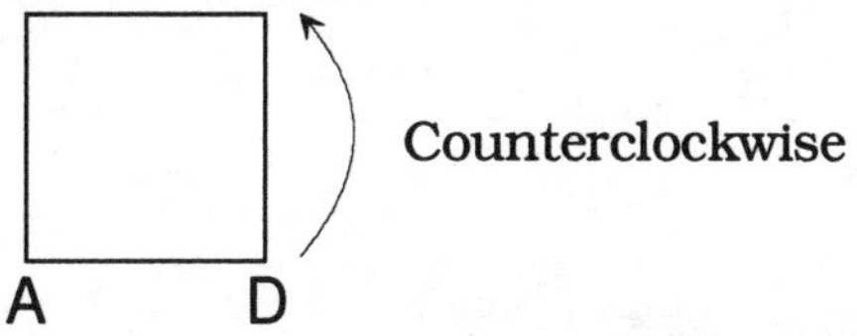


Three turns are needed, which equals 270°. The answer is D.

12. (B) By looking at the answers, it can be seen that the best approach is to work in reverse:

$3^4 = 81$

$4^4 = 256$

$5^4 = 625$

Since 576 is between 256 and 625 the answer is B.

13. (D) Every integer is a product of its primes:

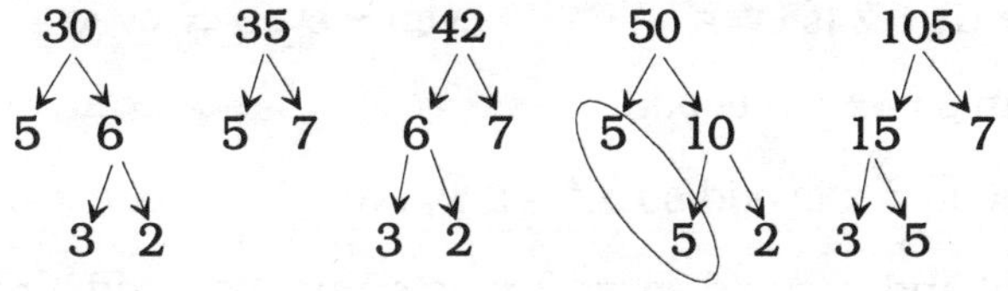


Only 50 has two common factors (5×5) which gives 25, a perfect square, (i.e., 50 = 2 × 25). The answer is D.

14. (C) 17 18 19 19 20 21

To find the average of the six numbers using the definition (sum the numbers and divide by 6) is easy, but time consuming. A much faster way to do it mentally would be to observe that the median is 19 and that on either side the numbers are "balanced" (i.e., the same distance from the center). Thus, each pair from the center has the same median or 19. The answer is C.

15. (A) $\frac{(0.5)(5.95)}{9.97}$

This is best solved by estimation:

$\frac{(0.5)(6)}{10} = \frac{3}{10}$ The answer is A.

16. (A) $-(-3)^2 - (-1)^2$

Remember PEMDAS, do powers before addition and subtraction:

$-(9) - (1) = -10$ The answer is A.

17. (B) The first step is to convert to the same unit, 1 oz = 8 fd (fluid drams).

$$4 \text{ oz} \times \frac{8 \text{ fd}}{1 \text{ oz}} = 32 \text{ fd}$$

A proportion would then be $\frac{.5}{1} = \frac{x}{32} \Rightarrow x = 16$.

10% of $16 is $1.60

16 – 1.60 = 14.40

The answer is B.

Alternatively:

$$\frac{\$.50}{\text{fd}} \times \frac{8 \text{ fd}}{\text{oz}} = \frac{\$4}{\text{oz}}$$

$$4 \text{ oz} \times \frac{\$4}{\text{oz}} = \$16$$

$$16 - 1.60 = 14.40$$

18. (C)

| | |
|---|---|
| (A) 3x is odd | (odd)(odd) ⇒ odd |
| therefore 3x + 1 is even | odd + odd ⇒ even |
| (B) 6x is even | (even)(odd) ⇒ even |
| therefore 6x + 2 is even | even + even ⇒ even |
| (C) 4x is even so 4x + 5 is odd | even + odd ⇒ odd |
| (D) $x^2$ is odd and x is odd so $x^2 + x$ is even | odd + odd ⇒ even |
| (E) $x^3$ is odd and x is odd so $x^3 + x$ is even | odd + odd ⇒ even |

The answer is C.

19. (E)

$$\frac{5}{4}\left(39 \div \frac{3}{16}\right) \Rightarrow \frac{5}{4}\left(\overset{13}{\cancel{39}} \times \frac{16}{\cancel{3}}\right)$$

$$= \frac{5}{\cancel{4}}(13 \times \overset{4}{\cancel{16}})$$

$$= 5(13 \times 4)$$

$$= 5(52)$$

$$= 260$$

The answer is E.

20. (C) A quick glance of the left side will show that everything cancels:

$$\frac{2}{\cancel{3}} \times \frac{\cancel{3}}{\cancel{5}} \times \frac{\cancel{5}}{\cancel{7}} \times \frac{\cancel{7}}{P} = \frac{2}{5}$$ (3s, 5s, and 7s cancel)

$$\frac{2}{P} = \frac{2}{5}$$

It is clear that P = 5. The answer is C.

21. (C) If 3 is the greatest common divisor (i.e., common factor) of s and t, then

$3A = s \qquad 3B = t$

where A and B are integers without a common factor. It follows:

$2 \cdot 3A = 2s$ and $2 \cdot 3B = 2t$

$6A = 2s$ and $6B = 2t$

6 is now the greatest common factor. The answer is C.

22. (C) 11, 13, 17, 19, 23, 29 are the six prime numbers between 10 and 30. The answer is C.

23. (E) A is at 2.014

B is at 2.026

Since distance is found by subtraction, 2.026 – 2.014 = .012.

The answer is E.

24. (E) A) $3\left(\frac{7}{21}\right) = 1$

B) and D) any fraction raised to a power gets smaller

C) the $\sqrt{3}$ is less than 2 so $\frac{\sqrt{3}}{2} < 1$

E) 3 is greater than the $\sqrt{8}$ so $\frac{3}{\sqrt{8}} > 1$

The answer is E.

25. (D) $\frac{39}{81}$ has a greatest common factor of 3, which yields $\frac{13}{27}$.

The answer is D.

26. (B)

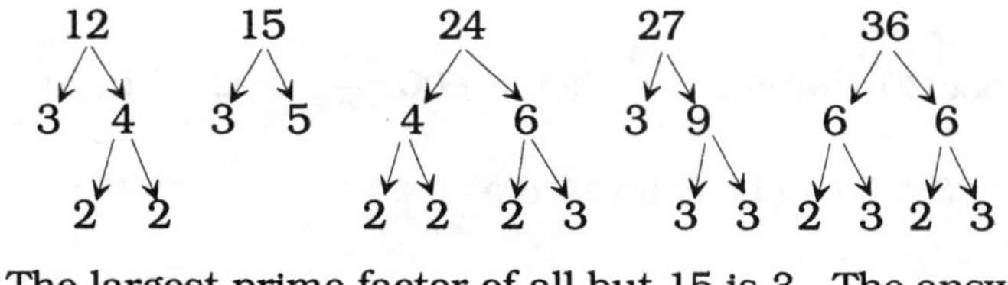


The largest prime factor of all but 15 is 3. The answer is B.

27. (C) If the ratio of men to women is 3:4 then the ratio of women to the class is 4:7 (3 + 4 = total).

$\frac{w}{56} = \frac{4}{7}$

$7w = 224$

$w = 32$

The answer is C.

28. (C) $\frac{2}{2} = 1;$ $1^2 = 1$ odd

$\frac{4}{2} = 2$ $2^2 = 4$ even

Since any number squared must be positive the answer is I and II which is C.

29. (C) Let P be the original price, then

$P - .25P = 90$

or

$P - \frac{1}{4}P = 90$

$\frac{3}{4}P = 90$

$3P = 360$

$P = 120$

Note: it is much easier to work with fractions than decimals.

The answer is C.

30. (B) The first year it decreased 200. The second year's decrease is then 400. The total decrease is 600. % decrease is $\frac{\text{change}}{\text{original}} = \frac{600}{2700} = \frac{2}{9}$.

$\frac{2}{9} = .22\overline{2}$ or approximately 22%. The answer is B.

31. (A) If 5 machines produce 300 jars per hour, then 10 machines produce 600 jars per hour.

$$\frac{5}{300} = \frac{10}{X} \Rightarrow X = 600$$

(arrows labelled 2: $5 \to 10$, $300 \to X$)

Now since 20 minutes is $\frac{1}{3}$ hour, $600 \times \frac{1}{3} = 200$. The answer is A.

32. (D) Ratios of 3:4:5 can be expressed as 3x:4x:5x, which is a total of 12x.

Since 3x = 5000, $\frac{3x}{5000} = \frac{12x}{T}$, and T = 20,000. The answer is D.

(arrows labelled 4: $3x \to 12x$, $5000 \to T$)

33. (D) The distance from A to B = |B – A| = |14 – (-2)| = | 14 + 2 | = 16.

Since C is a midpoint, it is half way from A or B, which is a distance of 8. C then is 14 – 8 = 6. ( or –2 + 8 = 6). Now since D is a midpoint, its distance from A or C is 4. D then is 6 – 4 = 2 (or –2 + 4 = 2).

The answer is D.

34. (D) For each power of 10 the decimal point moves one place. The desired value is 100.1, which requires moving four places to the right.

$10^4 = 10{,}000$. The answer is D.

35. (B) $\left(-\frac{1}{2}\right)^3 - \left(\frac{1}{2}\right)\left(\frac{1}{3}\right)$

A negative raised to an odd power remains negative.

$-\frac{1}{8} - \frac{1}{6} = \frac{-3-4}{24} = -\frac{7}{24}$

The answer is B.

36. (D) A reciprocal of a number N is $\frac{1}{N}$. For a fraction, it is the fraction flipped.

I. 4 is the reciprocal of $\frac{1}{4}$.

II. $-\frac{1}{2}$ is not the reciprocal of $\frac{1}{2}$

III. The reciprocal of $\sqrt{2} = \frac{1}{\sqrt{2}}$. On the surface this does not seem to be the reciprocal of $\frac{\sqrt{2}}{2}$, but if we rationalize we have $\frac{1}{\sqrt{2}} \cdot \frac{\sqrt{2}}{\sqrt{2}} = \frac{\sqrt{2}}{2}$.

The answer is D.

37. (C) 35% of $\frac{3}{4}$ of 160 is ?

"Of" means to multiply:

$\frac{3}{\cancel{4}} \times \overset{40}{\cancel{160}} = 3 \times 40 = 120$

$.35 \times 120 = 42$

A quick way to mentally do 35% of 120 is to break 35 into 10s and 5s:

10% of 120 = 12

30% of 120 = $3 \times 12 = 36$

5% of 120 is half of 10% = 6

$36 + 6 = 42$

The answer is C.

38. (B)

$6 = 2 \times 3$

$8 = 2 \times 4$

$9 = 3 \times 3$

$15 = 3 \times 5$

$35 = 5 \times 7$

Only 8 has 2 factors which are not both prime.

The answer is B.

39. (C) $\frac{6.06}{5.05}$ A fraction is a division problem:

$$5.05\overline{)6.06} \Rightarrow 505\overline{)606.0}$$

$$\begin{array}{r} 1.2 \\ 505\overline{)606.0} \\ \underline{505} \\ 101.0 \end{array}$$

The answer is C.

40. (A) $\left(\frac{1}{5}\right)^2 = \frac{1}{25} = 25\overline{)1.00}$ = .04

The answer is A.

41. (D) $\frac{(-20)(2.5)-(10)(-5)}{5} = \frac{(-50)-(-50)}{5} = \frac{-50+50}{5} = \frac{0}{5} = 0$

The answer is D.

42. (E) $\frac{-3-1+x}{3} = 2$

$-4+x = 6$

$x = 10$ The answer is E.

43. (C) $\frac{125}{10{,}000} = .0125 = 1.25\%$

The answer is C.

44. (B)

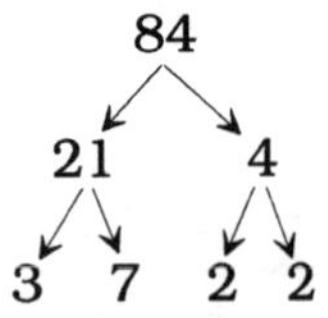


There are three unique prime factors, 2, 3, and 7.

The answer is B.

45. (A) The definition of being between implies <u>not</u> including the end points.

$\frac{96}{6} = 16$ $\frac{18}{6} = 3$

The number of integers between 16 and 3 is 12 (4 through 15).

Alternatively, simply listing them would suffice and be sufficiently fast enough: 24, 30, 36, 42, 48, 54, 60, 66, 72, 78, 84, 90 (12 numbers).

The answer is A.

46. (D) One way to compare fractions is to cross multiply:

| $\frac{4}{11}$ ✕ $\frac{2}{5}$ | $\frac{3}{8}$ ✕ $\frac{2}{5}$ | $\frac{1}{3}$ ✕ $\frac{2}{5}$ | $\frac{3}{7}$ ✕ $\frac{2}{5}$ | $\frac{9}{23}$ ✕ $\frac{2}{5}$ |
|---|---|---|---|---|
| 20 (22) | 15 (16) | 5 (6) | (15) 14 | 45 (46) |

$\frac{3}{7}$ produces the only larger cross product when compared to $\frac{2}{5}$.

Alternatively, most of the answers could be eliminated by other methods.

$\frac{2}{5} = \frac{4}{10}$ and $\frac{4}{10} > \frac{4}{11}$

$\frac{3}{8} = .375$ and $\frac{2}{5} = .40$

$\frac{1}{3} = .33\overline{3}$ and $\frac{2}{5} = .40$

This leave only 2 which actually require comparison by other means. Note: finding common denominators is a poor choice for comparison.

47. (C) This problem requires 150 to be broken down into pairs of factors. 6×25=150 so 6 and 25 are OK. 10×15=150 so 10 and 15 are OK. 12 is not a factor of 150.

The answer is C.

48. (C) Decimal places are located by counting the places of the numbers being multiplied. The $\sqrt{0.0036}$ has 4 decimal places so the product of .06×.06=.0036.

The answer is C.

49. (B) $\frac{2}{\frac{y}{z}} = 6$

$2 = 6\left(\frac{y}{z}\right)$ Multiply both sides by $\frac{y}{x}$.

$\frac{2}{6} = \frac{y}{z}$ Divide both sides by 6.

$\frac{1}{3} = \frac{y}{z}$

The answer is B. Note: y and z did not have to be found individually.

Since x = 2, a good alternate method would be to use the supplied answers. Divide 2 by each answer. It would be seen that $2 \div \frac{1}{3} = 6$.

50. (E) Converting the words to an equation, we have:

$P \times 15 = 40$

$P = \frac{40}{15} = 2\frac{10}{15} = 2\frac{2}{3}$

$2\frac{2}{3} = 266\frac{2}{3}\%$

Note: clearly 40 is more than twice 15 which implies greater than 200%, thus eliminating answers A, B, and C.

The answer is E.

51. (B) This is a comparison problem solved by a proportion.

$$4\left(\frac{20 \text{ miles}}{80 \text{ minutes}} = \frac{x}{60 \text{ minutes}}\right)4$$

x = 15 miles. The answer is B.

52. (A) $-1 - 1.1 = -2.1$

$-3$ is less than $-2.1$: $-3 < -2.1 < -2$. The answer is A.

53. (E) Laser speed: $\frac{200 \text{ characters}}{\text{second}}$.

Divide by 4 to get speed of bubble jet: $\frac{50 \text{ characters}}{\text{second}}$.

Divide by 5 to get speed of dot matrix: $\frac{10 \text{ characters}}{\text{second}}$.

Now convert from seconds to minutes:

$$\frac{10 \text{ chararacters}}{\cancel{\text{seconds}}} \times \boxed{\frac{60 \cancel{\text{seconds}}}{\text{minute}}} = \frac{600 \text{ characters}}{\text{minute}}.$$

The answer is E.

54. (D) $\frac{2}{4} : \frac{3}{3} : \frac{4}{2}$ ratios from the given

$\frac{1}{2} : 1 : 2$ reduced ratios, but not one of the answers

$2\left(\frac{1}{2} : 1 : 2\right)$ multiply by two

1:2:4 The answer is D.

55. (D) $5! - 4! = 5 \cdot 4 \cdot 3 \cdot 2 \cdot 1 - 4 \cdot 3 \cdot 2 \cdot 1$

Factor out $(4 \cdot 3 \cdot 2 \cdot 1)$: $4 \cdot 3 \cdot 2 \cdot 1 \cdot (5-1)$

$24(4) = 96$ The answer is D.

56. (D) $$\frac{0.005 \times \frac{20}{3} \times 24}{2 \times 0.0012 \times \frac{5}{6}}$$

$$\frac{0.005 \times \frac{20}{\not{3}} \times 24}{2 \times 0.0012 \times \frac{5}{\not{6}}} \times \frac{\not{6}^{\,2}}{\not{6}}$$ (clear fractions by multiplying by $\frac{6}{6}$)

$$\frac{0.005 \times \not{20}^{\,4} \times 24 \times \not{2}}{\not{2} \times 0.0012 \times \not{5}}$$ (do some canceling)

$$\frac{0.0050 \times 4 \times 24}{0.0012} \times \frac{10{,}000}{10{,}000}$$ (move decimal four places to the right)

$$\frac{50 \times 4 \times \not{24}^{\,2}}{\not{12}} = 400$$ The answer is D.

57. (D) The two possible combinations of signs are all positive and (-)(-)(+) to get a positive (largest) integer. The largest product of two different numbers in –10, -9, ..., 4, 5 is (-10)(-9) or 90. The largest possible positive number is 90·5 or 450.

58. (B) $A = 3\sqrt{2} \quad = \sqrt{2} + \sqrt{2} + \sqrt{2}$

$B = 2+2\sqrt{2} = \quad 2 + \sqrt{2} + \sqrt{2}$

$C = 3+\sqrt{2} \quad = \quad 2 + \quad 1 + \sqrt{2}$

By breaking A, B, and C into the above sums, it is easier to see which is larger. First note that B > C since $\sqrt{2} > 1$. Also B > A since $2 > \sqrt{2}$.

Now to compare A and C, to see which is the smallest, first drop the $\sqrt{2}$:

$A - \sqrt{2} \ ? \ C - \sqrt{2}$

$3\sqrt{2} - \sqrt{2} \ ? \ 3 + \sqrt{2} - \sqrt{2}$

$2\sqrt{2} \ ? \ 3$

In general to compare a square root with an integer or fraction, you can square both sides. (Squaring positive numbers does not change their order.)

$(2\sqrt{2})^2 \ ? \ 3^2$

$8 < 9$ so

$A < C$

Therefore the full order is B > C > A. The question asks for ascending order which is ACB. The answer is B.

59. (C) In this average problem it is best to work with the sum, not the average.

$$\frac{x+y+z}{3} = 200$$
$$x+y+z = 600$$

Therefore the sum of the three numbers is 600. If z, the largest is 250 then x + y = 350. For one number to be small, the other must be as large as possible. But the largest a <u>different</u> integer can be is 249, one less than 250. 350-249 is 101, which is the least the smallest number can be. The answer is C.

60. (A) This question is easy if you see the "trick." In this case each integer added to form N is the product of an integer and a multiple of ten. Each number added to N had zero as its units place, thus the units place of N must be 0. The answer is A.

61. (D) Recomputed average problems usually are most easily solved from the perspective of the sum (before the division produces the average). In this problem the sum of 10 numbers is 53·10 or 530. The sum of the 9 other numbers is 52·9 or 468. The difference is 530-468=62, which is the removed number. The answer is D.

Another way to compute the number is to determine what number must be added to the nine to increase the average from 52 to 53. (Note that the perspective has been changed deliberately from removal to addition.) To maintain the average just add the number 52, but to increase by 1 (to 53) we must add 10 more to the sum to counter the effect of averaging (division by 10). Therefore add the number 52+10 or 62.

62. (B) 40 out of 200 are grape and small is 20%. From 30% grape this leaves 10%, which are grape and large. From 50% small 30% are strawberry and small. There are then two ways to compute what percentage are strawberry and large: 1) 50% large – 10% large and grape leaves 40% large strawberry OR 2) 70% strawberry – 30% small strawberry leaves 40% large strawberry. The answer is B.

An alternate method which is applicable to the solution of many GMAT problems involves the use of a small table. For this problem the table might first be filled out like so:

| | 50% Small | 50% Large | |
|---|---|---|---|
| Grape (30%) | 40 | | |
| Strawberry (70%) | | ? | |
| | | | 200 |

The "?" is what we want to find, the 40 and 200 are the given amounts, and the percentages (for columns and rows) are also given. The table provides a visual organization of the math involved. Using the 50%s at the top, divide the 200 into its two groups of 100 each:

| | 50% Small | 50% Large | |
|---|---|---|---|
| Grape (30%) | 40 | | |
| Strawberry (70%) | | ? | |
| | ***100*** | ***100*** | 200 |

In the small column, we see there are 100 jars. We know that 40 are grape, so 60 must be strawberry:

| | 50% Small | 50% Large | |
|---|---|---|---|
| Grape (30%) | 40 | | |
| Strawberry (70%) | ***60*** | ? | |
| | 100 | 100 | 200 |

In the right most column we know that there are 200 jars total and that 70% are strawberry, which is 140:

| | 50% Small | 50% Large | |
|---|---|---|---|
| Grape (30%) | 40 | | |
| Strawberry (70%) | 60 | ? | ***140*** |
| | 100 | 100 | 200 |

This then implies that ? = 140 – 60, or 80:

| | 50% Small | 50% Large | |
|---|---|---|---|
| Grape (30%) | 40 | | |
| Strawberry (70%) | 60 | ***80*** | 140 |
| | 100 | 100 | 200 |

Thus the answer is 80 jars, which is 40% of 200. The answer is B.

The table above could have been filled in a different order with the same answer achieved. What is important is that this "spreadsheet" sort of table makes that solution process visual. You note that one number in a column can be computed if others are first found. This gives you a way to choose the most convenient solution path. Also the table can be filled out in the other directions, which providing a means to verify your computations.

63. (B) The rate is 800 miles for \$150. If the cost we pay is X dollars, then T miles at this rate suggests a proportion of the type $\frac{D_1}{\$_1} = \frac{D_2}{\$_2}$ or $\frac{D_1}{D_2} = \frac{\$_1}{\$_2}$. To solve the proportion for X, first cross multiply either:

$$\frac{800}{\$150} = \frac{T}{X} \quad \text{or} \quad \frac{800}{T} = \frac{\$150}{X}$$

$$800X = 150T$$

$$X = \frac{15}{80}T = \frac{3}{16}T$$

The answer is B.

64. (D) This also lends itself to the use of proportion. First compute the number of seconds gained per hour (60 minutes), given that 5 seconds are gained every 15 minutes:

$$3\left(\frac{5}{15} = \frac{x}{60}\right)3 \quad (\times 4)$$

x = 20 seconds per hour. In 12 hours it gains 20·12 = 240 seconds = 4 minutes.

The answer is 12:04, which is D.

65. (B) The total for food is \$250 and bread is \$50 or $\frac{1}{5}$ of food. Since food is 25% bread is $\frac{1}{5} \cdot 25\%$ or 5% of the total. The answer is B.

66. (D) Use a proportion:

$$10\left(\frac{25}{250} = \frac{10}{X}\right)10$$

$x = 100$

The answer is D.

67. (D) Given the sum of the odd numbers from 1 to 100 (1,3,5,..., 97, 99) the sum of the even numbers (2, 4, 6,..., 98, 100) will be 1 more for each number of 50. So the total will be 2550. The answer is D.

68. (B) The rate is b books for d dollars; this is a proportion:

$$\frac{b}{d} = \frac{10}{x} \quad \text{(first cross multiply)}$$

$$b \cdot x = d \cdot 10$$

$$x = \frac{10d}{b}$$

The answer is B.

69. (B) I. $\text{even}^{(\text{integer power} \geq 1)} = \text{even}$ – any even integer raised to a power ≥ 1 is always even.

II. $2^{(2-2)} = 2^0 = 1$ not even – an exception

III. $\text{odd}^{(\text{integer power} \geq 1)} = \text{odd}$ – any odd integer raised to a power ≥ 1 is always odd.

Thus the answer is B: I only.

70. (C) There are at least two ways to find the midpoint of two points on the number line: 1) find the difference between the numbers, take half and add to the smaller number 2) take the average of the two numbers.

Choice A: $\dfrac{-1.6+2.6}{2} = .5$ Choice B: $\dfrac{.2+3.4}{2} = 1.8$

Choice C: $\dfrac{-.3+3.5}{2} = 1.6$ Choice D: $\dfrac{.8+2.2}{2} = 1.5$

Choice E: $\dfrac{-.8+2.2}{2} = .7$

Therefore the correct answer is C.

71. (C) As the volume increases the % of alcohol proportionally decreases (i.e., as volume doubles the % alcohol drops to one-half. This problem is an inverse proportion:

$$\frac{3\text{ gallons}}{5\text{ gallons}} = \frac{x\%}{30\%}$$

$$5x = 3 \times 30 = 90$$

$$x = 18$$

The answer is C.

72. (B) The answer is the ratio of the amount of unsold blue ties to the amount of unsold ties. The amount of unsold blue ties is (one-quarter left of one-third) $\frac{1}{4} \cdot \frac{1}{3} = \frac{1}{12}$. The ratio is then $\dfrac{\frac{1}{12}}{\frac{1}{3}} = \frac{1}{12} \times \frac{3}{1} = \frac{1}{4}$.

The answer is B.

73. (B) Notice the question asks for "approximate %." Remember % savings is the savings divided by the higher cost. First estimate the savings:

209 + 89 – 249

210 + 90 – 250 = 50 (approximately)

Estimate the separate price:

209 + 89

300 (approximately)

Thus the approximate percent savings is:

$$\frac{50}{300} = \frac{1}{6} \approx 16\%$$

The correct answer is B.

74. (C) Before evaporation the salt was 30% of the mixture. If it was reconstituted with water only it would return to being 30%. But a quarter more salt is being added (2 of 8 gallons). So a quarter of 30%, or $7\frac{1}{2}\%$, is being added bringing the concentration to $37\frac{1}{2}\%$.

The answer is C.

Alternatively:

| | | |
|---|---|---|
| 30% of 8 gallons ⇒ (.3)(8) | = 2.4 | amount of salt in original solution |
| 30% of 2 gallons ⇒ (.3)(2) | = 0.6 | amount of salt in added solution |
| | 3.0 | total amount of salt |

$$\frac{3}{8} = 37\frac{1}{2}\%$$

75. (B) First compute percent that take the train and live outside:

40% of 40% = (.4)40% = 16%

Now subtract from 30%: 30% - 16% = 14%. The answer is B.

76. (D) Remember that %profit is $\frac{\text{change in price}}{\text{original price}}$. Compute the change in price (profit): 140 – 35 is 105. So %profit is:

$$\frac{105}{35} \cdot 100\% = 3 \cdot 100\% = 300\%$$

The answer is D.

77. (E) This class of problem (recomputed averages) involves re-computing the sum used in computing the average. The total of the 4 scores is 4·24 or 96. The new average would be:

$$24 + K = \frac{96 + \text{new score}}{5}$$

To compute the new score, multiply by 5 and subtract 96:

$$5(24 + K) = 96 + \text{new score}$$

$$120 + 5K = 96 + \text{new score}$$

$$24 + 5K = \text{new score}$$

In general most people familiar with recomputed averages know that to raise the average for N items by an amount of K, the total of N·K must be added to the N elements of the sum. In this case all 5K points must be added to an "average" (24 points) fifth game score or therefore 24+5K is the necessary score. The answer is E.

78. (C) This problem is not as difficult as it seems. To find the actual percentage of those voting for candidate X, compute the percent from each group and add the percents. Of the 70% who said that they would vote for candidate X, 80% did:

80% of 70% = (.8)(70%) = 56%

Of the 30% who said that they would not vote for candidate X, 10% did:

10% of 30% = (.1)(30%) = 3%

Those actually voting for:

56% + 3% = 59%

Notice that 80% and 10% were converted to their decimal equivalents (.8 and .1) to obtain an answer with % not %%. The answer is C.

79. (B) For this class of problem a drawn figure is the best first step:

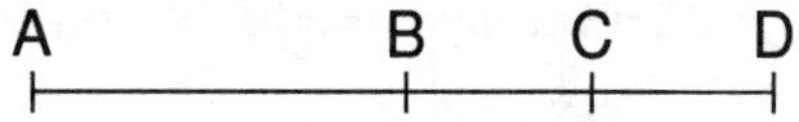


Draw the figure as described by the problem. Place the A and D first, then place the B, then place the C. Using the supplied proportions throw in some appropriate distances:

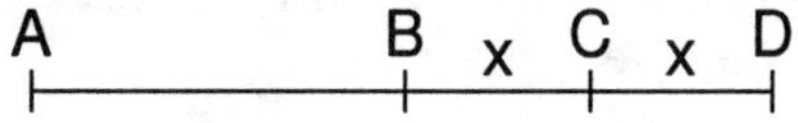


Since C is midway between B and D, we will choose x for BC and CD. This makes BD=2x which is the same as AB (remember B is the midpoint for AD):

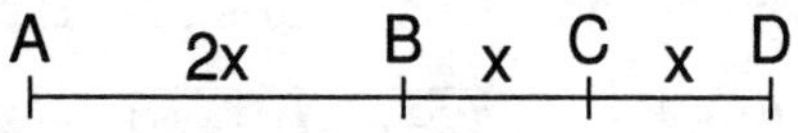


Now AC to AB $= \frac{AC}{AB} = \frac{3x}{2x} = \frac{3}{2}$. The answer is B.

80. (D) This problem involves the combination of the concepts of factor and exponent. First factor 18:

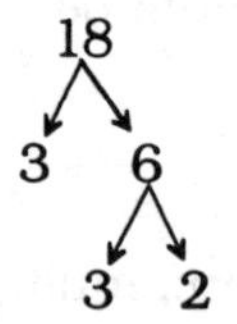


There are two factors of 3 in each 18.

Next we must combine this with exponentiation: $18^{10} = 2^{10} \cdot 3^{20}$. As a result, we see $3^{20}$ is the largest power of 3 to be found in $18^{10}$. The answer is D.

Alternatively, using $(AB)^x = A^x B^x$ property:

$$18^{10} = 3^{10} \cdot 6^{10} = 3^{10} \cdot 2^{10} \cdot 3^{10} = 2^{10} \cdot 3^{20}$$

81. (E) Here are the two possibilities: (x, y, z) = (odd, even, odd) and (even, odd, even).

Choice A: odd·even·odd=even    even·odd·even=even    NO

Choice B: odd+even+odd= → odd+odd=even    even+odd+even= → odd+even=odd    NO

Choice C: odd×even+odd= → even+odd=odd    even×odd+even= → even+even=even    NO

Choice D: (odd+even)odd= → odd×odd=odd    (even+odd)even= → odd×even=even    NO

Choice E: (odd+even)(even+odd)= → odd×odd=odd    (even+odd)(odd+even)= → odd×odd=odd    YES

Alternatively, <u>Choice A</u> must be even because one of the three consecutive integers is even. <u>Choice C</u> xy is even so z determines odd-even. <u>Choice D</u> if z is even then (x + y)z is even. This leaves B and E to be analyzed as above.

For those who are experts:

<u>Choice E</u>: Note that for both x+y and y+z, the sum of two consecutive integers is always odd. Further the product of odd numbers is odd. This means that E must be odd.

82. (C) Compute the interior: $\sqrt{(29-4)(19+6)} = \sqrt{25 \cdot 25}$

$= \sqrt{25^2}$

$\sqrt{x^2} = |x|$: $= 25$

83. (D) This problem is best solved using the properties of exponents:

$$\frac{2^{20}-2^{19}}{2}=\frac{2\left(2^{19}\right)-2^{19}}{2}=\frac{2^{19}(2-1)}{2}=\frac{2^{19}}{2}=2^{18}$$

There are several ways to solve the problem, but the key in this case is the step to convert $2^{20}-20^{19}$ to $2^{19}(2-1)$. This is called factoring, and is quite common in solving problems, but is the step most don't consider trying. It is not a trick problem, but a problem that requires the use of a tool most fail to employ.

Note: Don't fall into the trap of thinking that $2^{20}-2^{19}=2^{1}$.

84. (A) This class of problems involving inequalities requires care. There are at least two ways to proceed 1) use the fact that $\frac{1}{3^x}$ gets smaller as x increases and solve for the bottom of the fractions or 2) solve as an inequality. Let's first proceed as in #2:

$$\frac{1}{3^x}<.001$$

Multiply both sides by $3^x$: $\quad 1<.001\times 3^x$

Divide both sides by .001: $\quad 1000<3^x$

(note that the inequality, or "less than" sign, did not flip because both multiply/divide operations involved positive numbers ($3^x$ and .001). Now to solve note that $3^6=729$ and $3^7=2187$, so that 7 is the smallest integer x that satisfies $1000<3^x$ and $\frac{1}{3^x}<.001$.

The faster way takes account of the fact that as $3^x$ increases $\frac{1}{3^x}$ gets smaller. If we first note that $.001=\frac{1}{1000}$ then the inequality can be written as: $\frac{1}{3^x}<\frac{1}{1000}$

which implies $3^x>1000$. x=6 is too small so the least value of x is 7. The answer is A.

85. (B) Converting 0.40% to a fraction can be done by replacing the % with $\frac{1}{100}$:

$$0.40\%=\frac{0.40}{100}\times\frac{10}{10}=\frac{4}{1000}$$

Now reduce by dividing top and bottom by 4 to get $\frac{1}{250}$.

86. (D) First count the number of combinations of two options chosen from four. The following illustrates the <u>six</u> possibilities:

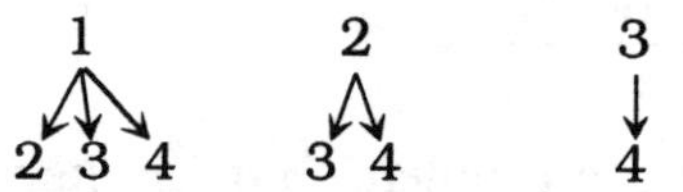


Second count the number of combinations of four things chosen from five. The following illustrates the <u>five</u> possibilities:

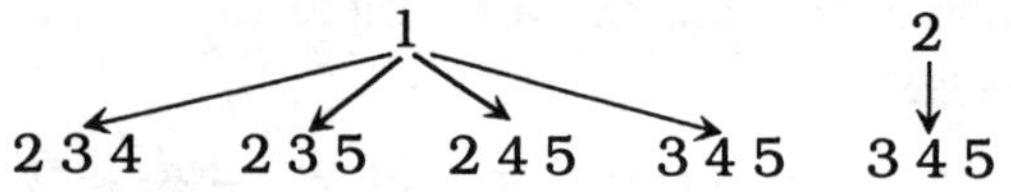


The buyer then has 6 times 5 or 30 ways to choose 2 options of 4 from category A and 4 options of 5 from category B.

The answer is D.

Alternatively, using combinations, we see:

$$\#\text{ of ways to choose 2 of 4 from A} = \frac{4!}{2!(4-2)!} = \frac{4!}{2!\cdot 2!} = \frac{\overset{2}{\cancel{4}}\cdot 3\cdot \cancel{2}\cdot 1}{(\cancel{2}\cdot 1)(\cancel{2}\cdot 1)} = 6$$

$$\#\text{ of ways to choose 4 of 5 from B} = \frac{5!}{4!(5-4)!} = \frac{5!}{4!\cdot 1!} = \frac{5\cdot \cancel{4}\cdot \cancel{3}\cdot \cancel{2}\cdot 1}{(\cancel{4}\cdot \cancel{3}\cdot \cancel{2}\cdot 1)(1)} = 5$$

Then multiply the two independent choices 5 and 6 to get 30 possible choices.

87. (E) In each case, these fractions simplify to integers:

$$\frac{2}{\frac{2}{3}} = \cancel{2}\cdot\frac{3}{\cancel{2}} = 3 \qquad \frac{4}{\frac{4}{5}} = \cancel{4}\cdot\frac{5}{\cancel{4}} = 5 \qquad \frac{5}{\frac{5}{6}} = \cancel{5}\cdot\frac{6}{\cancel{5}} = 6$$

Thus the problem becomes 3+5+6=14. The answer is E.

88. (A)

$$(\sqrt{3}+\sqrt{2})(\sqrt{3}-\sqrt{2}) = \sqrt{3}\sqrt{3} + \sqrt{3}(-\sqrt{2}) + \sqrt{2}\sqrt{3} + \sqrt{2}(-\sqrt{2})$$

$$= 3 - \sqrt{6} + \sqrt{6} - 2$$

Notice that $-\sqrt{6} + \sqrt{6}$ cancel out.

$$= 3 - 2$$

$$= 1$$

The answer is A.

89. (C) This is a units conversion problem and rate problem:

$$\frac{4800 \text{ revolutions}}{\cancel{\text{minute}}} \times \boxed{\frac{1\ \cancel{\text{minute}}}{60 \text{ seconds}}} = \frac{80 \text{ revolutions}}{\text{second}}$$

This conversion ratio = 1

The above conversion allows us to setup the rate equation:

$$T\ \cancel{\text{seconds}} \times \frac{80 \text{ revolutions}}{\cancel{\text{seconds}}} = 80T \text{ revolutions}$$

The answer is C.

90. (B) These types of problems are best solved by listing integer sums and their products:

| | |
|---|---|
| 1+2=3 | 1·2=2 |
| 0+3=3 | 0·3=0 |
| (-1)+4=3 | (-1)·4=-4 |
| (-2)+5=3 | (-2)·5=-10 |
| (-3)+6=3 | (-3)·6=-18 |

As you may well see the product will just get more and more negative, so –6 will never occur (i.e., -6 was bypassed as the product decreased). The answer is B.

91. (B) I. $-(3x^2+4)$ must be negative because $x^2 \geq 0$ for all x,

II. -(-x) = x so x positive makes this positive, and

III. $(-x)^3$ is not negative when x is negative: $(-(-1))^3 = 1^3 = 1$.

Therefore only I is always negative for $x \neq 0$. The answer is B.

92. (B) The question can also be phrased, "What is the greatest power of 5 less than 30,000?" So compute the powers of 5:

$5^3 = 125$ $5^4 = 625$ $5^5 = 3125$ $5^6 = 15{,}625$ $5^7 = 78{,}125$

The answer is N = 6, which is B.

Estimation could be used without sacrifice of accuracy for $5^6$ and $5^7$. Consider $5^5 \approx 3000$; therefore $5^6 \approx 15{,}000$, which is clearly under 30,000, and $5^7 \approx 75{,}000$, which is clearly over 30,000.

93. (D) "x exceeds y by" means "What is x – y?"

$$x - y = 1 + \frac{1}{2} + \frac{1}{4} + \frac{1}{8} - \frac{1}{2}\left(1 + \frac{1}{2} + \frac{1}{4} + \frac{1}{8}\right)$$

$$= 1 + \frac{1}{2} + \frac{1}{4} + \frac{1}{8} - \frac{1}{2} - \frac{1}{4} - \frac{1}{8} - \frac{1}{16}$$

Six fractions cancel and leave

$$= 1 - \frac{1}{16}$$

$$= \frac{15}{16}$$

The answer is D.

94. (E) Referring to the first page of the Arithmetic Review there are the two properties that have even results: **even ± even = even** and **odd ± odd = even**. This implies that if the difference of any two integers is even, then their sum will be even as well. Therefore x + y cannot be odd. The answer is E.

Alternatively, if you wish to eliminate answers, it is easy to eliminate A, B, C, and D with some well chosen values of x and y.

95. (D) $\dfrac{(13)(28)-(28)(6)}{13-6}=\dfrac{28\cancel{(13-6)}}{\cancel{13-6}}=28$ Factor out 28.

Long computations involving large numbers could be performed by hand, but are very tedious. The GMAT invites you to get bogged down with this type of work. But you should remember to look for numbers that cancel before multiplying within the numerator and denominator.

The answer is D.

96. (D) Distance is always the positive difference between two points (i.e., the absolute value of the difference). In this case:

$$\left|6+\sqrt{3}-\left(3-\sqrt{3}\right)\right|=3+2\sqrt{3}.$$

The answer is D.

97. (D) $\left(2^4\right)^2-1=16^2-1=256-1=255$ Now factor 255: $255 \div 5 = 51$, $255 = 5 \cdot 51 = 5 \cdot 3 \cdot 17$. So the greatest prime factor of 255 is 17.
The answer is D.

98. (A) Using the definition of average:

$$\frac{7+11+A+B}{4}=13$$
$$7+11+A+B=52$$
$$A+B=34$$

This is all we can determine regarding A and B, but this is enough. The average of (A + 2) and (B – 10) is:

$$\frac{(A+2)+(B-10)}{2}=\frac{(A+B)+2-10}{2}$$
$$=\frac{(A+B)-8}{2}$$

Substitute 34 for $A+B$:

$$=\frac{34-8}{2}$$
$$=\frac{26}{2}$$
$$=13$$

The answer is A.

99. (B) $\left(1-\frac{1}{4}\right)^2\left(1-\frac{1}{3}\right)^2=\left(\frac{3}{4}\right)^2\left(\frac{2}{3}\right)^2=\frac{\cancel{9}}{16}\times\frac{4}{\cancel{9}}=\frac{4}{16}=\frac{1}{4}$

The answer is B.

100. (D) $\frac{x}{12}$ cannot be an integer because x is not divisible by 4 as stated in the problem: $\frac{x}{12}=\frac{1}{3}\cdot\frac{x}{4}$. The answer is D.

# Algebra Review

Algebra involves the use of letters that represent unknown values (variables). These are combined with arithmetic operations to form expressions, equations, and inequalities.

## EXPRESSIONS

An expression is a combination of terms which when evaluated, represent a value.

EXAMPLE: $\frac{x+3}{2}$ is an expression. What is its value when x = 1, 2, and 3?

When x = 1, we have $\frac{1+3}{2} = \frac{4}{2} = 2$.

Thus when x = 1, the value of $\frac{x+3}{2} = 2$.

Similarly when x = 2, $\frac{2+3}{2} = \frac{5}{2}$.

And when x = 3, $\frac{3+3}{2} = \frac{6}{2} = 3$.

Since x is a variable, it can take on any value that produces a real number when the expression is evaluated. The set of allowable values of x is called the ***domain***. Consider the following expression:

$$\frac{2}{x-2}$$

If x = 2 then we would have $\frac{2}{2-2} = \frac{2}{0}$, which is undefined. Therefore the domain is all real numbers except 2.

The set of numbers that are produced when all values from the domain are evaluated is called the ***range***.

A ***function*** is an expression defined over a domain and range.

EXAMPLE: f(x) = x + 3

"f(x)" is read "function of x."

f(1) = 1 + 3 = 4

f(2) = 2 + 3 = 5

The property of functions is that for each value of x (domain) there is only one value of f(x) (range).

## COMPONENTS OF AN EXPRESSION

$$2x^2 + 3x - 1$$

coefficients (2, 3) constant (1)

***Coefficients*** multiply the term (i.e. how many of each). ***Constants*** are fixed values when the expression is used as a function.

EXAMPLE: $f(x) = 2x^2 + 3x - 1$

$$\begin{aligned} f(3) &= 2(3)^2 + 3(3) - 1 \\ &= 2(9) + 9 - 1 \\ &= 26 \end{aligned}$$

## ADDITION AND SUBTRACTION OF TERMS

In simplifying expressions a good first step is to combine like terms. 3x and 7x are like terms. Though the coefficients differ, the variables are the same. 3x and 7x combine to form 10x $(3 + 7 = 10)$. Combining like terms then involves addition of the coefficients.

EXAMPLE: x + 2x + 4x = 7x. x, 2x, and 4x are like terms and can be combined.

EXAMPLE: x + 2y + 3z. x, 2y, and 3z are not like terms and cannot be combined.

EXAMPLE: $x^2 + 4x + 3x^2 - x = 4x^2 + 3x$. 4x and –x are like terms. $x^2$ and $3x^2$ are also like terms. However, $3x^2$ and 4x are <u>not</u> like terms; the variable in $3x^2$ is $x^2$ whereas the variable in 4x is x. Put another way, since x is not equal to $x^2$ (their graphs are radically different) they cannot be combined. Like terms must match <u>both</u> letter and exponent.

## EXPONENTS (POWERS)

In algebra the word exponent is preferred over power (though they are the same).

Consider $2x^3 \Rightarrow 2(x)(x)(x)$. x is called the base and 3 is the exponent. (Note: as with powers, the exponent only applies to what it touches directly.)

DEFINITION: $x^n$ means x multiplied by itself n times (i.e. $x^n = x \cdot x \cdots x$, n times).

### Rules of Exponents

**RULE I**: $x^a x^b = x^{a+b}$, when multiplying like bases, add exponents.

EXAMPLE: $x^3 x^4 = x^{3+4} = x^7$.

**RULE II**: $(xy)^a = x^a y^a$, the exponent applies to everything within parentheses.

**RULE III**: $\dfrac{x^a}{x^b} = x^{a-b} = \dfrac{1}{x^{b-a}}$, when dividing like bases, subtract exponents.

EXAMPLE: $\dfrac{x^3}{x^5} = x^{3-5} = x^{-2}$

or Note: $x^{-2} = \dfrac{1}{x^2}$.

$\dfrac{x^3}{x^5} = \dfrac{1}{x^{5-3}} = \dfrac{1}{x^2}$

**RULE IV:** $x^{-a} = \dfrac{1}{x^a}$, compare with note in above example.

**RULE V:** $(x^a)^b = x^{ab}$, when raising an exponent to an exponent, multiply exponents.

EXAMPLE: $(x^2)^3 = x^{(2)(3)} = x^6$. This can also be seen as

$(x^2)^3 = (x^2)(x^2)(x^2) = x^{2+2+2} = x^6$ where $x^2$ is raised to the 3rd power and then the rule for multiplication of like bases is applied.

**RULE VI:** $x^0 = 1$, any non-zero number with an exponent of zero equals 1.

EXAMPLE: $5^0 = 1$

EXAMPLE: $(3x)^0 = 1$ when $x \neq 0$.

This can be seen more clearly from the following example. Consider $\dfrac{x^a}{x^a} = x^{(a-a)} = x^0$, but any non-zero number divided by itself equals 1. Therefore $x^0 = 1$.

Powers are the opposite (inverse) of roots. This relationship is expressed with exponents that are reciprocals. The inverse of $x^a$ is $\sqrt[a]{x}$, and $\sqrt[a]{x}$ is the same as $x^{\frac{1}{a}}$.

The inverse nature can be seen using Rule V above: $\left(x^a\right)^{\frac{1}{a}} = x^{(a)\left(\frac{1}{a}\right)} = x^1 = x$. What this says is that the nth root of x is simply x raised to the reciprocal of n.

EXAMPLE: $\sqrt[2]{x} = x^{\frac{1}{2}}$ and $\sqrt[3]{x} = x^{\frac{1}{3}}$.

In general $x^{\frac{a}{b}} = \left(x^a\right)^{\frac{1}{b}} = \sqrt[b]{x^a}$. (Note $\frac{a}{b} = a \cdot \frac{1}{b}$.)

EXAMPLE: $x^{\frac{2}{3}} = \sqrt[3]{x^2}$

Another important use of this property is switching the order of power and root:

$$\sqrt[b]{x^a} = \left(x^a\right)^{\frac{1}{b}} = x^{\frac{a}{b}} = \left(x^{\frac{1}{b}}\right)^a = \left(\sqrt[b]{x}\right)^a$$

Therefore $\sqrt[b]{x^a} = \left(\sqrt[b]{x}\right)^a$.

EXAMPLE: $\sqrt[3]{27^2} = \left(\sqrt[3]{27}\right)^2 = (3)^2 = 9$

## MULTIPLICATION OF SINGLE TERMS

EXAMPLE: Multiply the terms $(2x^2)(3x)$ to get a single combined term.

SOLUTION: First multiply numbers (coefficients) together, then multiply letters (variables) together (adding exponents). That is $2 \cdot 3 = 6$ and $x^2 \cdot x = x^3$: $(2x^2)(3x) = 6(x^2)(x) = 6x^{2+1} = 6x^3$.

## SINGLE TERMS RAISED TO AN EXPONENT

EXAMPLE: Apply the rule $(xy)^a = x^a y^a$ to simplify $(2x^2)^3$.

SOLUTION: $(2x^2)^3 = 2^3(x^2)^3 = 8x^6$

Alternatively, since the exponent is an integer, $(2x^2)^3 = (2x^2)(2x^2)(2x^2)$ can be used: $(2 \cdot 2 \cdot 2)(x^2x^2x^2) = 8x^{2+2+2} = 8x^6$.

## DIVISION WITH SINGLE TERMS

EXAMPLE: Simplify $\frac{4x^3y}{2xy^2}$, the division of two terms.

In dividing variables with exponents, determine whether the numerator or denominator has the larger exponent. Using the rule of exponent division, subtract the smaller exponent from the larger exponent.

$$\frac{x^3}{x} = \frac{x^{3-1}}{x^{1-1}} = \frac{x^2}{1} = x^2 \text{ and } \frac{y}{y^2} = \frac{y^{1-1}}{y^{2-1}} = \frac{1}{y}$$

$$\frac{4x^3y}{2xy^2} = \frac{2x^{3-1}}{1y^{2-1}} = \frac{2x^2}{y}$$

## FACTORS OF EXPRESSIONS

Recall from the arithmetic section, a factor is a number that divides into another number evenly. In algebra each term is composed of factors, since each element of a term is multiplied together to produce the term. For example the term $2x^2$ has the factors 2, x, 2x, $x^2$, and $2x^2$. Each of these "numbers" divides evenly into $2x^2$.

When factoring multi-term expressions, look for what is common to each term (the greatest common factor).

EXAMPLE: Factor $2x^2y - 6xy^3$.

SOLUTION: 2xy is common to both terms. This can be seen as follows:

$$2x^2y - 6xy^3 = \underline{2xxy} - \underline{(2)}(3)\underline{xy}yy$$

Therefore, it can be factored out. That which remains stays inside the parentheses: $2x^2y - 6xy^3 = 2xy(x - 3y^2)$.

## Distributive Property of Multiplication for Multi-Term Expressions

EXAMPLE: Multiply $2x(x + 3)$.

SOLUTION: Multiply each term of one by each term of the other.

$$2x(x + 3) = (2x)(x) + (2x)(3)$$
$$= 2x^2 + 6x$$

EXAMPLE: $-(x - 3)$

SOLUTION: Remember, a negative sign in front of parentheses is equivalent to multiplying by $-1$:

$$(-1)(x - 3) = -x + (-1)(-3) = -x + 3$$

EXAMPLE: $(x + 3)(x + 2)$

SOLUTION: Here both expressions have multiple terms. A good way to remember to multiply all terms is FOIL, which stands for First, Outside, Inside, Last.

$$(x + 3)(x - 2) = x^2 - 2x + 3x - 6$$
$$= x^2 + x - 6$$

Note: The product is a second degree polynomial (i.e. highest power is 2). This is useful to recognize when the reverse process, factoring, is needed.

EXAMPLE: Use FOIL in reverse to factor $x^2 - 2x - 3$.

SOLUTION: (x )(x ) F_ _ _ (First)

(x 1)(x 3) F_ _ L (Last)

Since the product of the "Last" is -3, either 1 or 3 is negative (-). Since the sum of "Inside" and "Outside" is $-2x$, the 3 is negative.

$(x + 1)(x - 3)$

## Factoring the Difference of Two Squares

This factoring method applies only to the difference of two squares.

EXAMPLES: $x^2 - 16$, $x^2 - 25$, and $x^4 - 81$

Whenever the expression to be factored appears in the general form $a^2 - b^2$, the factored form is $(a + b)(a - b)$.

EXAMPLES: $a^2 - b^2 = (a + b)(a - b)$

$x^2 - 16 = (x + 4)(x - 4)$

$x^2 - 25 = (x + 5)(x - 5)$

$x^4 - 81 = (x^2 + 9)(x^2 - 9)$ (Notice that $x^2 - 9$ is also the difference of two squares and can be factored further.)

$x^4 - 81 = (x^2 + 9)(x^2 - 9) = (x^2 + 9)(x + 3)(x - 3)$

## Factoring a Trinomial Square

A trinomial square has the general form $a^2 \pm 2ab + b^2$. The middle term is twice the product of the square roots of the first and last terms.

EXAMPLE: $a^2 + 2ab + b^2 = (a + b)(a + b) = (a + b)^2$

EXAMPLE: $x^2 + 4x + 4 = (x + 2)(x + 2) = (x + 2)^2$

EXAMPLE: $a^2 - 2ab + b^2 = (a - b)(a - b) = (a - b)^2$

EXAMPLE: $x^2 - 10x + 25 = (x - 5)(x - 5) = (x - 5)^2$

## Division with Multi-Terms

EXAMPLE: $\dfrac{x^2 + 5x - 14}{x - 2}$

SOLUTION: Problems of this form are predominately done by factoring and cancellation. First factor $x^2 + 5x - 14$: $x^2 + 5x - 14 = (x - 2)(x + 7)$.

Then cancel, if possible: $\dfrac{(x - 2)(x + 7)}{x - 2} = x + 7$.

## Simplifying Multi-Term Expressions

EXAMPLE: Simplify 3X - (-2X + 5) + (3X - 2).

SOLUTION: The first step is to remove all parentheses:

3X + 2X – 5 + 3X – 2

Then combine like terms:

8X - 7

EXAMPLE: 3x(4x + 7) - 2(5x- 8) - 12

SOLUTION: Remove parentheses by using the distributive property:

$12x^2 + 21x - 10x + 16 - 12$

Combine like terms:

$12x^2 + 11x + 4$

# EQUATIONS

An ***equation*** describes two quantities that are equal (i.e. each side equals the other). The solution of an equation is the value of variable(s) that make the equation true. We say that an equation is in balance when both sides have the same value.

# LINEAR EQUATIONS

The exponent of the variable(s) being 1 characterizes linear equations (i.e., $y = 2x + 1$ is linear because the exponent of both the x and the y is 1). They are called linear because their graph is a line.

## Linear Equations with One Variable

Isolating the variable on one side solves linear equations with one variable. To isolate the variable, do inverse operations on both sides until the variable is by itself.

EXAMPLE: Solve for x: $\frac{3}{4}x + 5 = 17$.

SOLUTION:

$$\frac{3}{4}x + 5 = 17$$

$$\underline{\quad -5 = -5}$$ Subtract 5 from both sides.

$$\frac{3}{4}x \quad = 12$$

$$4 \cdot \frac{3}{4}x = 4 \cdot 12$$ Multiply both sides by 4.

$$3x = 48$$

$$\frac{3x}{3} = \frac{48}{3}$$ Divide both sides by 3.

$$x = 16$$

EXAMPLE: Solve for x: $\frac{3x-4}{5} = 4$.

SOLUTION:

$$5 \cdot \frac{3x-4}{5} = 5 \cdot 4$$ Multiply both sides by 5.

$$3x - 4 = 20$$

$$\underline{\quad +4 \quad +4}$$ Add 4 to both sides.

$$3x \quad = 24$$

$$\frac{3x}{3} = \frac{24}{3}$$ Divide both sides by 3.

$$x = 8$$

EXAMPLE: $3x + 4 = x - 2$

SOLUTION: Since the variable is on both sides, it is necessary to eliminate it from one of the sides.

$$\begin{array}{rl} 3x + 4 = & x - 2 \\ \underline{-x \quad = } & \underline{-x} \\ 2x + 4 = & -2 \end{array}$$

Subtract x from both sides.

$$\begin{array}{l} 2x + 4 = -2 \\ \underline{\quad -4 = -4} \\ 2x \quad = -6 \end{array}$$

Subtract 4 from both sides.

$$\frac{2x}{2} = \frac{-6}{2}$$

Divide both sides by 2.

$x = -3$

EXAMPLE: $\frac{1}{2}x + \frac{2}{3}x = 28$

SOLUTION: To clear multiple fractions, multiply all terms by the LCM (least common multiple) of the denominators. In this case, 6 is the LCM.

$$\overset{3}{\cancel{6}} \cdot \frac{1}{\cancel{2}}x + \overset{2}{\cancel{6}} \cdot \frac{2}{\cancel{3}}x = 6 \cdot 28$$

Multiply each term by 6.

$3x + 4x = 168$

$7x = 168$

Combine like terms.

$$\frac{7x}{7} = \frac{168}{7}$$

Divide both sides by 7.

$x = 24$

Note: Mental math techniques can often speed up multiplication. For instance when multiplying 6 and 28: (6)(28) = (6)(30 - 2) = 180 - 12 = 168 or (6)(28) = (6)(20 + 8) = 120 + 48 = 168. Dividing the number into a multiple of 10 and a single-digit integer is easier to do in your head.

## Simultaneous Linear Equations

The simplest of simultaneous equations consists of two equations with two variables.

Note: a single linear equation with 2 variables has multiple solutions, thus necessitating at least two equations for a unique solution.

EXAMPLE: $x + y = 8$

$x - y = 2$

These equations must be solved together to produce a common solution. There are several ways to find the solutions. Following are the two most popular methods.

## Elimination Method

The concept here is to combine (by addition) the two equations together so as to eliminate one of the variables.

EXAMPLE:

$$\begin{array}{r} x + y = 8 \\ \underline{x - y = 2} \\ 2x \quad = 10 \end{array}$$

Notice: The y's cancelled during the addition because they had the same coefficients with opposite signs.

$x = 5$

Now substitute 5 for x in either equation to solve for y:

$$\begin{array}{rl} 5 + y = 8 & \qquad 5 - y = 2 \\ y = 3 & \qquad -y = -3 \\ & \qquad y = 3 \end{array}$$

## Substitution Method

This method requires rewriting an equation so that a variable is on one side by itself. This rewriting gives us a value to substitute into other equations.

Let's apply this concept to the equations $x + y = 8$ and $x - y = 2$, once again. Using the first equation and isolating the variable y we get $y = 8 - x$. (We subtracted x from both sides to isolate y.) Now substitute $8 - x$ for y in the second equation:

$$x - (8 - x) = 2$$

$$x - 8 + x = 2$$

$$2x = 10$$

$$x = 5$$

Substitute 5 for x as before and you'll find $y = 3$. To check each solution, plug both numbers into both equations. If the solution is correct both equations will balance.

In most cases just adding two equations will not eliminate one of the variables. Consider the following example.

EXAMPLE: What value of x and y satisfies $2x + y = 7$ and $x - 2y = 6$ simultaneously?

SOLUTION: If we add them together, neither variable cancels. This can be resolved by remembering what made them cancel in the first example, same coefficients with opposite signs. We can modify one of the equations to establish this condition. If we multiply the first equation by 2, we have

$4x + 2y = 14$

Now adding this new equation with the second we have

$$\begin{array}{r} 4x + 2y = 14 \\ \underline{x - 2y = 6} \\ 5x \qquad = 20 \\ x \qquad = 4 \end{array}$$

Substituting $x = 4$ into the second equation:

$$4 - 2y = 6$$

$$-2y = 2$$

$$y = -1$$

| CHECK: | $2x + y = 7$ | $x - 2y = 6$ | Check with x = 4 and y = -1. |
|---|---|---|---|
| | $2(4)-1 = 7$ | $4 - 2(-1) = 6$ | |
| | $8 - 1 = 7$ | $4 + 2 = 6$ | |
| | $7 = 7$ | $6 = 6$ | (Checks out okay.) |

## QUADRATIC EQUATIONS

The exponent of the variable being 2 characterizes quadratic equations. Linear equations are limited to exponents of one. Quadratic equations can have exponents up to 2.

Solvable quadratic equations always have two solutions. (They will be the same solution if the polynomial is a perfect square.) The general form for a quadratic is $ax^2 + bx + c = 0$.

EXAMPLE: What values of x satisfy the equation $x^2 + 4x + 3 = 0$?

SOLUTION: This is solvable by factoring (reverse FOIL).

(x )(x ) F _ _ _

(x 1)(x 3) F _ _ L

(x + 1)(x + 3) The middle term is (+) and last term is (+).

Then using the property $a \cdot b = 0 \rightarrow a = 0$ or $b = 0$, then

$x + 1 = 0$ or $x + 3 = 0$

$x = -1$ or $x = -3$

x + 1 and x + 3 are the factors and -1 and -3 are the solutions (roots). Either root will satisfy the equation:

| For $x = -1$ | For $x = -3$ |
|---|---|
| $(-1)^2 + 4(-1) + 3 = 0$ | $(-3)^2 + 4(-3) + 3 = 0$ |
| $1 - 4 + 3 = 0$ | $9 - 12 + 3 = 0$ |
| $0 = 0$ | $0 = 0$ |

If the equation does not equal zero, move everything to one side and set it equal to zero.

EXAMPLE: What values of x make $2x^2 = 9x + 5$ a true statement?

SOLUTION: Subtract 9x + 5 from both sides:

$2x^2 - (9x + 5) = 9x + 5 - (9x + 5)$

$2x^2 - 9x - 5 = 0$

then factor: $(2x + 1)(x - 5) = 0$

$2x + 1 = 0$ or $x - 5 = 0$

$2x = -1$ $x = 5$

$x = -\frac{1}{2}$

# INEQUALITIES

An inequality illustrates quantities that are not equal. An inequality states that one quantity is greater than (or less than) another.

### Symbols

- $a \neq b$    a and b are not equal
- $a > b$    a is greater than b
- $a < b$    a is less than b
- $a \geq b$    a is greater than or equal to b
- $a \leq b$    a is less than or equal to b

## Simple Operations with Inequalities

To this point in algebra we have worked with equalities. An equation (equality) can be readily manipulated and still be correct. Some manipulations performed have been adding/subtracting from both sides and multiplying/dividing both sides. We have done this repeatedly and not destroyed the equality. However, such manipulations on inequalities require a little more care.

Consider the inequality $1 > 0$. If we multiply both sides by $-1$ the result is $-1 > 0$, which is not correct. What must we do to insure that the truth of an inequality is not broken during manipulations necessary for solution?

### Addition/Subtraction with Inequalities

The same number or variable may be added or subtracted from both sides and the inequality will not be affected.

| Rule | Example |
|---|---|
| If $a > b$ | $5 > 2 \quad c = 3$ |
| Then $a + c > b + c$ | $5 + 3 > 2 + 3$ |
| So: | $8 > 5$ |
| If $a < b$ | $7 < 10 \quad c = -1$ |
| Then $a - c < b - c$ | $7 - 1 < 10 - 1$ |
| So: | $6 < 9$ |

## Multiplication/Division with Inequalities

The same number or variable may be multiplied/divided on both sides of an inequality. However, if the number/variable that is multiplied/divided is negative the inequality reverses (i.e., a "greater than" becomes "less than," and vice versa) when both sides of an inequality are multiplied (or divided) by a negative number.

| Rule | Example | |
|---|---|---|
| If $a > b$ and $c > 0$<br>Then $ca > cb$ | $5 > 3$<br>$2(5) > 2(3)$<br>$10 > 6$ | $c = 2$ |
| If $a > b$ and $c < 0$<br>Then $ca < cb$ | $5 > 3$<br>$-2(5) < -2(3)$<br>$-10 < -6$ | $c = -2$ |
| If $a > b$ and $d > 0$<br>Then $\frac{a}{d} > \frac{b}{d}$ | $12 > 4$<br>$\frac{12}{2} > \frac{4}{2}$<br>$6 > 2$ | $d = 2$ |
| If $a > b$ and $d < 0$<br>Then $\frac{a}{d} < \frac{b}{d}$ | $12 > 4$<br>$\frac{12}{-2} < \frac{4}{-2}$<br>$-6 < -2$ | $d = -2$ |

## Solving Simple Inequalities

Solving an inequality means finding all values that make the inequality true.

EXAMPLE: Find the solution set for $2x + 5 > 7$.

SOLUTION: $2x + 5 > 7$

$\quad -5 \quad -5$ Subtract 5 from both sides.

$\frac{2x}{2} > \frac{2}{2}$ Divide both sides by 2.

$x > 1$ is the solution set (i.e., x is all values greater than 1).

EXAMPLE: Find all values that make $-x + 2 < 5$ true.

SOLUTION: $-x + 2 < 5$

$\quad -2 \quad -2$ Subtract 2 from both sides.

$-x < 3$

$(-1)(-x) > 3(-1)$ Multiply both sides by $-1$.

$x > 3$

## Solving More Complex Inequalities

Applying the rules from the previous section, more complex inequalities can be solved. Here are some examples.

EXAMPLE: Solve for x: $3x + 2 > x + 10$.

SOLUTION: $3x + 2 > x + 10$

$\underline{\quad -2 \qquad -2}$ Subtract 2 from both sides.

$3x \quad > x + 8$

$\underline{-x \qquad -x \quad}$ Subtract x from both sides.

$\frac{2x}{2} > \frac{8}{2}$ Divide both sides by 2.

$x > 4$

EXAMPLE: Solve for x: $-5x - 2 > -x + 18$.

SOLUTION: $-5x - 2 > -x + 18$

$\underline{\quad +2 \qquad +2}$ Add 2 to both sides.

$-5x \quad > -x + 20$

$\underline{+x \qquad +x \quad}$ Add x to both sides.

$\frac{-4x}{-4} < \frac{20}{-4}$ Divide both sides by –4.

$x < -5$

Remember that the inequality sign reverses directions when both sides are multiplied/divided by a negative number.

## Range Inequalities

Range inequalities are essentially two inequalities together in one statement. In general the solution of range inequalities takes the form $a < x < b$, where a and b are numbers and x is the variable. To solve range inequalities you may convert it to two inequalities or apply all algebraic operations to the larger single statement. Let's look at these examples.

EXAMPLE: $-2 < x < -1$, this one is already in the solution form. It reads, "x is greater than -2 but less than –1."

EXAMPLE: Given $-2 < x < -1$, what is the range of 3x?

SOLUTION: Since 3x is 3 times x, multiply everything by 3: $(3)(-2) < 3x < (3)(-1)$ or

$-6 < 3x < -3$.

EXAMPLE: Solve for the range of x that satisfies $1 < x - 2 < 4$.

SOLUTION: We add 2 to everything to find x: $1 + 2 < x - 2 + 2 < 4 + 2$ or

$3 < x < 6$.

$1 < x - 2 < 4$

$\underline{+2 \qquad +2 \;\; +2}$ Add 2 to each side.

$3 < x \qquad < 6$

# ADDITIONAL ALGEBRAIC TOPICS

The rest of the section on algebra covers a diverse group of topics. Such topics as rate problems, sets, probability, combinations, and symbolic algebra may appear on the GMAT. These topics tend to use algebra in their solution and application.

## RATE

A rate can be thought of as a relationship of one unit of measure to another (i.e., something per something).

EXAMPLE: A rate can be the occurrence of an event over a period of time (i.e., $\frac{\text{miles}}{\text{hour}}, \frac{\text{feet}}{\text{second}}, \frac{\text{shirts washed}}{\text{day}}$).

## DISTANCE

The basic formula is distance = rate × time (D = Rt).

EXAMPLE: How far does a car travel at a speed (rate) of 40 MPH in 2 hours and 15 minutes?

$$15 \text{ minutes} = \frac{1}{4} \text{ hour}$$

$$2 \text{ hours } 15\text{min.} = 2\frac{1}{4} \text{ hours} = \frac{9}{4} \text{ hours}$$

$$D = \frac{\overset{10}{\cancel{40}}\text{ miles}}{\cancel{\text{hour}}} \times \frac{9}{\cancel{4}}\cancel{\text{hour}}$$

D = 90 miles

NOTE: time units (i.e., hours) cancel leaving answer units in miles.

## PRICE (COST)

Another form of rate is monetary per unit(s).

The basic formula is sale price = rate × number of units

EXAMPLE: If eggs sell for \$2.50 per dozen, what is the cost of 54 eggs?

54 = 4 1/2 dozen

$$C = \frac{\overset{1.25}{\cancel{\$2.50}}}{\cancel{\text{dozen}}} \times \frac{9}{\cancel{2}}\cancel{\text{dozen}}$$

C = (1.25)(9) = 9(1) + 9(.25) -- a good technique for mental math is to split the multiplication into parts as shown

C = 9 + 2.25 = \$11.25

Again notice that the dozen units cancel leaving \$.

# WORK

The basic formula is:

Work = Rate × Time

Where rate is the amount of work that one man can do in a unit of time (i.e., what part of the job) and work is in terms of the amount of job completed.

EXAMPLE: If two men can do a job in five hours, what percent of the job can one man do in 1 hour and 30 minutes? (Assume each man works at the same rate.)

SOLUTION: Step 1: find the rate of one man.

If 2 men take 5 hours, it is clear that one man will take longer to do the job, not shorter. This implies an inverse proportion:

$$2\left(\frac{2\text{ men}}{1\text{ man}} = \frac{x}{5\text{ hours}}\right)2$$

x = 10 hours: it takes one man 10 hours.

Step 2: Apply the formula work = rate × time.

If it takes one man 10 hours to do a job, then his rate is $\frac{1}{10}$ (he can do $\frac{1}{10}$ of the job in 1 hour). Now since 1 hour and 30 minutes is $\frac{3}{2}$ hours we have work $= \frac{1}{10} \cdot \frac{3}{2} = \frac{3}{20} = 15\%$.

A variation of the same situation could be:

EXAMPLE: How long would it take one man to complete 60% of the job (that takes 2 men 5 hours to complete)?

SOLUTION: The rate is still $\frac{1}{10}$ and since $60\% = \frac{6}{10}$, we have

$$\frac{6}{10}J = \frac{1}{10}J \cdot t.$$

Multiplying by 10 to clear the fractions we have 6J = J·t and 6 hours = t.

EXAMPLE: If a job that takes 12 men 6 hours to complete, then two men working for 24 hours will complete what % of the job?

SOLUTION: First setup the inverse proportion to determine how long, x hours, the job would take two men:

$$\frac{12}{2} = \frac{x}{6} \Rightarrow 2x = 72;$$ where x is the time for two men to do the job

x = 36 hours

Since it would take 36 hours for two men to complete the job, two men could complete $\frac{24}{36} = \frac{2}{3} = 66\frac{2}{3}\%$ of the job in 24 hours.

### Work (Different Rates)

When multiple units work together, the individual rates of working alone are combined to calculate the result of working together. The basic formula is $\frac{1}{T}+\frac{1}{S}=\frac{1}{J}$, where T is for Tom and S is for Sam. $\frac{1}{T}$ represents Tom's rate of work and $\frac{1}{S}$ the rate for Sam. $\frac{1}{J}$ is their combined rate (the amount of the job they complete together in a unit of time).

EXAMPLE: If Tom can do a job in 4 hours and Sam can do the same job in 2 hours, how long will it take them to complete the job if they work together?

SOLUTION: Tom's rate is $\frac{1}{4}$ and Sam's is $\frac{1}{2}$.

$$\frac{1}{4}+\frac{1}{2}=\frac{1}{J}$$

$$\cancel{4}J\frac{1}{\cancel{4}}+\overset{2}{\cancel{4}}J\frac{1}{\cancel{2}}=4\cancel{J}\frac{1}{\cancel{J}},$$ clear the fractions by multiplying by 4J.

$J + 2J = 4$

$3J = 4$

$J = \frac{4}{3} = 1$ hour 20 minutes

## INTEREST

Simple interest is based on a time frame of one year (i.e., annual). The basic formula is interest is equal to the products of principle, rate and time: $I = P \times R \times t$.

EXAMPLE: What is the interest on \$5000 invested at 5% for two years?

SOLUTION: $I = 5000 \times \frac{5}{100} \times 2$

Notice that using the fractional form of percent makes cancellation possible and avoids multiplication with decimals.

$I = 5000 \times \frac{5}{100} \times 2$

$I = 50 \times 5 \times 2$

$I = 500$

Alternately, 5% for 2 years is equivalent to 10% for 1 year (an inverse proportion) and 10% of 5000 is 500.

EXAMPLE: How much must be invested for 3 months at 4% to earn $120 in simple interest?

SOLUTION: Since a year has 12 months, three months equals $\frac{3}{12} = \frac{1}{4}$ year.

$$I = P\,R\,t$$

$$120 = P\left(\frac{4}{100}\right)\left(\frac{1}{4}\right)$$

$$120 = \left(\frac{P}{100}\right)$$

$$12{,}000 = P$$

Compound interest is computed on the principle and any accumulated interest over the unit of the compounding time specified.

EXAMPLE: What is the final value of a $10,000, 6 month CD, which has a specified interest rate of 6% compounded quarterly?

SOLUTION: Compounded quarterly is code for compounded every three months.

$$I = \overset{100}{\cancel{10000}}\left(\frac{\cancel{6}}{\cancel{100}}\right)\left(\frac{3}{\underset{2}{\cancel{12}}}\right)$$

$$I = 100\left(\frac{3}{2}\right) = 150$$

The interest of $150 for the first three months is added to the principle before computing the interest for the second quarter.

$$I = \overset{101.50}{\cancel{10{,}150}}\left(\frac{\cancel{6}}{\cancel{100}}\right)\left(\frac{3}{\underset{2}{\cancel{12}}}\right)$$

$$I = 101.50\left(\frac{3}{2}\right)$$

$$I = \frac{304.50}{2}$$

$$I = 152.25$$

Total = 10,000 + 150 + 152.25 = 10302.25

## CONVERSION OF UNITS

Conversion of units deals with equivalent rates with a change of unit measure.

EXAMPLE: $\frac{30\text{feet}}{\text{second}} = \frac{?\,\text{yards}}{\text{minute}}$

SOLUTION: The above conversion requires the change of two units, feet to yards and seconds to minutes. To change each unit we can multiply by a conversion factor that equals one.

$$\frac{\overset{10}{\cancel{30}}\cancel{\text{feet}}}{\cancel{\text{second}}} \times \boxed{\frac{1\text{ yard}}{\cancel{3}\cancel{\text{feet}}}} \times \boxed{\frac{60\cancel{\text{ seconds}}}{1\text{ minute}}} =$$

equals 1
(1 yard = 3 feet)

equals 1
(1 minute = 60 seconds)

Note that feet cancel feet and seconds cancel seconds.

$$10\text{ yards} \times \frac{60}{\text{minute}} = \frac{600\text{ yards}}{\text{minute}}$$

## ADDITIONAL BUSINESS FORMULAS

### Profit

**Profit = Sale price – Cost, or simply P = S – C**

EXAMPLE: A merchant made a $40 profit on an item he sold for $120. What was the percent profit?

SOLUTION: $\%\text{profit} = \frac{\text{profit}}{\text{original cost}}$

$$P = S - C$$
$$40 = 120 - C$$
$$C = 120 - 40 = 80$$

$$\%\text{profit} = \frac{40}{80} = 50\%$$

### Sale Price

**Sale Price = List - %discount (List)**

Since the list price represents 100% of list we also have:

**Sale Price = (100% - %discount) (List)**

EXAMPLE: An item discounted by 20% sold for $100. What was the original price of the item?

A) 80 B) 120 C) 125 D) 180 E) 124

SOLUTION: $(100\% - 20\%)\ L = \$100$

$.8L = \$100$

$$L = \frac{\$100}{.8}$$

$L = \$125$

The answer is B.

## MIXTURE

In a mixture problem, various quantities of different substances are combined to form a mixture.

EXAMPLE: A nut mixture is to be made of 4 pounds of peanuts at $2.00 per pound and 2 pounds of cashews at $5.00 per pound. What is the price per pound of the mixture?

SOLUTION: Total cost $= 4\ (\$2.00) + 2\ (\$5.00)$

$= \$8 + \$10 = \$18$

Total Weight $= 4 + 2 = 6$ lb

Using a proportion we can take $18 per 6 pounds and convert it into price per pound:

$$3\left(\frac{18}{6} = \frac{X}{1}\right)3$$

$X = \$3$ per pound.

Solution mixture type problems involve percent concentrations. Consider the following example.

EXAMPLE: Ten liters of water are added to 40 liters of a solution that is 20% alcohol and water. What percent of the new solution is alcohol?

SOLUTION: $$\text{Percent} = \frac{\text{part}}{\text{whole}} = \frac{\text{alcohol}}{\text{final solution}}$$

We need to find the amount of alcohol since only water is to be added.

Volume of alcohol = 20% of 40 liters = 8 liters

The total solution volume is 40 + 10 = 50 liters

$$\frac{8}{50} = \frac{16}{100} = 16\%$$ (Note the shortcut used to find the percent.)

An alternate method involves the use of inverse proportion. As the water increases in the solution the % alcohol decreases so

$$\frac{40}{50} = \frac{X}{20}$$

$80 = 5X$

$16 = X$

# SETS

A set is a collection of elements. Some examples are the set of integers, the set of odd integers, the set of even integers, and the set of primes.

## OPERATIONS ON SETS

Consider the sets A and B: A = {1, 2, 3} and B = {3, 4, 5}. The ***intersection*** (i.e. what is in A and B) is the set {3}. This is denoted as follows $A \cap B = \{3\}$. The ***union*** (i.e. what is in A or B) is the set {1, 2, 3, 4, 5}. This is denoted as follows $A \cup B = \{1, 2, 3, 4, 5\}$.

## VENN DIAGRAMS

Sets and operations on sets can be described in pictorial form by what are called Venn diagrams.

EXAMPLE: Let A be the set of seniors. Let B be the set of business majors.

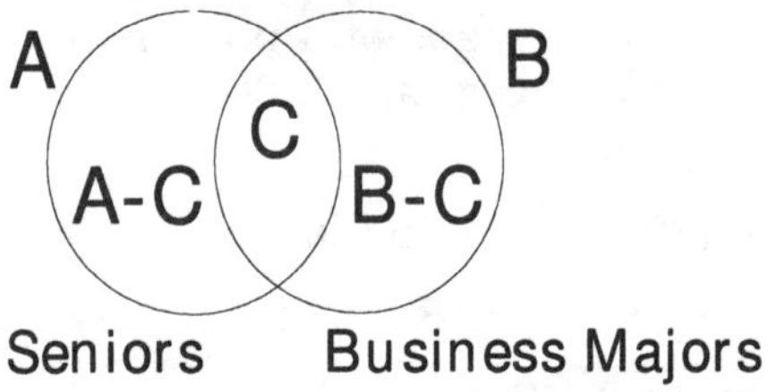


Note that $C = A \cap B$. By way of introduction, note that A – C stands for the part of A outside of C. The same goes for B – C. Also notice that the set C consists of all business majors who are also seniors. It follows that A - C is the set of seniors who are not business majors and that the set, B – C, contains all of the business majors who are not seniors.

To see a little more of the manipulation of sets, the union of A and B can be seen as follows:

$$
\begin{aligned}
A \cup B &= (A - C) + C + (B - C) \\
&= A - C + C + B - C \\
&= A + B - C
\end{aligned}
$$

From this we see the general rule that $A \cup B = A + B - A \cap B$.

## Application of VENN Diagrams

EXAMPLE: Given that 40% of all students are business majors, 30% of all students are seniors, and 10% are senior business majors, what percent are neither seniors nor business majors?

SOLUTION: First we'll assign some variables. Let S = seniors, let B = business majors, and let I = senior business majors (i.e. $I = S \cap B$).

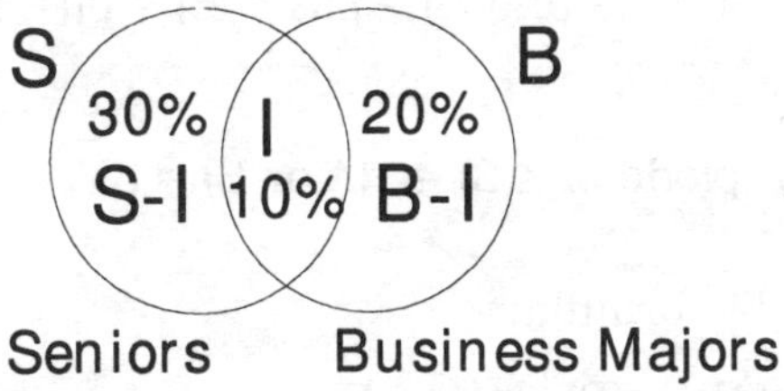


Use a Venn diagram and the following calculations:

$S - I = 40\% - 10\% = 30\%$

$B - I = 30\% - 10\% = 20\%$

The union of S and B represents all students who are seniors, business majors, or both. From the diagram and the calculations, $A \cup B = (S - I) + I + (B - I) = 30\% + 10\% + 20\% = 60\%$. Therefore 40% are neither.

This could also be solved by the formula $S \cup B = S + B - I = 40\% + 30\% - 10\% = 60\%$. And once again we see that 40% are neither seniors nor business majors.

# PROBABILITY

Probability describes the chance that an event, E, will occur. A probability of zero means it cannot happen. A probability of one means it must happen. Therefore probability is always between zero and one (i.e. $0 \le p \le 1$) or a fraction. p(E) reads, "the probability that event E will occur" and is computed by

$$p(E) = \frac{\text{set of chance outcomes}}{\text{set of all outcomes}}$$

EXAMPLE: Consider one roll of a die (six sided with each side equally likely). What is the chance of the result being an odd number?

SOLUTION: Set of odd = {1, 3, 5} set of odds

Set of all = {1, 2, 3, 4, 5, 6} set of all

$p(E) = \frac{3}{6} = \frac{1}{2}$, half of the time a fair die is rolled the number will be odd.

Similarly it can be shown that $p(\text{even}) = \frac{1}{2}$.

# COMBINATION PROBABILITY (MULTIPLE EVENTS)

Operations on sets are used in determining the probability of a combination of events given the probability of simpler events. Given the events A and B (both sets of many simpler events), the chance that the outcome is in both events (i.e., intersection) is denoted by $p(A \cap B)$. The chance that the outcome is in either or both events involves the union: $p(A \cup B)$. Probability theory says that $p(A \cup B) = p(A) + p(B) - p(A \cap B)$. This comes straight from set theory.

EXAMPLE: Given the roll of one die (with six sides), let event A = {1, 3, 5}, the odd number event, and let B = {1, 2, 3}, the event that the roll is less than 4. What then is the likelihood that a roll will be both odd and less than four?

SOULTION: $p(\text{odd and} \le 3) = p(A \text{ and } B) = p(A \cap B) = p(\{1,3\}) = \dfrac{\{1,3\}}{\{1,2,3,4,5,6\}} = \dfrac{2}{6} = \dfrac{1}{3}$

Additionally, $p(\text{odd or} \le 3) = P(A \text{ or } B) = p(A \cup B) = \dfrac{\{1,2,3,5\}}{\{1,2,3,4,5,6\}} = \dfrac{4}{6} = \dfrac{2}{3}$.

Alternately, by formula:

$p(A \cup B) = p(A) + p(B) - p(A \cap B) =$

$$\frac{\{1,3,5\}}{\{1,2,3,4,5,6\}} + \frac{\{1,2,3\}}{\{1,2,3,4,5,6\}} - \frac{\{1,3\}}{\{1,2,3,4,5,6\}} = \frac{3}{6} + \frac{3}{6} - \frac{2}{6} = \frac{4}{6} = \frac{2}{3}.$$

If A and B have no elements in common then they are said to be ***mutually exclusive*** and it follows that $p(A \cup B) = p(A) + p(B)$ (i.e., no intersection).

## INDEPENDENT EVENTS

Events are ***independent*** if neither has an effect on the outcome of the other. Take for example the outcome of two tossed coins. These can be done simultaneously or one coin could be flipped twice in succession. In either case there are four possible outcomes:

| Coin A | Coin B |
|---|---|
| H | H |
| H | T |
| T | H |
| T | T |

The probability of coin A being a head is one-half, $p(A{=}H) = \frac{1}{2}$, similarly $p(B{=}H) = \frac{1}{2}$. When events A and B are independent then $p(A \text{ and } B) = p(A \cap B) = p(A)p(B)$. Therefore the probability of getting two heads is $p(A)p(B) = \left(\frac{1}{2}\right)\left(\frac{1}{2}\right) = \frac{1}{4}$. This is also clearly visible from the chart of the four possible outcomes. Only one out of four has both heads.

We also know that $p(A \text{ or } B) = p(A \cup B) = p(A) + p(B) - p(A \cap B)$. In this case, the probability of getting at least one head is $p(A) + p(B) - p(A \cap B) = \frac{1}{2} + \frac{1}{2} - \frac{1}{4} = \frac{3}{4}$. The chart also shows this where three out of the four outcomes have at least one head.

EXAMPLE: Given three coins, what is the probability of all tails?

SOLUTION: This is p(A and B and C) = p(A)p(B)p(C) = $\left(\frac{1}{2}\right)\left(\frac{1}{2}\right)\left(\frac{1}{2}\right) = \frac{1}{8}$.

This can be verified from this chart of three coins:

| Coin A | Coin B | Coin C | |
|---|---|---|---|
| H | H | H | |
| H | H | T | |
| H | T | H | |
| H | T | T | 8 possibilities |
| T | H | H | |
| T | H | T | |
| T | T | H | |
| T | T | T | ⇐ all tails = $\frac{1}{8}$ |

## COMBINATIONS

There are many instances where knowledge of the number of possible combinations can be determined without listing and counting them all. When choosing from two mutually exclusive sets A and B, where set A has X elements and set B has Y elements, then the total number of combinations is X times Y.

EXAMPLE: John has 4 shirts and 3 pairs of pants. How many different outfits (combinations) does he have to choose between?

SOLUTION: (4)(3) = 12.

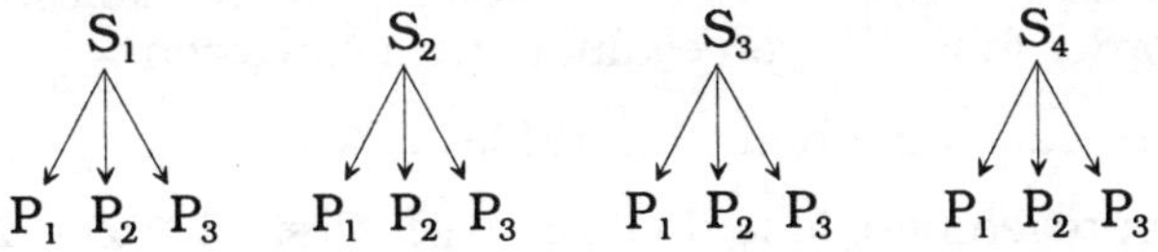


## ORDERING THE OBJECTS OF A SET

Once again it is possible to know how many different ways a set of objects can be ordered without listing and counting them all. The number of ways the objects of a set can be ordered is calculated by the use of factorial, n!. For a set of n elements:

$$n! = n(n - 1)(n - 2)...(n-(n-1)) \qquad \text{(note: } n-(n-1) = 1\text{)}.$$

EXAMPLE: If set A has 4 elements, the number of ways of ordering them is

$$\begin{aligned} 4! &= (4)(4 - 1)(4 - 2)(4 - 3) \\ &= (4)(3)(2)(1) \\ &= 24 \end{aligned}$$

## COMBINATIONS WITHIN ONE SET

Given a set of n elements, the number of possible r element combinations taken from n is denoted $\binom{n}{r}$ and is computed by $\binom{n}{r} = \frac{n!}{r!(n-r)!}$.

EXAMPLE: How many different combinations of 3 numbers can be taken from 4 numbers?

SOLUTION: $\binom{4}{3} = \frac{4!}{3!(4-3)!} = \frac{(4)(3)(2)(1)}{(3)(2)(1)(1)} = \frac{4}{1} = 4$ (i.e. for the set {ABCD} the possible sets of 3 are {ABC}, {ABD}, {ACD}, {BCD} = 4 sets).

EXAMPLE: How many combinations of 2 numbers can be selected from a set of 4?

SOLUTION: $\binom{4}{2} = \frac{4!}{2!(4-2)!} = \frac{\overset{2}{(4)}(3)(2)(1)}{(2)(1)(2)(1)} = \frac{6}{1} = 6$

Once again use the set {ABCD}: {AB}, {AC}, {AD}, {BC}, {BD}, {CD} = 6 combinations.

## SYMBOLIC ALGEBRA

Symbolic algebra deals with assigning a symbol to a relationship of variables in an expression. In general the relationship is defined and then you are expected to apply the relationship.

EXAMPLE: If A ⊙ B = 3A – B then what are 2 ⊙ 3 and 4 ⊙ 1?

SOLUTION: 2 ⊙ 3 = 3(2) - 3 = 6 - 3 = 3, and

4 ⊙ 1 = 3(4) - 1 = 12 - 1 = 11.

Sometimes you are asked to apply the relationship multiple times. In these instances exercise care in the order in which you evaluate the expression.

EXAMPLE: If A ¤ B = 2(A + B) then what is (3 ¤ 2) ¤ 1?

SOLUTION: The approach here is to do it in stages first (3 ¤ 2) = 2(3 + 2) = 2(5) = 10. Then using this result: 10 ¤ 1 = 2(10 + 1) = 2(11) = 22. Therefore (3 ¤ 2) ¤ 1 = 22.

## Practice – Algebra

1. If $y = 3x^2 - 2x$ and $x = -3$, then $y =$

   A. -33 B. -21 C. 21 D. 24 E. 33

2. Which of the following is equivalent to $7 - 5x < 32$?

   A. $x < -5$ B. $x < 5$ C. $x > -5$ D. $x > 5$ E. $x > 25$

3. If $-3 < x < -2$, then $3x$ could be:

   A. -9 B. -7 C. -5 D. 6 E. 7

4. If $2x = 3y = 20$, then $12xy =$

   A. 240 B. 400 C. 600 D. 800 E. 1200

5. A tank which is $\frac{2}{3}$ full becomes $\frac{7}{8}$ full after 10 gallons is added to it. What is the capacity of the tank?

   A. 24 gal. B. 32 gal. C. 36 gal. D. 48 gal. E. 64 gal.

6. The following pair of simultaneous equations has how many solutions?

   $x - y = 3$
   $3x = 3y + 9$

   A. None B. One C. Two D. Three E. Infinitely Many

7. The following pair of simultaneous equations has how many solutions?

   $x - y = 4$
   $2x = 2y - 6$

   A. None B. One C. Two D. Three E. Infinitely Many

8. If Q and R are integers and $Q^2R$ is a positive odd integer, which of the following need not be true:

   A. Q is positive
   B. R is positive
   C. R is odd
   D. Q + R is even
   E. QR is odd

9. If $x^2 + x - 6 = 0$ and $x^2 - 5x + 6 = 0$, then $x =$

   A. -3 B. -2 C. 0 D. 2 E. 3

10. On a particular trip, a person traveled in 3 stages.

Stage 1: $\frac{1}{5}$ of the trip

Stage 2: $\frac{3}{4}$ of the trip

Stage 3: 10 miles

How long was Stage 2?

A. 100 mi. B. 120 mi. C. 150 mi. D. 160 mi. E. 200 mi.

11. A 20% tax is paid on all income over $2,000. If a person's net income was $14,000, what was his income before taxes?

A. $18,000 B. $17,000 C. $16,000 D. $13,600 E. $12,000

12. Sam can complete a certain job in 6 hours. If Sam and Tom work together, they can complete the job in 2 hours. If Tom works alone for 2 hours, what fraction of the job is left to complete?

A. $\frac{1}{8}$ B. $\frac{1}{6}$ C. $\frac{1}{4}$ D. $\frac{1}{3}$ E. $\frac{1}{2}$

13. If $x \neq 0$ and $x = \sqrt{2xy - y^2}$, then in terms of y, x =

A. $\frac{y}{2}$ B. y C. 2y D. -y E. y – 2

14. If $A \neq 0$ and $2A = 3B$ and $5C = 4A$, what is the ratio of C to B?

A. $\frac{5}{2}$ B. $\frac{5}{4}$ C. $\frac{5}{6}$ D. $\frac{6}{5}$ E. $\frac{4}{5}$

15. If $y = 2x$ and $z = 4y$, then $x + y + z =$

A. 7x B. 8x C. 9x D. 10x E. 11x

16. An importer bought a particular batch of items at a price of 3 for one dollar. He later sold the entire batch at 5 for 2 dollars. If his profit was 100 dollars, how many items did he sell?

A. 250 B. 500 C. 1000 D. 1500 E. 3000

17. A train traveled x miles in the first 48 minutes. If it completed the next 100 miles in y minutes, what was its average speed in miles per hour for the entire trip?

A. $\frac{4}{5}x+\frac{6000}{y}$

B. $\frac{5}{4}x+\frac{6000}{y}$

C. $\frac{x+100}{60(48+y)}$

D. $\frac{60x+6000}{48+y}$

E. $\frac{xy+4800}{60y}$

18. An importer can sell an item at a 40% discount from list price and still make a 20% profit. What percent of the cost would the gross profit be if he sold the item at list price?

A. 50% B. 60% C. 100% D. 150% E. 200%

19. A sales promotion says buy 3 tickets, get 2 free. Using this promotion, a family of 5 will save what percent of the amount if they would have purchased 5 tickets at the regular price?

A. 20% B. $33\frac{1}{3}$% C. 40% D. 60% E. $66\frac{2}{3}$%

20. Working independently, Ralph can do a job in 9 hours. Sarah, working independently, can do the same job in 6 hours. If Ralph works for 6 hours, how many hours will it take Sarah to complete the job?

A. $\frac{1}{3}$ B. $\frac{2}{3}$ C. 2 D. 3 E. 4

21. A factory worker produces x units per work day. In a month with 23 work days, he was sick for y days. At what daily rate must he work the remainder of the month in order to maintain his normal average of x units per day for the month?

A. 23x B. 23x – y C. $\frac{23x}{y}$ D. $\frac{23x}{23-y}$ E. $\frac{y}{23x}$

**For questions 22 and 23:** If $x \neq 2$ and $\frac{x^2-4}{y}=\frac{x-2}{2}$, then:

22. y =

A. x + 2 B. x + 4 C. 2x + 2 D. 2x + 4 E. 2x – 4

23. x =

A. y – 4 B. 2y – 8 C. $\frac{y-4}{2}$ D. $\frac{y+4}{2}$ E. 2y + 8

24. A company has budgeted \$2,400 for employee raises. The 3 part-time employees will receive the same raise. The 2 full-time employees will each receive 50% more than a part-time employee's raise. What amount did each full-time employee receive?

A. \$200 B. \$400 C. \$500 D. \$600 E. \$800

25. $x^3 - \left(\frac{x}{2}\right)^3 =$

A. $x^3 - x$ B. $\frac{x^3-1}{8}$ C. $\frac{1}{8}$ D. $\frac{7x^3}{8}$ E. $\frac{x^3}{2}$

26. If $\frac{x}{y} = 4$, then $\frac{2y}{x} =$

A. $\frac{1}{4}$ B. $\frac{1}{2}$ C. 1 D. 2 E. 4

27. If $x = 1 + \frac{1}{2} + \frac{1}{4} + \frac{1}{8}$ and $y = 1 + \frac{1}{2}x$, then $y - x =$

A. 1 B. $\frac{1}{2}$ C. $\frac{1}{4}$ D. $\frac{1}{8}$ E. $\frac{1}{16}$

28. Given x and y are integers, if x is a perfect square and y is a perfect cube such that $20 < y < 30$, and $(x - y)^2 = 4$, then $x =$

A. 4 B. 9 C. 16 D. 25 E. 29

29. A student received a score of 74 on a 50-question test. The scoring process is to add 3 points for correct answers and subtract 1 point for incorrect answers. How many questions did he answer correctly if he answered all 50 questions?

A. 19 B. 29 C. 30 D. 31 E. 39

30. $\sqrt{72x^5} =$

A. $36x^4\sqrt{2x}$
B. $18x^2\sqrt{2x}$
C. $6x^2\sqrt{2x}$
D. $6x^2\sqrt{12x}$
E. $6x\sqrt{2x}$

31. How many milliliter of pure alcohol must be added to a 100-milliliter solution that is 10% alcohol in order to produce a solution that is 25% alcohol?

A. 5 B. 10 C. 15 D. 20 E. 25

32. If $x + y = 8$ and $\frac{x}{y} = 3$, then $\frac{1}{x} + \frac{1}{y} =$

A. $\frac{1}{4}$ B. $\frac{3}{8}$ C. $\frac{5}{8}$ D. $\frac{2}{3}$ E. $\frac{5}{6}$

33. If $x + y = 4$ and $(xy)^3 = 27$, $\frac{1}{x} + \frac{1}{y} =$

A. $\frac{2}{3}$ B. $\frac{3}{4}$ C. $\frac{5}{6}$ D. $\frac{4}{3}$ E. $\frac{9}{4}$

34. Train A leaves the station at 8 a.m. at a speed of 30 miles per hour. Train B leaves the same station, in the same direction, on a parallel track at 10 a.m. at a speed of 50 miles per hour. At what time will train B overtake train A?

A. 12:30 p.m. B. 1:00 p.m. C. 2:00 p.m. D. 3:00 p.m. E. 4:00 p.m.

35. Train A leaves the station at 8 a.m. at a speed of 30 miles per hour. Train B leaves at 9 a.m., in the opposite direction, at a speed of 40 miles per hour. What time will it be when the trains are 170 miles apart?

A. 10:00 a.m. B. 10:30 a.m. C. 11:00 a.m. D. 12:00 p.m. E. 1:00 p.m.

36. Train A leaves station x for station y at 8 a.m. at a speed of 50 miles per hour. Train B leaves station y for station x on a parallel track at 9 a.m. at a speed of 60 miles per hour. At 12 noon, the two trains pass each other. How far apart are the 2 stations x and y?

A. 330 mi. B. 360 mi. C. 380 mi. D. 440 mi. E. 500 mi.

37. A train traveled from Oshkosh to Bemidji, a distance of 60 miles, at an average speed of 30 miles per hour. On the return trip it averaged 20 miles per hour. What was the average speed of the entire trip?

A. 20 B. 24 C. 25 D. 26 E. 30

38. A boy has 25 coins in nickels and dimes. The value of the coins is $1.90. How many nickels does he have?

A. 9 B. 11 C. 12 D. 13 E. 17

39. If $x^2 - x - 3 = 3$, then x <u>could</u> equal:

A. -1 B. 0 C. 2 D. 3 E. 4

40. A company bought a batch of switches which it believed were $\frac{4}{5}$ usable. This would then be a cost of $1.25 per usable switch. It was later found that $\frac{1}{3}$ of the switches were defective. What was the actual cost of a usable switch?

A. $1.00 B. $1.20 C. $1.50 D. $1.75 E. $3.00

41. An employee had an average salary of \$60,000 over the last 3 years. If his second year was $1\frac{1}{3}$ of the first, and the third year was twice the second year, what was his salary the first year?

A. \$20,000 B. \$24,000 C. \$30,000 D. \$36,000 E. \$40,000

42. The sum of 4 consecutive odd integers is –8. What is the largest of the 4?

A. 0 B. -1 C. 1 D. 3 E. -5

43. A shipper charges x dollars per pound per mile for packages. What is the cost to ship 10 packages, each weighing 3 pounds, at distance of y miles?

A. 30xy B. $\frac{10x}{3y}$ C. $\frac{xy}{30}$ D. $\frac{30x}{y}$ E. $\frac{x}{30y}$

44. A basketball team has a record of 50 wins and 10 losses. If it has ¼ of its games left to play, how many games must it win in the remaining games, to have a final record of 80% wins?

A. 10 B. 12 C. 14 D. 16 E. 20

45. If $(-8)^{3x} = -2$, then x =

A. $\frac{1}{9}$ B. $\frac{1}{6}$ C. $\frac{1}{3}$ D. -3 E. 3

46. The average of 3 numbers is (A – 4). If one of the numbers is A, what is the average of the other two numbers?

A. A – 1 B. A – 2 C. A – 6 D. A – 4 E. 2A – 12

47. If $(25)^{5-x} = 5^{x+4}$, then x =

A. -3 B. -2 C. 2 D. 3 E. 6

48. An employee received a raise of 5% plus a Christmas bonus of \$1,200. This is equivalent to an overall 8% raise. What was his original salary?

A. \$24,000 B. \$30,000 C. \$36,000 D. \$40,000 E. \$48,000

49. For all numbers A, A↑ = 2A + 1 and A↓ = A – 2, what is the value of (A↑ - A↓)↑ if A = -3?

A. -2 B. -1 C. 0 D. 1 E. 2

50. If $(x+2)\left(3-\frac{2}{x}\right)=0$, then x could be:

A. 6 B. 2 C. $\frac{3}{2}$ D. $\frac{2}{3}$ E. $\frac{1}{2}$

51. At Xerba Corporation's headquarters there are five meeting rooms. Four rooms have white boards, three have projection screens, and two have video conferencing equipment. If one room has only a white board, another has only a projection screen, and only one has all three, what else is in the other room with video conferencing equipment?

A. A projection screen
B. A white board
C. No other equipment
D. Video conferencing equipment
E. Cannot be determined

52. John has two delivery jobs. In the morning, he delivers the *Wall Street Journal* to homes, and during the day he is a private courier for several local businesses. In his PDA (personal data assistant) he stores and sorts his daily activities by zip code. In all he works in ten different zip codes. He recently noticed that his two jobs only overlap in one zip code. If he delivers *The Journal* in three zip codes, to how many zip codes does his courier business take him?

A. 5 B. 6 C. 7 D. 8 E. 9

## Solutions – Algebra

1. E If $y = 3x^2 - 2x$ and $x = -3$, then by substituting $-3$ for x we have:

$$\begin{aligned} y &= 3(-3)^2 - 2(-3) \\ &= 3(9) + 6 \\ &= 27 + 6 \\ &= 33 \end{aligned}$$

2. C Which of the following is equivalent to $7 - 5x < 32$?

$$\begin{array}{rcl} 7 - 5x &<& 32 \\ \underline{-7} & \underline{<} & \underline{-7} \end{array} \quad \text{Subtract 7 from both sides.}$$

$$-5x < 25$$

$$\frac{-5x}{-5} > \frac{25}{-5} \quad \text{Divide by -5.}$$

$$x > -5$$

Note: the inequality changes direction when divided by a negative.

3. B If $-3 < x < -2$, then to find the boundaries of 3x, we can multiply everything by 3. This results in $-9 < 3x < -6$. Thus, 3x could be -7.

4. D If $2x = 3y = 20$, then $12xy =$

SOLUTION 1: $12xy = (2)(2x)(3y)$ intuitive factoring

$$= 2(20)(20) = 800$$

SOLUTION 2: If $2x = 20$, then $x = 10$, and if $3y = 20$, then $y = \frac{20}{3}$

$$\begin{aligned} 12xy &= 12(10)\left(\frac{20}{3}\right) \\ &= 4(10)(20) \\ &= 800 \end{aligned}$$

5. D SOLUTION 1: Proportion Method. Let x represent $\frac{2}{3}$ full, then x + 10 represents $\frac{7}{8}$ full.

$$\frac{\frac{2}{3}}{\frac{7}{8}} = \frac{x}{x+10}$$

$$\frac{7}{8}x = \frac{2}{3}(x+10)$$

$$21x = 16(x + 10) \quad \text{Multiply both sides by 24.}$$

$$21x = 16x + 160$$

$$5x = 160$$

$$x = 32$$

Now, 32 represents $\frac{2}{3}$ full, so

$$\frac{2}{3}F = 32$$

$$2F = 96$$

$$F = 48$$

SOLUTION 2: Let T equal the full-tank, then,

$$\frac{2}{3}T + 10 = \frac{7}{8}T$$

$$16T + 240 = 21T \quad \text{Multiply each term by 24, to clear fractions.}$$

$$240 = 5T$$

$$48 = T$$

6. E Elimination method – step 1: line up variables.

multiply each term by 3:

$$x - y = 3 \rightarrow 3x - 3y = 9$$

subtract 3y from both sides:

$$3x = 3y + 9 \rightarrow 3x - 3y = 9$$

Now the two equations are the same and there can be any number of solutions (i.e., elimination of one variable eliminates all).

Alternate solution using the substitution method:

If x - y = 3, then x = y + 3. Then substitute y + 3 for x into the second equation:

$$3(y + 3) = 3y + 9$$

$$3y + 9 = 3y + 9$$

$$0 = 0$$

Therefore, y could be anything.

7. A Elimination method – step 1: line up variables.

$$x - y = 4$$
$$2x = 2y - 6$$

multiply each term by 2; subtract 2y from both sides

$$2x - 2y = 8$$
$$2x - 2y = -6$$

There are no values for x and y that solve both equations simultaneously.

Alternate solution using the substitution method:

If x - y = 4, then x = y + 4. Then substitute y + 4 for x into the second equation:

| | |
|---|---|
| $2(y + 4) = 2y - 6$ | |
| $2y + 8 = 2y - 6$ | subtract 2y from both sides |
| $8 = -6$ | which cannot be made true |

Therefore no solution exists.

8. A $Q^2$ is always positive, so for $Q^2R$ to be positive, R must be positive. This eliminates B. For $Q^2R$ to be odd, both $Q^2$ and R must be odd, so C is eliminated. Now if $Q^2$ is odd, Q must be odd, and an odd + odd = even, which eliminates D. Also an (odd)(odd) = odd, which eliminates E. The answer is A, Q does not have to be positive.

9. D SOLUTION 1: Factoring.

| | |
|---|---|
| $x^2 + x - 6 = 0$ | $x^2 - 5x + 6 = 0$ |
| $(x - 2)(x + 3) = 0$ | $(x - 2)(x - 3) = 0$ |

The factor in common is x - 2. Since x - 2 = 0, x = 2.

SOLUTION 2: Since both polynomials equal 0, they are equal to each other.

| | |
|---|---|
| $x^2 + x - 6 = x^2 - 5x + 6$ | |
| $x - 6 = -5x + 6$ | Subtract $x^2$ from both sides. |
| $6x = 12$ | Add 5x + 6 to both sides. |
| $x = 2$ | Divide both sides by 6. |

10. C The sum of the 3 stages equals the entire trip. Let T be the length of the entire trip:

$$\frac{1}{5}T + \frac{3}{4}T + 10 = T$$

| | |
|---|---|
| $4T + 15T + 200 = 20T$ | Multiply each term by 20, to clear fractions. |
| $200 = T$ | Subtract 19T from both sides. |

Since stage 2 is $\frac{3}{4}T$, then stage 2 is 150 miles. The answer is C.

11. B We can use the equation:

$$\text{Net} = \text{Gross} - \text{Tax}$$
$$14{,}000 = G - .20(G - 2000)$$
$$14{,}000 = G - .2G - 400$$
$$13{,}600 = .8G$$
$$17{,}000 = G$$

12. D Using the rate formula for work we have:

$$\frac{1}{S} + \frac{1}{T} = \frac{1}{J}$$ Let S = Sam, T = Tom, and J = job.

$$\frac{1}{6} + \frac{1}{T} = \frac{1}{2}$$

$$T + 6 = 3T$$ Multiply by 6T, to clear fractions.

$$6 = 2T$$
$$3 = T$$

Tom's rate is then $\frac{1}{3}$. If he works for 2 hours, using work = rate × time, we have $\frac{1}{3} \times 2 = \frac{2}{3}$. So Tom completes $\frac{2}{3}$ of the job. That leaves $\frac{1}{3}$ of the job left.

Alternatively, since together they could complete the job in 2 hours, only Sam's amount didn't get done when Tom worked for 2 hours alone. Since Sam's rate is $\frac{1}{6}$, we have $\frac{1}{6} \times 2 = \frac{1}{3}$ of the work left to complete.

13. B To find x in terms of y, x must be isolated from y.

$$x = \sqrt{2xy - y^2}$$

The first step is to remove the $\sqrt{\phantom{x}}$ by squaring both sides.

$$x^2 = 2xy - y^2$$

The resulting quadratic can be solved by setting it equal to 0.

$$x^2 - 2xy + y^2 = 0$$

Factoring gives us:

$$(x - y)(x - y) = 0$$

Since both factors are the same

$$x = y$$

14. D B and C can be expressed in terms of A, from the givens: 2A = 3B and 5C = 4A. By doubling 2A = 3B, we have 6B = 4A. Since 4A is common:

$$6B = 4A = 5C$$

We wish to isolate $\frac{C}{B}$ so we divide 6B = 5C by 5B:

$$\frac{6B}{5B} = \frac{5C}{5B}$$

$$\frac{6}{5} = \frac{C}{B}$$ This yields the desired ratio.

15. E A look at the answers shows everything is in terms of x. If y = 2x and z = 4y, then z= 4(2x) = 8x. Therefore:

$$x + y + z =$$

$$x + 2x + 8x = 11x$$

16. D The solution can be found by using the equation:

Profit = Sale Price - Cost

The sale price is the price per item times the number of items: $S = \frac{\$2}{5}N$.

Note: $\frac{5}{2}$ is not used since S is a dollar amount and 5 and N are units which will cancel leaving dollars. Similarly: $C = \frac{\$1}{3}N$.

$$P = S - C$$

$$100 = \frac{2}{5}N - \frac{1}{3}N$$

$$1500 = 6N - 5N$$ Multiply by 15, to clear fractions.

$$1500 = N$$

17. D The basic formula we can use is Distance = Rate × time (D = R·t). D = x + 100 and t = 48 + y. Now substituting we have:

$$x + 100 = R(48 + y)$$

$$\frac{x+100}{48+y} = R \qquad \left(R = \frac{D}{t}\right)$$

But the time is in minutes and has to be converted to hours. Using the basic conversion method, we multiply our answer by:

$$\boxed{\frac{60\ \text{min.}}{1\ \text{hr.}}} \times \frac{x+100\ \text{mi.}}{48+y\ \text{min.}} = \frac{60x+6000\ \text{mi.}}{48+y\ \text{hr.}}$$

Thus we multiplied the answer by the equivalent of 1. Minutes cancel which brings us to the above result.

18. C If we let L be the list price and C be the cost, then a 40% discount would be .6L (discount is based on list price) and a 20% profit would be 1.2C (profit is based on cost). So we have:

$$.6L = 1.2C$$

$$L = 2C$$

Percent profit is found by the change over the original cost. The original cost is C and since the sale price is 2C, the change is 2C – C = C. This gives us:

$$\frac{C}{C} = 1 = 100\%$$

19. C Using the promotion 5 tickets can be purchased for the price of 3 regular tickets. Letting S = sale price and R = regular price, we have:

$$5S = 3R$$

$$S = \frac{3}{5}R$$

The sale price is $\frac{3}{5}$ of the regular price so the savings is $\frac{2}{5} = 40\%$.

20. C This is a two step work problem. The formula is work = rate × time. The amount of work that Ralph produces is $\frac{1}{9} \times 6 = \frac{2}{3}$ where $\frac{1}{9}$ is his rate and 6 the number of hours. If Ralph completes $\frac{2}{3}$ of the job, then $\frac{1}{3}$ is left for Sarah to finish. We have:

$$\frac{1}{3} = \frac{1}{6} \times T\text{, where } \frac{1}{6} \text{ is Sarah's rate.}$$

Multiplying by 6, T = 2.

21. D The basic equation of work still applies to this problem: W = RT. The amount of work is W = 23x (23 days times x units per day). The time is T = 23 - y (23 days minus the sick days). Thus:

$$23x = R(23 - y)$$

$$\frac{23x}{23 - y} = R$$

22. D If $x \neq 2$, solving for y:

$$\frac{x^2 - 4}{y} = \frac{x - 2}{2}$$

$y(x - 2) = 2(x^2 - 4)$ Cross multiply.

$y(x - 2) = 2(x - 2)(x + 2)$ Factor right side.

$y = 2(x + 2)$ Divide by x - 2.

$y = 2x + 4$

23. C If $x \neq 2$, solving for x:

$$\frac{x^2 - 4}{y} = \frac{x - 2}{2}$$

| | |
|---|---|
| $y(x - 2) = 2(x^2 - 4)$ | Cross multiply. |
| $y(x - 2) = 2(x - 2)(X + 2)$ | Factor right side. |
| $y = 2(x + 2)$ | Divide by x - 2. |
| $y = 2x + 4$ | |
| $y - 4 = 2x$ | |
| $x = \frac{y - 4}{2}$ | |

24. D There are two variables, P = part time and F = full time. There are also two equations which can be established:

| | |
|---|---|
| $3P + 2F = 2400$ | Total of raises |
| $F = 1.5P$ | Relationship of raises. |

Substituting 1.5 P for F in the first equation:

$$3P + 2(1.5P) = 2400$$

$$3P + 3P = 2400$$

$$6P = 2400$$

$$P = 400$$

The question asks for the full time raise. Since F = 1.5P:

$$F = 1.5(400)$$

$$F = 600$$

25. D $x^3 - \left(\frac{x}{2}\right)^3 =$

| | |
|---|---|
| $x^3 - \frac{x^3}{8}$ | Expand fraction (top and bottom). |
| $\frac{8x^3 - x^3}{8}$ | Common denominator. |
| $\frac{7x^3}{8}$ | The answer. |

26. B The object here is to manipulate $\frac{x}{y} = 4$ into $\frac{2y}{x}$.

Starting with $\frac{x}{y} = 4$

| | |
|---|---|
| $x = 4y$ | Multiply both sides by y. |
| $1 = \frac{4y}{x}$ | Divide by x. |
| $\frac{1}{2} = \frac{2y}{x}$ | Divide by 2. |

Alternate method: If $\frac{x}{y} = 4$, then $\frac{y}{x} = \frac{1}{4}$. Multiply by 2 and we have: $\frac{2y}{x} = 2\left(\frac{1}{4}\right) = \frac{1}{2}$.

27. E If $x = 1 + \frac{1}{2} + \frac{1}{4} + \frac{1}{8}$ and $y = 1 + \frac{1}{2}x$. To find y - x, substitute for x in the second equation:

$$y = 1 + \frac{1}{2}\left(1 + \frac{1}{2} + \frac{1}{4} + \frac{1}{8}\right)$$

$$y = 1 + \frac{1}{2} + \frac{1}{4} + \frac{1}{8} + \frac{1}{16}$$

If we now compare y to x, we see that everything cancels except $\frac{1}{16}$.

28. D The only integer between 20 and 30 which is a perfect cube is 27, which is $(3^3)$. Now if $(x - y)^2 = 4$, then x - y must equal 2 or -2:

| | | |
|---|---|---|
| $(x - 27) = 2$ | or | $x - 27 = -2$ |
| $x = 29$ | | $x = 25$ |

Since x is a perfect square, x = 25.

29. D If we let C equal the number correct and I equal the number incorrect, we can establish two equations:

| | |
|---|---|
| $C + I = 50$ | total equation |
| $3C - I = 74$ | value equation |
| $4C = 124$ | |
| $C = 31$ | |

30. C To simplify $\sqrt{72x^5}$, we look for perfect squares under the radical. The best choice is: $\sqrt{2 \cdot 36 \cdot x^2 x^2 x}$. 36, $x^2$, and $x^2$ can be removed leaving:

$$6xx\sqrt{2x}$$

$$6x^2\sqrt{2x}$$

31. D This is a mixture problem which can be solved by establishing an algebraic equation from the information given. 10% of 100 is the initial amount of alcohol. If x is the amount of alcohol to be added, then 25% of (100 + x) is the final amount of alcohol. Decimals or fractions can be used to establish the equation:

$$.1(100) + x = .25(100 + x)$$

or

$$\frac{1}{10}(100) + x = \frac{1}{4}(100 + x)$$

$$10 + x = 25 + \frac{1}{4}x$$

$$\frac{3}{4}x = 15$$

$$3x = 60$$

$$x = 20$$

32. D With two equations of this type, substitution is the easiest method. If $\frac{x}{y} = 3$, then $x = 3y$. Now substituting into $x + y = 8$, we have:

$$3y + y = 8$$

$$4y = 8$$

$$y = 2$$

If $y = 2$, then $x = 6$.

$$\frac{1}{x} + \frac{1}{y} = \frac{1}{6} + \frac{1}{2} = \frac{1}{6} + \frac{3}{6} = \frac{4}{6} = \frac{2}{3}$$

33. D Recognizing that 27 equals $3^3$ we have:

$$(xy)^3 = 3^3$$

$$xy = 3$$ Take the cube root of both sides.

$$x = \frac{3}{y}$$ Divide both sides by y.

Now substituting into $x + y = 4$, we have:

$$\frac{3}{y} + y = 4$$

$$3 + y^2 = 4y$$ Multiply each term by y.

$$y^2 - 4y + 3 = 0$$ Set Equal to 0.

$$(y - 1)(y - 3) = 0$$ Factor.

$$y = 1 \text{ or } y = 3$$

Using $x + y = 4$, if $y = 1$, then $x = 3$, or if $y = 3$, then $x = 1$. In either case:

$$\frac{1}{x} + \frac{1}{y} = \frac{1}{3} + \frac{1}{1} = \frac{4}{3}$$

34. B The basic formula is $D = Rt$. With two trains we have:

$$D_A = R_A t_A \qquad D_B = R_B t_B$$

Since both trains will travel the same distance:

$$R_A t_A = R_B t_B$$

Using the given, $R_A = 30$ and $R_B = 50$.

Train B leaves 2 hours later, so relative to train A, its time is $T_A - 2$. Putting these together we have:

$$30t_A = 50(t_A - 2)$$
$$30t_A = 50t_A - 100$$
$$100 = 20t_A$$
$$5 = t_A$$

If $t_A = 5$ and $t_B = t_A - 2$, then $t_B = 5 - 2 = 3$. 3 + 10 a.m. = 1 p.m.

35. C The basic formula is $D = Rt$. With the trains traveling in opposite directions, the distance of 170 miles is $D_A + D_B$. Since $D_A = R_A t_A$ and $D_B = R_B t_B$, we have $170 = R_A t_A + R_B t_B$. Also, since train B leaves one hour later, $t_B = t_A - 1$. We now have:

$$170 = 30t_A + 40(t_A - 1)$$
$$170 = 30t_A + 40t_A - 40$$
$$210 = 70t_A$$
$$3 = t_A$$

Add 3 hours to the time train A leaves (8 a.m.) and the answer is 11:00 a.m.

36. C The basic formula is $D = Rt$. With two trains we have $D_A = R_A t_A$ and $D_B = R_B t_B$. The distance the stations are apart is $D_A + D_B$. This gives us:

$$D_A + D_B = R_A t_A + R_B t_B$$

Using the given, $R_A = 50$ and $R_B = 60$. Train B leaves one hour later so $t_B = t_A - 1$. If they pass at 12 noon, train A was traveling for 4 hours and train B for 3 hours. Putting this together we have:

$$D_A + D_B = 50(4) + 60(3)$$
$$= 200 \quad + 180$$
$$= 380 \text{ miles}$$

37. B The basic formula is D = Rt. The trip from Oshkosh to Bemidge can be represented by:

$$60 = 30t_o \qquad \text{(where } t_o = \text{time out)}$$

$$2 = t_o$$

The return trip is:

$$60 = 20t_B \qquad \text{(where } t_B = \text{time back)}$$

$$3 = t_B$$

The total time for the round trip is $t_o + t_B = 2 + 3 = 5$.

The average speed is then:

$$120 = R(5)$$

$$24 = R$$

Note: avoid the trap of averaging the two speeds (i.e., $\frac{30+20}{2} = 25$).

38. C Two equations can be formed from the given information. Let N equal the number of nickels and D equal the number of dimes, giving us a total for N + D = 25. The value of a nickel is .05 and a dime is .10. This gives us:

$$.05N + .10D = 1.90$$

We can eliminate decimals by multiplying by 100:

$$5N + 10D = 190$$

If we multiply N + D = 25 by -10, we have:

$$-10N - 10D = -250$$

Combining the two equations by addition:

$$\begin{array}{rl} 5N + 10D = & 190 \\ \underline{-10N - 10D = } & \underline{-250} \\ -5N \quad = & -60 \\ N \quad = & 12 \end{array}$$

Note: there are 13 dimes (25 – 12 = 13) be careful to label each to avoid confusion (i.e., N = nickel and D = dime is better than X and Y labels).

39. D If $x^2 - x - 3 = 3$, then:

$$x^2 - x - 6 = 0$$

Remember, quadratics may have two solutions.

$$(x + 2)(x - 3) = 0$$

$$x = -2 \text{ or } x = 3$$

Since 3 is the only one offered, the answer is D.

40. C The basic formula is Total Cost = Number of Switches × Rate per Switch. If we let N be the total number of switches and since the total cost does not vary, we have:

Original Actual

$$\frac{4}{5}N(1.25) = \frac{2}{3}N(x) \quad (\frac{1}{3} \text{ defective means } \frac{2}{3} \text{ usable})$$

The N's cancel and evaluating the left side we have:

$$1 = \frac{2}{3}x$$

$$3 = 2x$$

$$\frac{3}{2} = x$$

$$\frac{3}{2} = 1.5 \text{ or } \$1.50$$

Alternate method: as the number of usable switches decreases the cost per switch increases. This suggests the use of an inverse proportion:

$$\frac{\frac{4}{5}N}{\frac{2}{3}N} = \frac{x}{1.25}$$

$$\frac{4}{5}N(1.25) = \frac{2}{3}N(x) \qquad \text{after cross multiplication}$$

Then the solution follows as above.

41. D If his average was \$60,000, then his total for 3 years is \$180,000. This can be expressed as:

$$x + 1\frac{1}{3}x + 2\frac{2}{3}x = 180{,}000$$

$$5x = 180{,}000$$

$$x = 36{,}000$$

42 C Let x equal the first, then:

$$x + (x + 2) + (x + 4) + (x + 6) = -8$$

$$4x = -20$$

$$x = -5$$

x + 6 is the largest giving -5 + 6 = 1.

43. A 10 packages weigh 30 pounds. At x dollars per pound, we have 30x. This is for each mile so for y miles we have 30xy.

44. C 60 games have been played which represents $\frac{3}{4}$ of the games:

$$60 = \frac{3}{4}G$$

$$240 = 3G$$

$$80 = G$$ So there are a total of 80 games.

80% equals $\frac{4}{5}$ so,

$\frac{4}{5}$ of 80 = 64. So they must win 64 games.

If their record is 50 wins, they need to win 14 more.

45. A If $(-8)^{3x} = -2$, then to evaluate the exponent x, we need to find a common base: $-8 = (-2)^3$. Replace –8 with $(-2)^3$:

$$\left((-2)^3\right)^{3x} = -2$$ Multiply the exponents.

$$(-2)^{9x} = (-2)^1$$ Now that the bases are the same,

$$9x = 1$$ equate the exponents and solve.

$$x = \frac{1}{9}$$

46. C Let x and y be the other two numbers, then:

$$\frac{x + y + A}{3} = A - 4$$

$$x + y + A = 3A - 12$$ Multiply each term by 3.

$$x + y = 2A - 12$$ Subtract A from both sides.

$$\frac{x + y}{2} = \frac{2A - 12}{2}$$ Divide by two to get the average.

$$= A - 6$$ So A – 6 is the average of x and y.

47. C If $25^{5-x} = 5^{x+4}$, then to evaluate the exponent x, we need to find a common base: $25 = 5^2$. Replace 25 with $5^2$:

$$(5^2)^{5-x} = 5^{x+4}$$

$$5^{2(5-x)} = 5^{x+4}$$

$$2(5 - x) = x + 4$$ equate the exponents

$$10 - 2x = x + 4$$

$$6 = 3x$$

$$2 = x$$

48. D Let x be his original salary, then:

$$.05x + 1200 = .08x$$

Multiply each term by 100, to clear decimals:

$$5x + 120{,}000 = 8x$$
$$120{,}000 = 3x$$
$$40{,}000 = x$$

49. D This problem is a sample of symbolic algebra. The A↑ and A↓ operations can be viewed as either functions of A or rules to be applied. In this problem the order of operation is important.

$(A\uparrow - A\downarrow)\uparrow = (\,(2A + 1) - (A - 2)\,)\uparrow$ (apply ↑ and ↓ rules to A)

$= 2\,(\,(2A + 1) - (A - 2)\,) + 1$ (apply ↑ rule)

The second step involves taking the value ( (2A + 1) – (A – 2) ) and applying the ↑ operation to it. One could then substitute A = -3 and compute the value.

A better alternative is to evaluate at each step:

$(A\uparrow - A\downarrow)\uparrow = (\,(2A + 1) - (A - 2)\,)\uparrow$

$= (\,(2(-3) + 1) - (-3 - 2)\,)\uparrow$ (replace A with –3)

$= (\,(-6 + 1) - (-5)\,)\uparrow$

$= (\,(-5) - (-5)\,)\uparrow$

$= (\,0\,)\uparrow$ (this is not going to be zero)

$= (2(0) + 1)$

$= 1$

The answer is D.

50. D In this problem the function is already factored: $(x+2)\left(3-\frac{2}{x}\right)=0$.

Therefore for the function to be zero either x + 2 or $3-\frac{2}{x}$ is zero. For x + 2 to be zero, x = -2. (Note that answer B is a trap; be careful to not look at x + 2 and assume x = 2.) For $3-\frac{2}{x}$ to be zero:

$$3-\frac{2}{x}=0$$

$3x-2=0$ Multiply each term by x.

$$3x=2$$
$$x=\frac{2}{3}$$

The answer is D.

51. B

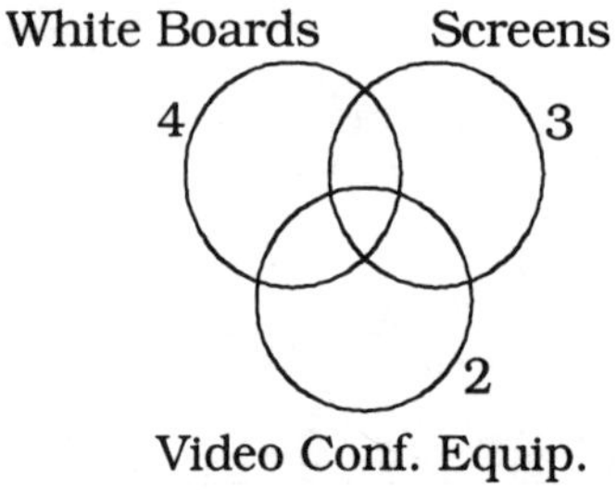


This problem is ideal for a Venn diagram. Draw three circles, one for each type of equipment. Just outside of the circles write the number of rooms for each type.

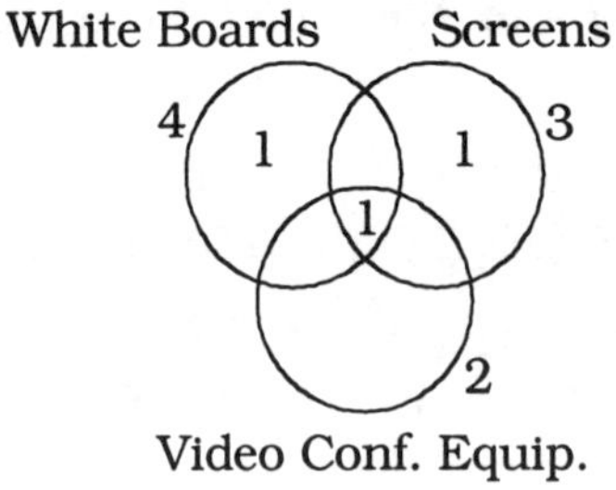


Since only one has a white board only, put a 1 in that circle. Likewise, since only one room has only a projection screen put a 1 in that circle. Since only one room has all three features, put a 1 in the intersection of the three circles.

Two rooms remain unknown. Notice that only two of four white board equipped rooms are on the chart. So the two remaining rooms must have white boards. Also notice that one room with a screen is not on the chart. These facts imply that a 1 needs to go where the white board and screens circles intersect, and another 1 goes into the intersection of the white boards and video conferencing equipment circles. The final diagram is as follows:

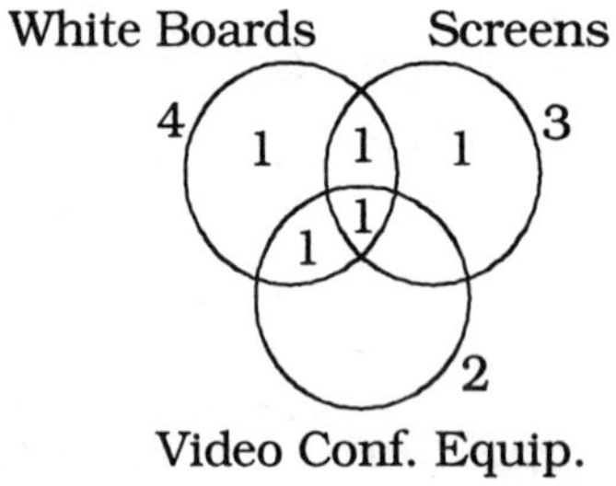


The answer is B, the other room equipped for video conferencing also has a white board.

52. D This problem is also ideal for a Venn diagram. In this case draw two circles one for each job. Put a 1 in the intersection for the number of zip codes the two jobs share. Put a 3 next to the circle for paper delivery and a 10 which represents the total.

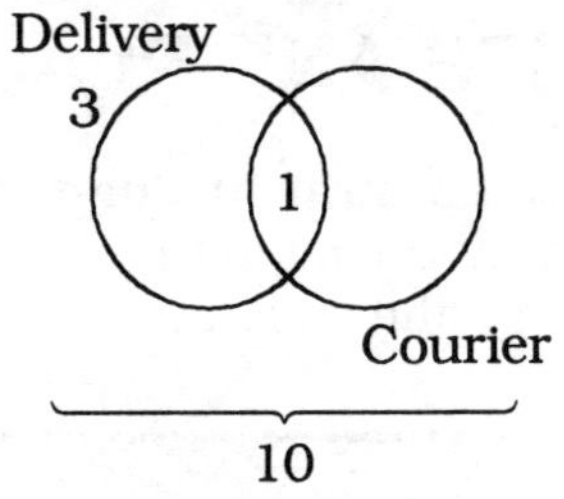


The numbers in the paper delivery circle must sum to 3, therefore put a 2 in the paper delivery circle (2+1=3). Since all three parts must sum to 10, place a 7 in the courier circle.

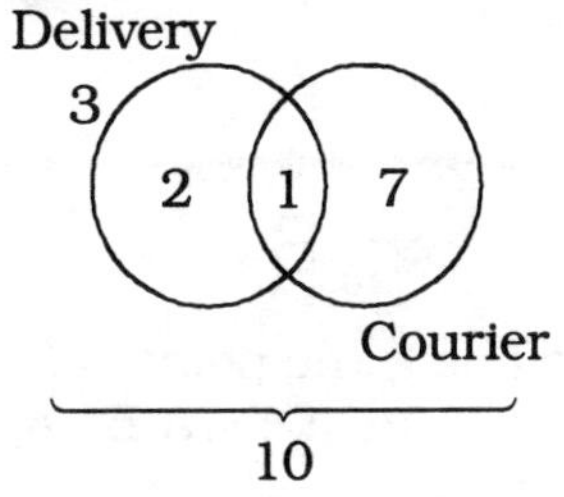


The total for the courier circle is 8. The answer is D.

# Geometry Review

## LINES AND PLANES

A ***"line"*** in geometry is considered a straight line that continues infinitely in opposite directions. A line can be denoted by the points it contains (i.e. line CD) or a single letter (i.e. line $\ell$). A line is considered one-dimensional.

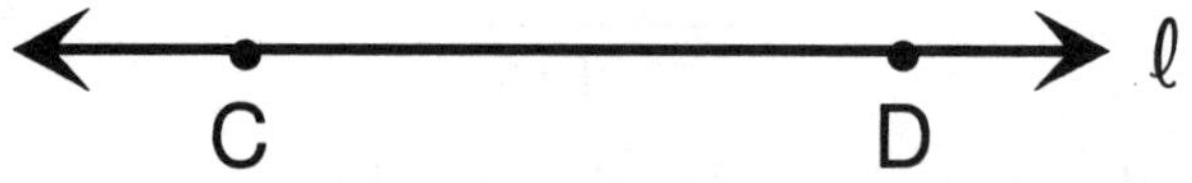


A ***line segment*** is a subset of a line and is a denoted by $\overline{CD}$. It has a fixed length with endpoints C and D. A line segment has a positive length. This is denoted by $|C - D|$ or $|D - C|$.

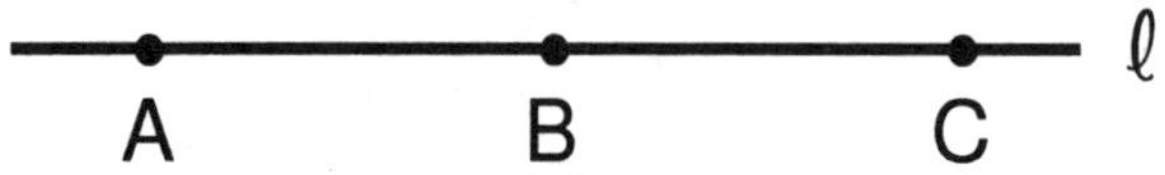


Given that A, B, and C lie on the line $\ell$, the point B is the ***midpoint*** of the line segment AC if B divides AC into 2 equal segments (i.e. $|A\text{-}B| = |B\text{-}C|$).

A ***plane*** is a flat surface, which extends without boundaries. It is considered to be two-dimensional (i.e. a point on a plane requires 2 coordinates to specify its location, see Coordinate Geometry).

## LINES AND ANGLES

An ***angle*** is the opening formed by two intersecting lines. The point of intersection is called the ***vertex***.

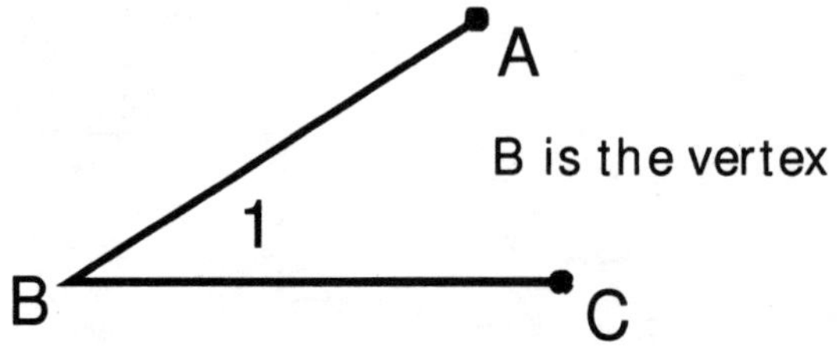


The above angle can be identified 4 ways: $\angle ABC$, $\angle CBA$, $\angle B$, and $\angle 1$. (Note: When 3 points are used, the middle is always the vertex.)

Angles use rotational measure to determine size. One full rotation (i.e. a complete circle) is 360°.

# TYPES OF ANGLES

Angles are classified by their measure. ***Acute*** angles have an angle measure smaller than 90°. ***Obtuse*** angles are greater than 90° but less than 180°. A ***right angle*** is an angle of precisely 90°. For completeness, an angle that measures 180° is called a ***straight angle***.

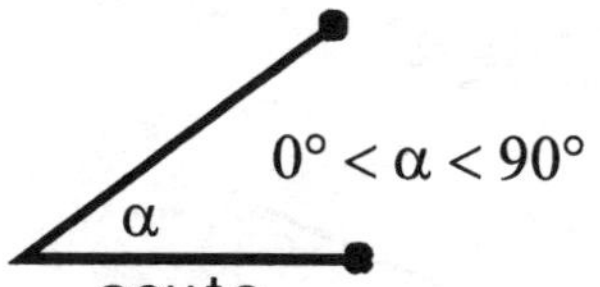


acute

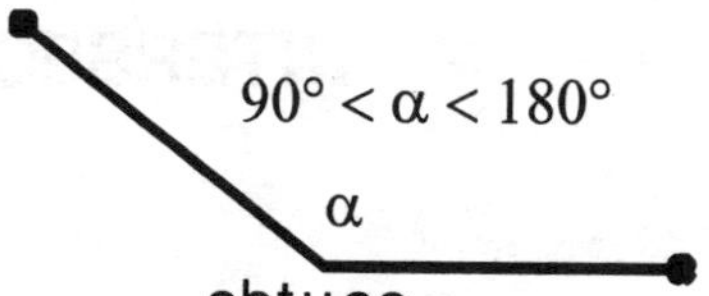


obtuse

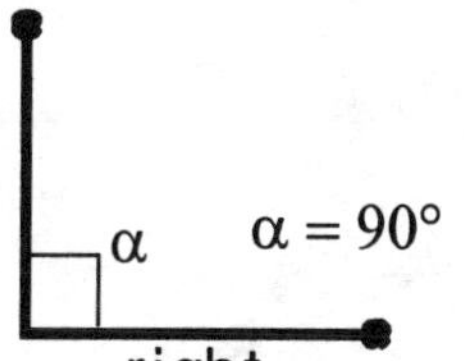


right
Note: a box by itself denotes a right angle.

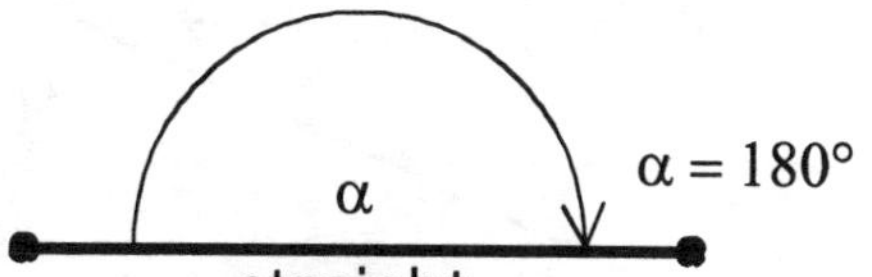


straight
Note: this is half way around a circle.

### Supplementary Angles

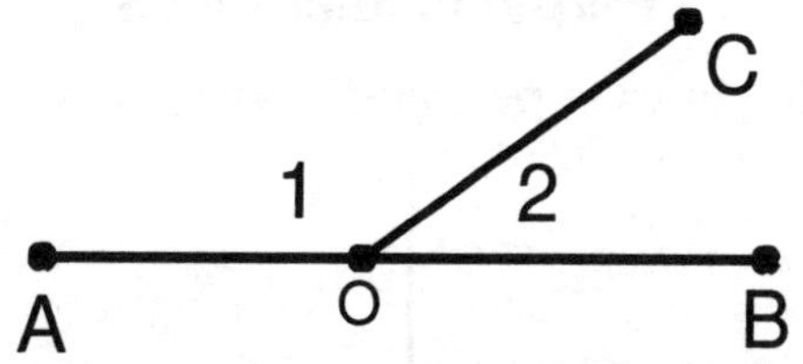


The lines AB and OC lie in the same plane and intersect at point O. Since ∠AOB is a straight angle, it follows that ∠AOC (∠1) plus ∠COB (∠2) = 180°. When two angles together form a straight angle, the angles are said to be ***supplementary***. In this case ∠1 and ∠2 are supplementary angles. They are also ***adjacent angles*** because they share a common side (OC).

Consider the following figure:

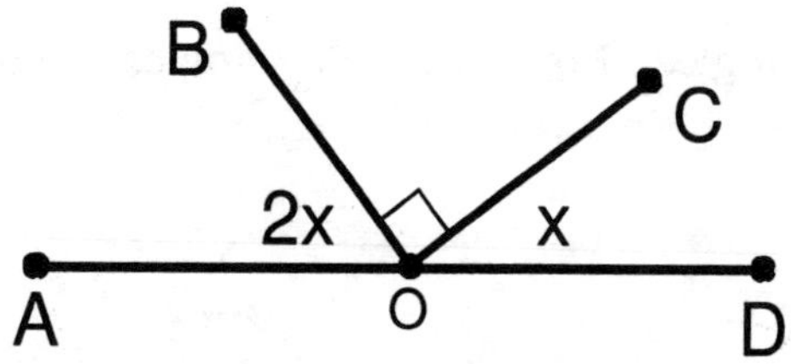


What is the measure of the two unknown angles (AD is a line segment)? First note that ∠AOB + ∠BOC + ∠COD = 180°. Since ∠BOC = 90° it follows that ∠AOB + ∠COD = 90°. Now using the fact that ∠AOB = 2x and ∠COD = x, we solve as follows:

$$2x + x = 90°$$
$$3x = 90°$$
$$x = 30°$$
$$\angle AOB = 2x = 2(30°) = 60°$$
$$\angle COD = x = 30°$$

## INTERSECTING LINES

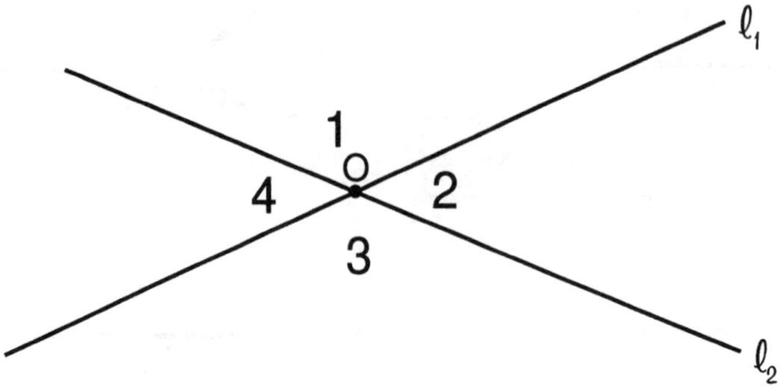


Lines $\ell_1$ and $\ell_2$ intersect at point O, where they form four angles. The opposite angles are equal and known as ***vertical angles*** ($\angle 1 = \angle 3$ and $\angle 2 = \angle 4$). Also note: $\angle 1 + \angle 2 = 180°$ (line $\ell_2$) and $\angle 2 + \angle 3 = 180°$ (line $\ell_1$).

### Perpendicular Lines

A special case of intersecting lines is ***perpendicular lines*** (denoted $\ell_1 \perp \ell_2$).

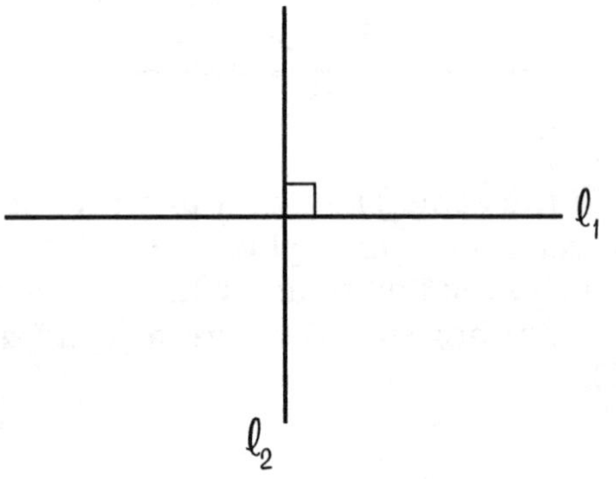


These lines meet at right angles. Notice that all 4 angles are 90°.

## Parallel Lines

Two lines in the same plane that never meet are called ***parallel lines***.

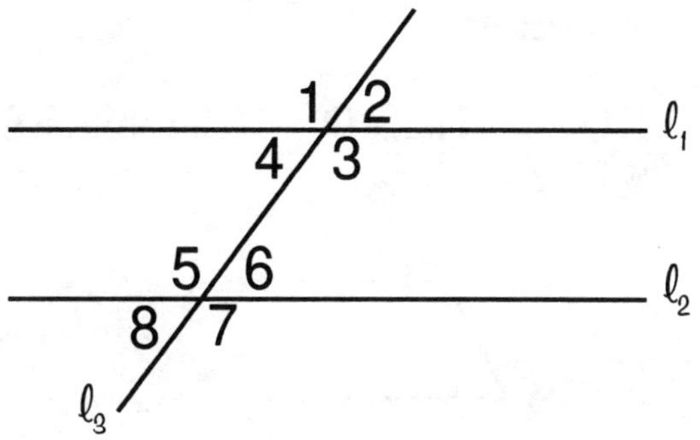


We denote $\ell_1$ is parallel to $\ell_2$ with $\ell_1 \parallel \ell_2$. $\ell_3$, which intersects $\ell_1$ and $\ell_2$ is called a ***transversal***. Eight angles are created by this intersection, but all have only one of two measures. Take note that $\angle 1 = \angle 3$ and $\angle 2 = \angle 4$ since they are vertical angles. Also angles 1, 2, 3, and 4 are identical to their ***corresponding angles*** 5, 6, 7, and 8. ($1 \Rightarrow 5$, $2 \Rightarrow 6$, $3 \Rightarrow 7$, $4 \Rightarrow 8$). In addition, $\angle 3 = \angle 5$ and $\angle 4 = \angle 6$ and each pair are called ***alternate interior angles***. And finally, $\angle 1 = \angle 7$ and $\angle 2 = \angle 8$ with each pair called ***alternate exterior angles***.

A word of caution: when you see similar drawings, do not assume lines are parallel unless stated (i.e. $\ell_1 \parallel \ell_2$).

# TRIANGLES

A triangle is a flat figure (i.e. lies in a plane) formed by joining 3 segments at their endpoints. Three angles are formed.

## PROPERTIES OF TRIANGLES

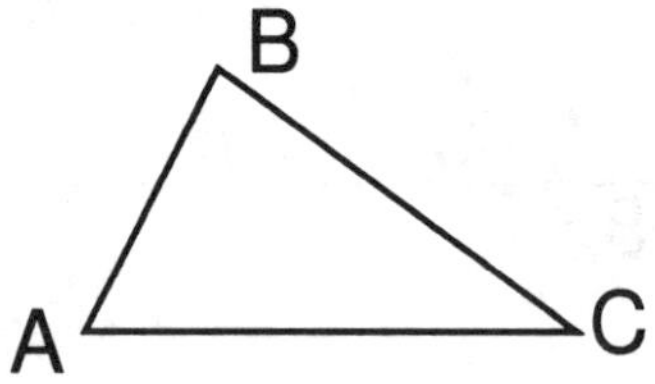


The sum of the angles equals 180° (i.e. $\angle A + \angle B + \angle C = 180°$). Angles opposite longer sides are larger than angles opposite shorter sides (i.e. if $BC > AB$, then $\angle A > \angle C$). It follows that angles opposite equal sides are equal (i.e. if $AB = BC$, then $\angle C = \angle A$).

EXAMPLE: Regarding the figure to the right, what is the relationship between $\angle A$ and $\angle C$?

SOLUTION: Line segment AB is opposite $\angle C$ and BC is opposite $\angle A$. Since the two segments are equal the angles are equal: $\angle A = \angle C$.

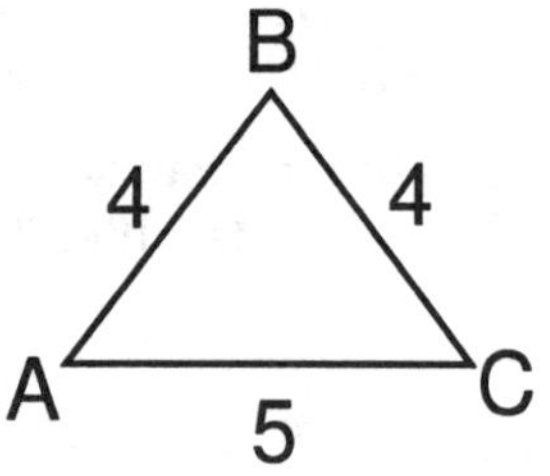


EXAMPLE: Regarding the figure to the right, what is the relationship between $\angle B$ and $\angle C$?

SOLUTION: Line segment AC is opposite $\angle B$ and AB is opposite $\angle C$. Since line segment AC is larger than line segment AB then $\angle B > \angle C$.

The length of any two sides is always longer than the third side ($AB + BC > AC$). This is sometimes quoted as, "The shortest distance between two points is a straight line." Mathematicians know it as the <u>Triangle Inequality</u>. You should remember that since AC is the shortest path from A to C, the distance from A to B and then from B to C must be longer, unless B is placed on the line segment AC.

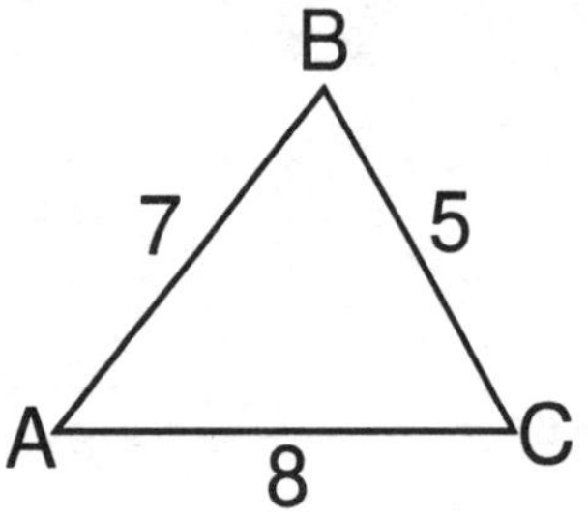


$5 + 7 > 8$

$5 + 8 > 7$

$7 + 8 > 5$

Also $\angle B > \angle C > \angle A$

### Similarity Property

If two triangles have the same angles, then the sides are proportional.

For example the given triangles $\Delta ABC$ and $\Delta DEF$, illustrated to the right, are similar because their angles are equal:

$$\angle A = \angle D,\ \angle B = \angle E,\ \text{and } \angle C = \angle F$$

Therefore their sides are proportional:

$$\frac{AB}{DE} = \frac{BC}{EF} = \frac{CA}{FD}$$

In this case the proportionality constant is 2:

$$\frac{5}{10} = \frac{7}{14} = \frac{8}{16}$$

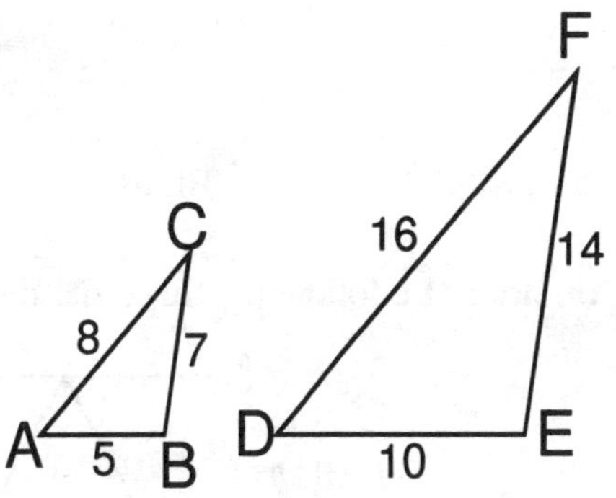


## CLASSIFICATION OF TRIANGLES

### By Angles

- ***Acute*** - all angles less than 90°.
- ***Right*** - one angle equals 90°. (Note: the sum of the other 2 angles also equals 90°.)
- ***Obtuse*** - one angle is greater than 90°. (Note: the sum of the other 2 angles is less than 90°.)

### By Sides

- ***Scalene*** - no sides are equal. (Note: also no angles are equal.)
- ***Isosceles*** - 2 sides are equal. (Note: opposite angles of the equal sides are equal.)

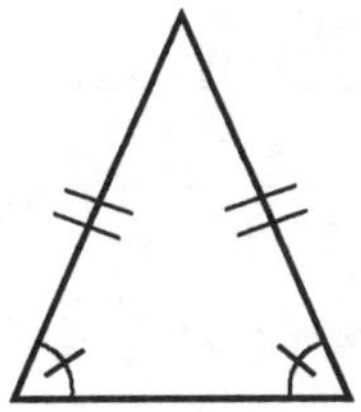

- ***Equilateral*** - all sides are equal. (Note: all angles are equal.)

$\angle A + \angle B + \angle C = 180°$ and since $\angle A = \angle B = \angle C$ then if $\angle A = X$ we have

$$X + X + X = 180°$$
$$3X = 180°$$
$$X = 60°$$

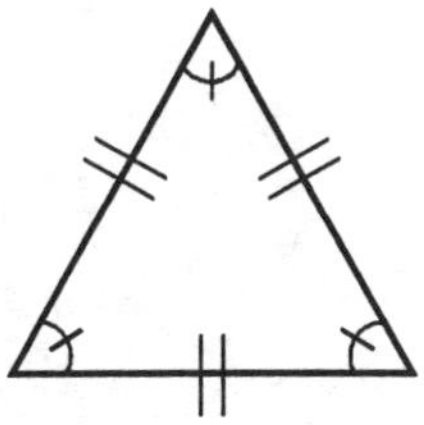

Therefore all angles of an equilateral triangle equal 60°.

## AREA OF A TRIANGLE

The formula for area of a triangle is $\frac{1}{2}bh$ or $\frac{bh}{2}$ where b is the length of the base and h is the height (or altitude) of the triangle. The height <u>must always</u> be measured perpendicular ($\perp$) to the base.

Acute 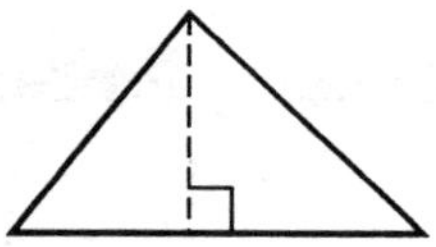 H is inside

Obtuse 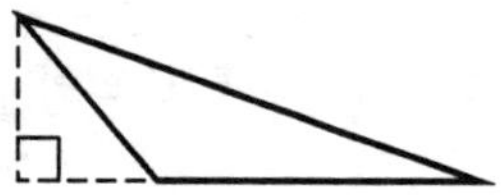 H is outside

Right 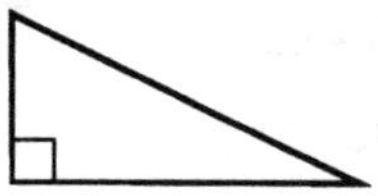 H is one side (or leg)

Consider the following three triangles:

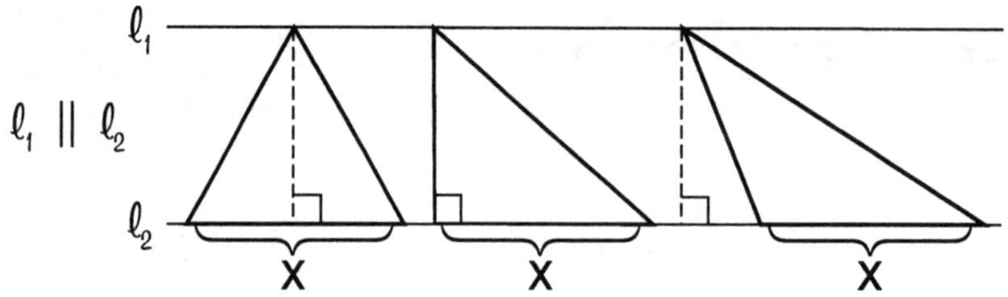


All three triangles have the same area since the bases are equal and the height of each is the same.

EXAMPLE: What is the area of the following triangle?

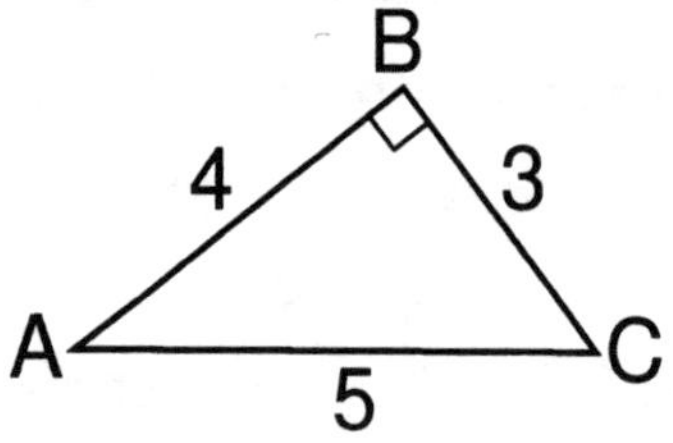


SOLUTION: If the altitude were drawn from point B to AC (that is to use AC as the base), the altitude would still not be known.

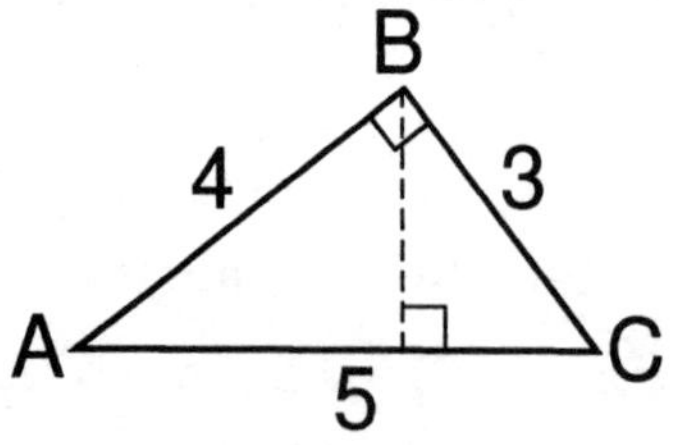


However, if the triangle is rotated such that AB is the base, the height would BC.

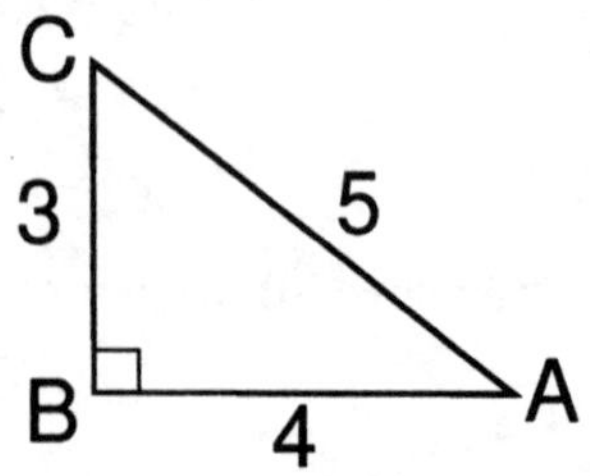


$A = \frac{1}{2}(3)(4) = 6$, so the area of this right triangle is 6.

# PYTHAGOREAN THEOREM

The Pythagorean theorem is concerned with the algebraic relationship between the legs and hypotenuse of a right triangle. The ***legs*** of a right triangle are the shorter sides that are attached at a right angle. The longer side of a right triangle, which is opposite the right angle, is called the ***hypotenuse***. For this discussion **a** and **b** will be the measures of the lengths of the legs and **c** the measure of the length of the hypotenuse.

## The Pythagorean Theorem

$$a^2 + b^2 = c^2$$

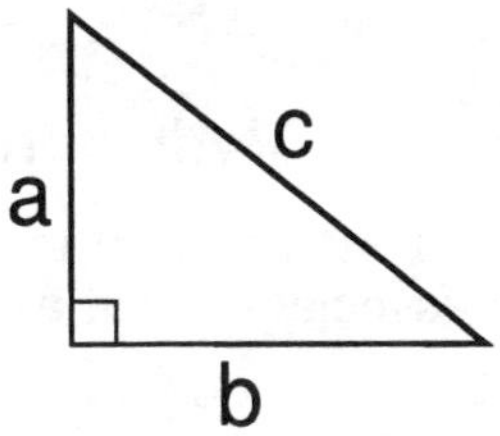


This relationship, $a^2 + b^2 = c^2$, holds for all right triangles drawn in the plane. This relationship is the foundation for distance calculations.

EXAMPLE: What is the length of the hypotenuse of the right triangle with leg lengths of 3 and 4?

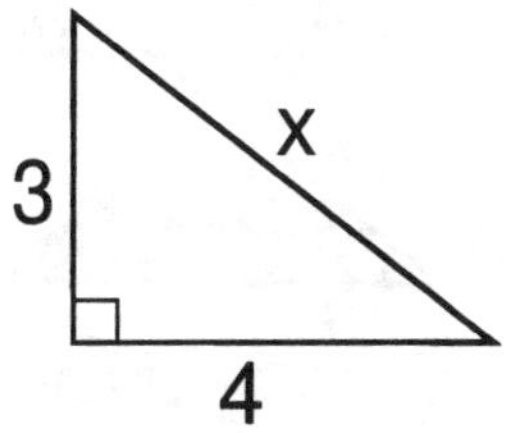


SOLUTION:

$$3^2 + 4^2 = X^2$$
$$9 + 16 = X^2$$
$$25 = X^2$$
$$5 = X$$

EXAMPLE: What is the length of the unknown side of the following right triangle?

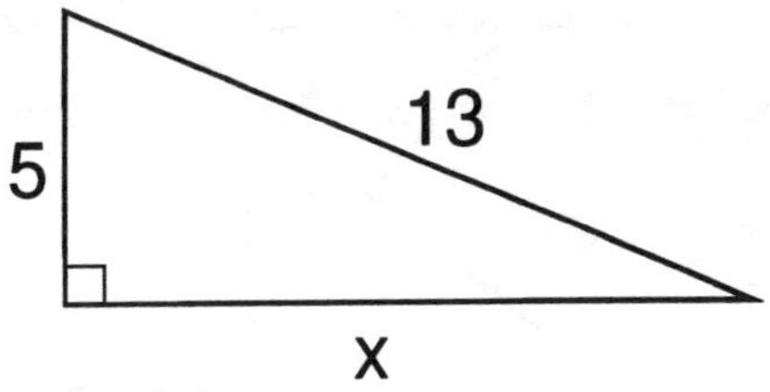


SOLUTION: (Note: the unknown is not the hypotenuse.)

$$5^2 + X^2 = 13^2$$
$$25 + X^2 = 169$$
$$X^2 = 169 - 25 = 144$$
$$X = 12$$

EXAMPLE: What is the length of the unknown side of the following right triangle?

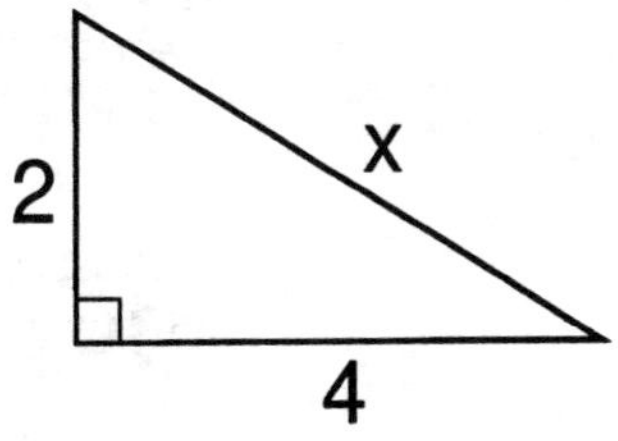

SOLUTION: The unknown is the hypotenuse so...

$$2^2 + 4^2 = X^2$$
$$4 + 16 = X^2$$
$$20 = X^2$$
$$2\sqrt{5} = X$$

Notice that sides are not always integers. Roots, such as $2\sqrt{5}$, occur quite frequently.

## Pythagorean Triples

A ***Pythagorean triple*** is a set of three integers that satisfy the Pythagorean equation. As a result each triple is associated with a right triangle with integer sides.

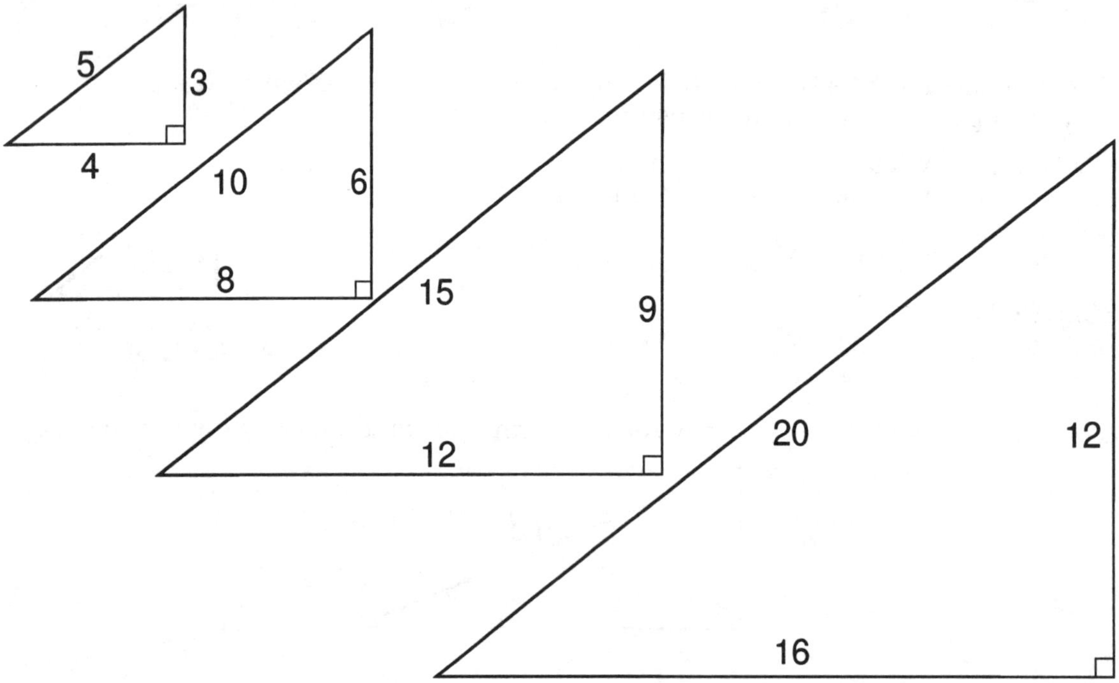


All of the above triangles are triples. Notice the relationship of the corresponding sides. Each is a multiple of the 3, 4, 5 triple (i.e. (2)(3) = 6, (2)(4) = 8, (2)(5) = 10). It can be shown that any multiple of a triple is also a triple (a similar triangle). Therefore, the next in this series would be (5)(3) = 15, (5)(4) = 20, (5)(5) = 25. Let's see if this is a triple:

$$15^2 + 20^2 = 25^2$$
$$225 + 400 = 625 \quad \text{Yes, it is.}$$
$$625 = 625$$

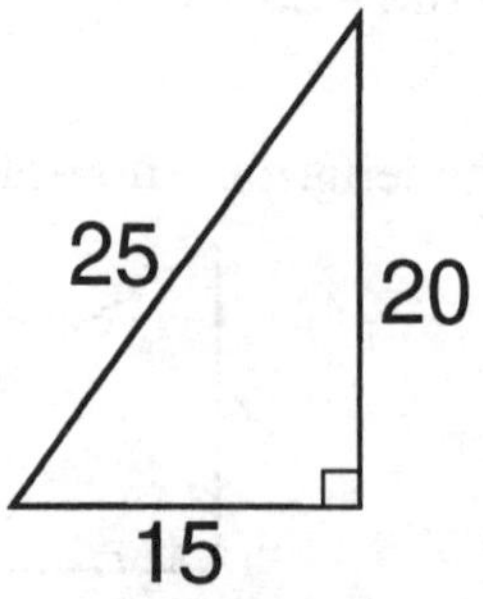

This is called the 3, 4, 5 family of triples. The GMAT predominately uses only three other families of triples.

| 5, 12, 13 | 8, 15, 17 | 7, 24, 25 |
|---|---|---|
| $5^2 + 12^2 = 13^2$ | $8^2 + 15^2 = 17^2$ | $7^2 + 24^2 = 25^2$ |
| $25 + 144 = 169$ | $64 + 225 = 289$ | $49 + 576 = 625$ |
| $169 = 169$ | $289 = 289$ | $625 = 625$ |

EXAMPLE: A 17 ft. ladder is placed 8 ft. from a building as shown. How tall is the building?

SOLUTION: This is easily seen as the 8, 15, 17 triple and therefore the building is 15 ft. tall.

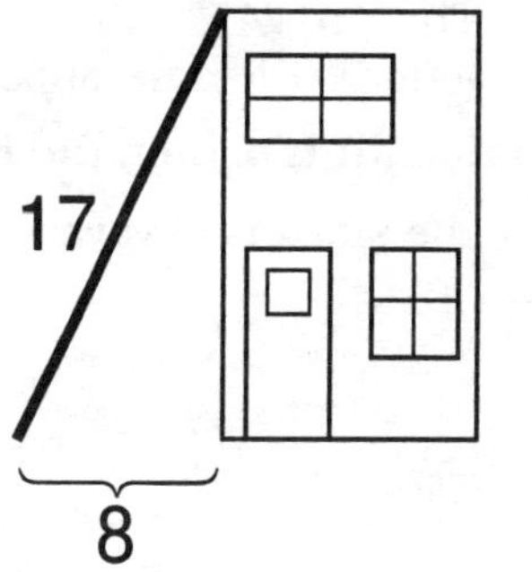


## SPECIAL RIGHT TRIANGLES

There are two special right triangles. They are known by their angles: 30°, 60°, 90° and 45°, 45°, 90°. These triangles have so many convenient features that all drafting kits (for engineering drawings) include one of each. The GMAT makes use of these features in problems. Knowing these features will increase the speed at which you solve the associated problems.

### The 30°-60°-90° Triangle

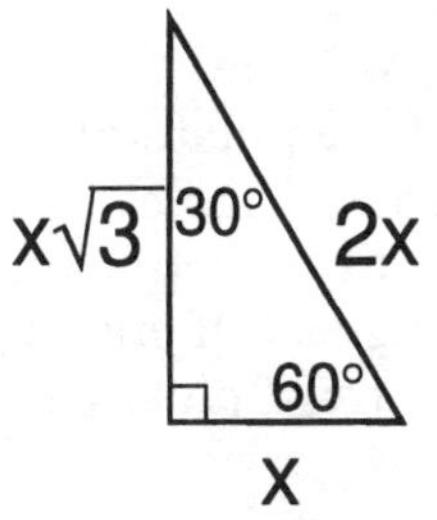


Given that the length of the side opposite the 30° angle is x, then the side opposite the right angle (hypotenuse) is 2x, and the side opposite the 60° angle is $x\sqrt{3}$ (i.e. the ratio of the sides is always x, $x\sqrt{3}$, 2x). For example:

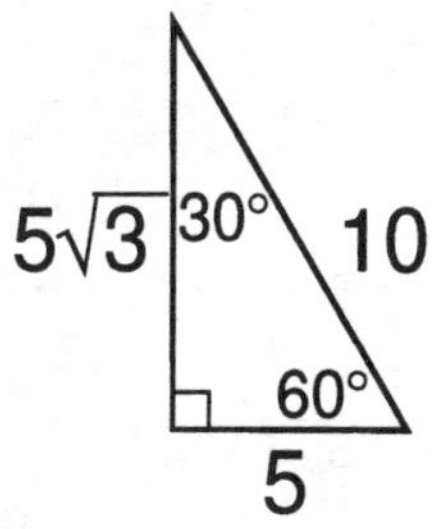

## The 45°-45°-90° Isosceles Triangle

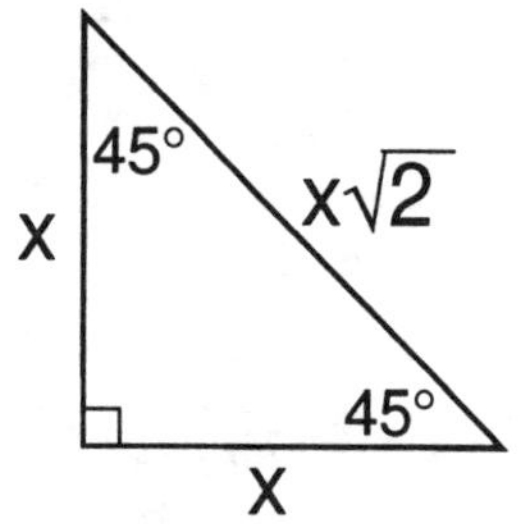


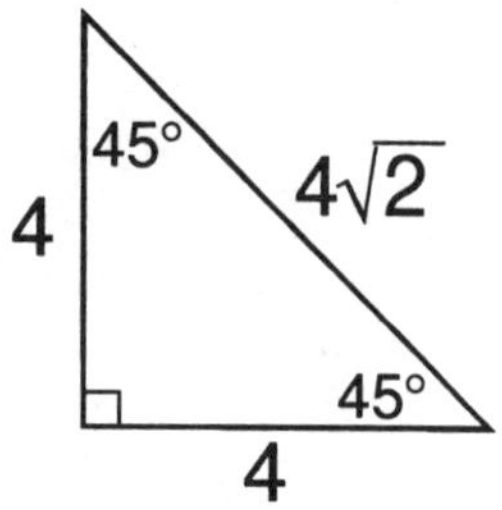


The 45°, 45°, 90° triangle is isosceles since two legs are equal in length (they are opposite angles of the same measure). If the leg's length is x then the hypotenuse is $x\sqrt{2}$ in length (i.e. the ratio of the sides is always x, x, $x\sqrt{2}$). For example:

## Application of The 30°-60°-90° Triangle

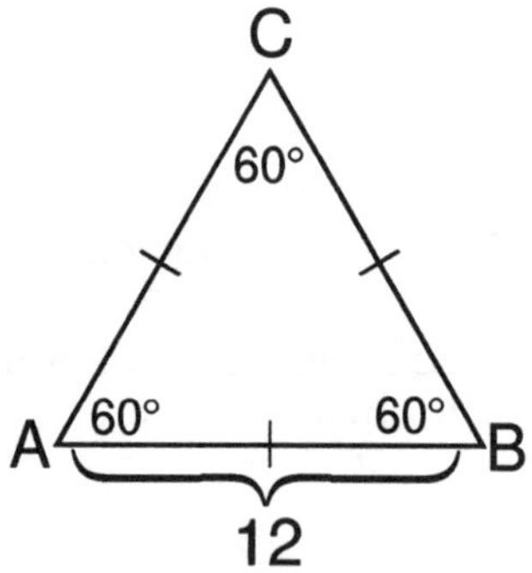


EXAMPLE: Given ΔABC is equilateral, and the base equals 12, what is its area?

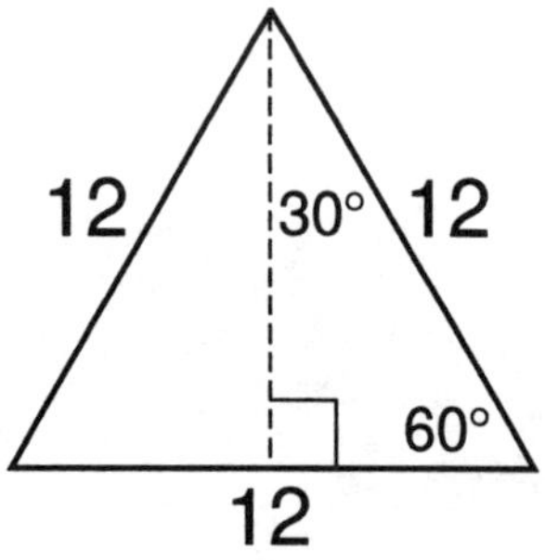


SOLUTION: Since the triangle is equilateral, it is also equiangular and each angle equals 60°. Drawing the altitude divides the triangle into two 30°, 60°, 90° triangles. (If one angle is 90°, and the other 60°, the third must be 30°.)

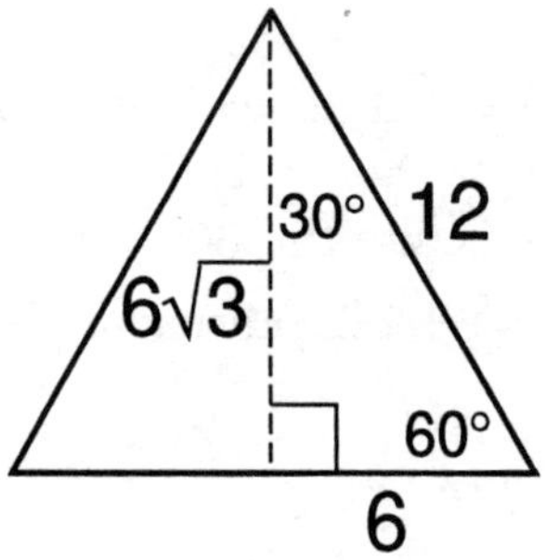


Since both hypotenuses are 12, the ratios 6, $6\sqrt{3}$, 12 can be applied (x, $x\sqrt{3}$, 2x) to both triangles. The area can be calculated using the formula $\frac{1}{2}bh$: $\frac{1}{2}(12)(6\sqrt{3}) = 36\sqrt{3}$.

(Remember: The base of the equilateral triangle is 12 not 6.)

# QUADRILATERALS

A quadrilateral is a flat figure (i.e. lies in a plane) surrounded by four line segments connected only at their endpoints. Four angles are formed.

## PROPERTIES OF QUADRILATERALS

The sum of the interior angles equals 360°. Consider any quadrilateral ABCD. The line segment AC divides the quadrilateral into two triangles. Since each triangle's angles sum to 180°, the two triangles' angles sum to 360°.

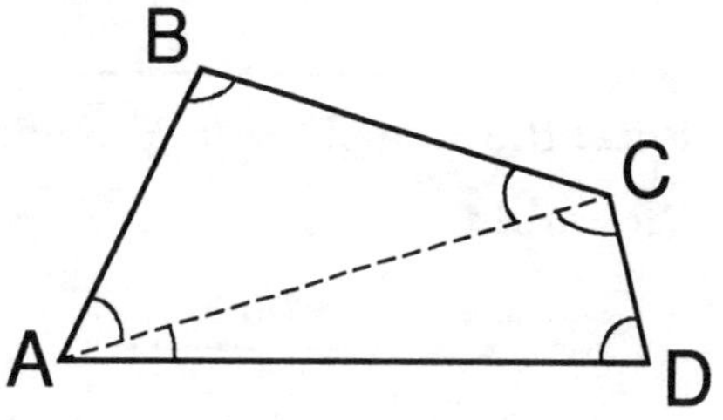


## SPECIAL QUADRILATERALS

Here we discuss five special quadrilaterals:

1. Parallelogram
2. Rectangle
3. Rhombus
4. Square
5. Trapezoid

**Parallelogram**

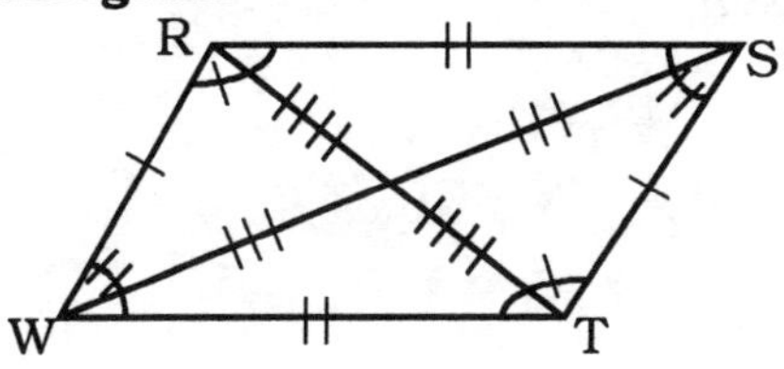


**Properties**

1. Opposite sides are parallel, $\overline{RS} \parallel \overline{WT}$ and $\overline{RW} \parallel \overline{ST}$.
2. Opposite sides are equal, $\overline{RS} = \overline{WT}$ and $\overline{RW} = \overline{ST}$.
3. Opposite angles are equal, $\angle R = \angle T$ and $\angle S = \angle W$.
4. Diagonals, $\overline{RT}$ and $\overline{SW}$, bisect each other.

**Rectangle**

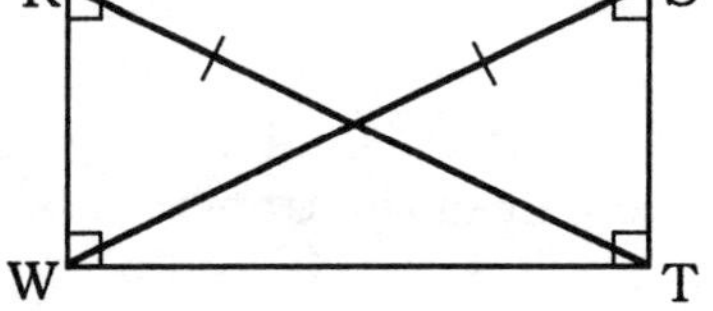


**Properties**

All parallelogram properties plus:

1. <u>All</u> vertex angles are equal ($\angle R$, $\angle S$, $\angle T$, $\angle W$) (right angles).
2. Diagonals are equal.

**Rhombus**

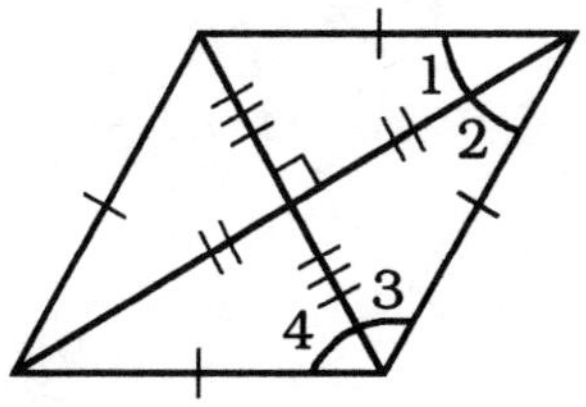


**Properties**

All parallelogram properties plus:

1. <u>All</u> sides are equal.
2. Diagonals are perpendicular and bisect vertex angles ($\angle 1 = \angle 2$ and $\angle 3 = \angle 4$).

**Square**

**Properties**

All parallelogram, rhombus, and rectangle properties.

**Note:** the area of the four quadrilaterals above is the base times the height.

**Trapezoid**

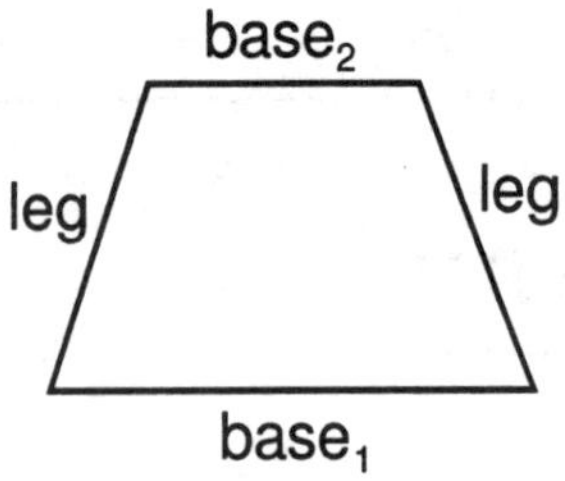


**Properties**

1. One pair of parallel sides (called ***bases***).
2. The other sides are called ***legs***.

The area of a trapezoid is "the average of the bases" times "the height" or $\frac{1}{2}(b_1 + b_2)h$.

(Note: sometimes dividing the trapezoid into simpler figures is a good alternate method for determining the area.)

EXAMPLE: Find the area of the following trapezoid:

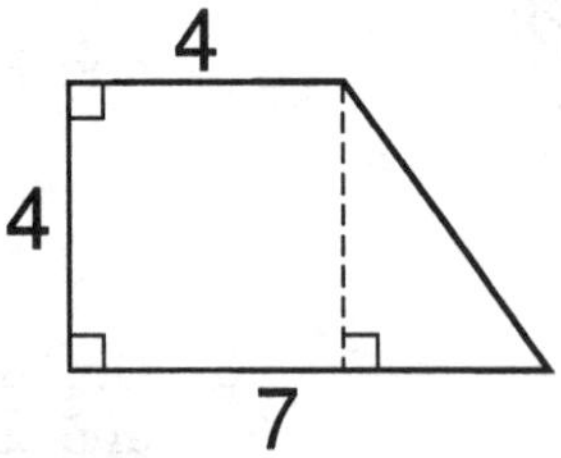


SOLUTION: Divide the trapezoid into a rectangle and a right triangle. (This can be done because two angles are right angles.) Area of rectangle = (b)(h) = (4)(4) or 16. Area of triangle is 0.5(b)(h) =0.5(3)(4) = 6. (Note: base of triangle equals 7 - 4 = 3). Therefore the area of the trapezoid is 16 + 6 = 22.

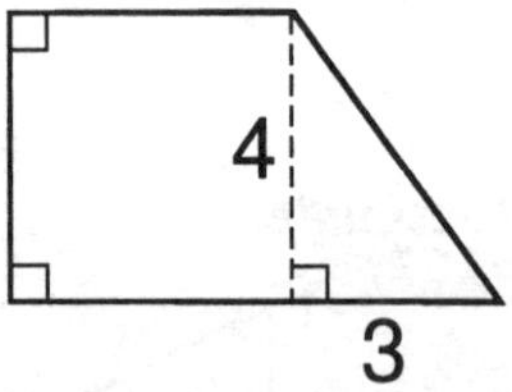


The perimeter of the above trapezoid is obtained using a similar method. The hypotenuse of the triangle is 5 (3, 4, 5 triple). The perimeter of the trapezoid is then the sum 4 + 7 + 5 + 4 or 20.

# POLYGONS

A polygon is a flat figure (i.e. lies in a plane) that is formed by many line segments (poly means many) joined at their endpoints. This section will deal only with convex polygons (all vertices point out).

EXAMPLE: This is a convex polygon: 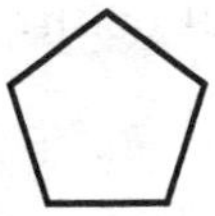

Versus a concave polygon: 

By the way, triangles and quadrilaterals are three-sided and four-sided polygons, respectively.

# PROPERTIES OF POLYGONS

The sum of the angles of any polygon is given by the formula 180°(n - 2), where n is the number of sides. This is illustrated in the following drawings:

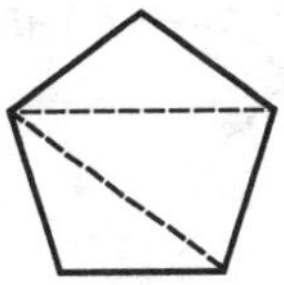

5 sides

3 triangles

$180°(5 - 2) = 540°$

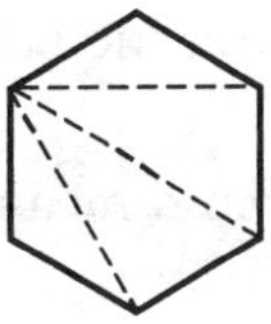

6 sides

4 triangles

$180° (6 - 2) = 720°$

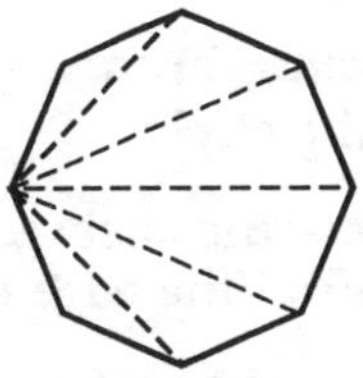

8 sides

6 triangles

$180° (8 - 2) = 1080°$

Interestingly a six-sided figure can be divided into two quadrilaterals. The sum of the angles is then 360°+ 360°= 720°. 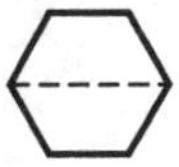

## Regular Polygons

Regular polygons have equal sides and equal angles. Two examples are the square and equilateral triangle.

We know the sum of the angles is 180°(n-2) and that each angle is equal. So the angular measure for each regular polygon is $\frac{180°(n-2)}{n}$.

EXAMPLE:

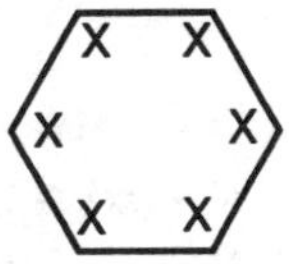


regular hexagon

$$x = \frac{180°(6-2)}{6} = 120°$$

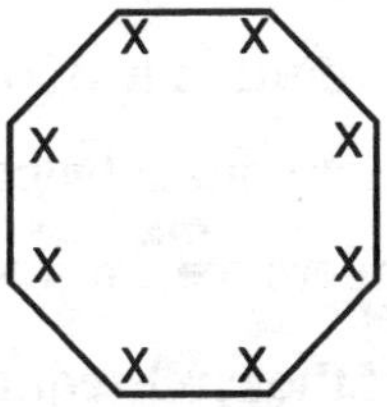


regular octagon

$$x = \frac{180°(8-2)}{8} = 135°$$

# CIRCLES

A circle is a flat closed figure (i.e. lies in a plane) with all its points equidistant from a central point.

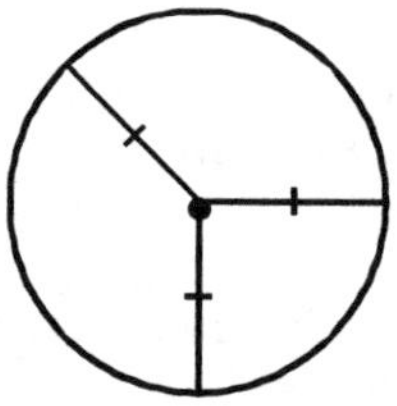

## PARTS OF A CIRCLE

- ***Radius*** - the distance from the center to the outside edge
- ***Chord*** - a segment with endpoints on the circle
- ***Diameter*** - a chord which passes through the center of the circle
- ***Tangent*** - a line which touches the outside edge of the circle at only one point
- ***Circumference*** - the distance around the outside of the circle
- ***Arc*** - the distance between two points measured around the edge of the circle

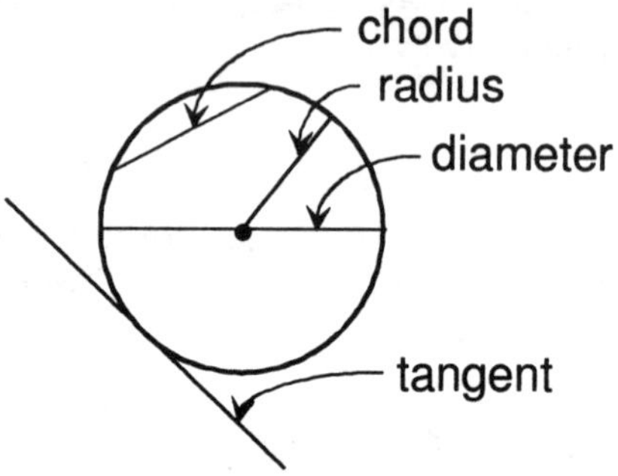


Arcs can be measured in linear measure (i.e. inches, cm, feet, etc.) or degrees. There are two arcs between two points (either direction around the center). If they are not equal, the shorter arc is called the minor arc and the larger the major arc. Arc AB is denoted $\overset{\frown}{AB}$.

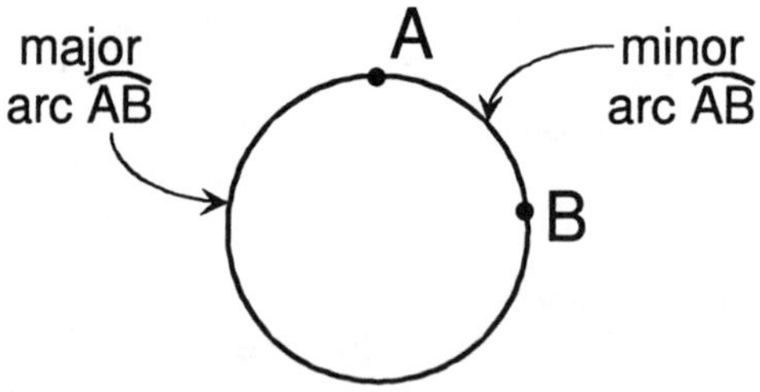


- ***Concentric circles*** are circles with the same center.

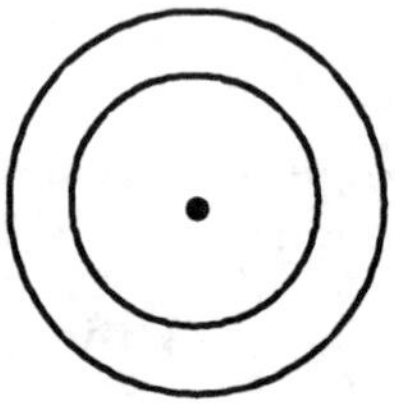

## PROPERTIES OF CIRCLES

- One revolution is 360° of arc.
- Diameter equals twice the radius (i.e. $d = 2r$).
- Circumference equals $\pi$ times the diameter (i.e. $C = \pi d = 2\pi r$).
- Area of the circle equals $\pi$ times the radius squared (i.e. $A = \pi r^2$).

Note: $\pi$ is an irrational number (i.e., it has no exact fractional representation). Its approximations, 3.14 or $\frac{22}{7}$, are rarely used in calculations except to distinguish it from 3 in comparison problems.

- The diameter is perpendicular (⊥) to its tangent. (Notice the right angle at point of intersection, the tangent point.)

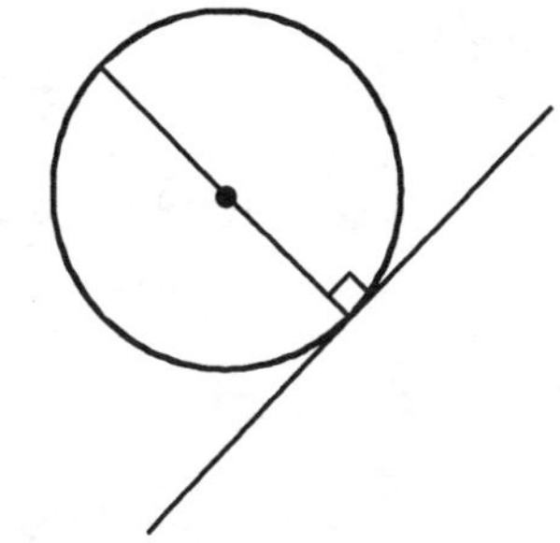

- A diameter which is perpendicular (⊥) to a chord, bisects the chord. Notice that AC = BC and $\widehat{AD}=\widehat{BD}$.

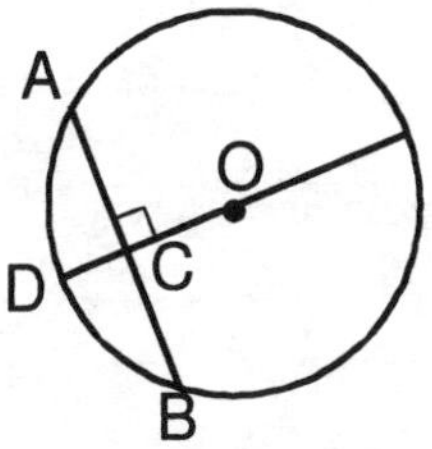


- A central angle (vertex at the center of the circle) measures the same degrees as the arc it intercepts.

$$\angle AOB = 90°$$

$$\widehat{AB}=90°$$

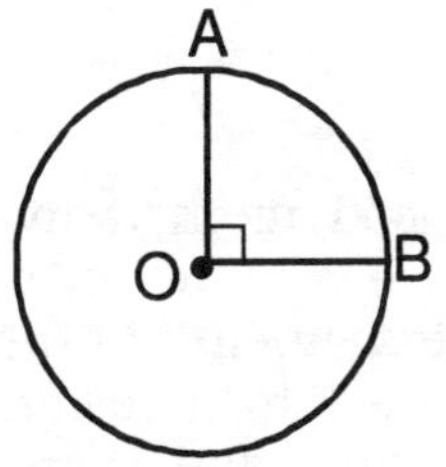


- An inscribed angle (vertex on the outside edge) measures half the arc it intercepts.

$$\angle X = \angle Y = \angle Z = \frac{1}{2}90° = 45°$$

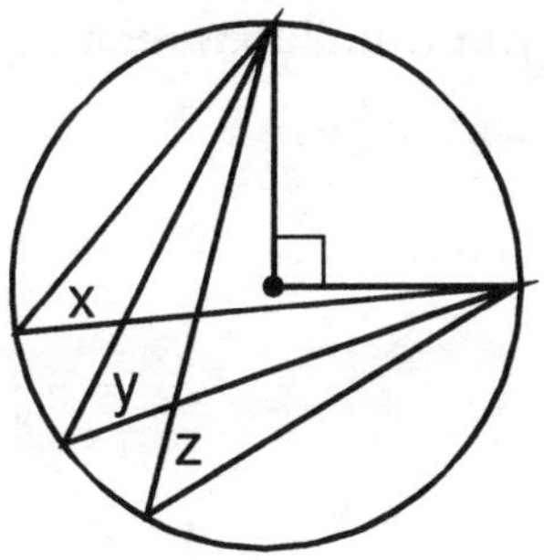


- An inscribed angle with endpoints on a diameter has a measure of 90°. This can easily be seen since a diameter is a straight angle (180°), its inscribed angle equals 90°.

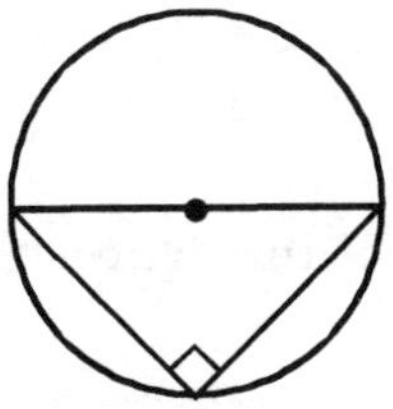

- The opposite angles of an inscribed quadrilateral are supplementary (i.e. 180°).

$$\angle 1 + \angle 3 = 180°$$

$$\angle 2 + \angle 4 = 180°$$

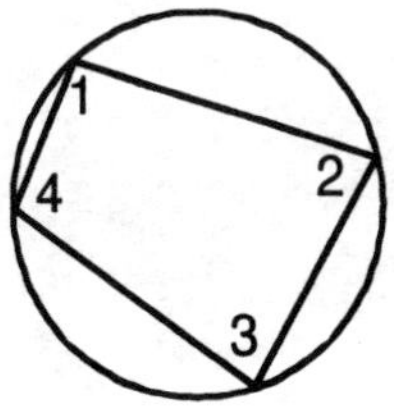

# MIXED FIGURES IN A PLANE

This is an example of a mixed figure:

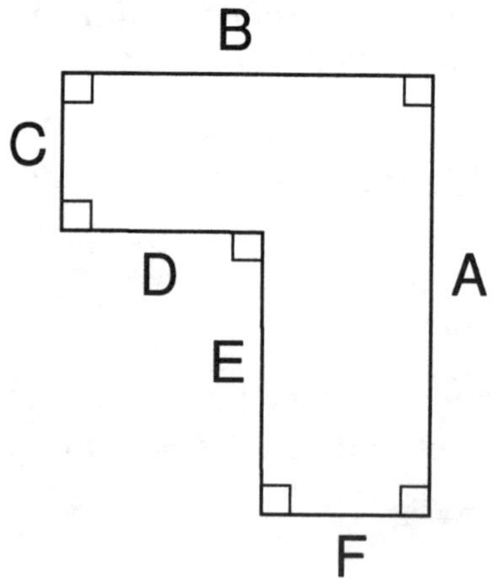


## PERIMETER

A good method to find the perimeter of this figure is to modify it as shown. Moving the two line segments to the dashed lines converts the figure into a rectangle. Do the "line moving" mentally and then compute the perimeter as you would for a rectangle.

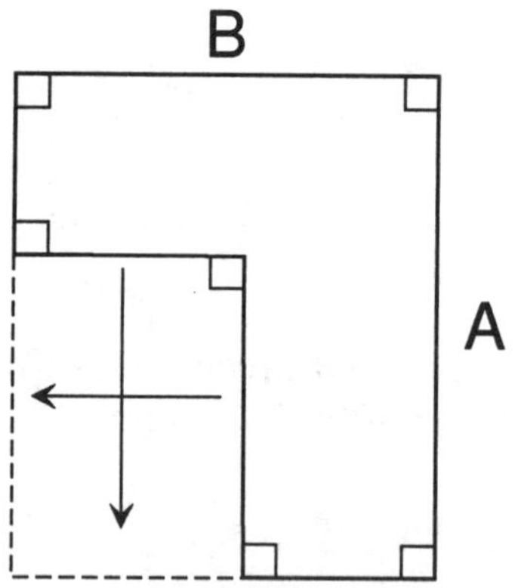


**perimeter = 2A + 2B**

## AREA

Divide the figure into two rectangles as shown.

area = (C)(D) + (A)(F)

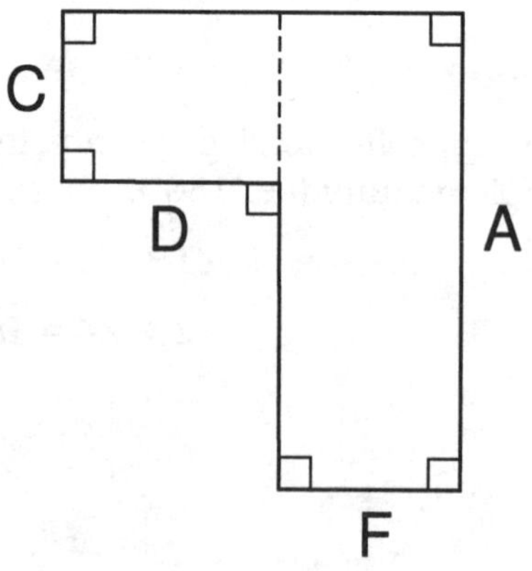

or area = (C)(B) + (E)(F)

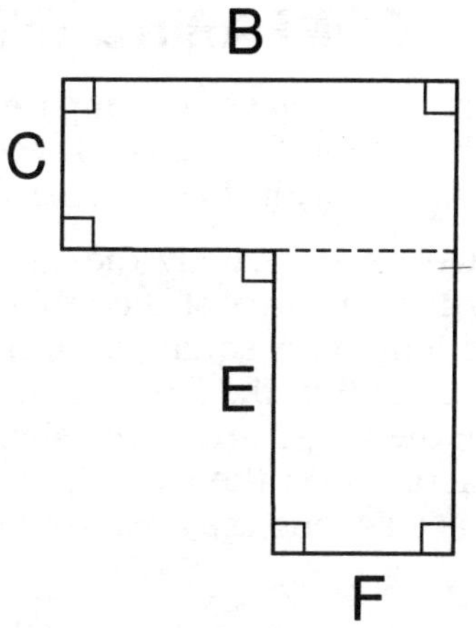


The following example is very popular with the GMAT.

EXAMPLE: What is the perimeter and area of an area rug in a rectangular room if the rug's edges are two feet from the wall? The length of the room is 20ft and the width is 14ft.

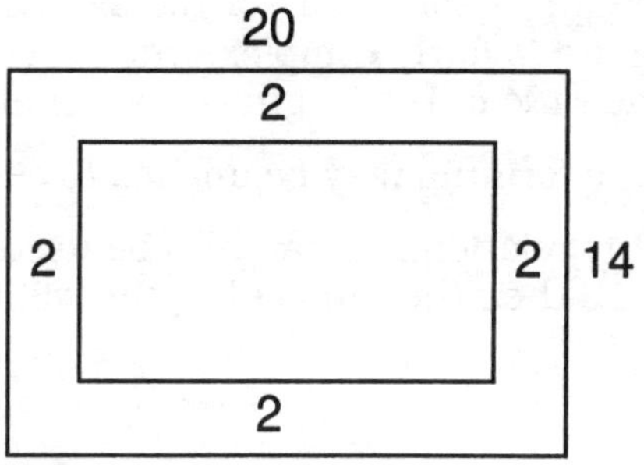


SOLUTION: Since the room is 20ft long, the rug length can be calculated as 20 - 4 = 16ft (subtract 2 from both ends). Similarly the rug width is 14 - 4 = 10ft.

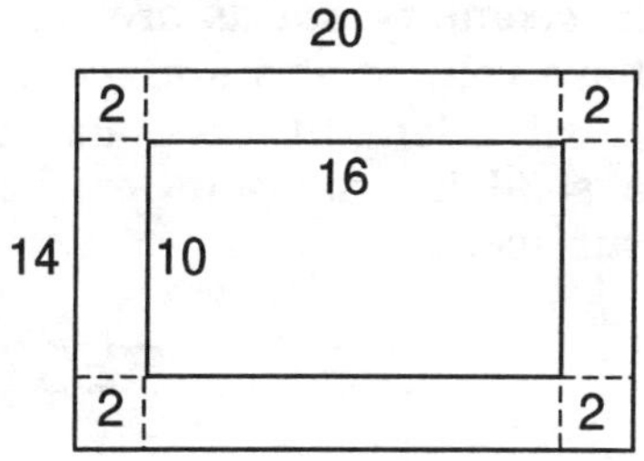


Perimeter = 2L + 2W $\qquad$ Area = LW

= 2(16) + 2(10) $\qquad$ = (16)(10)

= 52 ft. $\qquad$ = 160 sq. ft.

EXAMPLE: A racetrack is composed of two semicircles connected by two straightaways. The straightaway equals 500ft and the width is 100ft. What are the perimeter and the area?

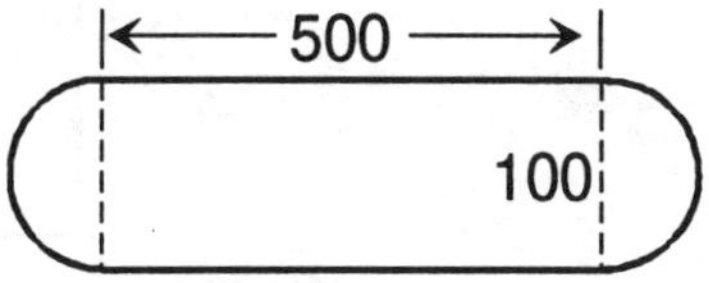


SOLUTION: The perimeter is composed of two straightaways, 2(500) = 1000, and two half circles (i.e. a whole circle), $C=\pi d=100\pi$. The perimeter of the track is $1000 + 100\pi$ ft.

The area is composed of a rectangle and two half circles (once again a whole circle). The area of the rectangle = (500)(100) = 50,000 sq. ft. and the area of the circle = $\pi(\frac{100}{2})^2 = 2500\pi$ sq. ft. The area enclosed by the track = $50{,}000 + 2500\pi$ sq. ft.

## COMPARING THE AREAS OF SIMILAR FIGURES

There are many ways to compare areas of similar figures. This section contains some helpful hints and formulas. These represent specific facts that are tested on the GMAT and familiarity with these properties can increase your performance.

If two figures are exactly the same except one is scaled down, the area of one can be used to find the area of the other. Consider the instance of one square that has sides twice as long as a square with an area of 16 square feet. The long way to solve the problem is to find the length of one side of the smaller box, double the length and then compute the larger area. The short way is to know that if the sides are twice as long the area is four times the size. The four comes from squaring the two. If the sides were three times as long the area would then be nine times larger.

In general the relationship is $\frac{A_1}{A_2} = \left(\frac{S_1}{S_2}\right)^2$. (A is the area and S is the corresponding length of some part of the similar figures.) This relationship is really handy when the figure is fairly complex or if the equation for the area is unknown. All that is needed is the ratio of the lengths of two similar sides or arcs of the two figures.

This formula may be applied to circles as well.

This relationship can also be used in reverse. If the area of similar figures has a ratio of 9:16 then the ratio of lengths will be 3:4, the square root of the area ratio.

## SOLIDS

In geometry ***solids*** are three-dimensional objects. Unlike figures in the plane, solids have volume and surface area. ***Surface area*** of a solid is analogous to the perimeter (surface length) of a planar figure; it is the measure of the edge of the solid. ***Volume*** of a solid is analogous to the area of a figure, it is the space enclosed by the solid's surface.

## RECTANGULAR SOLIDS (BOXES)

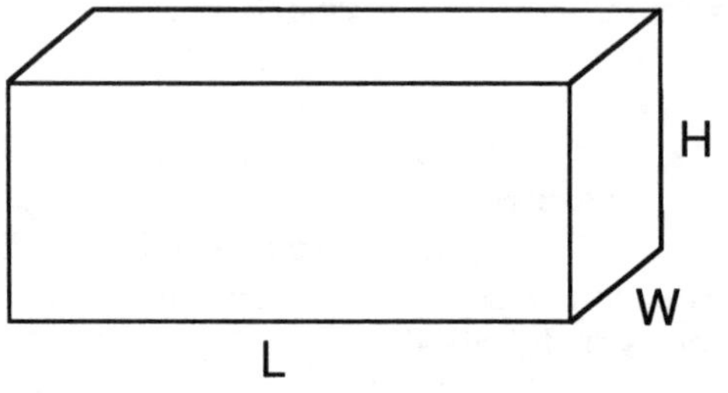


$$\text{Volume} = \text{Area}_{\text{Base}} \bullet \text{Height} = L \cdot W \cdot H$$

Note: Area of the base, which is a rectangle, equals $L \cdot W$.

The surface area is the area of all the sides. There are six sides (three pairs of equal sides). Thus the formula for surface area is as follows:

| front & back | top & bottom | left & right |
|---|---|---|
| 2LH | + 2LW | + 2WH |

## Cube

A ***cube*** is a rectangular solid with all dimensions the same (i.e. L = W = H). Therefore the volume of a cube is $V = (s)(s)(s) = s^3$ where s is the length of any edge. The surface area of a cube is 6 times the area of any side:

$$\text{Surface area} = 6s^2$$

EXAMPLE: Given the volume of a cube is 125 cubic inches, what is the surface area?

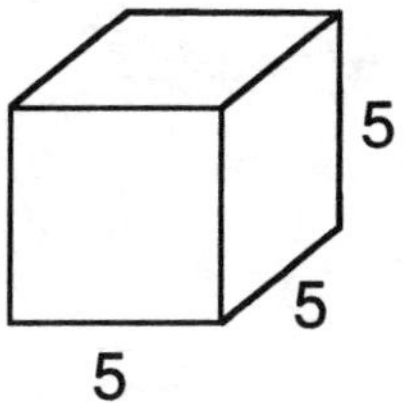


SOLUTION: Since volume equals $s^3$, the length of each edge is found by taking the cube root, $\sqrt[3]{125} = 5$ inches. The area of one side is (5)(5) = 25 and the surface area of the cube is 6(25) = 150 sq. in.

## CYLINDER (CAN)

$$\text{Volume} = \text{Area}_{\text{Base}} \bullet \text{Height} = \pi r^2 h$$

Note: area of the base, which is a circle, equals $\pi r^2$.

The surface area can be seen to be composed of two circles and a rectangle.

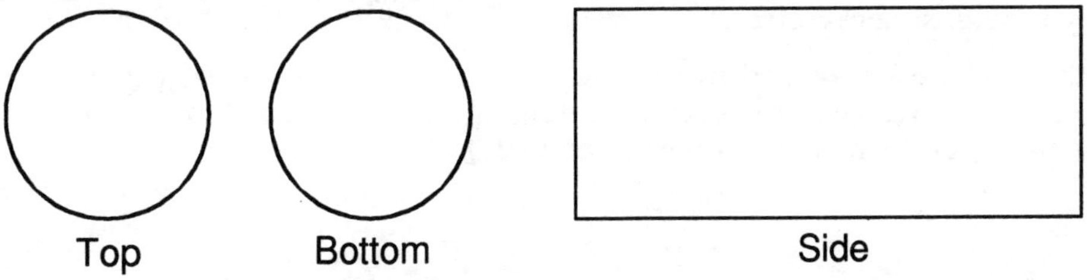


The length of the rectangle is the circumference of the circle, $2\pi r$, and the height is h. So the rectangle has an area of $2\pi rh$. Therefore the surface area is $2\pi r^2 + 2\pi rh$.

EXAMPLE: A 4 inch high by 6 inch wide label is to be placed around a can. The label completely covers the vertical side of the can. What is the volume of the can?

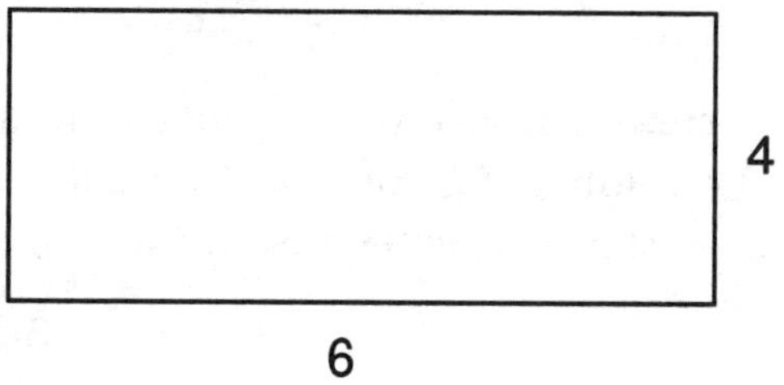


SOLUTION: Since the width of the label equals the circumference of the lid, we have:

$$C = 2\pi r$$

$$r = \frac{C}{2\pi} = \frac{6}{2\pi} = \frac{3}{\pi}$$

Using the radius we can find the area of the lid:

$$A = \pi r^2$$

$$A = \pi\left(\frac{3}{\pi}\right)^2 = \frac{9\pi}{\pi^2} = \frac{9}{\pi}$$

Now the volume can be calculated via:

$$V = \text{Area}_{\text{Base}} \bullet \text{Height}$$

$$= \frac{9}{\pi}(4) = \frac{36}{\pi}$$

## VOLUME OF SIMILAR SOLIDS

Just as similar planar figures can be compared via ratios of sides and areas, so can similar solids. The ratio equation in this case has a cubic power instead of a square power:

$$\frac{V_1}{V_2} = \left(\frac{S_1}{S_2}\right)^3$$

The implication is that if one solid has sides with twice the length, then its volume will be 2 cubed or eight times the volume of the smaller. This goes for cubes, rectangular solids, cylinders, spheres, etc.

This ratio can also be applied in reverse. If the volume of one object is 27 times the volume of a similar object, the corresponding sides and dimensions will be three times the dimensions of the smaller (three cubed is 27).

# Coordinate Geometry Review

Coordinate geometry involves a plane (i.e. flat surface) with two perpendicular axes.

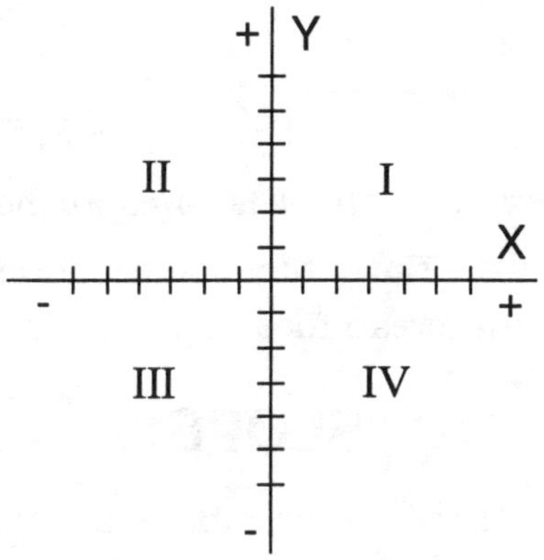


By convention, the ***x-axis*** is always horizontal and the ***y-axis*** is vertical. The four quadrants formed are numbered as shown above. Each axis is considered a number line. For the x-axis, moving right is positive and left negative. For the y-axis, moving up is positive and down negative. The intersection of the two axes is called the ***origin***. The value of each axis is zero at this intersection.

Each point on the coordinate plane is identified by its X and Y coordinates (X, Y). By convention, the X is always first. The coordinates are called an ordered pair. The origin then has coordinates (0, 0).

In the figure to the right are the signs of each ordered pair by quadrant.

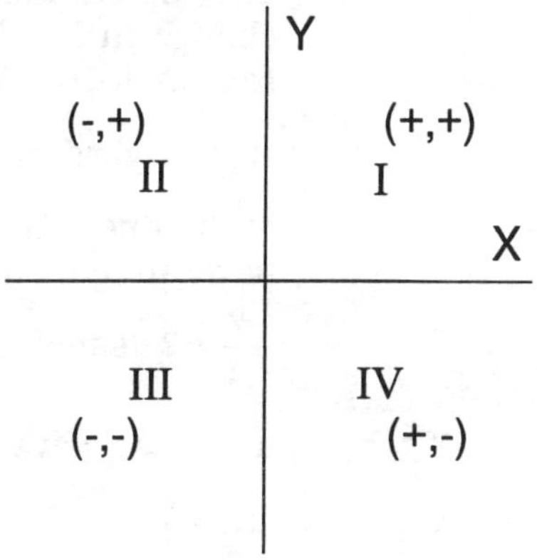


## DISTANCE BETWEEN POINTS

If two points are not displaced horizontally or vertically, the distance between them can be found using the Pythagorean theorem.

EXAMPLE: What is the distance between A and C and between B and C?

SOLUTION: The distance from A to C can be seen to be the hypotenuse of the right triangle shown to the right. The distance of each leg is found by subtracting the corresponding coordinates and taking the absolute value (distance is always positive).

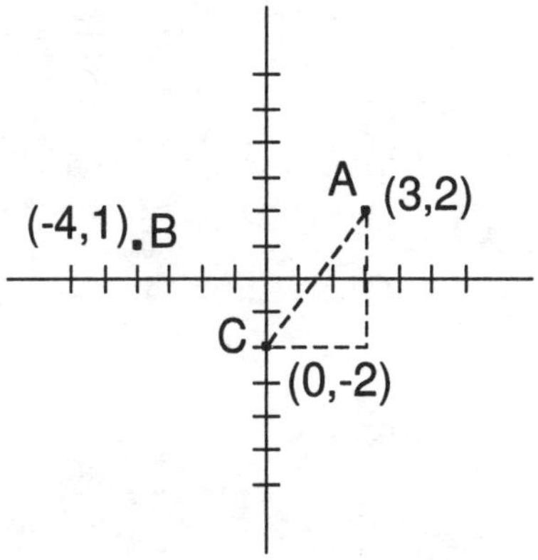

$$|AC|^2 = |X_A - X_C|^2 + |Y_A - Y_C|^2$$
$$= |3-0|^2 + |2-(-2)|^2$$
$$= 3^2 + 4^2$$
$$= 9 + 16$$
$$= 25$$
$$|AC| = 5$$

$$|BC|^2 = |X_B - X_C|^2 + |Y_B - Y_C|^2$$
$$= |0-(-4)|^2 + |-2-1|^2$$
$$= 4^2 + 3^2$$
$$= 16 + 9$$
$$= 25$$
$$|BC| = 5$$

If a grid is available, an alternate method is to count horizontally and vertically and then apply the distance formula. **Note:** the distance formula, $\sqrt{(x_1 - x_2)^2 + (y_1 - y_2)^2}$, is derived directly from the Pythagorean theorem.

## SLOPE

The ***slope*** (slant) of a line is defined as the ratio of the change in Y to the change in X (rise over run: $\frac{\text{change in Y}}{\text{change in X}} = \frac{\text{rise}}{\text{run}}$).

EXAMPLE: What is the slope of this line?

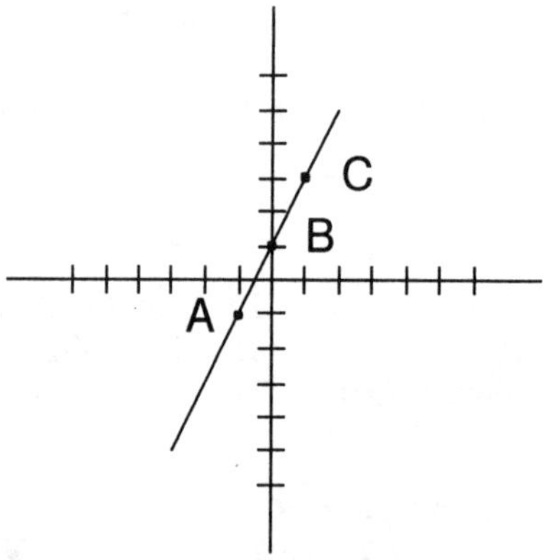


SOLUTION: To find the slope, pick any two points and determine the change in Y, the change in X, and divide. Let's consider from A to B. We have to go up 2 and right 1 yielding $\frac{2}{1} = 2$ which is the slope of the line. Alternately from B to A. We have to go down 2 and left 1 giving $\frac{-2}{-1} = 2$ (same answer as above). From A to C, we have $\frac{4}{2} = 2$ (again the same) and so on.

EXAMPLE: What is the slope of this line?

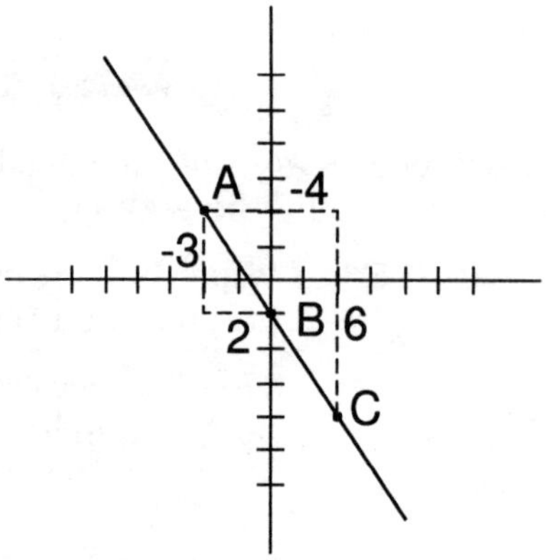


SOLUTION: Notice that the slope is computed to be the same no matter which two points are used in the computation.

$$A \rightarrow B = \frac{-3}{2} = -\frac{3}{2}$$

$$C \rightarrow A = \frac{6}{-4} = -\frac{3}{2}$$

# IMPORTANT SLOPE CONCEPTS

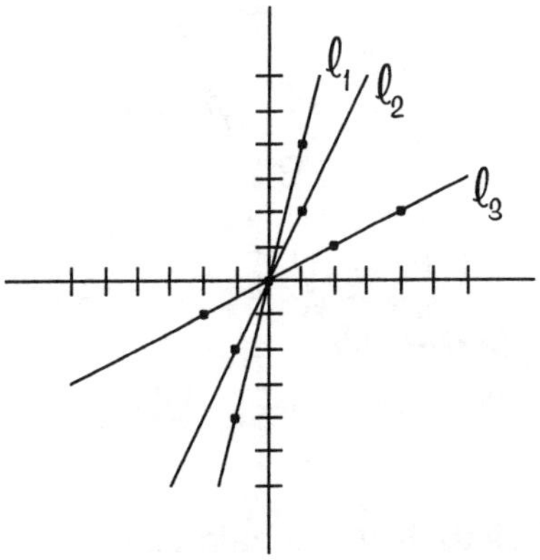


Given the three lines in the above figure, it can be seen that the steeper the line (i.e. $\ell_1$ is the steepest and $\ell_3$ is the least steep) the greater the magnitude of the slope.

$$\text{slope of } \ell_1 = \frac{4}{1} = 4 \qquad \text{slope of } \ell_2 = \frac{2}{1} = 2 \qquad \text{slope of } \ell_3 = \frac{1}{2}$$

A line that is perfectly horizontal (i.e. parallel to the x-axis) has a slope of zero.

As a line continues to rotate down (clockwise, see $\ell_4$ below), its slope turns negative.

$$\text{slope of } \ell_4 = \frac{-2}{4} = -\frac{1}{2}$$

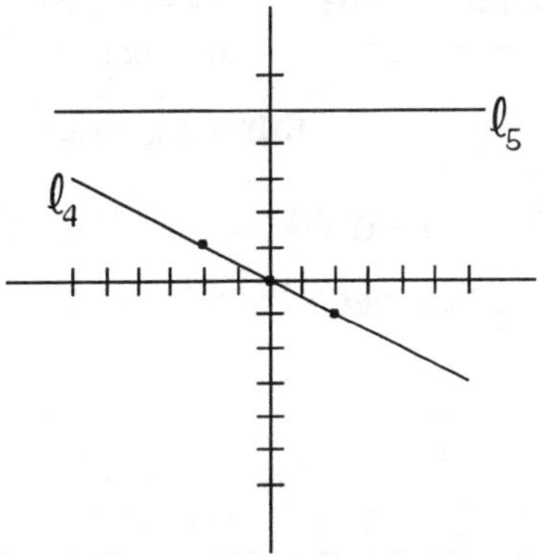


$$\text{slope of } \ell_5 = 0$$

Lastly, a vertical line (i.e., a line parallel to the y-axis) has no slope or the slope is said to be "undefined." This is easily seen since a vertical line has no change in x (i.e., $x_1 - x_2 = 0$) and division by zero is undefined.

# LINEAR EQUATIONS

Each line in the coordinate plane can be defined by a linear equation. The general form is Ax + By + C = 0, where A and B are coefficients and C is a constant. **Note**: the equation has two variables and the exponent of each is 1. This is a characteristic of all linear equations.

When working with slope a more common form of the equation is y = mx + b, where m is the slope and b is a constant equal to the ***y-intercept*** (i.e., where the line intercepts the y-axis). The equation y = mx + b is said to be in ***slope-intercept form***.

It can be seen that the slope of the line below is two and the y-intercept is 1. Therefore m = 2 and b = 1 and we have the equation y = 2x + 1.

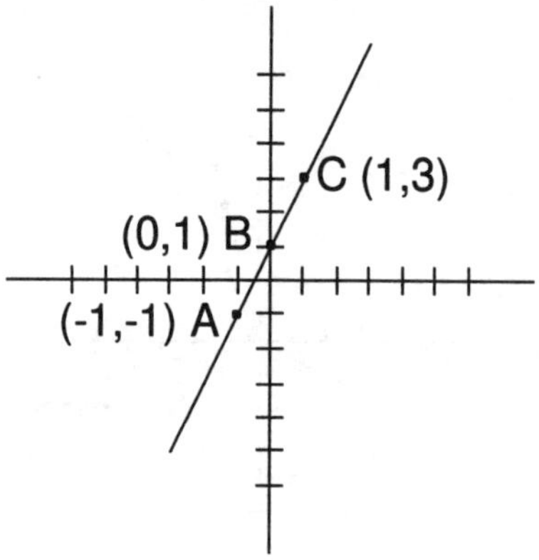


Each point on the line must satisfy (i.e., balance) the equation. Below we test each point. In general this is a good way to check that you picked the correct slope and intercept.

| Check point A (-1, -1): | Check point B (0, 1): | Check point C (1, 3): |
|---|---|---|
| -1 = 2(-1) + 1 | 1 = 2(0) + 1 | 3 = 2(1) + 1 |
| -1 = -2 + 1 | 1 = 0 + 1 | 3 = 2 + 1 |
| -1 = -1 | 1 = 1 | 3 = 3 |

If the y-intercept is not specifically identified (as seen in the figure to the right), the equation can be derived from the slope equation $m = \frac{y - Y_1}{x - X_1}$. Multiplying both sides by $(x - X_1)$, we have $m(x - X_1) = (y - Y_1)$.

To determine the line's equation we need the slope, m, and any point, $(X_1, Y_1)$.

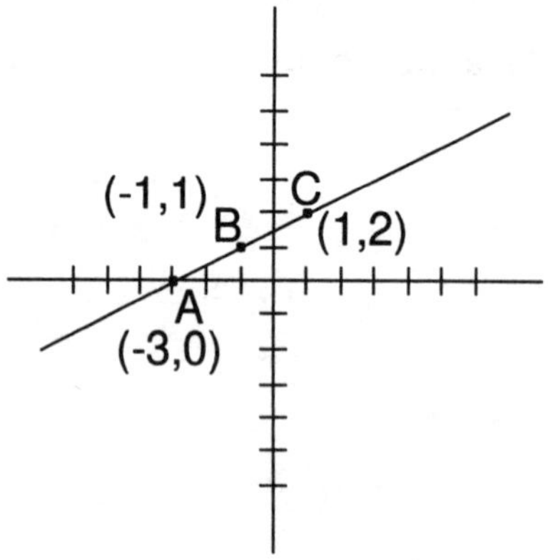


First calculate the slope: $m = \frac{(Y_A - Y_B)}{(X_A - X_B)} = \frac{(0-1)}{(-3-(-1))} = \frac{-1}{-2} = \frac{1}{2}$. Then plug one point back in to solve:

| Use point A (-3, 0): | Use point B (-1, -1): | Use point C (1, 2): |
|---|---|---|
| $y - 0 = \frac{1}{2}(x - (-3))$ | $y - 1 = \frac{1}{2}(x - (-1))$ | $y - 2 = \frac{1}{2}(x - 1)$ |
| $y = \frac{1}{2}(x + 3)$ | $y - 1 = \frac{1}{2}x + \frac{1}{2}$ | $y - 2 = \frac{1}{2}x - \frac{1}{2}$ |
| $y = \frac{1}{2}x + \frac{3}{2}$ | $y = \frac{1}{2}x + \frac{1}{2} + 1$ | $y = \frac{1}{2}x + 2 - \frac{1}{2}$ |
| | $y = \frac{1}{2}x + \frac{3}{2}$ | $y = \frac{1}{2}x + \frac{3}{2}$ |

# QUADRATIC EQUATIONS

A quadratic equation does not describe a straight line but rather a "U" shaped curve called a parabola. In general a quadratic equation takes the form of $y = ax^2 + bx + c$. The "U" shape is caused by the $x^2$ term.

EXAMPLE: Plot $y = x^2$ on a coordinate plane.

| Points on the Graph of $y = x^2$ | |
|---|---|
| X | Y |
| 0 | 0 |
| 1 | 1 |
| 2 | 4 |
| -1 | 1 |
| -2 | 4 |

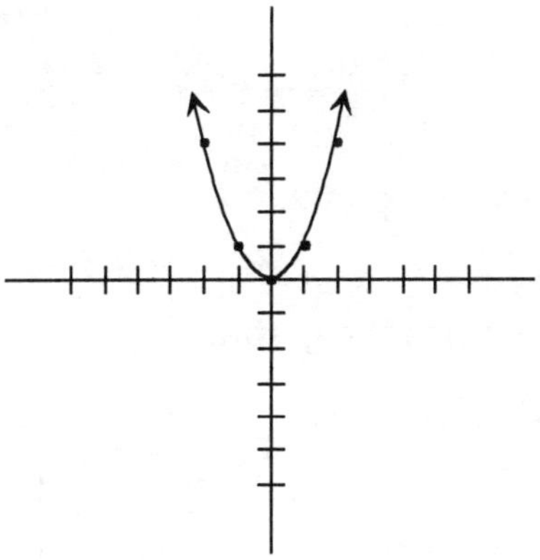

The addition of a constant will cause the graph to slide up or down vertically:

EXAMPLE: $y = x^2 + 3$

| Points on the Graph of $y = x^2 + 3$ | |
|---|---|
| X | Y |
| 0 | 3 |
| 1 | 4 |
| 2 | 7 |
| -1 | 4 |
| -2 | 7 |

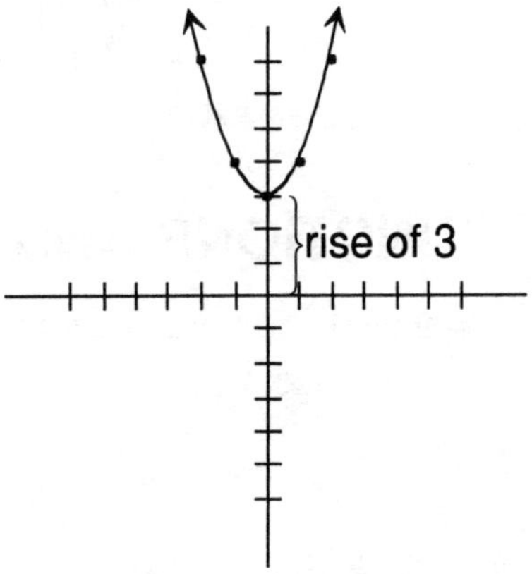


A constant of +3 causes a rise of 3.

EXAMPLE: $y = x^2 - 2$

| Points on the Graph of $y = x^2 - 2$ | |
|---|---|
| X | Y |
| 0 | -2 |
| 1 | -1 |
| 2 | 2 |
| -1 | -1 |
| -2 | 2 |

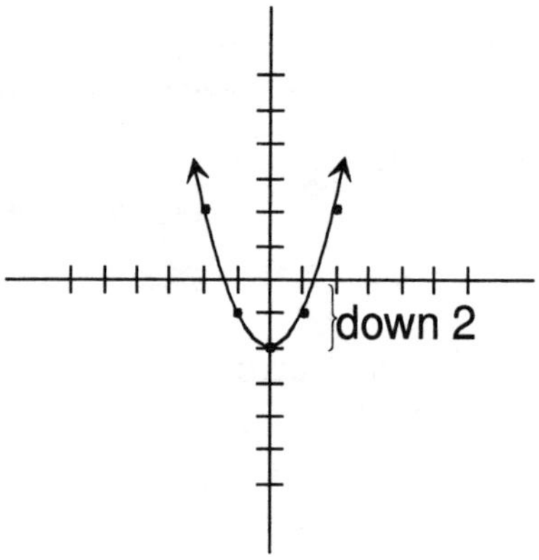


A constant of -2 causes a drop of 2.

A negative coefficient inverts the graph:

EXAMPLE: $y = -x^2 - 2$

| Points on the Graph of $y = -x^2 - 2$ | |
|---|---|
| X | Y |
| 0 | -2 |
| 1 | -3 |
| 2 | -6 |
| -1 | -3 |
| -2 | -6 |

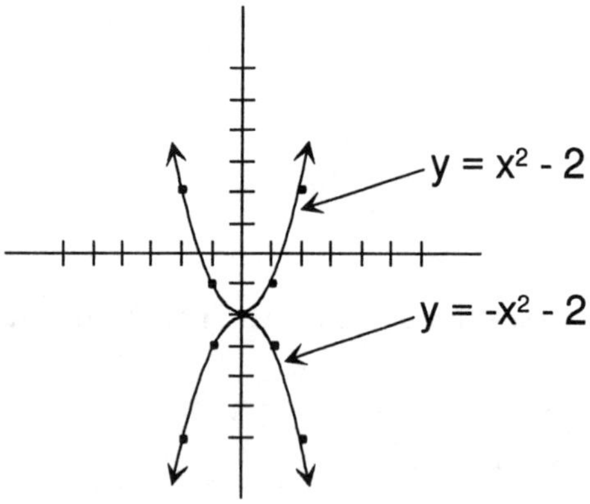


## FUNCTIONS AND GRAPHS

Consider the equation $y = 2x + 1$. $f(x)$ may be substituted for y giving $f(x) = 2x + 1$ (i.e. a linear function).

| Points on the Line $f(x) = 2x + 1$ | |
|---|---|
| X | Y |
| -2 | -3 |
| -1 | -1 |
| 0 | 1 |
| 1 | 3 |
| 2 | 5 |

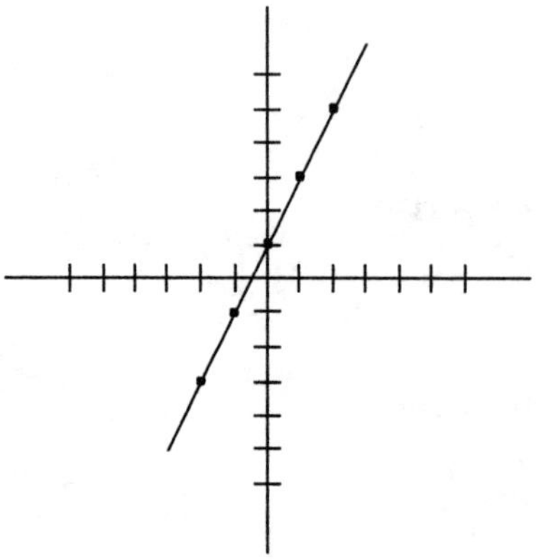

The equation $y = x^2 - 1$ becomes the function $f(x) = x^2 - 1$.

| Points on the Parabola $f(x) = x^2 - 1$ | |
|---|---|
| X | Y |
| -2 | 3 |
| -1 | 0 |
| 0 | -1 |
| 1 | 0 |
| 2 | 3 |

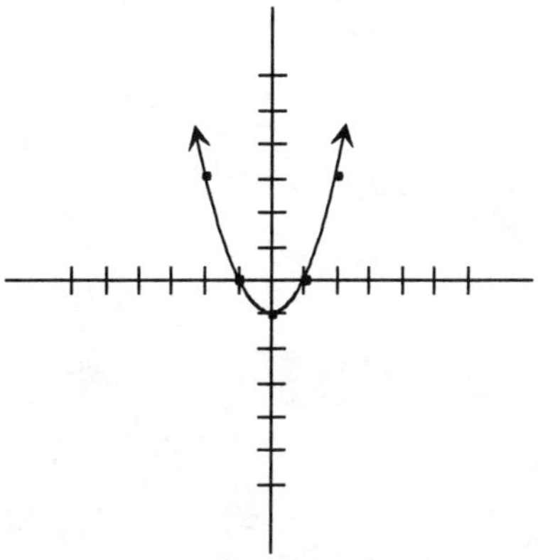

## Finding the X-intercepts of a Parabola (Finding the Roots)

Finding values of x which satisfy the equation f(x) = 0 in general is called finding the roots. Let f(x) = 0, or what values of x satisfy $x^2 - 1 = 0$?

By factoring we have (x + 1)(x - 1) = 0, which tells us x = -1 or x = 1. (To make the product (x + 1)(x – 1) equal zero, one of the two factors must be zero. The only number that makes x + 1 zero is x = -1, and x = 1 is required to make x – 1 zero.)

In general factoring is the best way to find the roots of a quadratic equation.

# Practice – Geometry

1.

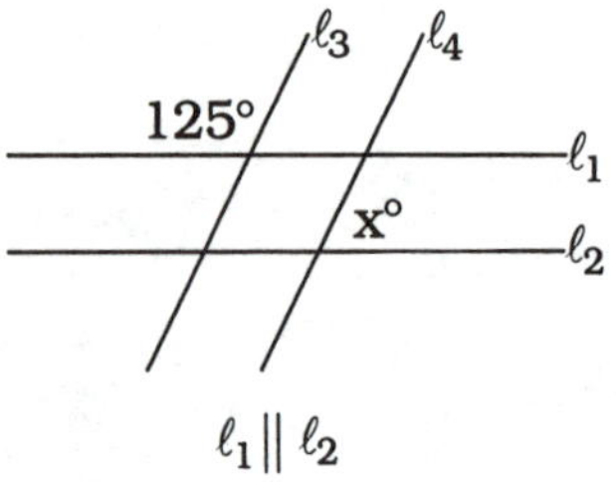


What is the value of x?

A. 45 B. 55 C. 75 D. 235 E. cannot be determined

2.

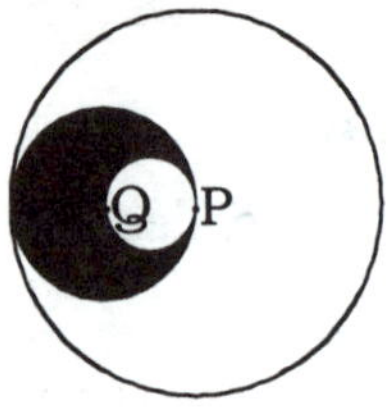


P is the center of the big circle. Q is the center of the medium circle. What fraction of the big circle is shaded?

A. $\frac{1}{16}$ B. $\frac{1}{8}$ C. $\frac{3}{16}$ D. $\frac{1}{4}$ E. $\frac{3}{8}$

3.

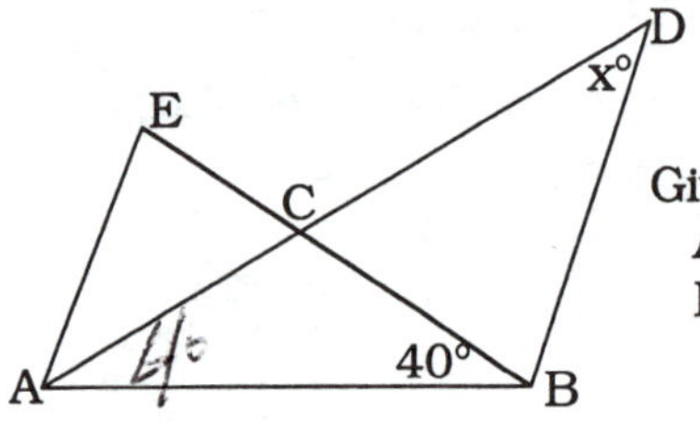


Given:
AC = BC
BD = CD

Not Drawn to Scale

What is the value of x?

A. 10 B. 15 C. 20 D. 30 E. 40

4.

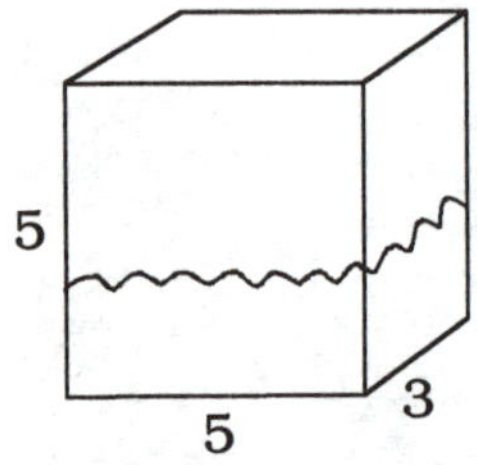


The fish tank to the left is filled with water to a depth of 2 feet. If the tank is rolled over on its largest side, what will be the depth of the water in feet?

A. $\frac{5}{6}$ B. $\frac{6}{5}$ C. $\frac{5}{3}$ D. $\frac{5}{2}$ E. 3

5. 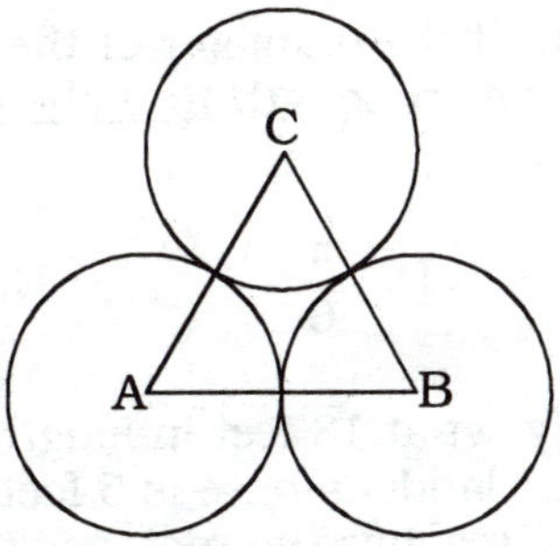


A, B and C are the centers of 3 equal circles which are tangent. If the area of the 3 circles is $108\pi$, what is the perimeter of $\Delta ABC$?

A. 9 B. 18 C. 24 D. 36 E. 72

6. 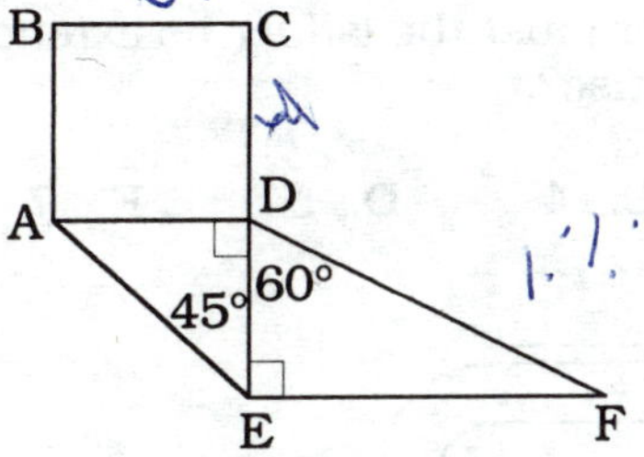


The area of square ABCD = 16. What is the area of $\Delta DEF$?

A. $4\sqrt{3}$ B. 8 C. $8\sqrt{3}$

D. $16\sqrt{3}$ E. 16

7. 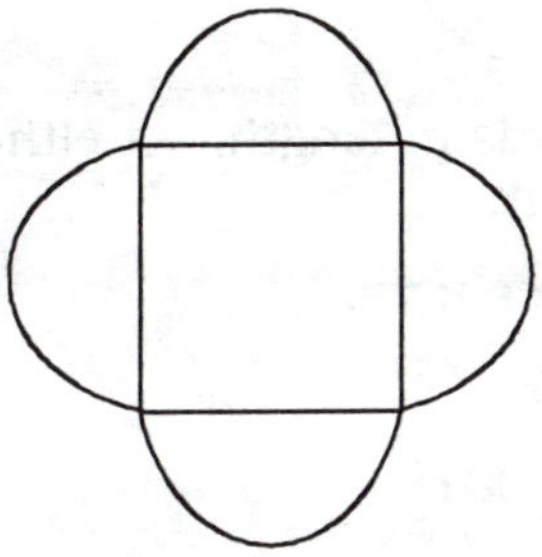

The picture to the left represents the top view of an advertising pillar for a soda company. There is a semicircle on each side of the central square. The square has an area of 36 sq. ft. If the pillar has a height of 10 ft., what is the volume of the sign in <u>cu. ft.</u>?

A. 540 B. $360 + 90\pi$ C. $360 + 180\pi$

D. $540\pi$ E. $540 + 180\pi$

8. A right cylindrical container has a radius of 1 and a height of 2. If the container is $\frac{3}{4}$ full, how many containers with a radius of $\frac{1}{4}$ and height of 4 can be filled to capacity from the first container?

A. 3 B. 4 C. 6 D. 9 E. 12

9. A square garden has a border y feet wide on all sides. If the dimensions along the inside of the border are x all around, what is the area of the border?

A. $y(2x + y)$ B. $2y(x + y)$ C. $2y(2x + y)$ D. $4y(x + y)$ E. $4(x + y)$

10. 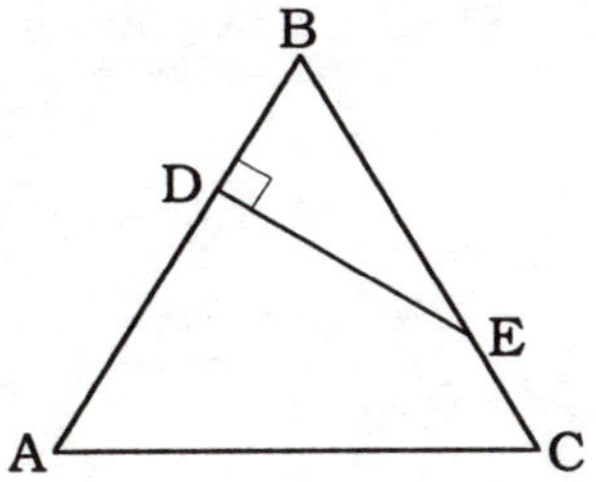


$\Delta ABC$ is equilateral with sides of length 6. BD = 2. What is the area of ADEC?

A. $16\sqrt{3}$ B. $18-2\sqrt{3}$ C. $9-2\sqrt{3}$

D. $7\sqrt{3}$ E. $5\sqrt{3}$

11. A circular bicycle sprocket has 54 teeth around. If the diameter of the sprocket is 9 inches, from tooth tip to tooth tip, what is the arc length in inches between two tooth tips?

A. $\frac{3\pi}{2}$ B. $\frac{\pi}{2}$ C. $\frac{\pi}{3}$ D. $\frac{\pi}{6}$ E. $\frac{\pi}{18}$

12. 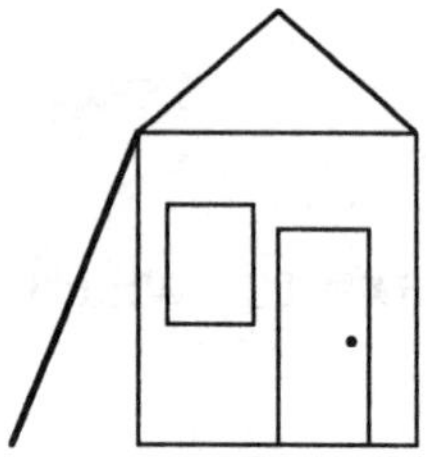

An extension ladder initially set at 13 feet in length is leaned against a house. The ladder's base is 5 feet from the house while the top just reaches the roof, as shown. If the base of the ladder is then moved 4 more feet from the house, how much longer must the ladder be extended to reach the roof of the house?

A. 2 B. 3 C. 4 D. 5 E. 7

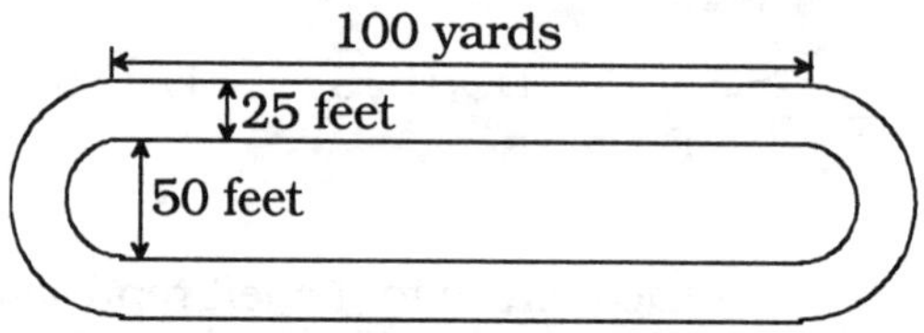


The running track above has straightaways 100 yards in length. At either end is a semicircle. The track has a constant width of 25 ft.

**Questions 13-15 refer to the figure above.**

13. How many feet is it around the outside of the track?

A. 800 B. $200 + 50\pi$ C. $200 + 100\pi$
D. $600 + 50\pi$ E. $600 + 100\pi$

14. How many more feet is it around the outside of the track than the inside?

A. 50 B. 100 C. $50\pi$ D. $100\pi$ E. $200\pi$

15. What is the area of the track, excluding the infield?

A. 5,000 sq. ft. + $1{,}875\pi$ sq. ft.
B. 15,000 sq. ft. + $1{,}875\pi$ sq. ft.
C. 15,000 sq. ft. + $2{,}500\pi$ sq. ft.
D. 15,000 sq. ft. + $7{,}500\pi$ sq. ft.
E. 16,875 sq. ft.

16. 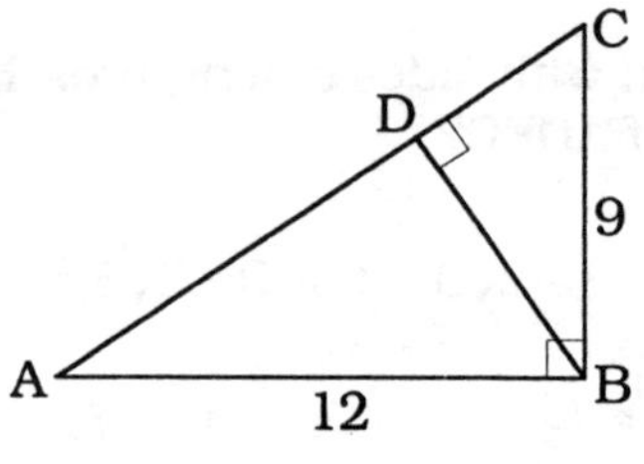


In the drawing above, what is the length of BD?

A. $\frac{16}{9}$ B. $\frac{18}{5}$ C. $\frac{36}{5}$ D. $\frac{48}{5}$ E. $\frac{7}{3}$

17. The sum of the interior angles of a 10 sided figure is how many times larger than the sum of the interior angles of a quadrilateral?

A. 2.5 B. 4 C. 5 D. 6 E. 7.5

18. 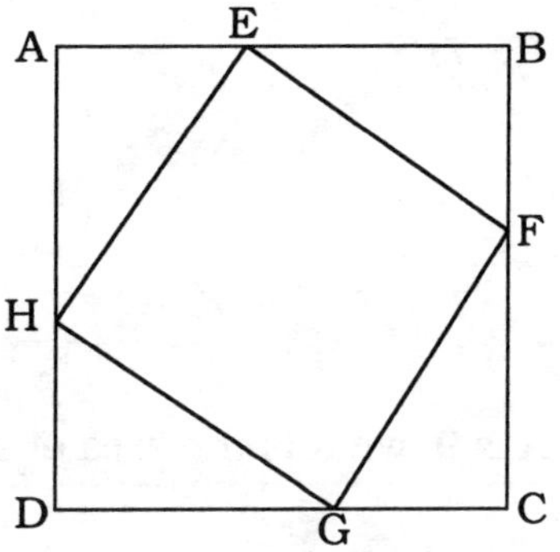


Square EFGH is inscribed in square ABCD. If the ratio of AE to EB is $\frac{3}{4}$, what is the ratio of the area of EFGH to the area of ABCD?

A. $\frac{3}{7}$ B. $\frac{9}{16}$ C. $\frac{4}{7}$

D. $\frac{5}{7}$ E. $\frac{25}{49}$

19. 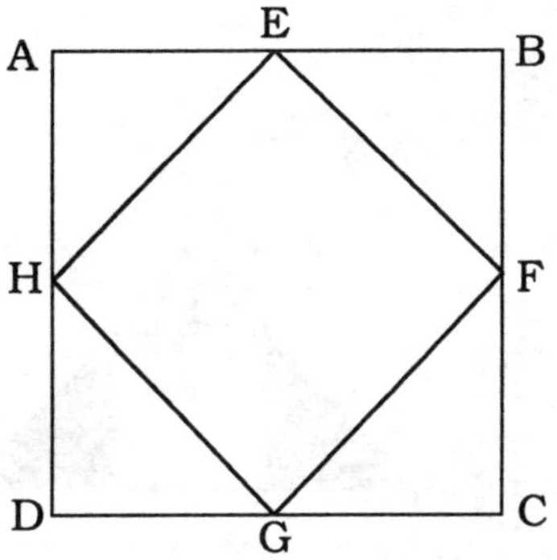


Square EFGH is inscribed in square ABCD. E is the midpoint of AB. If AB equals x, then in terms of x, EF =

A. $\frac{1}{4}x$ B. $\frac{1}{2}x$ C. $\frac{x\sqrt{2}}{2}$

D. $\frac{2x}{\sqrt{2}}$ E. $x\sqrt{2}$

20. 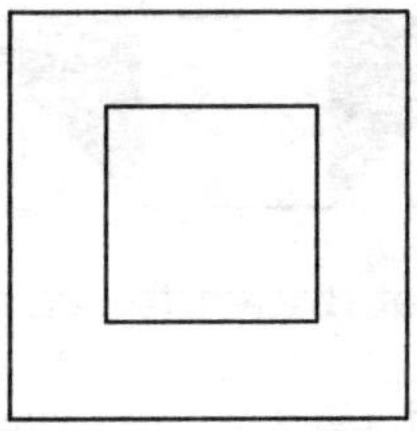

(Not drawn to scale.)

In the picture to the left, there is a $\frac{1}{2}$ inch border on all sides between the small square and the large square. If the area of the small square equals 1 sq. in., what is the ratio of the area of the small square to the area of the large square?

A. $\frac{1}{9}$ B. $\frac{1}{4}$ C. $\frac{4}{9}$

D. $\frac{1}{2}$ E. $\frac{2}{3}$

21. 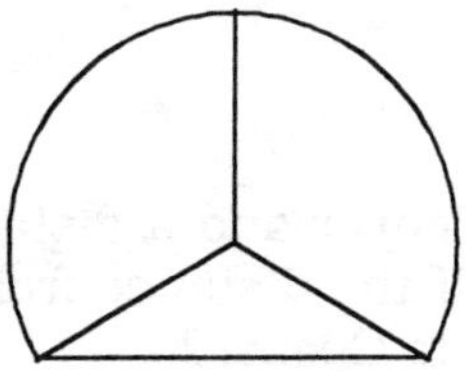

The sign outside a triathlon sports store is the picture of an equal angular tri-spoke racing wheel mounted on a flat base at the end of 2 spokes. If the length of a spoke is 12 inches, what is the perimeter of the sign?

A. $16\pi$ B. $12 + 16\pi$ C. $12\sqrt{3} + 16\pi$

D. $24\pi$ E. $12\sqrt{3} + 24\pi$

22. 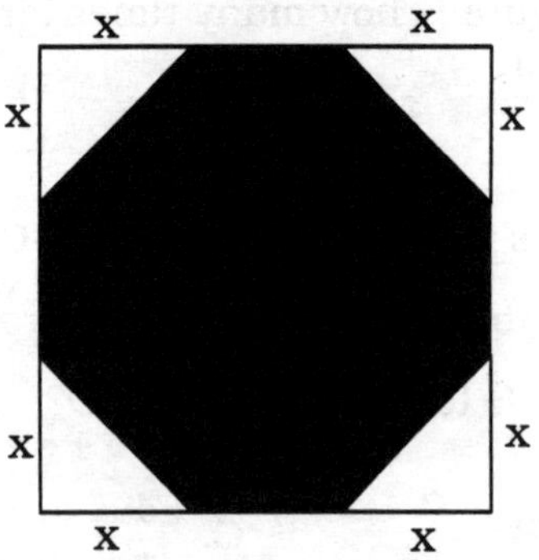


The square to the left has sides of length 3x. What is the area of the shaded region?

A. $3x^2$ B. $4x^2$ C. $5x^2$

D. $6x^2$ E. $7x^2$

23. 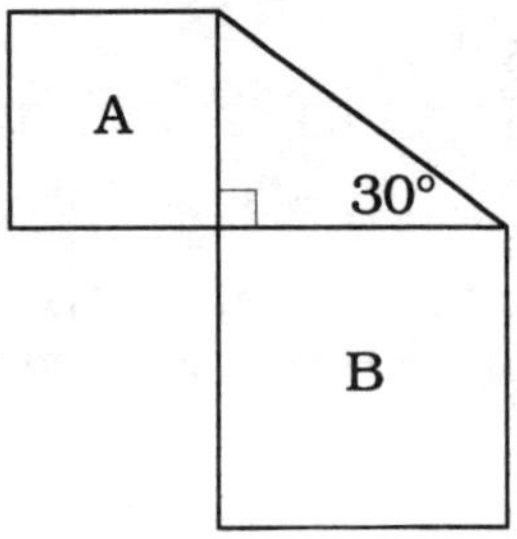


If the area of square A is 9, what is the area of square B?

A. 12 B. 16 C. 25 D. 27

E. 36

24. What is the area of the shaded region formed by connecting the vertices of the regular octagon to the right?

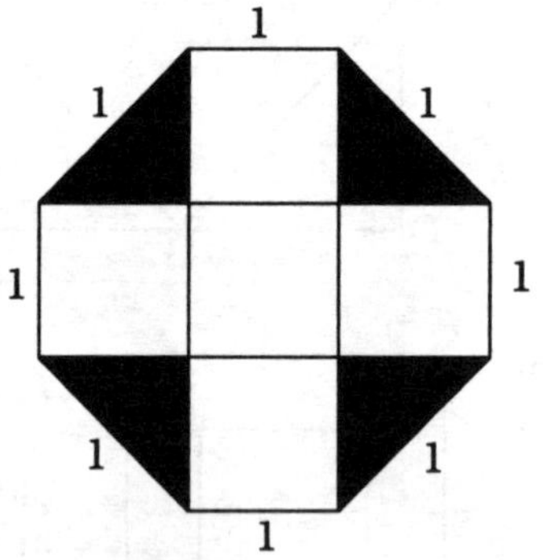

Not drawn to scale.

A. $\frac{\sqrt{2}}{2}$ B. 1 C. $\sqrt{2}$

D. 2 E. $\frac{3\sqrt{2}}{2}$

25. 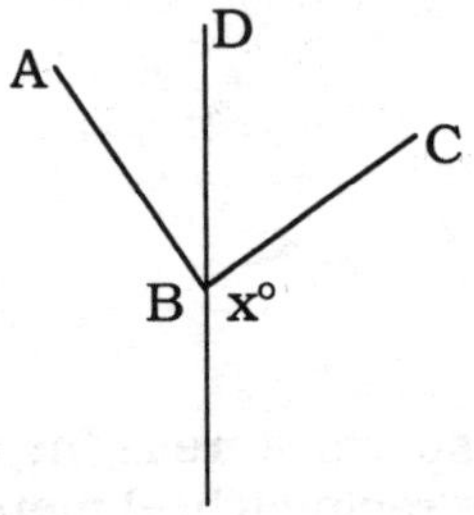


If $\angle ABC$ is a right angle, and $\angle ABD = 35°$, what is the value of x?

A. 115 B. 125 C. 135

D. 145 E. 155

26. Aston is due west of Cooper. Butler is due south of Cooper and a distance of 7 miles more from Cooper than Aston is from Cooper. If the distance from Aston to Butler is 13 miles, how many miles is it from Butler to Cooper?

A. 5 B. 6 C. 8 D. 12 E. 20

27. Dave and Alice both took trips to town. Dave traveled 4 miles north, then 15 miles east, then 4 miles north again. If Alice started from the same place but took the directly straight route, what distance (in miles) did Alice travel?

A. 17 B. 18 C. 20 D. 21 E. 23

28. 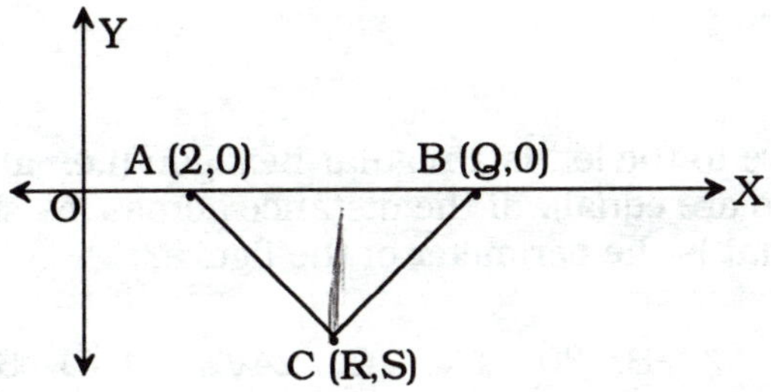


Given the x, y coordinate system to the left, what is the area of ΔABC?

A. $\frac{R(Q-2)}{2}$ B. $\frac{S(Q-2)}{2}$

C. $\frac{S(R-2)}{2}$ D. $\frac{-S(Q-2)}{2}$

E. $\frac{Q(R-2)}{2}$

29. 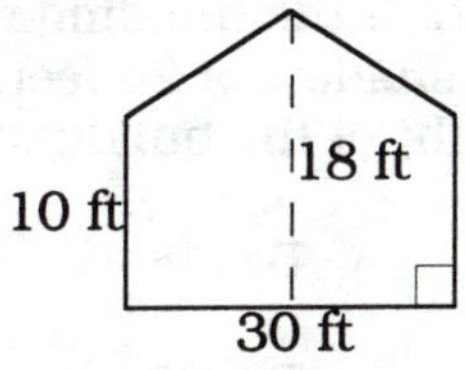


The picture to the left represents the front of a symmetric house. What is the area of the front?

A. 180 B. 270 C. 390

D. 420 E. 540

30. 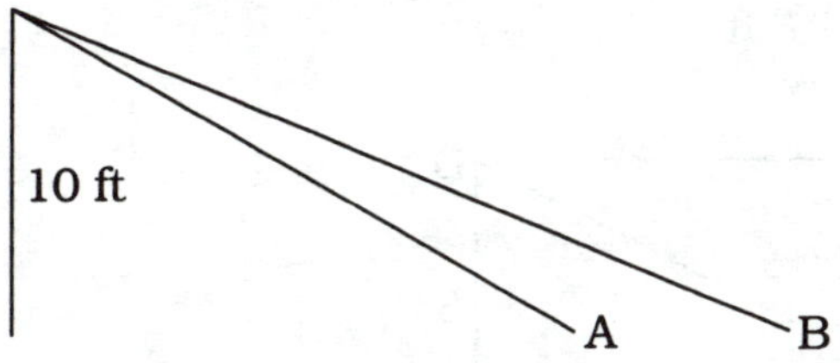


Two ropes are stretched from a pole to the ground at points A and B. The rope to point A is 20 feet. The rope to point B is 26 feet. The pole is 10 feet tall. What is the distance from A to B?

A. 6 B. $10\sqrt{3}$ C. 14

D. $24-10\sqrt{3}$ E. $24-10\sqrt{2}$

31. 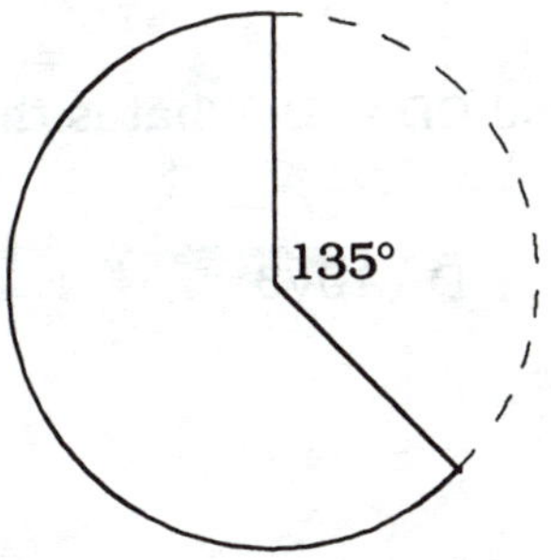


A circle has a perimeter of $24\pi$. A 135° slice is removed as shown to the left. What is the perimeter of the figure with the slice removed?

A. $15\pi$ B. $24\pi$ C. $15\pi + 12$

D. $15\pi + 24$ E. $24\pi + 12$

32.

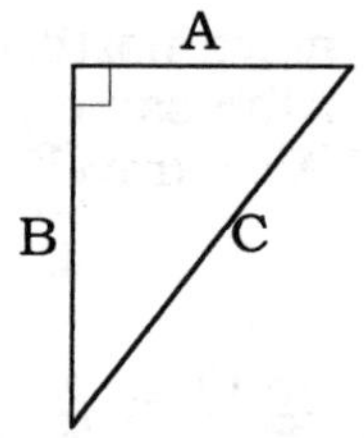


The area of the triangle to the left equals 30. If B = 2A + 2, what is the value of C?

A. 10 B. $5\sqrt{5}$ C. $5\sqrt{6}$ D. 13 E. 17

33.

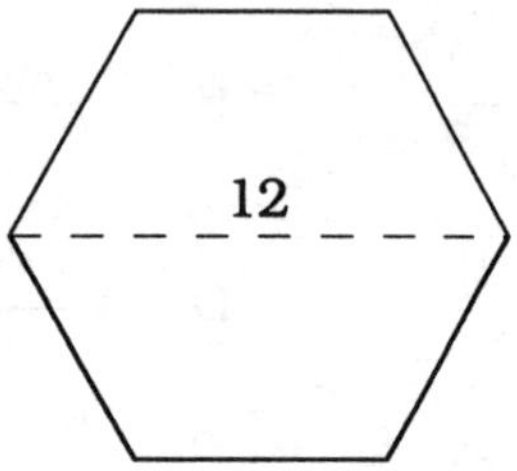


The figure to the left is a regular hexagon (i.e., all angles and sides are equal). If the distance across (as shown) is 12, what is the perimeter of the figure?

A. 24 B. 30 C. $24\sqrt{2}$ D. 36
E. $24\sqrt{3}$

34.

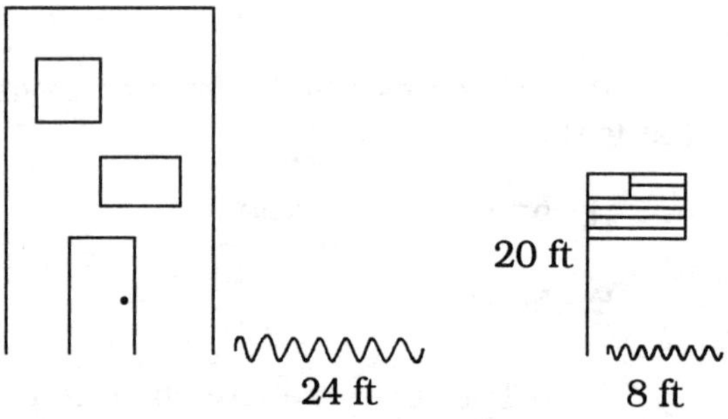


A 20 foot flag pole casts a shadow of 8 feet. If the building next to it casts a shadow of 24 feet, what is the height of the building?

A. 40 B. 48 C. 60
D. 64 E. 80

35.

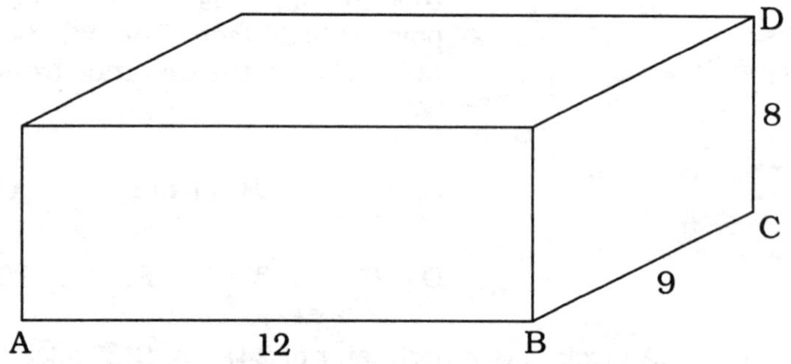


In the rectangular solid above, AB = 12, BC = 9 and CD = 8. What is the length of AD?

A. 15 B. $9\sqrt{3}$ C. 17 D. $10\sqrt{3}$ E. 20

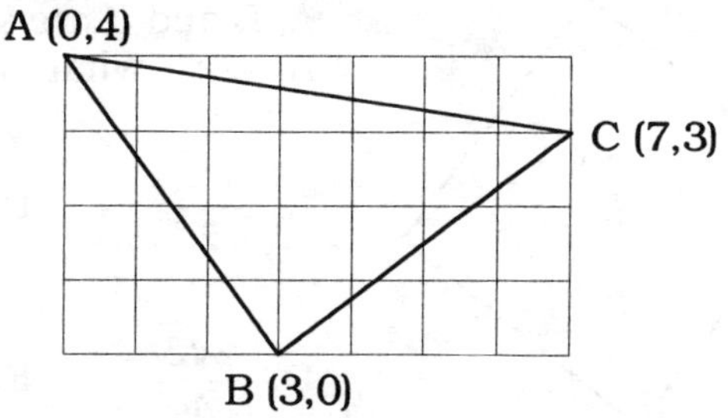


36. In the grid above, what is the perimeter of $\Delta ABC$?

A. 15 B. $12\sqrt{2}$ C. $10+5\sqrt{2}$ D. $15\sqrt{2}$ E. $10+7\sqrt{2}$

37. In the grid above, what is the measure of angle ABC?

A. 60° B. 80° C. 90° D. 100° E. cannot be determined

38. 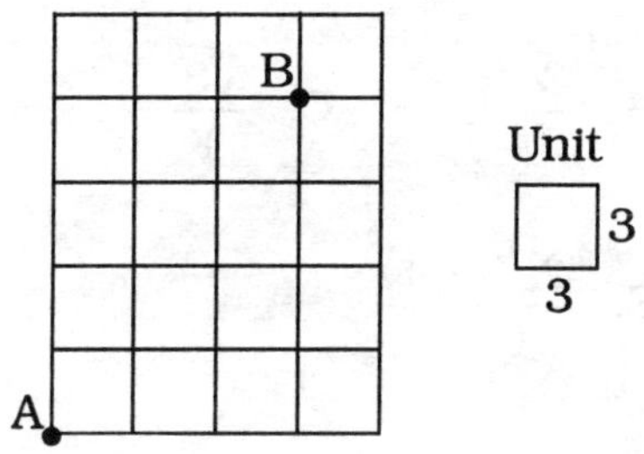


In the figure to the left, what is the length from A to B?

A. 5 B. $9\sqrt{2}$ C. 15 D. $12\sqrt{2}$ E. 18

39. 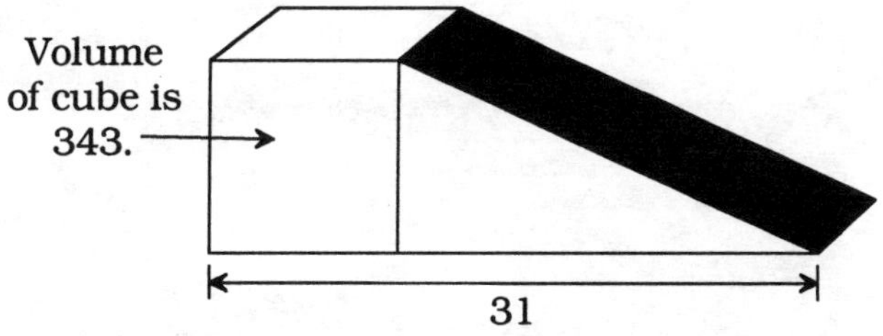


In the figure above, the volume of the cube is 343 cubic inches. What is the area of the shaded region in square inches?

A. 135 B. 175 C. 225 D. 360 E. 600

40. If the volume of a cube equals its surface area (units excluded), then what is the area of one side?

A. 6 B. 16 C. 36 D. 64 E. 216

41. 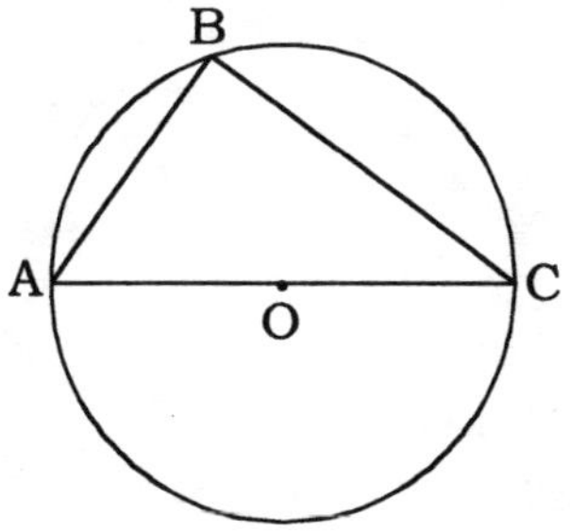


Triangle ABC is inscribed in the circle with center O. If AB = 12 and BC = 16, what is the area of the circle?

A. $10\pi$ B. $20\pi$ C. $100\pi$ D. $400\pi$

E. cannot be determined

42.

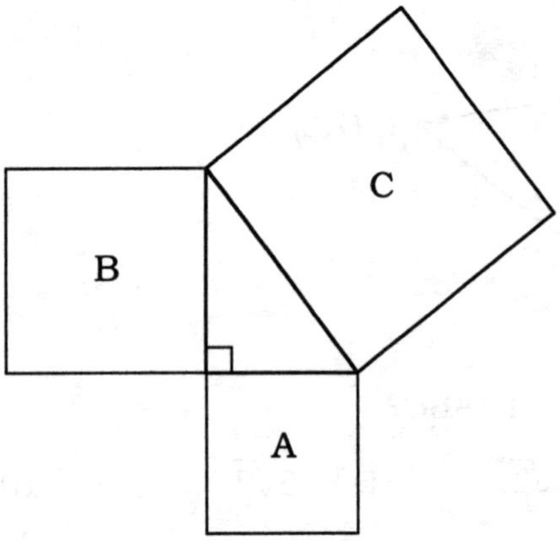


A, B and C are squares. If the ratio of C to A is 4:1, what is the ratio of B to A?

A. $\frac{\sqrt{3}}{2}$ B. $\frac{3}{2}$ C. $\frac{\sqrt{3}}{1}$

D. $\frac{2\sqrt{3}}{1}$ E. $\frac{3}{1}$

43.

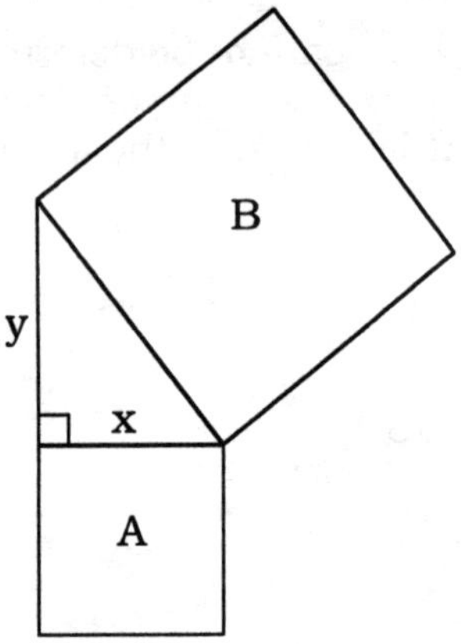


A and B are squares. If the ratio of B to A is 4:1, what is the ratio of y to x?

A. $\frac{\sqrt{3}}{2}$ B. $\frac{3}{2}$ C. $\frac{\sqrt{3}}{1}$

D. $\frac{2\sqrt{3}}{2}$ E. $\frac{2\sqrt{3}}{1}$

## Solutions – Geometry

1. E The problem is a trap. It states $\ell_1 \parallel \ell_2$ but not $\ell_3 \parallel \ell_4$. Therefore, the answer is E, x cannot be determined.

2. C Let x be the radius of the small circle. Then the radius of the medium circle is 2x and the radius of the large circle is 4x. The area of the shaded region is the area of the medium minus the small circle or:

$$\pi(2x)^2 - \pi x^2 = \pi 4x^2 - \pi x^2 = 3\pi x^2$$

The area of the large circle is $\pi(4x)^2 = 16\pi x^2$. The fraction shaded is then:

$$\frac{3\pi x^2}{16\pi x^2} = \frac{3}{16}$$

3. C Since AC = BC, then $\Delta$ABC is isosceles and $\angle$ACB = 100°. From this, $\angle$BCD = 80° (supplementary). Now since BD = CD, then $\Delta$BCD is also isosceles and $\angle$BDC = 20°.

4. B SOLUTION 1: The volume of the water in the tank = $5 \times 3 \times 2 = 30$.

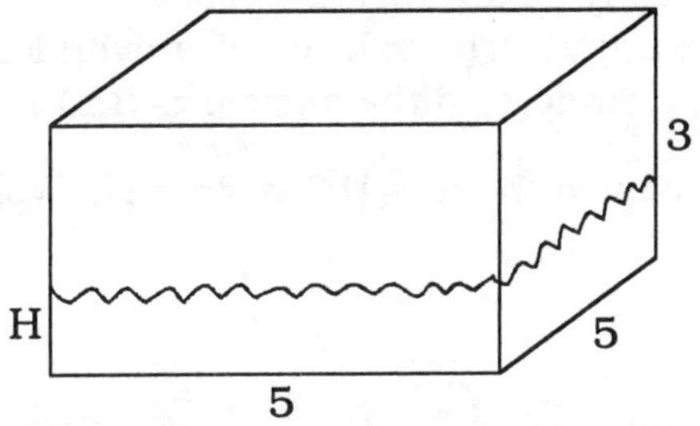


The picture above represents the tank flipped on its largest side and H is the height of the water. Since the volume of the water is 30 it follows:

$$30 = 5 \times 5 \times H$$

$$30 = 25 \times H$$

$$\frac{30}{25} = H$$

$$\frac{6}{5} = H$$

SOLUTION 2: Since the original height of the tank is 5 and the water is 2, the tank is $\frac{2}{5}$ full. When turned onto the biggest side, the height is 3.

$\frac{2}{5}$ of 3 = $\frac{6}{5}$.

5. D Since the area of the 3 circles is $108\pi$, we have :

$$3\pi r^2 = 108\pi$$
$$r^2 = 36 \qquad \text{Dividing by } 3\pi.$$
$$r = 6$$

Each side of the triangle equals 2r. This gives a total of 6r for the triangle or $6 \times 6 = 36$.

6. C Since the area of the square is 16, each side is equal to 4. It follows that if AD = 4, then since $\Delta ADE$ is an isosceles, 45°-45°-90°, right triangle, DE = 4. Also since $\Delta DEF$ is a 30°-60°-90° right triangle, $EF = 4\sqrt{3}$. The area of $\Delta DEF$ is:

$$\text{The area of } \Delta DEF = \frac{4 \times 4\sqrt{3}}{2}$$
$$= 8\sqrt{3}$$

7. C The volume of the rectangular portion of the pillar is area of base times height or $10 \times 36 = 360$. This already eliminates answers A, D and E. The 4 half cylinders equals 2 whole cylinders. The volume of a cylinder is $\pi r^2 H$ or $\pi(3)^2 \times 10 = 90\pi$. But there are 2 cylinders so the answer is $360 + 180\pi$

8. C The volume of the first container is $\pi r^2 h$ or $\pi(1)^2 2 = 2\pi$. The volume of its contents is $\frac{3}{4} \times 2\pi = \frac{6\pi}{4} = \frac{3\pi}{2}$.

The volume of the second container is $\pi\left(\frac{1}{4}\right)^2 4 = \frac{4\pi}{16} = \frac{\pi}{4}$. The number of second containers which can e filled can be found by dividing the first by the second or $\frac{\frac{3\pi}{2}}{\frac{\pi}{4}} = \frac{3\pi}{2} \cdot \frac{4}{\pi} = 6$.

9. D

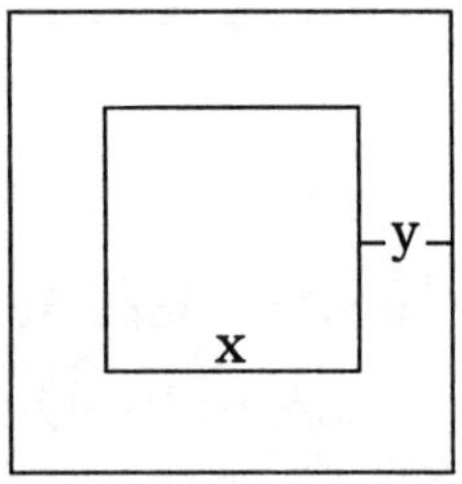


The area of the border can be found by subtracting the area of the inner square from the area of the outer square. One side of the outside square equals x + 2y (add y to both sides of x), so we have:

$$(x+2y)^2 - x^2 = x^2 + 4xy + 4y^2 - x^2 \qquad \text{expand by FOIL}$$
$$= 4xy + 4y^2 \qquad \text{cancel } x^2$$
$$= 4y(x+y) \qquad \text{factor out } 4y$$

10. D The area of ADEC can be found by subtracting the area of $\Delta BDE$ from $\Delta ABC$.

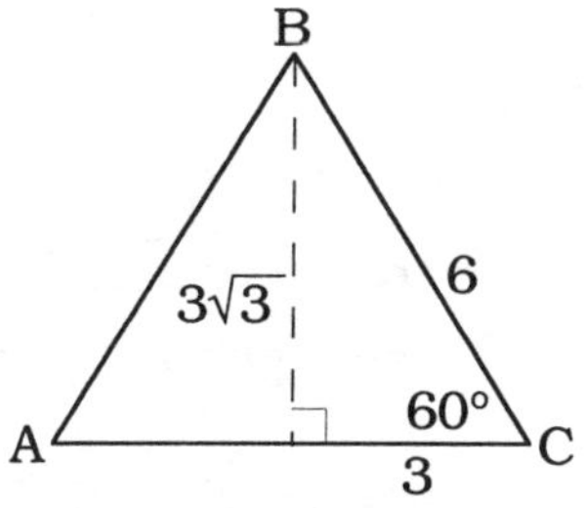


Drawing an altitude from B to AC, creates a 30°-60°-90° right triangle, which gives the altitude to be $3\sqrt{3}$.

The area of $\Delta ABC = \frac{6 \times 3\sqrt{3}}{2} = 9\sqrt{3}$.

$\Delta BDE$ is also a 30°-60°-90° right triangle. Its area is: $\frac{2 \times 2\sqrt{3}}{2} = 2\sqrt{3}$.

$\Delta ABC - \Delta BDE = 9\sqrt{3} - 2\sqrt{3} = 7\sqrt{3}$.

11. D The circumference of the sprocket is $\pi D = 9\pi$. Since there are 54 teeth, $9\pi = 54t$, $t = \frac{9\pi}{54} = \frac{\pi}{6}$.

12. A The ladder, ground and the wall of the house form a right triangle:

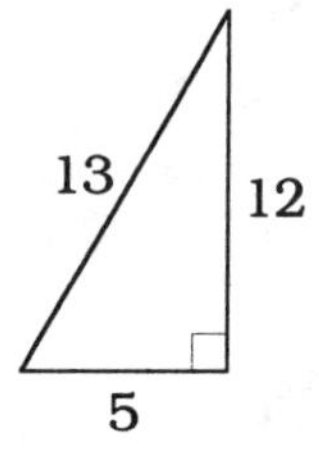


This is 5-12-13 Pythagorean Triple, so the height of the house is 12. If the ladder is extended so that it is 4 more feet from the house, this forms a new triangle and a new Pythagorean Triple 9-12-15. 15 - 13 = 2, so the ladder must be extended 2 feet.

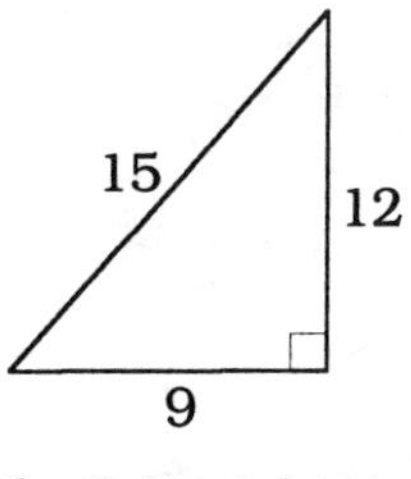


13. E 100 yards = 300 feet, so the 2 straightaways equal 600 ft. The 2 ends can be put together to form a circle with a diameter of 100 feet. The circumference $C = \pi D$ or $100\pi$. The combined answer is $600 + 100\pi$.

14. C The difference around the outside of the track from the inside is the difference in the distance around the 2 semicircles (the straightaways are the same). The outside distance is the circle with diameter 100: $C = \pi D$ or $100\pi$. The inside distance is the circle with diameter 50: $C = \pi D = 50\pi$. The difference is then $100\pi - 50\pi = 50\pi$.

15. B

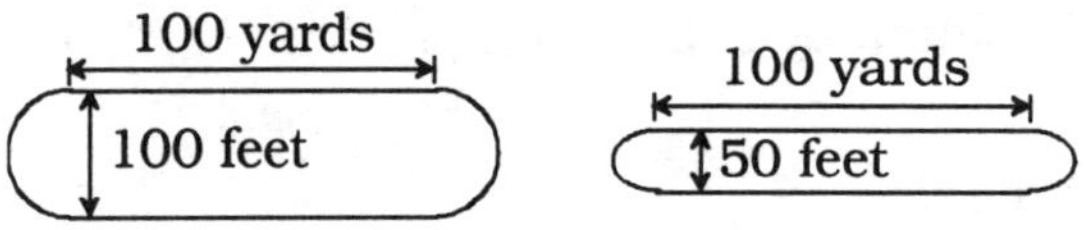


Each figure can be divided into a rectangle and a circle.

Area of Rectangle:

$100 \times 300 = 30{,}000$

Area of Circle:

$\pi r^2 = \pi(50)^2$

$= 2500\pi$

Area of Rectangle:

$50 \times 300 = 15{,}000$

Area of Circle:

$\pi r^2 = \pi(25)^2$

$= 625\pi$

The difference is $15{,}000 + 1{,}875\pi$.

16. C ABC is a 9-12-15 Pythagorean Triple. Therefore AC = 15. The area of a triangle is $\frac{bh}{2}$. This could be:

$$\frac{AB \times BC}{2} \quad \text{OR} \quad \frac{AC \times BD}{2}$$

It follows that:

$$AB \times BC = AC \times BD$$
$$12 \times 9 = 15 \times BD$$
$$108 = 15BD$$
$$\frac{108}{15} = BD$$
$$\frac{36}{5} = BD$$

17. B The sum of the angles of any polygon is (S - 2)(180) where S is the number of sides. (10 – 2)(180) = 1,440.

$$(4 - 2)(180) = 360$$
$$\frac{1{,}440}{360} = 4$$

18. E

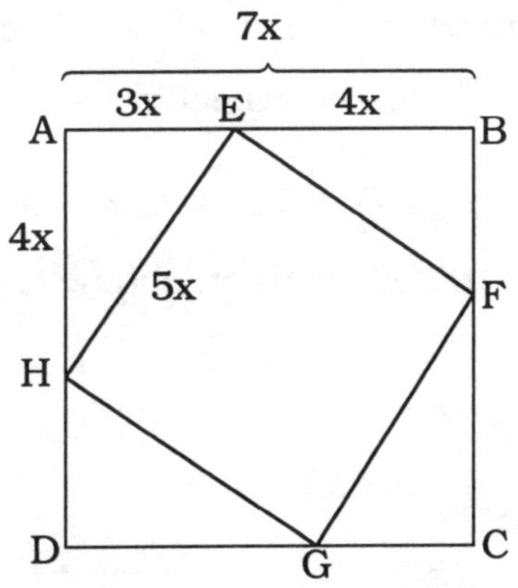


From the ratio $\frac{AE}{EB} = \frac{3}{4}$, let AE = 3x and EB = 4x. Since ABCD is a square, EB = AH. Now ΔAEH is a right triangle 3x, 4x, 5x, so the length of EH is 5x.

$$\frac{(5x)^2}{(7x)^2} = \frac{25x^2}{49x^2} = \frac{25}{49}$$

19. C

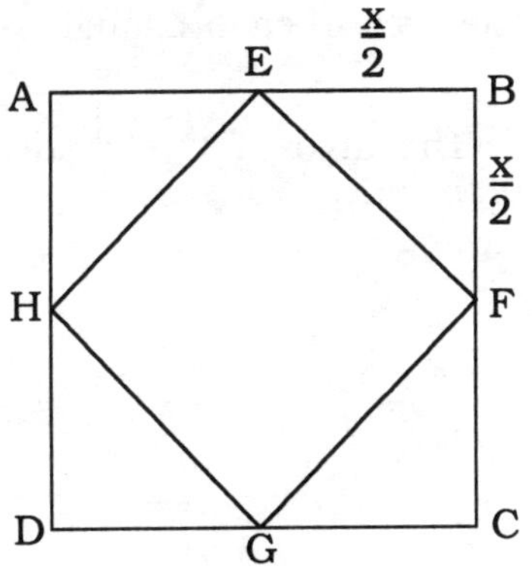


If AB = x, then EB = $\frac{x}{2}$ and BF = $\frac{x}{2}$. ΔEBF is a 45°-45°-90° right isosceles triangle and therefore EF = $\frac{x}{2}\sqrt{2} = \frac{x\sqrt{2}}{2}$.

20. B

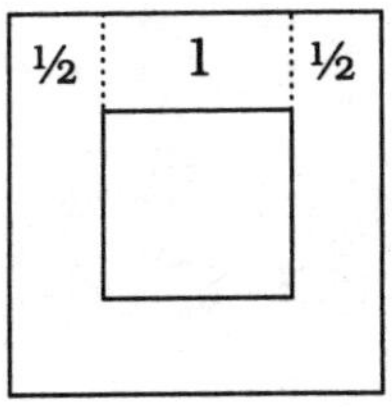


The small square with area 1 sq. in. has a side length of 1 in. From the drawing above the length of a side of the big square is 2. The area of the big square is 4 and the ratio of small to big is $\frac{1}{4}$.

21. C Since a spoke is a radius, the circumference of a whole wheel would be $2\pi r = 2 \times \pi \times 12 = 24\pi$. But only $\frac{2}{3}$ of the wheel exists around, and therefore, the circular portion of the sign is $\frac{2}{3} \times 24\pi = 16\pi$. The triangle at the bottom of the figure is an isosceles triangle with an obtuse angle of 120°, $\frac{1}{3}$ of 360°.

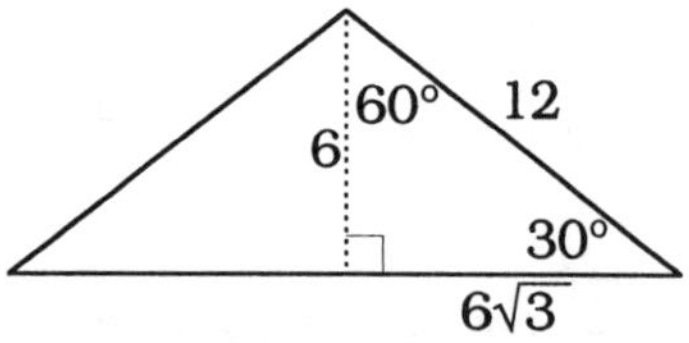


If an altitude is drawn, we have a 30°-60°-90° right triangle and the side opposite the 60 angle equals $6\sqrt{3}$. This makes the base of the sign $12\sqrt{3}$ and the perimeter $12\sqrt{3} + 16\pi$.

22. E The area of the square is $(3x)^2 = 9x^2$. The area of each triangle is $\frac{x^2}{2}$. The area of the 4 triangles is $\frac{4x^2}{2} = 2x^2$. The area of the shaded region is $9x^2 - 2x^2 = 7x^2$.

23. D

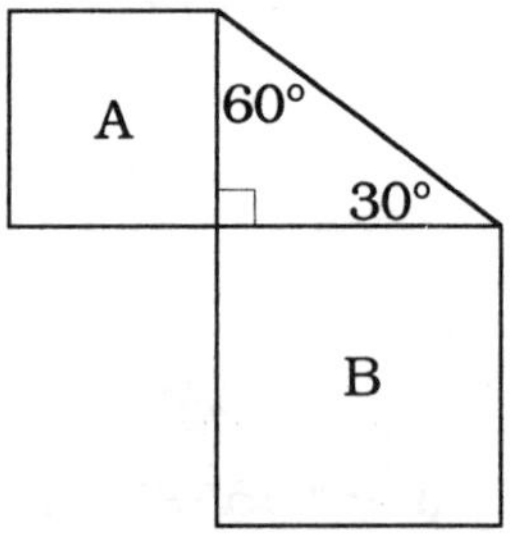


The triangle is a 30°-60°-90° right triangle and the side opposite the 30° angle is $\sqrt{9} = 3$. Then for the side opposite the 60° angle is $3\sqrt{3}$. The area of square B is then: $(3\sqrt{3})(3\sqrt{3}) = 27$.

24. B

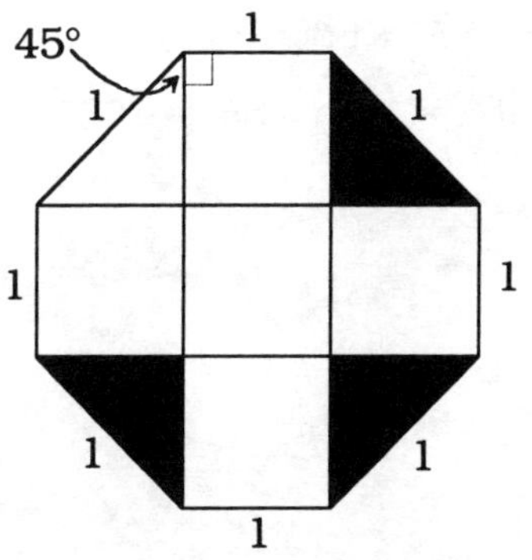


A regular octagon has angles of 135°:

$$\frac{(S-2)(180°)}{S} = \frac{(8-2)(180°)}{8} = 135°$$

The grid then divides each angle into 90° and 45°. This makes each triangle a 45°-45°-90° right triangle.

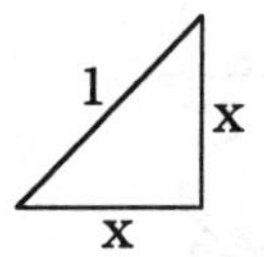


Now let x be a leg and we have:

$$x^2 + x^2 = 1^2$$

$$2x^2 = 1$$

$$x^2 = \frac{1}{2}$$

$$x = \sqrt{\frac{1}{2}}$$

$$x = \frac{1}{\sqrt{2}}$$

The area of a triangle is $\frac{bh}{2}$:

$$= \frac{\frac{1}{\sqrt{2}} \times \frac{1}{\sqrt{2}}}{2}$$

$$= \frac{\frac{1}{2}}{2}$$

$$= \frac{1}{4}$$

There are 4 triangles so $4 \times \frac{1}{4} = 1$.

25. B

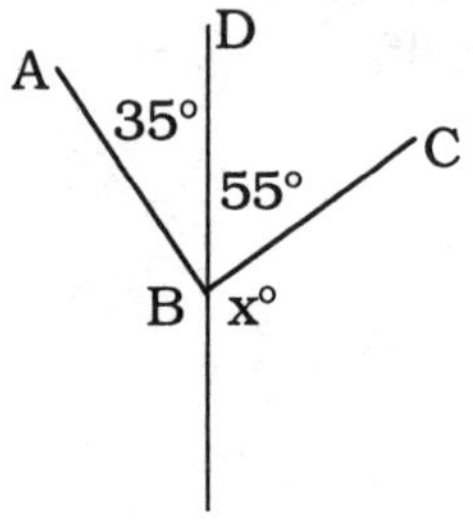


Since $\angle ABD = 35°$ and $\angle ABC = 90°$,

then $\angle DBC = 90° - 35° = 55°$.

It then follows that $x = 180° - 55° = 125°$.

26. D

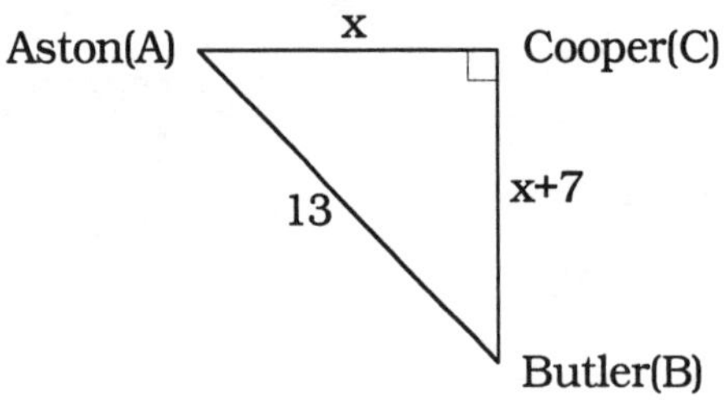


The drawing above represents the 3 towns as stated. If we let AC = x, then BC = x + 7 and $(AC)^2 + (BC)^2 = 13^2$ or:

$$x^2 + (x + 7)^2 = 13^2$$

$$x^2 + (x + 7)(x + 7) = 169$$

$$x^2 + x^2 + 14x + 49 = 169$$

$$2x^2 + 14x - 120 = 0$$

$$2(x^2 + 7x - 60) = 0$$

$$(x + 12)(x - 5) = 0$$

Since distance must be positive, x = 5 and x + 7 = 12.

Note: a hypotenuse of 13 could imply a 5-12-13 Pythagorean triple. This would then make x = 5 and it would then follow that x + 7 would indeed be 12.

27. A

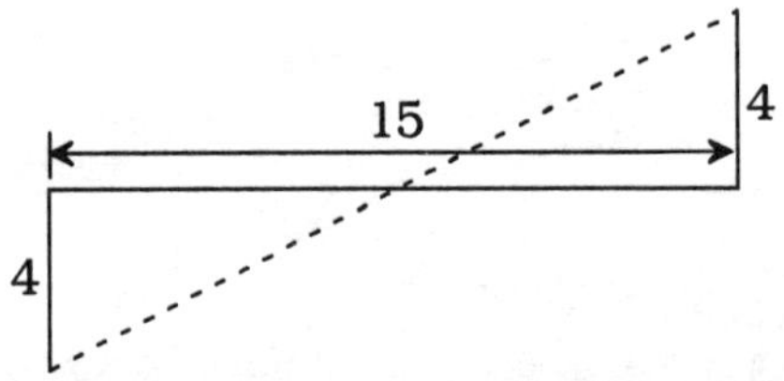


The picture above represents the routes of Dave and Alice as stated. It can be rearranged into the right triangle below:

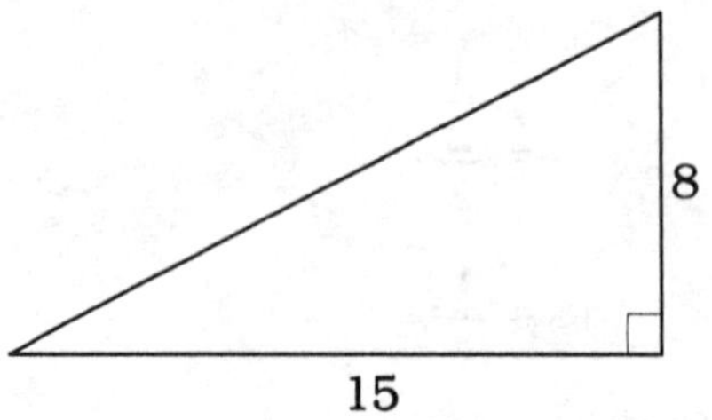


Identifying the 8-15-17 right triangle, Alice traveled 17 miles.

28. D Since A and B are on the x axis, AB is determined by subtracting the x coordinates of each point, therefore AB = Q - 2. The height of $\Delta ABC$ is the positive distance from C to the x-axis. This would be the absolute value of the y coordinate of C, which is $|S|$, but since S is negative, $|S| = -S$. The correct answer is D, $\frac{-S(Q-2)}{2}$.

29. D SOLUTION 1:

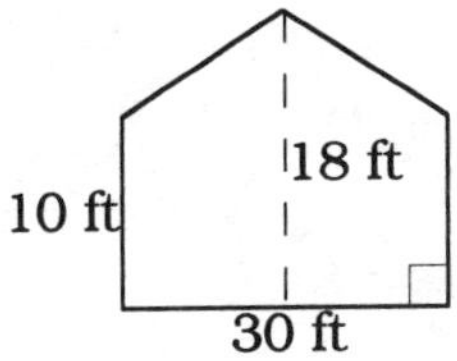


The figure can be divided into 2 equal trapezoids. The area equals:

$\frac{1}{2}(b_1 + b_2)h = \frac{1}{2}(10 + 18)15 = 210$. Therefore, the total area = 420.

SOLUTION 2:

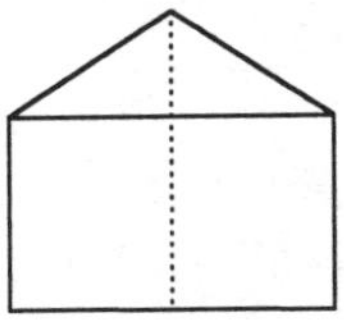

The figure can be divided into a triangle and a rectangle. The area of the rectangle is $10 \times 30 = 300$. The area of the triangle is $\frac{1}{2} \times 30 \times 8 = 120$. The total is 420.

30. D

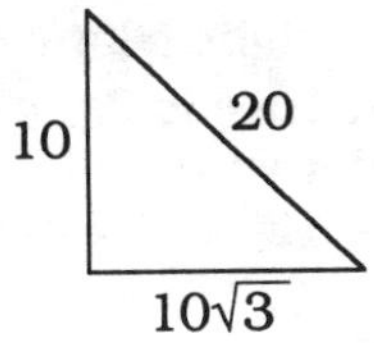


Rope A forms a right triangle with the hypotenuse twice one leg. Therefore it is a 30°-60°-90° triangle and the other leg equals $10\sqrt{3}$.

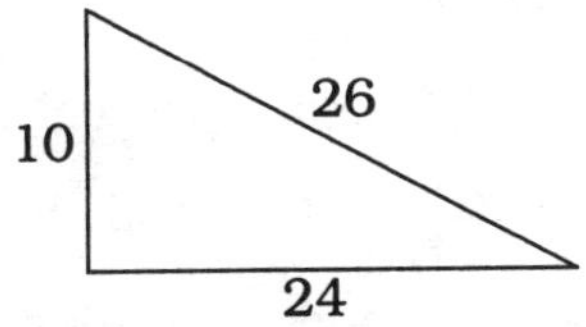


The second triangle is twice the Pythagorean Triple 5-12-13. Therefore the leg is 24 and the answer is D, $24 - 10\sqrt{3}$.

31. D $\frac{135°}{360°} = \frac{3}{8}$, which is the amount of the circle missing. Therefore $\frac{5}{8}$ remains:

$$\frac{5}{8} \times 24\pi = 15\pi$$

To find the radius we use:

$$2\pi r = 24\pi$$

$$r = 12$$

Since the angle is formed by 2 radii, the total perimeter is $15\pi + 24$.

32. D Area of a triangle equals $\frac{bh}{2}$ or $\frac{A(2A+2)}{2} = \frac{2A(A+1)}{2} = A(A+1)$

Now: $A(A + 1) = 30$

$A^2 + A - 30 = 0$ solve as a quadratic

$(A + 6)(A - 5) = 0$

Since A must be positive, A = 5.

$B = 2(5) + 2$

$= 12$

We now have a 5-12-13 triangle and C = 13.

33. D SOLUTION 1:

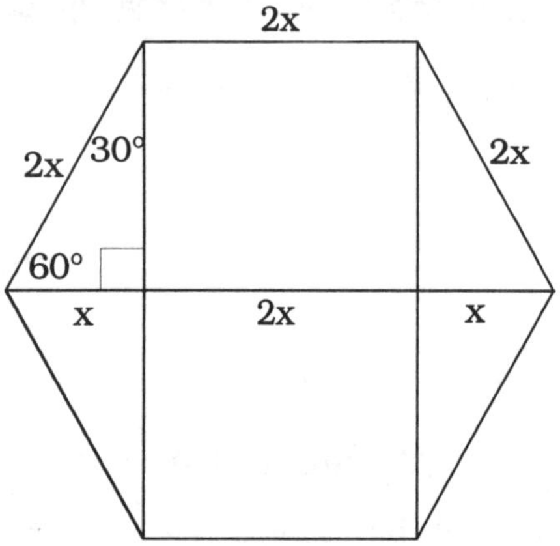


The size of each angle of the hexagon can be calculated using the formula (S - 2)(180°) = (6 - 2)(180°) = 720°. Then dividing by 6, each angle equals 120°. Drawing an altitude, we create a 30°-60°-90° right triangle. If we let the side opposite the 30° angle be x, then the hypotenuse is 2x and therefore each side of the hexagon is 2x. From this we can derive the distance across as x + 2x + x = 4x. But this equals 12, therefor 4x = 12, and x = 3. One side is then 2 × 3 = 6 and 6 sides is 6 × 6 = 36.

SOLUTION 2:

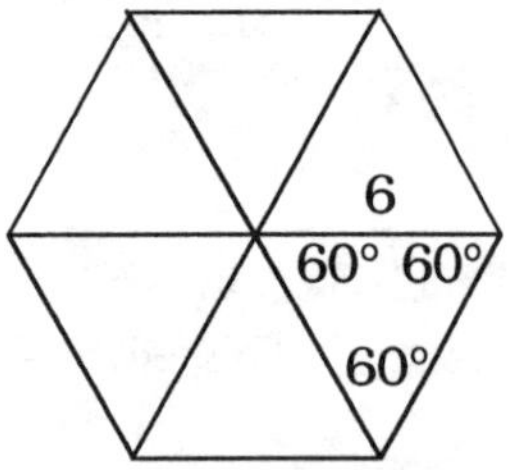


Drawing 3 diagonals creates 6 isosceles triangles. The central angle is $\frac{360°}{60} = 60°$ and therefore each triangle is equilateral. Since one diagonal equals 12, one side of a triangle equals 6 and 6 × 6 = 36.

34. C The shadow of an object is proportional to its height, therefore $\frac{20}{8} = \frac{H}{24}$ is the proportion. Since 24 is 3 times 8, A must be 3 times 20 which equals 60.

35. C

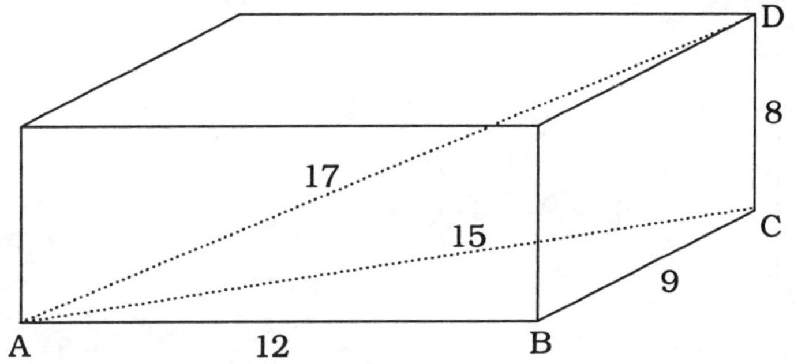


$\triangle ABC$ is a 9-12-15 right triangle, so AC = 15. This gives $\triangle ACD$ as an 8-15-17 right triangle, so AD = 17.

36. C

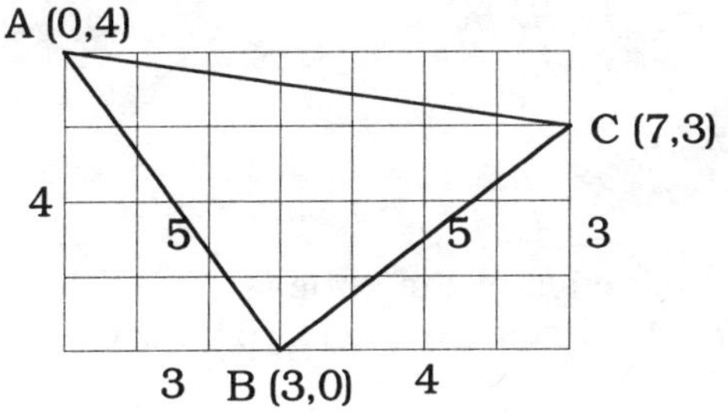


AB can be calculated by forming a 3-4-5 right triangle, so AB = 5. Similarly BC can also be found by forming a 3-4-5 right triangle. AC can be found by the Pythagorean Theorem:

$$1^2 + 7^2 = (AC)^2$$

$$50 = (AC)^2,$$

$$\text{and } AC = \sqrt{50} = 5\sqrt{2}$$

The answer is $10 + 5\sqrt{2}$.

37. C

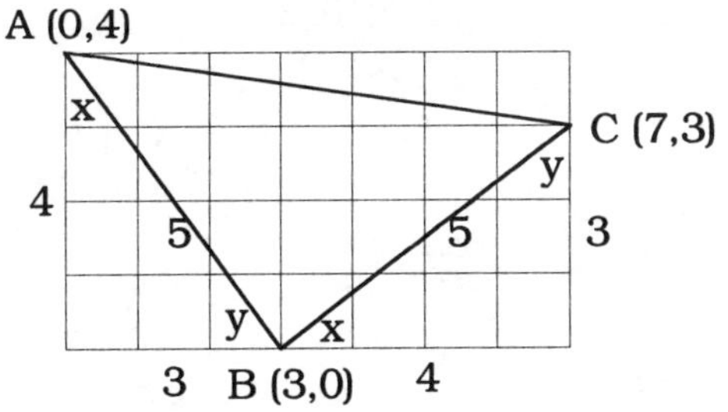


There are two 3-4-5 right triangles labeled above. If we label $\angle x$ opposite the side of length 3 and $\angle y$ opposite the side of length 4, we see that $\angle y + \angle ABC + \angle x = 180°$ (straight angle). It can further be seen that from either 3-4-5 right triangle that $\angle x + \angle y = 90°$, and therefore $\angle ABC = 90°$.

38. C

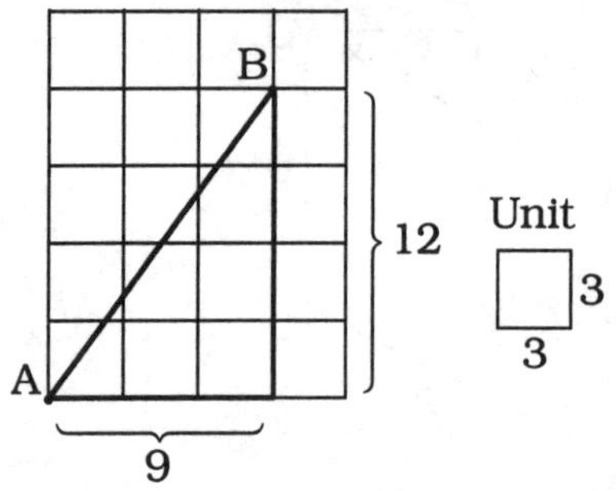


AB is a diagonal line segment. By making a right triangle as shown above, AB is part of a 9-12-15 right triangle and AB = 15.

39. B

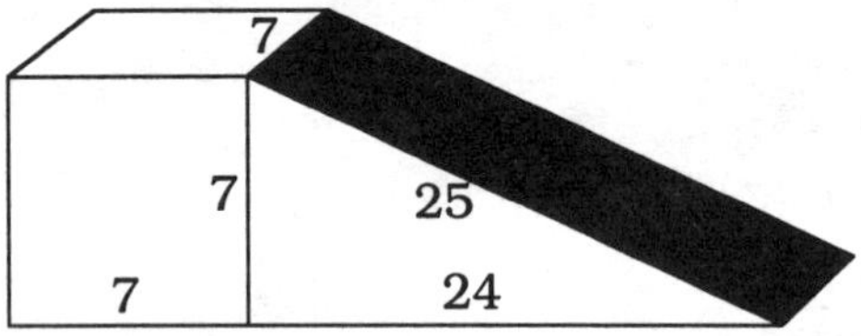


The cube root of 343 is 7, so each edge of the cube is 7. Subtracting 7 from 31 equals 24. This gives a 7-24-25 right triangle. The area of the shaded rectangle is $7 \times 25 = 175$.

40. C The volume of a cube is $S^3$. The area of one side is $S^2$ and the surface area of a cube is $6S^2$. Since they are equal we have:

$$S^3 = 6S^2$$

$$S^3 - 6S^2 = 0$$

$$S^2(S - 6) = 0$$

Since S cannot equal 0, $S - 6 = 0$ and $S = 6$. The area of one side is then $6 \times 6 = 36$.

41. C

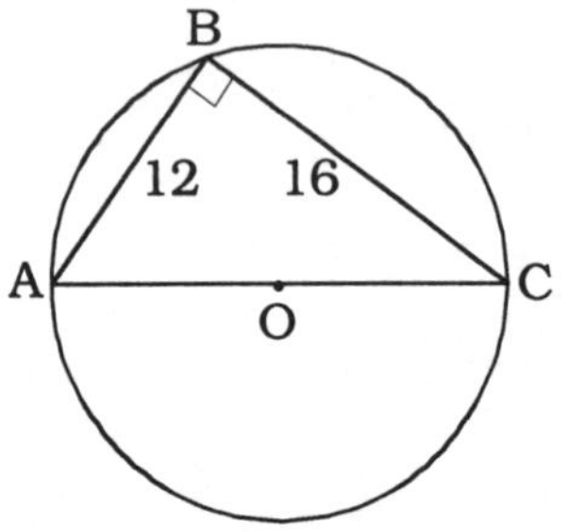


Since AC is a diameter, and an inscribed angle equals half its arc, $\angle B = 90°$ (a right angle).

Therefore $\Delta ABC$ is a 12-16-20 right triangle and AC = 20. This gives a radius of 10. The area is $\pi r^2 = \pi(10)^2 = 100\pi$.

42. E For any right triangle $A^2 + B^2 = C^2$. If we let the area of A be $x^2$, then the area of C is $4x^2$. We now have $x^2 + B^2 = 4x^2$ or $B^2 = 3x^2$. The ratio of B to A is $\frac{3x^2}{x^2} = \frac{3}{1}$.

43. C

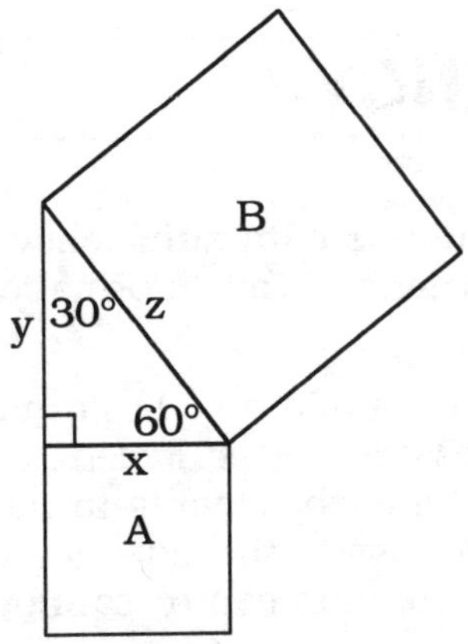


From the drawing $A = x^2$. Then, since B is four times A, $z^2 = 4x^2$ and $z = 2x$. This makes the triangle a 30°-60°-90° since the hypotenuse is twice the leg. The side opposite the 60 is then $x\sqrt{3}$. So $y = x\sqrt{3}$. The ratio of $\frac{y}{x}$ is then $\frac{x\sqrt{3}}{x} = \frac{\sqrt{3}}{1}$.

# DATA SUFFICIENCY

A portion of the quantitative section of the **GMAT** contains data sufficiency questions. These are designed to measure your ability to determine if the information given is sufficient to enable you to solve a specific problem.

Each question is composed of a problem and two pieces of additional information. The two pieces of additional information, potentially necessary and sufficient to lead to a unique solution, are in the form of two statements. Your objective is to decide which statement, or statement combination, is sufficient to answer the question. **DO NOT** solve the problem. The question asks only whether a solution can or cannot be found, using a combination of the supplied statements.

First determine what you need to solve the problem; what is missing from the problem statement that must be supplied? Then examine the two statements to see if what is lacking is supplied. If not, the answer is that there is not sufficient information for a unique solution. If what is lacking is supplied somewhere in the two statements, then the sufficiency of the two statements must be further analyzed.

Keep in mind that even if a question is accompanied by an illustration:

1. No inferences regarding length, measure, etc. may be made unless you are instructed to do so.
2. The illustration applies to the initial question only, not to the additional statements.

EXAMPLE: Is ABCD a parallelogram?

1. AB is parallel to CD.
2. AB = CD

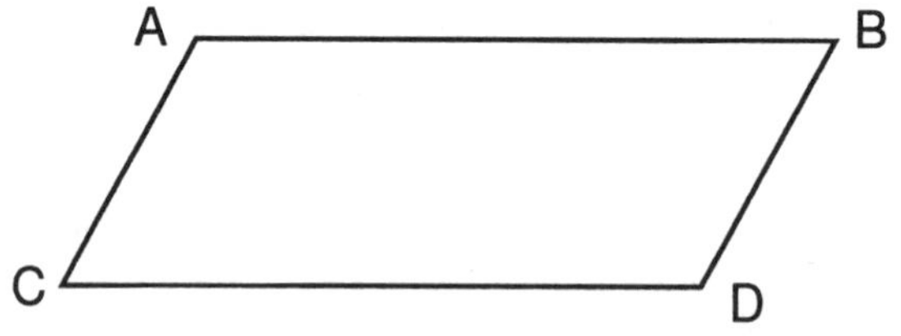


Although the illustration appears to be a parallelogram, no conclusion should be reached based on the figure exclusively.

ANALYSIS: The problem presents the question: what are the properties of a parallelogram?

Statement (1) alone is insufficient to prove the quadrilateral is a parallelogram. If two sides are parallel, the figure is at least a trapezoid but not necessarily a parallelogram.

Statement (2) alone is insufficient as well. Two opposite sides being equal in length is not sufficient to make a quadrilateral a parallelogram.

The combination of (1) and (2) provides sufficient information according to the theorem: "If two sides of a quadrilateral are parallel and equal, then the quadrilateral is a parallelogram."

The solution to this problem was achieved only by knowing the concepts. Data sufficiency requires rapid recall of principles to tersely stated problems.

All data sufficiency questions have five multiple-choice answers. You must click on the oval preceding the correct combination of statements. Here are the five possible answers.

(A) If statement (1) ALONE is sufficient, but statement (2) alone is not sufficient to answer the question asked.

(B) If statement (2) ALONE is sufficient, but statement (1) alone is not sufficient to answer the question asked.

(C) If BOTH statements (1) and (2) together are sufficient, but NEITHER ALONE is adequate.

(D) If EACH statement ALONE is sufficient. Either is adequate to answer the question independent of the other.

(E) If the question cannot be answered, even if (1) and/or (2) are used. Either there is not enough information or there is uncertainty in the answers which statements (1) and/or (2) provide.

The correct answer to the parallelogram problem is (C). You should keep in mind that all data sufficiency questions only ask you to determine what is sufficient; no numerical solution is requested.

For the **GMAT CAT** there is a strategy to keep in mind. If one of the two statements is clearly sufficient or insufficient, some answers can be eliminated, increasing the likelihood of a correct guess. For instance, in the previous problem statement (1) is certainly not sufficient. Answer (A) is therefore incorrect, and additionally answer (D) is also wrong. The only good candidates are (B), (C), and (E). Further if it is clear that statement (2) is insufficient, by itself, (B) is eliminated and the answer is either (C) or (E). The odds now are a very attractive 50%. Even if you are not certain that (1) and (2) together are sufficient, your odds are much higher to guess the correct answer. More on this strategy is to follow.

EXAMPLE: A square is bounded by two semicircles, forming a "region". What is the area of the region?

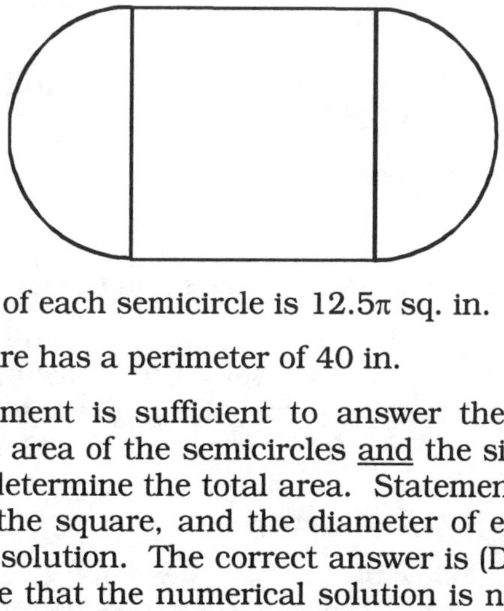

(1) The area of each semicircle is $12.5\pi$ sq. in.

(2) The square has a perimeter of 40 in.

ANALYSIS: Either statement is sufficient to answer the question. Statement (1) provides the area of the semicircles and the side of the square making it possible to determine the total area. Statement (2) provides the length of one side of the square, and the diameter of each semicircle, which also leads to the solution. The correct answer is (D); either statement may be used. Notice that the numerical solution is not requested; although the correct answer is $(100 + 25\pi)$ sq. in.

Let's say you are not certain that (1) is sufficient by itself, but are certain that (2) is. What answers can be eliminated? First (A) can be eliminated, since (B) is a possibility. (E) can be eliminated because you know that it can be solved. Further (C) can be eliminated since you know that (2) is sufficient alone. Now your odds once again are 50%! The only good candidates are (B), (2) alone, or (D), (1) or (2) alone. Now you decide whether you think (1) is sufficient alone or insufficient alone. Then choose either (B) or (D).

You see, you don't have to know it all or know it cold, to demonstrate that you know something. From what you do know eliminate other answers, then consult your feelings or take your best hunch. Once you have applied your knowledge and reduced the number of answers, you have increased your odds. Since you must answer every question on the **GMAT CAT**, it is best to reduce the number of answers and then apply your best instinct.

Another pertinent point is that knowledge of the precise equation is not needed to get the correct answer. In the previous problem you just need to know that given the area of the semicircle you can find the radius or diameter uniquely, and then use the diameter to determine the area of the square unambiguously. That is all! You don't need to know whether you multiply or divide by $\pi$, or if you need the square or square root.

As you proceed through the data sufficiency section, keep in mind that some questions cannot be answered. The stated information is insufficient; more data specific to the problem would be needed. For example:

What was the percent decrease of annual earnings of the XYZ Company?

(1) Last year's earnings were greater than this year's earnings.

(2) The sum of last year's and this year's earnings are $150,000.

ANALYSIS: This question is unanswerable; even if both statements are used. There is insufficient data to find a solution. Therefore, the answer is (E).

Some data sufficiency questions have statements that lead to inconsistencies. In this case, no specific answer is obtained because different answers are possible.

EXAMPLE: Is $r > s$?

(1) $2 < r < 9$

(2) $0 < s < 7$

ANALYSIS: From statement (1), r lies between 2 and 9 (non-inclusive). From statement (2), s lies between 0 and 7 (non-inclusive).

If $r = 7$ and $s = 2$ then $r > s$.

If $r = 3$ and $s = 6$ then $r < s$.

Therefore, an inconsistency exists and the answer must be (E).

The task of analyzing each question is made more difficult by the possibility that yet more information is necessary to uniquely solve the problem. Your ability to foresee the process of solution without actually solving the problem is what is being determined. Therefore your mastery of mathematical concepts and methods of solution should be refined to help make finding the correct answer as easy as possible. Following is a set of sample test questions for data sufficiency.

Remember, while doing the following sample questions, to eliminate all answers which your knowledge precludes with certainly, then use your instincts to pick the best answer from what remains. Practicing your use of knowledge and instinct here will save you valuable time when you take the test. Since the **GMAT CAT** does not let you skip questions, answer each one as soon as you know that you have applied your best knowledge and best instincts. To spend any additional time is pointless. Use what you know to its fullest, for what you don't know use your best instinct, then mark the best answer, and move to the next question.

## Sample Data Sufficiency Test Questions

Each of the following problems contains a question and two additional statements. Your objective is to decide which statement or statement combination has sufficient data to answer the initial question. Keep in mind that no inferences should be made about any figure supplied with the question unless you are provided with specific information.

You are not asked to actually solve the question, only to decide which data is sufficient. At the conclusion of the section the answers are supplied and each problem is analyzed and solved (if possible). Read the solution for each carefully, because data sufficiency represents a cross-section of arithmetic, algebra and geometry.

Possible answers to choose:

(A) If (1) alone is sufficient and (2) alone is insufficient.
(B) If (2) alone is sufficient and (1) alone is insufficient.
(C) If (1) and (2) together are sufficient, but neither alone is sufficient.
(D) If each statement alone is sufficient.
(E) If the problem cannot be solved uniquely; (1) and (2) are insufficient.

1. What is the area of the rectangle?

(1) X + Y = 15

(2) X is twice as long as Y.

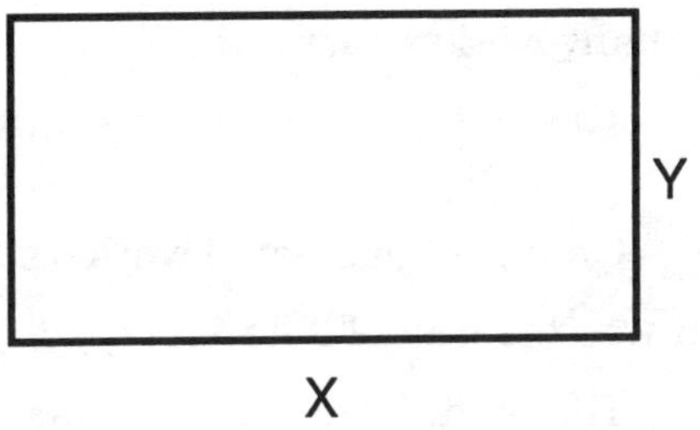


2. The right triangle shown has a hypotenuse of 10 meters. What is the length of $\overline{BC}$?

(1) AB is the longest side of triangle ABC.

(2) ∠A is $\frac{1}{2}$ the measure of ∠B.

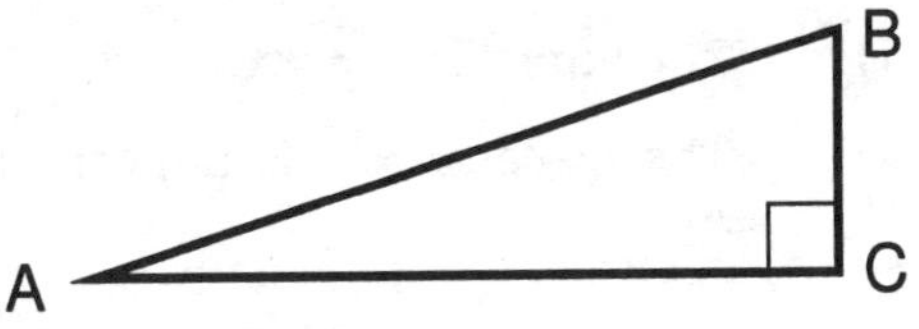


3. When will Y overtake X?

(1) X left 2 hours earlier than Y from the same place.

(2) X is traveling 10 MPH slower than Y.

4. What is the longest side of this triangle?

(1) The perimeter is 37.

(2) ∠R and ∠T are complementary.

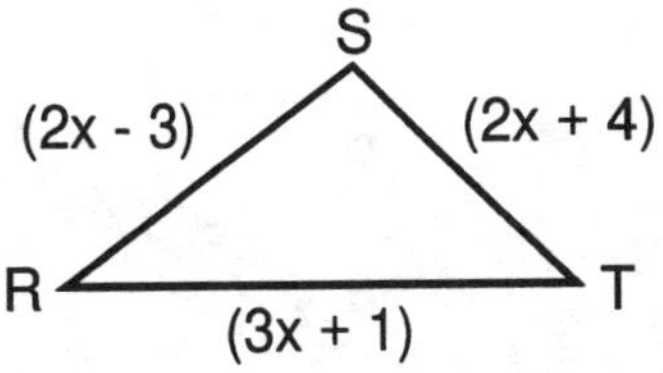


$x > \frac{3}{2}$

(A) If (1) alone is sufficient and (2) alone is insufficient.
(B) If (2) alone is sufficient and (1) alone is insufficient.
(C) If (1) and (2) together are sufficient, but neither alone is sufficient.
(D) If each statement alone is sufficient.
(E) If the problem cannot be solved uniquely; (1) and (2) are insufficient.

5. How old is Larry?

(1) The ratio of the present age of Larry:Joan is 5:4.

(2) 6 years ago Larry was as old as Joan is now.

6. Is triangle ABC a right triangle?

(1) AC is a diameter.

(2) AC < AB + BC

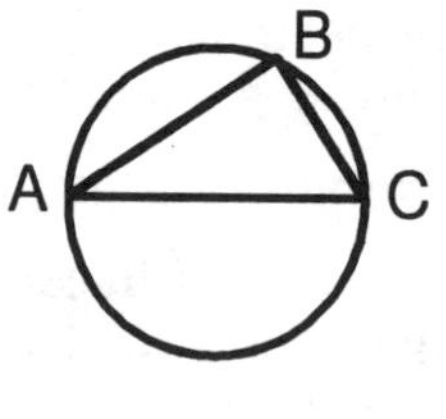


7. What is the ratio of X:Y?

(1) $X^2 - Y^2 = 36$

(2) $2X - 3Y = 0$

8. How many workers are required to unload a truck? (All work at the same rate).

(1) The amount of time presently required to unload a truck is 3 hours and 12 minutes.

(2) On a previous day 8 workers took 2 hours to unload a similar truck.

9. What was the cost of 2 dozen eggs?

(1) The profit based on cost was 15%.

(2) Each dozen contains 12 eggs.

10. Is the polygon shown an isosceles triangle?

(1) The sum of $\angle A + \angle C = 78$.

(2) The bisector of $\angle B$ is perpendicular to AC.

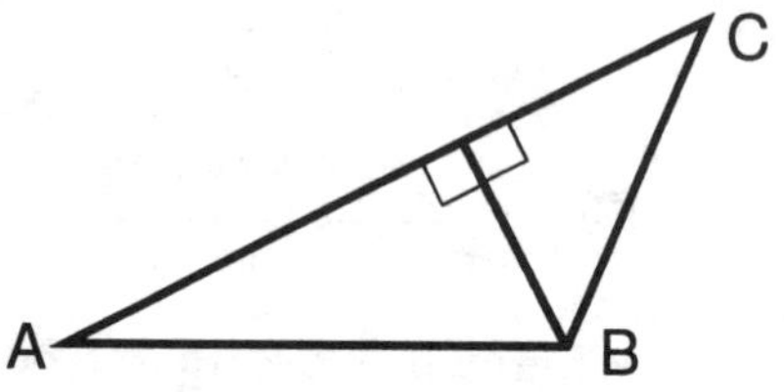


11. Is the integer X divisible by 6?

(1) X is divisible by 3.

(2) X is divisible by 12.

(A) If (1) alone is sufficient and (2) alone is insufficient.
(B) If (2) alone is sufficient and (1) alone is insufficient.
(C) If (1) and (2) together are sufficient, but neither alone is sufficient.
(D) If each statement alone is sufficient.
(E) If the problem cannot be solved uniquely; (1) and (2) are insufficient.

12. What is the area of rhombus ABCD?

(1) AB = 13 in.

(2) AC = 10 in.

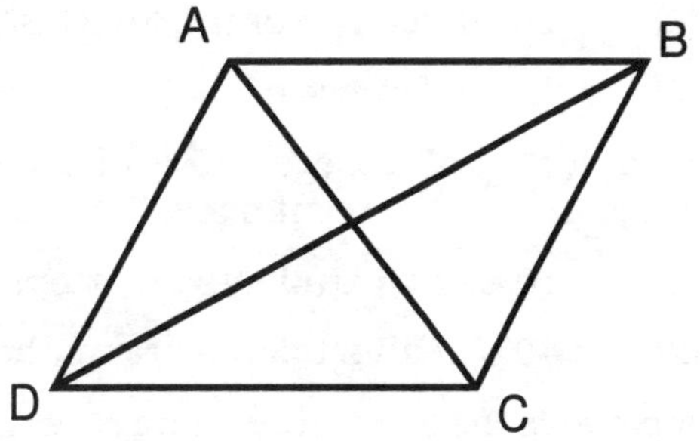


13. A man invests part of $4,000 for one year at 5%, the remainder at 6%. How much was invested at 5%?

(1) The total annual interest earned was $225.

(2) The investment at 5% earned more than the previous year's interest.

14. What is the surface area of a cube?

(1) The area of the base is 16 square feet.

(2) The diagonal of the cube, ED, is $4\sqrt{3}$ feet.

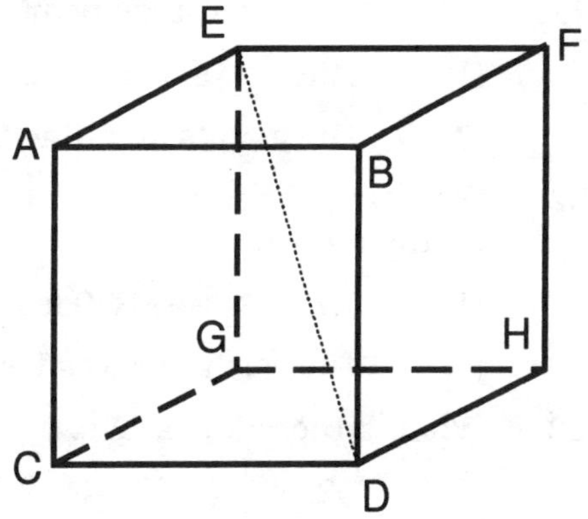


15. How many minutes are needed to fill an empty fish tank?

(1) 2/5 of the tank can be filled in one minute.

(2) The fish tank holds 20 gallons.

16. What is the area of the shaded region?

(1) Triangle AOB is equilateral.

(2) Arc AB = $4\pi$ cm

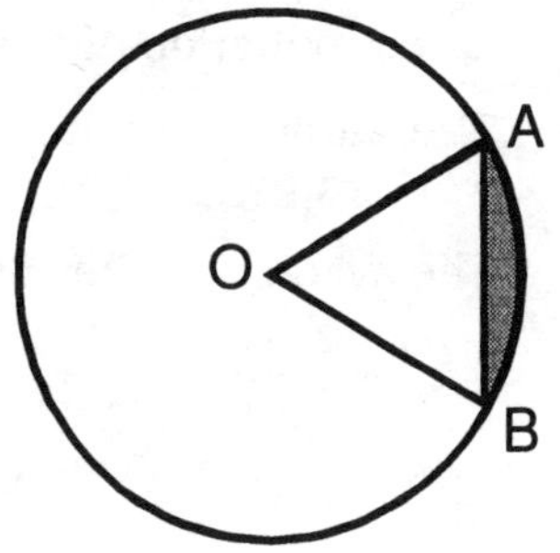


17. How much greater is the cost of an orange than an apple?

(1) The ratio of oranges:apples in 5 lb. bags of each is 3:2.

(2) Apples cost $.80/lb.

(A) If (1) alone is sufficient and (2) alone is insufficient.
(B) If (2) alone is sufficient and (1) alone is insufficient.
(C) If (1) and (2) together are sufficient, but neither alone is sufficient.
(D) If each statement alone is sufficient.
(E) If the problem cannot be solved uniquely; (1) and (2) are insufficient.

18. What is the sum of two integers?

(1) The difference of the integers is 5.

(2) The difference of their squares is 55.

19. In a technical college, 25% of all science majors elect to "minor" in another subject. What percent of students at the college study only science?

(1) 60% of all students are science majors.

(2) 40% of all students are mathematics majors.

20. A circle is inscribed in a square. What is the area of the shaded region?

(1) The circumference of the circle is $12\pi$ in.

(2) The ratio of the diagonal of the square to one side of the square = $\sqrt{2}:1$.

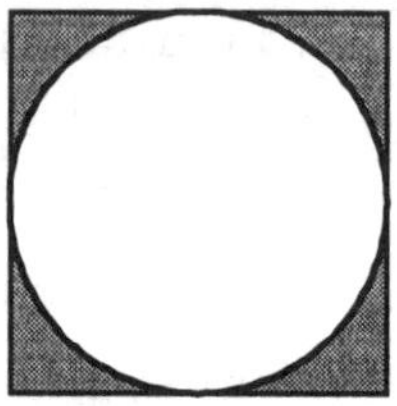

21. A 6 ft. tall man stands near a tree on a sunny day. How tall is the tree?

(1) The man's shadow is 1/5 as long as the height of the tree.

(2) The man is standing 20 feet from the tree.

22. What was the dealer cost of an item? It sold for $270, which was a 10% discount off the regular price.

(1) The cost was $50 less than the regular price.

(2) The sale price was less than the average of the cost and the regular price.

23. What is the value of X?

(1) $X^2 - 7X = -6$

(2) $X > 4$

24. What were the earnings of an accountant in 1982?

(1) The average earnings for 1980, 1981 and 1982 was $40,000.

(2) The 1982 earnings were 15% more than 1981.

25. What is the production of a factory per 5 day work week?

(1) The number of items produced daily is 400% times the number of workers.

(2) The average worker produces 20 items per week.

## Solutions to Sample Test Questions for Data Sufficiency

1. (C) Since X + Y = 15, and X = 2Y, then by substitution:

$2Y + Y = 15$, so $Y = 5$ and $X = 10$

The area = XY = 50

2. (B) Angle A + angle B = $90^0$. Since they are in a ratio of 1:2, a 30°-60°-90° triangle is formed.

Side BC = 1/2(10) = 5m.

The fact that the hypotenuse is the longest side provides no information to solve the problem.

3. (E) Since the distance traveled by both is the same, the following table of information is possible:

| | RATE | TIME | d |
|---|---|---|---|
| X | R | T | same |
| Y | R+10 | T-2 | same |

Considering that (Rate)(Time) = Distance:

For X: (R)(T) = Distance traveled, and

For Y: (R + 10)(T - 2) = Distance traveled.

Then R(T) = (R + 10)(T - 2). There are too many unknowns, and the question can not be solved.

4. (D) Statement (1) is sufficient because the value of X can be found:

$(2X-3) + (2X+4) + (3X+1) = 37$ Then $X = 5$ and each side may be compared. (The longest side is RT.)

Statement (2) implies that ∠S is a right angle. Since this is the largest angle, then $\overline{RT}$ is the longest side.

5. (C) Both statements are needed to complete this diagram.

| | PAST | PRESENT |
|---|---|---|
| Larry | $\frac{5}{4}X - 6$ | $\frac{5}{4}X$ |
| Joan | X-6 | X |

Solving $\frac{5}{4}X - 6 = X$

$$\frac{1}{4}X = 6$$

$$X = 24$$

Joan is 24, Larry is 30. Six years ago Joan was 18, Larry was 24.

6. (A) Statement (1) provides enough information. Angle ABC is a right angle, because it is inscribed in a semicircle. Statement (2) is too general since <u>all</u> triangles must have the sum of 2 sides greater than the third side.

7. (B) Statement (2) is rearranged: $2X-3Y = 0$.

Then 2X = 3Y. The ratio of $\frac{X}{Y} = \frac{3}{2}$.

Although statement (1); $X^2 - Y^2 = 36$ can be factored as $(X+Y)(X-Y) = 36$, that information is not useful.

8. (C) Both statements are needed. Statement (2) gives the number of worker-hours to complete the job:

8 workers (2 hours) = 16 worker-hours.

Let X = the number of workers required.

$$16 \text{ W-H} = (X)(3 \text{ hr., } 12 \text{ min.}) = (X)(3\ 1/5 \text{ hr.}) = \frac{16X}{5}$$

Solving: X = 5 workers

9. (E) Not enough information about the cost or profit is supplied to solve the problem.

10. (B) Statement (1) is insufficient since it does not provide any information about each angle. Statement (2) is adequate based on the theorems and properties of isosceles triangles.

11. (B) Integers divisible by 3 may not always be divisible by 6. For example:

$\frac{9}{3} = 3$ but $\frac{9}{6}$ = not an integer

All integers divisible by 12 are also divisible by 6 (6 is a factor of 12).

12. (C) Using this information, AX = CX = 5 (diagonals bisect each other and are perpendicular).

BX = 12 in.

allow use of $C^2 = a^2 + b^2$. Then BD = 24 in., and

the area = $\frac{1}{2}(AC)(BD) = \frac{1}{2}(10)(24) = 120$ sq. in.

13. (A) Letting X = amount invested at 5%

($4,000 - X) = amount invested at 6%

Using I = PRT

Interest @ 5% = X(.05)(1) = .05X

@ 6% = (4,000 - X)(.06)(1) = 240 - .06X

$225 = .05X + 240 - .06X

.01X = 15

Therefore X = $1,500

Statement 2 is not sufficient

14. (D) Statement (1) shows each side of the cube has an area of 16 sq. feet. The surface area can be found by multiplying the area of one side by 6.

16 sq. ft. (6) = 96 sq. ft.

Statement (2) utilizes the formula:

Prism Diagonal = $\sqrt{\text{length}^2 + \text{width}^2 + \text{height}^2}$

If X = length (or width or height) then:

$4\sqrt{3} = \sqrt{x^2 + x^2 + x^2} = \sqrt{3x^2} = x\sqrt{3}$, and X = 4, then, one side = 16 sq. ft. and the surface area can be easily found.

15. (A) Statement (1) shows the filling rate is 2/5 tank per minute or 1/5 tank per 1/2 minute. That means the empty tank is filled using a total of 5 (1/2 minute intervals) = 2 1/2 minutes. The volume of the tank is irrelevant unless you know the fill rate.

16. (C) The equilateral triangle describes that $\angle AOB = 60^{0}$. The arc length in statement (2) would be 1/6 the circumference. Total circumference is $24\pi$ cm, then the radius = 12 cm. From that information the area of the sector = 1/6 ($144\pi$ sq. cm) = $24\pi$ sq. cm. The area of equilateral triangle = $36\sqrt{3}$ sq. cm. The solution is found by subtracting (sector - area triangle AOB) = ($24\pi - 36\sqrt{3}$) sq. cm.

17. (E) A 5 lb. bag of apples has two-thirds as many apples as a 5 lb. bag of oranges has oranges. Now if we knew how much each bag or pound of fruit cost we could determine the ratio of costs. Unfortunately we are only given this data for apples not oranges. Thus (1) and (2) together do not provide enough information for a solution.

18. (C) Let X = one integer and Y = the other integer.

Statement (1) provides X - Y = 5. Statement (2) is $X^2 - Y^2 = 55$.

Since $X^2 - Y^2 = (X + Y)(X - Y)$ (the difference of two squares) and knowing that X - Y = 5:

$$\begin{aligned} 55 &= X^2 - Y^2 \\ &= (X - Y)(X + Y) \\ &= 5(X + Y) \\ 11 &= X + Y \end{aligned}$$

19. (A) From statement 1 we see that 60% of all students are science majors. If we subtract 25% of the science students who are double majors we end up with:

60% - .25(60%) = 45%

Statement (2) does not help us determine science majors, except by limiting the number to 60%.

20. (A) The circumference, $12\pi$ in., yields the diameter by solving $C = \pi d$: d = 12 in. The diameter, of the inscribed circle, is the length of one side of the square.

The area of the circle is $36\pi$ sq. in. The area of the square = 144 sq. in. The solution is ($144 - 36\pi$) sq. in.

Statement (2) merely restates the relationship of the hypotenuse to a leg of any 45°-45°-90° triangle.

21. (E) Two similar triangles are formed, and all the information supplied is inserted:

$$\frac{\text{MAN HEIGHT}}{\text{MAN SHADOW}} = \frac{\text{TREE HEIGHT}}{\text{TREE SHADOW}}$$

$$\frac{\text{6 FT.}}{X/5} = \frac{X}{\text{TREE SHADOW}}$$

This problem cannot be solved because a complete proportion cannot be written without knowing the length of the man's shadow.

22. (A) Let X be the dealer cost, then the regular price was \$(X + 50). The 10% sale price equals 90% of regular price 0.90 (X + 50) = \$270.

Solving: X = \$250

Information about the average in statement (2) is not helpful.

23. (C) Statement (1) is rearranged and factored:

$X^2 - 7X + 6 = 0 \qquad (X - 6)(X - 1) = 0$

The roots are X = +6 and X = +1.

Statement (2) gives the domain of X. Without this domain to limit the answer, the answer provided by (1) would not be unique, therefore (2) is necessary.

24. (E) Not enough information is supplied. At best, if X = 1981 earnings then:

$$\frac{(1980) + X + 1.15X}{3} = 40{,}000$$

The solution can go no further unless you know how the value of 1980 earnings relates to the other years.

25. (E) The problem is insolvable because it depends on knowing the number of workers. Although the production of one worker is known, no correlation can be made about factory production.

# Graph and Data Interpretation

The mathematics section of the GMAT contains questions about graphs and data tables. Types of graphs include:

1. LINE GRAPHS 2. BAR GRAPHS 3. CIRCLE GRAPHS

Several helpful hints about answering this type of question include:

A. Always read all information carefully.

B. Observe the entire graph or table. Often information is contained around the perimeter of the illustration.

C. Determine the units used; be certain to answer using the same units.

D. Do not make guesses based on "feelings" about the illustration, and try not to be hasty in making decisions.

E. Verify your answer as much as possible. Often data you extract from graphs are estimations, try to be as accurate as possible.

## PRACTICE PROBLEMS – GRAPH AND DATA INTERPRETATION

PERCENTAGE OF GROSS INCOME PAID AS INCOME TAX

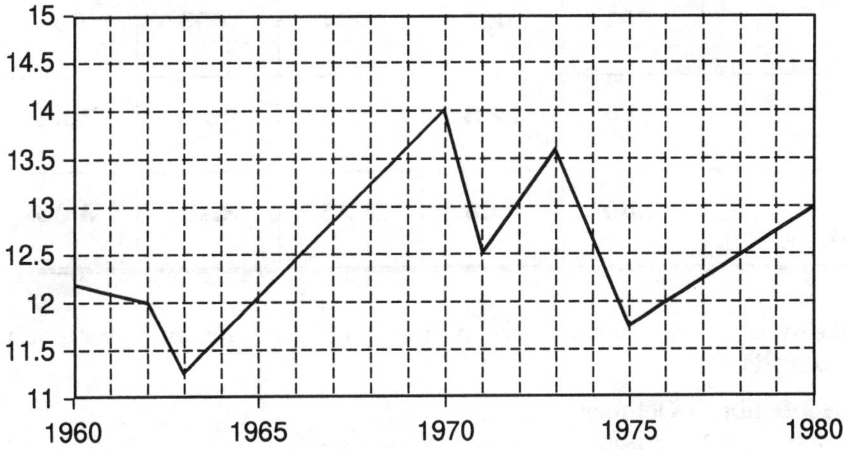


1. In what year was the percentage of after tax income the greatest?

(A) 1975
(B) 1973
(C) 1970
(D) 1966
(E) 1963

2. Between what two years was the increase in taxes paid the greatest?

(A) 1963 - 65
(B) 1965 - 68
(C) 1970 - 72
(D) 1971 - 73
(E) 1975 - 80

3. What would be the net (after tax) income of a wage earner in 1973 with a gross income of $15,000?

(A) $12,520
(B) $12,960
(C) $13,130
(D) $13,470
(E) $13,815

4. How much did a 1976 wage earner need to earn to have a net take-home of $20,000? (Round answer to nearest hundred.)

(A) $22,700
(B) $22,500
(C) $22,100
(D) $21,750
(E) $21,320

REGIONAL CONSUMPTION OF HEATING FUELS
September 1978 – February 1979

| **FUEL** | **MONTHLY CONSUMPTION** | | | | | |
|---|---|---|---|---|---|---|
| (In thousands) | **SEPT** | **OCT** | **NOV** | **DEC** | **JAN** | **FEB** |
| **COAL** (Tons) | **.001** | **.002** | **.004** | **.005** | **.008** | **.100** |
| **OIL** (Gallons) | **10.0** | **12.3** | **17.5** | **20.8** | **23.2** | **23.9** |
| **GAS** (Cubic Feet) | **1.50** | **1.88** | **2.25** | **3.12** | **3.80** | **3.92** |

5. Between what two consecutive months did oil have the greatest increase in consumption?

(A) September - October
(B) October - November
(C) November - December
(D) December - January
(E) January - February

6. The increase of gas consumption between September and November is what percent of the September use?

(A) 25%
(B) 30%
(C) 40%
(D) 50%
(E) 150%

7. If the average price per 1/2 ton coal during the 6 month period (Sept. - Feb.) was $30; what total amount was spent for coal as a fuel from September through February?

(A) $4,850
(B) $5,215
(C) $5,760
(D) $6,520
(E) $7,200

GRADUATE POST-COLLEGE CAREER CHOICES OF THREE SCHOOLS

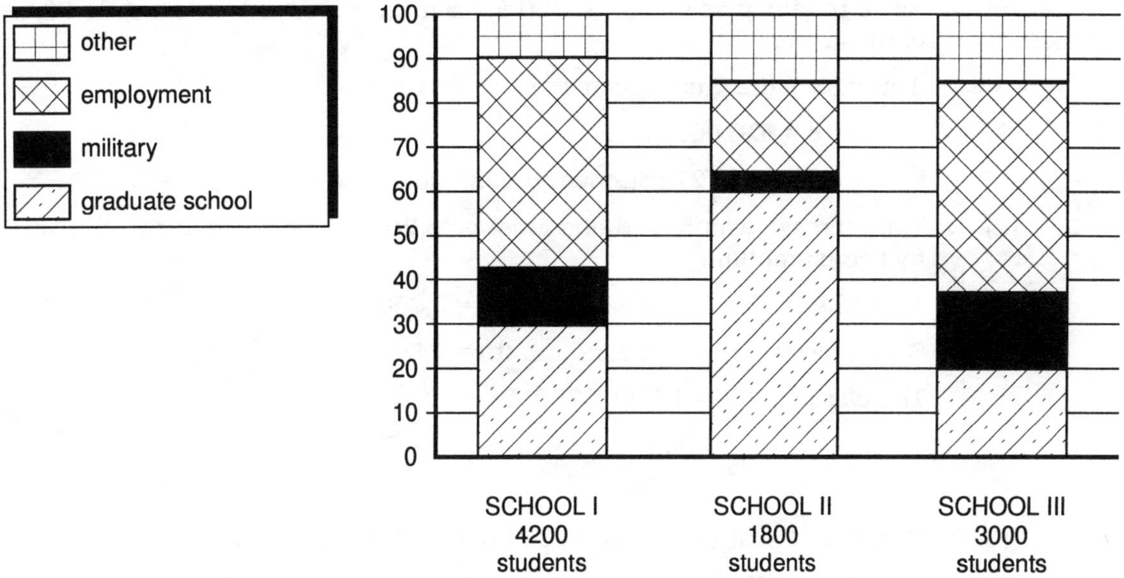


8. Which college had the highest number of students pursue advanced study in graduate school?

(A) School I
(B) School II
(C) School III

9. How many students from School III entered the military?

(A) 485
(B) 510
(C) 540
(D) 620
(E) 635

10. Which represents a larger number of students: those from School I choosing employment; or those from School III who chose the military?

(A) School I
(B) School III

## ANSWERS AND EXPLANATIONS
## GRAPH AND DATA INTERPRETATION

1. (E) The percentage of the tax paid was the lowest in 1963, therefore, the after tax income was the greatest.

2. (D) Between 1971 and 1973 the slope of the graph is the steepest, indicating the sharpest increase.

3. (B) The percent of tax paid is about 13.6%; therefore 86.4% of $15,000 represents the take home pay. Then: 0.864 ($15,000) = $12,960.

4. (A) Since the tax percentage is 12.0%, then the $20,000 take home is 88.0% of the gross.

   Letting x = the gross income

   .88x = $20,000 then

   x = $22,727 rounded to $22,700

5. (B) The increase was 5.2 (thousands) or 5,200 gallons, the greatest rise in fuel consumption.

6. (D) November = 2.25 (thousand cu. ft.) = 2,250

   September = 1.50 (thousand cu. ft.) = 1,500

   Therefore: 2,250 - 1,500 = 750

   $$\% = \frac{750}{1{,}500} = 50\%$$

7. (E) The sum of coal used was 0.120 (thousand) = 120 tons.

   At $30 per 1/2 ton ($60 per ton) the price paid was $7,200.

8. (A) 30% of 4,200 = 1,260 students

   60% of 1,800 = 1,080 students

   20% of 3,000 = 600 students

   30% of 4,200 exceeds all the others, and School I is the answer.

9. (C) Those choosing the military were (38 - 20)% = 18% of the total.

   18% (3,000 students) = 540 students

10. (A) School I employment was (90 - 42)% or

    48% of 4,200 = 2,016 students.

    School III was (38 -20)% = 18% x 3,000 = 540.

    School I > School III by a ratio of almost 4:1.

# Useful Formulas and Key Math Vocabulary

## Frequently Used Formulas

| | |
|---|---|
| The sum of all angles in a triangle | $\angle A + \angle B + \angle C = 180°$ |
| Pythagorean Theorem: | $c^2 = a^2 + b^2$ |
| Ratio of the sides of a 30°-60°-90° triangle | $x,\ x\sqrt{3}\ ,\ 2x$ |
| Ratio of the sides of a 45°-45°-90° triangle | $x,\ x,\ x\sqrt{2}$ |
| Area of a Parallelogram: | $A = bh$ |
| Area of a Triangle: | $A = \frac{1}{2}bh$ |
| Area of an equilateral Δ | $A = \frac{s^2}{4}\sqrt{3}$ |
| Area of a Rhombus: | $A = \frac{1}{2}(d_1 \cdot d_2)$ |
| Area of a Trapezoid: | $A = \frac{1}{2}(h)(b_1 + b_2)$ |
| Area of a Circle: | $A = \pi r^2$ |
| Circumference of a Circle: | $C = 2\pi r$ |
| Sum of complementary angles | 90° |
| Sum of supplementary angles | 180° |
| Sum of interior angles of a polygon: | 180° (N-2) |
| Sum of exterior angles of a polygon | 360° |
| Ratio of areas of similar figures: | $\frac{A_S}{A_L} = \left[\frac{S_S}{S_L}\right]^2$ |
| Ratio of volumes of similar figures: | $\frac{V_S}{V_L} = \left[\frac{S_S}{S_L}\right]^3$ |
| Volume of a right prism: | $V = L \cdot W \cdot H$ |
| Volume of a cylinder: | $V = \pi r^2 H$ |

## Mathematics Key Words

After completing the mathematics review you should be able to define these words. If you can not, take a moment to find the information in the text.

Integer
Whole Number
Prime Number
Mixed Number
Signed Number
Factors
Exponent
Square Root
Progression
Difference of Two Squares
Perimeter
Man-Hours
Direct Variation
Inverse Variation
Venn Diagram
Proportion
Inequality
Bisector
Vertical Angles
Corresponding Angles
Alternate Interior Angles
Complementary
Supplementary
Isosceles Triangle
Perpendicular Bisector
Polygon
Parallelogram
Trapezoid
Rhombus
Sector
Circumference
Absolute Value
Quadratic Equation